BOWATER

A history

Sir Eric Vansittart Bowater, 1895–1962.

BOWATER
A history

W. J. READER

RESEARCH BY RACHEL LAWRENCE JUDY SLINN
HUGO BARNACLE ROCHELLE MCDONALD

GENERAL ADVISER ROBERT KNIGHT

CAMBRIDGE UNIVERSITY PRESS

CAMBRIDGE

LONDON   NEW YORK   NEW ROCHELLE
MELBOURNE   SYDNEY

Published by the Press Syndicate of the University of Cambridge
The Pitt Building, Trumpington Street, Cambridge CB2 1RP
32 East 57th Street, New York, NY 10022, USA
296 Beaconsfield Parade, Middle Park, Melbourne 3206, Australia

First published 1981

Printed in Great Britain at
the University Press, Cambridge

Library of Congress catalogue
card number: 81–7681
British Library cataloguing in publication data
Reader, W. J.
Bowater.
1. Bowater Corporation – History
2. Paper making and trade – Great Britain – History
I. Title
338.7'6762'0941   HD 9831.9.B/

ISBN 0 521 24165 0

Contents

Illustrations

Tables

Preface

The Board of the Bowater Corporation commissioned this book to mark the centenary of the foundation in 1881, by William Vansittart Bowater, of a paper merchant's business in the City of London, carried on by himself and, later, by his sons and grandsons. This was the direct ancestor of the business nowadays carried on in the United Kingdom, North America and many other places by the Corporation, its subsidiaries and associates. Bowater's first manufacturing enterprise, a newsprint mill at Northfleet on the Thames, was set up in the mid-twenties, and it is from this period that the modern history of Bowater may be said to run. The founder of Bowater in its modern form, Sir Eric Vansittart Bowater (1895–1962), is the central character in my narrative.

For the research on which the narrative is based I am indebted to Rachel Lawrence, Judy Slinn and Hugo Barnacle in the United Kingdom and to Rochelle McDonald in Newfoundland. I am deeply grateful for their work and for their support, which has frequently gone far beyond anything I had a reasonable right to call for. For the plan of the book, for the writing, and for the general picture of Bowater's progress, light and shade alike, I alone am responsible. I should also like to thank Elizabeth O'Beirne-Ranelagh for taking so much trouble in editing the text, and William Davies and the staff of the Cambridge University Press generally for making it a pleasure to publish under their imprint.

Robert Knight, throughout, has been my guide and my assistants' guide to the affairs of the business to which he devoted almost the whole of his working life. He has answered questions without end and has reviewed the text for factual accuracy with the meticulous care which is characteristic of him. I have him to thank also for the reconstruction of Bowater's early accounts, leading to the estimates of consolidated profits for the years before 1947 which appear in Appendix II Table 1; for very detailed and painstaking work on

paper and pulp prices (Appendix I Table 8); and, with help from
K. C. Saunders, for the Glossary of technical terms (Appendix IV).
Joan Binns, Mr Knight's secretary, as well as providing for us a large
number of files and documents from the Bowater records, has given
us much other help, from research in the British Library to the
transcription of very long taperecorded interviews. I imagine she
won't mind if she never sees a tape cassette again.

Other members of Bowater's staff, on both sides of the Atlantic,
have been unfailingly helpful. I should particularly like to record my
thanks to:

The Chairman of the Corporation, Lord Erroll of Hale, and the
Managing Director, C. F. Popham, for finding time to read and
comment on my very long typescript; the Secretary of the Corporation, D. A. Rees, and members of his staff, T. H. Aucott,
Maggie Hunt, Barbara Moore, Alan Scouler and Connie Slevin
(Barbara Moore has typed the entire text and a great many
amendments to it); D. J. Parsons and Mary Hoare for help with
illustrations, with dating the original establishment of W. V.
Bowater & Sons, and answering numerous queries; Dianne
Howard and Ron Jones for help with post-1962 newsprint statistics; Lydia Lamb for typing and much other help.

George Baker, Karen Dinnage, H. J. Kennard, Richard Martin,
Ann Saker, Stanley Smith and Geoffrey Young, for a great deal of
help in tracing documents and answering queries.

The Executive Vice-President, A. E. Balloch, and the General
Counsel, T. G. Hart, of Bowater Inc., Old Greenwich, Conn.; the
President and the Secretary of Bowater Mersey (Nova Scotia),
Robert Weary and H. J. Dyer; the Secretary of Bowater New-
foundland, Frank Bursey; the Secretary of Bowater Southern,
Robert L. Wright, and the public relations officer, Ed Haws, of
Bowater Carolina, all for much varied assistance.

I am extremely grateful to Sir Henry Chisholm, Jack Miles and
Sir Godfrey Morley for reading the typescript with great care and
commenting on it perceptively and constructively, and to Dervish
Duma for answering numerous queries and providing documents
and photographs. Moira Reay-Mackey, by talking to me and by
giving me access to private correspondence, has greatly widened
and deepened my understanding of Eric Bowater.

Outside Bowater circles altogether, I should like to acknowledge
help from institutions and individuals as follows:

The Bank of England Records Office, for help with papers relating to Bowater's business at Northfleet and in Newfoundland;
the trustees of the Beaverbrook Papers and the House of Lords

Record Office; the Manchester Statistical Society, for the use of
A. P. Wadsworth's paper 'Newspaper circulations 1800–1954';
Geoffrey Bensusan, for help with early dates; Burnham Gill,
Provincial Archivist at St Johns, Newfoundland; Sir Eric
Cheadle, for access to records of the Newsprint Supply Co.; the
Hon. T. Harmsworth; Tom Kelly, keeper of *Daily Mail* records;
Percy Roberts, Chairman and Chief Executive of Mirror Group
Newspapers, for access to minute books; Ian D. Reid, for access
to Reid Newfoundland papers; J. G. Rustad, Chairman of Price
& Pierce, for statistics; Dr Percy Sykes; Dr Denis Williams.
Sir Eric Bowater's widow, Lady Margaret Bowater, and his cousins
Sir Noel and Sir Ian, as well as some forty-five other individuals
with special knowledge of Bowater and its history, all of whose
names are set out in the Bibliography, have been kind enough to
express themselves frankly and at length in interviews. I am very
grateful to all of them. Interviews provide evidence of character,
motive and personal relationships which is rarely available from
documents, and they sometimes correct impressions which documents convey. The narrative would have been much poorer without
these numerous conversations, and I very much hope that none who
took part will feel that he or she has been misrepresented in the use I
have made of what was said.

December 1980   W. J. READER

CHAPTER ONE

The publishing revolution and the family firm 1880–1914

For the Eleventh Edition of the *Encyclopaedia Britannica*, 1911, Lord Northcliffe, the founder of the *Daily Mail*, wrote a note on 'Price of newspapers'. Looking back over the previous half-century, he observed that the growth of the cheap newspaper – he meant newspapers priced in England at a halfpenny, or a penny at most – had been practically simultaneous 'throughout the civilized world', notably in the United States, France and Great Britain. 'The general tendency in newspaper production', he went on, 'as in all other branches of industry, has in recent times been towards the lowering of prices while maintaining excellence of quality, experience having proved the advantage of large sales with a small margin of profit over a limited circulation with a higher rate of profit.'

Northcliffe was writing from personal knowledge, describing a revolution in the publishing industry in which he was himself a leader and in which the development of cheap newspapers was neither the earliest nor the largest feature. During the 1880s and 1890s, in spite of the 'Great Depression' which darkened some regions of the economic landscape and in spite of the sluggishness which some historians have discerned in some branches of British industry, material welfare generated by earlier phases of the Industrial Revolution was spreading through society as real wages rose.[1] In these circumstances, Alfred Harmsworth (Lord Northcliffe 1905), born in 1865, his three-years-younger brother, Harold (Lord Rothermere 1914), and other enterprising businessmen, mostly young, were showing that large and profitable businesses could be founded on selling periodicals designed for a reading public not previously catered for; a public newly able to afford periodicals along with other products designed for and advertised to them, such as Sunlight Soap, Cadbury's Cocoa, Wills' cigarettes, patent medicines, ready-made clothes, cheap railway tickets to the seaside – all the delights of an emerging consumer society.

This was not a highly educated public. Until 1870 there was no provision in England for universal schooling, and, in the eighties and nineties, the system was still far from complete, so that, for many moderately prosperous people on the ill-defined frontier between the upper working class and the lower middle class, reading must have been almost as much of a novelty as reading matter. Nevertheless, they had an enormous appetite for information, served brightly, briefly and simply and for entertainment, and this was the essential discovery made by George Newnes (1851–1910) who launched *Tit-Bits* – tit-bits, that is, of information – in 1881.

Newnes had a great many imitators and competitors, amongst whom two were pre-eminent: Alfred Harmsworth, a contributor to *Tit-Bits*, and C. A. Pearson (1866–1921), a Wykehamist who, at the age of nineteen, became its manager. Each decided that, what Newnes could do, he could do as well or better. Harmsworth launched *Answers to Correspondents – Answers –* in 1888 and Pearson launched *Pearson's Weekly* in 1890. Around his original success, each of these pioneers built a range of other periodicals. Some, like Newnes' *Review of Reviews* (1890) and *Strand Magazine* (1891), were aimed rather higher in the market; others, if anything, lower, like Harmsworth's *Comic Cuts* (1890) and Pearson's *Dan Leno's Comic Journal* (1898). There were periodicals for women – *Home Chat* (Harmsworth, 1895) – Sunday periodicals, periodicals for boys, and periodicals for special interest groups, and in this field W. I. Iliffe, a printer and stationer of Coventry, was turning his attention to the possibilities first of cycling – Alfred Harmsworth worked for him on *Bicycling News* in the mid-eighties – then of motoring (*The Autocar,* 1895), and eventually of flying (*Flight,* 1909).

A variant of periodical publishing was the publication of 'part-works': this is, the publication at fixed intervals – a fortnight, perhaps, or a month – of parts of a self-contained work: an account of a war in progress, perhaps, or an encyclopaedia, or a 'self-educator' – intended eventually to be bound permanently and kept. The advantages of the plan were – and are – two-fold: the publisher sees a rapid return on his outlay and the buyer is able to buy the complete work by instalments. Part-works were nothing new and old-established publishers like Cassells had plenty of experience of them. Harmsworth joined in with enthusiasm, starting with *Sixty Years a Queen* in ten sixpenny parts in 1897 and going on with *Nelson and his Times*, also in ten sixpenny parts. *With the Flag to Pretoria* (thirty parts) followed, and when the Boers failed to surrender in a sensible manner, forty-two parts of *After Pretoria*. These mirrored the imperial pride of the day: so too, in a way, did *Japan's Fight for Freedom* in sixty parts. For those seeking to improve themselves or their children he published the *Harmsworth Encyclopaedia* in forty parts, starting in March 1905; the *Harmsworth Self-Educator* in forty-eight parts, starting in October of the same year; the *Children's Encyclopaedia* (Spring 1908) and many more. For children there was a string of 'annuals' in the early 1900s – *Playbox*, *Puck*, *Schoolgirls' Own*, *Tiger Tim*'s and others – and, in November 1910, women were favoured with the first of forty-eight parts of *Everywoman's Encyclopaedia*.[2]

The sheer volume of this form of publishing – periodicals and part-works – must have been immense, though precisely how immense is impossible to say because sales or circulation figures are hard to come by. There are, however, one or two indicators. Newnes, in 1891, was claiming sales of 500,000 copies a week for *Tit-Bits* and, at about the same time, a chartered accountant certified net sales of 1,000,000 a week for all Harmsworth publications.[3] Periodicals had never been sold in anything like these numbers before, just as soap had never been sold in the quantities in which Lever Brothers were selling it.

In 1896, Alfred Harmsworth, still aiming at the mass market, launched the *Daily Mail*, a daily paper designed not for highly educated, leisured gentlemen interested in public affairs and with hours to spare for reading about them, but for clerks and workmen on their way to work and for women. In so far as any newspapers had reached this kind of readership before, they had generally been Sunday papers, sensational then as now in the selection and treatment of news and radical in politics, if they had any, and when the *Daily Mail* was launched there were two, perhaps three, mass-circulation Sunday papers – *News of the World*, *Lloyd's Weekly News*, *Reynolds' News* – which had been founded as far back as the mid-century. As a daily, however, and in its price – a ha'penny – the *Daily Mail* was the leader, by a long way, in the development of a new kind of journalism.

It soon had competitors. In 1900 Pearson launched the *Daily Express* and Edward Hulton the *Daily Dispatch*. Then in 1904 Harmsworth converted the *Daily Mirror* launched for 'gentlewomen' in the previous year, and a failure, into the first illustrated daily, and a success. The circulation figures for London halfpenny dailies, so far as they are known or can be guessed, rose in the early 1900s far above any figure previously attained. The *Daily Express*, after an initial print of 800,000, fell back to about 250,000: still, for its time, a high figure, and the circulation of the *Daily News*, driven down to a halfpenny in 1904, seems to have risen well over 500,000 before 1914. The *Mail*, at the head of them all, built up a steady daily circulation of 750,000 (after one million, briefly, during the Boer War) and the *Mirror*, by 1912, seems to have gone higher, though not lastingly. The *Mail*'s success was phenomenal, and until the late 1920s it had no serious rival.[4]

Between 1881 and 1911 the number of authors, editors and journalists recorded in the Census of England and Wales rose by more than 300 per cent.[5] Here is another indication, wider in its scope and probably more reliable than circulation figures, of the success of popular periodicals, halfpenny papers, and mass-market publishing generally. This publishing revolution set in motion processes by which information and ideas could penetrate more rapidly, widely and deeply into society than ever before. There was simplification, distortion, triviality, but a mind-broadening engine of great power had come into action, unparalleled until the development of broadcasting and television. The modern mass-media had been born, and despite sneers from on high – later directed also at television – there can be no reasonable doubt that the widening diffusion of the printed word enormously expanded the general knowledge and awareness of the mass of the population, just as the contemporary development of other consumer goods raised their general standard of living.

To reach their market, Northcliffe and publishers like him relied on cheap, abundant supplies of papermaking material; on machinery for converting it into paper cheaply and quickly; and on printing machinery to match the papermakers' output. Mass-market publishers have the same requirements today, and so far as papermaking is concerned they are met in very similar ways. Developments in the underlying technology of papermaking, during the period of this book, have been in matters of speed, size and quantity, not in the engineering principles of the machinery or in the general nature of papermaking material.

Broadly speaking, the new publishers of the 1880s and 1890s found papermaking machinery waiting for them which was adequate for their purpose or could readily be made so. Paper was already being made in large quantities on plant of a kind first developed, very early in the nineteenth century, by John Gamble, the stationer brothers Henry and Sealy Fourdrinier and the versatile engineer Bryan Donkin who had a hand in many other things as well, including an early process for canning food, and who became FRS.*

* John Gamble, dates unknown; H. Fourdrinier 1766–1854; S. Fourdrinier, d. 1847; B. Donkin, 1768–1855.

The Fourdrinier machine took in at one end a wet pulp – 99 per cent water – of cellulosic material and passed it in a thin layer first over wire mesh, then on to endless travelling felts which carried it between pressure rolls, and then to a final drying between heated rollers, the object of these successive processes being to expel nearly all the water from the pulp and convert it into a continuous sheet of paper which could be wound on to a reel. The process is much the same, in essentials, today as it was in the nineteenth century, but whereas a machine of 1890 would produce paper 100 inches wide at between 100 and 200 feet a minute,[6] a machine in 1980, 380 feet long, was capable of producing paper 364 inches wide at 3,000 to 3,250 feet a minute.

Fourdrinier machines and rotary presses guaranteed that paper could be produced and printed rapidly and in large quantities. Cheapness they did not by themselves guarantee. The papermakers' product could only be cheap if they could find a cheap and abundant source of cellulose fibre. Rag had been used for centuries but, by the 1860s, it was too scarce and expensive for newsprint. The papermakers turned first to esparto grass and straw, then to wood pulp, especially in the eighties after chemical methods of treating the raw wood produced a better quality cellulose. In a combination of 'mechanical' pulp and 'sulphite' pulp – that is, pulp produced purely by grinding and pulp produced by chemical 'cooking' – the papermakers found what they needed for the newsprint end of their trade, where the mass production and the mass sales lay.

They also found themselves dependent on imports of pulp, because there was no adequate timber in the United Kingdom. Pulp at first came chiefly from Scandinavia and other parts of Northern Europe, then additionally and increasingly from Canada and, in time, paper, especially newsprint, began to come also. In 1900, 487,742 tons of wood pulp were imported, a figure six times as great as in 1887.[7] Reliance on imported raw material and competition in their finished product became facts of permanent and growing significance to the British papermakers, particularly the makers of newsprint.

The use of wood pulp for papermaking was the key development which enabled publishers to realise the full potential of their suppliers' and printers' machinery. Northcliffe had no doubt of its importance. 'From 1875 to 1885', he wrote for the *Encyclopaedia Britannica*, 'paper cheapened rapidly and it has been estimated that the introduction of wood pulp trebled the circulation of newspapers in England.'

Harold Harmsworth, even more than his brother, was impressed by the importance of cheap paper for their joint enterprises, and, as Alfred's business manager, he was able to put his ideas into practice. He 'saw that the clue to their success was in buying raw material' – that is, paper – 'at the lowest possible price and selling it at a profit in processed form', and he had the early periodicals printed as cheaply as possible on the cheapest possible paper, coloured, if necessary, to hide its badness. In dealing with his brother, Harold was quite open. 'Our bad paper and cheap printing', he wrote to Alfred in 1892, 'will not stand much in the way of small type.' Four years later, accordingly, he proposed to have the *Daily Mail* printed on cheap, tinted, paper. This was too much for Alfred. He had a large investment in the paper emotionally, as well as financially, and no doubt felt that he was solidly enough established to permit his greatest venture a measure of luxury. Moreover, he wanted to flatter his readers and, at some time, he might want to publish illustrations. The *Daily Mail* was printed on good, white, paper.

The Harmsworth enterprises, taken all in all, were by this time among the largest British businesses. There were two other news-papers besides the *Mail* – the *Evening News*, bought in 1894, and the *Daily Record* of Glasgow, bought the following year – and fourteen periodicals. Harmsworth Brothers Ltd, formed in 1896 to take over everything except the newspapers, claimed to be the biggest periodical publishing house in the world.[8]

The owners of this imposing assembly bought some or all of their most important raw material – paper – through an agent, and it was said in the office 'that when Harold had a couple of minutes to spare he would send for the paper agent and knock off another two-and-a-half per cent discount'.[9] The agent who suffered that disconcert-ing treatment probably belonged to a small firm in the City of London, appointed to the agency about 1890.[10] The name of the firm was W. V. Bowater & Sons.

Of Bowaters' earliest days little is known and that little is founded chiefly on oral traditions, sometimes conflicting. William Vansittart Bowater (1838–1907) was born into a Midland family of good social standing and with numerous branches. Several of his rela-tions of various generations were officers in the army, including two who became generals – John Bowater (1741–1813), a great-uncle, and Sir Edward Bowater (1787–1861), a distant cousin who was equerry to the Prince Consort. William himself went into trade, which suggests strongly that his father could not finance any more genteel career. He joined James Wrigley & Sons of Manchester and Bury, papermakers.

W. V. Bowater's reputation is thoroughly unpleasant. He seems to have been hard-drinking, bad-tempered, and tyrannical. All three characteristics are suggested by the story which is told of his downfall at Wrigleys. He came back from lunch drunk one afternoon in the seventies and went to sleep in his office. A policeman entered to warn him, apparently quite politely, that the street door was open. 'Don't you know better than to wake an Englishman

William Vansittart Bowater in the 1890s.

when he's asleep?' shouted Bowater, and he hustled the constable downstairs into the street. Wrigleys sacked him and he moved to London.

In February 1881 he was in business at 31 London Wall. During the same year he moved to 91 Queen Street and in 1883 to 28 Queen Street, a handsome Georgian house where the firm remained until 1899.[11] In 1885 he was listed in the first annual issue of the *Directory of Papermakers* as one of forty-four 'Paper Makers' London Representatives' and, on another page, he advertised 'Fine and Common Printings, News, Long Elephants, Cartridges, Engine Sized Writings, Fine Glazed and Unglazed Browns, Caps, and Mill Wrappers'. In 1886, in case anyone had missed the point, he described himself as 'Paper Makers' Agent and Wholesale Stationer' and, a couple of years later, he announced a line of business which was to become important: 'Waste Papers Bought and Sold'.

W. V. Bowater's advertisement in *The Paper Makers' Monthly Journal*, 15 November 1881. *British Library*

The business, at a comparatively modest level, must have been prosperous for, at the end of 1889, perhaps with the Harmsworth agency in view, W. V. Bowater took three of his five sons into partnership.[12] The eldest, Thomas Vansittart, was twenty-seven; Frank was twenty-three; Frederick, twenty-two. The family firm, typical of English business practice of the day, was complete. There was no suggestion of incorporation or limited liability.

This was not yet a business fitted for large-scale dealings in newsprint, which figures only incidentally in its list of wares alongside the Long Elephants, Cartridges, Engine Sized Writings. It was not, indeed, fitted for large-scale dealings in anything, rather the

Nos. 27 and 28 Queen Street, drawn by Hanslip Fletcher in 1929.
Guildhall Library

reverse. 'Can the Manufacturer do without the Agent?' enquired
the *Paper Trade Review* in 1889 and, in discussing the question,
gave an account of the paper agent's functions, which no doubt
suited W. V. Bowater's business as well as that of any of his
forty-odd London competitors.[13]

Why, it was being asked, have paper agents at all? Why shouldn't
manufacturers deal direct with buyers of their products? The *Review's* answer, first, was that the manufacturer should not attempt
to be a dealer as well. 'The proper manufacture of paper . . . fully
absorbs the whole intelligence and attention of the maker, and to
attempt both' – that is, both manufacture and dealing – 'often
means doing so at the expense of one or other of the branches, each
of which requires a peculiar knowledge and handling.'

'Let us see', the *Review* went on,

why the dealer is necessary as between maker and consumer (wholesale or retail). The consumer cannot possibly supply all his wants from one maker and, consequently, would have to visit several before getting all he wants. Again, should only a small quantity be needed, the dealer must of necessity be resorted to, who, by having several such demands, is able to take from the maker an amount that it pays to produce and, on the other hand, can obviate the necessity of the customer having to go to half-a-dozen places to fill up what he wants, not to mention the saving of time by all being to hand when wanted. This last-named fact often gives the dealer an advantage over the maker, especially where time is an object. The maker cannot (with a view to loss of interest, warehouse room, &c.) keep an assorted stock, and so is liable to be without the very thing wanted, and recourse must be had at once to the dealer to save time and money. The price quoted by the dealer is not higher than at the makers, and indeed often less, as having large parcels on hand . . . he is able to dispose of them, if need be, in small quantities at a much lower rate than the maker would supply . . . In short, the dealer, by having a quantity of relatively small orders, can send a large one to the maker, who is enabled to execute it at a low rate, and yet with profit, owing to the quantity.

Whoever wrote this passage cannot have been thinking of the Harmsworths, needing paper for a million copies of periodicals a week, or of Edward Lloyd, whose *Lloyd's Weekly News* was probably already selling nearly 900,000 copies every Sunday and who also owned the *Daily Chronicle*. Mass-market publishers and owners of mass-circulation papers, like the Harmsworths and Edward Lloyd, had to find far more paper than any previous paper-user had ever needed and the terms on which they found it were crucial to the health of their enterprises.

Broadly speaking, the users had two options open to them, not necessarily mutually exclusive, and they will be seen exercising them again and again throughout the period we are dealing with. On the one hand, they could attempt to play suppliers off against each other in the market. As demand grew, there were relatively few suppliers who could meet it and the users always feared monopoly – newspaper owners seem to have been nervous of it as early as 1889[14] – which might lead them to consider the other alternative, building their own paper mills.

Harold Harmsworth's early activities seem to represent a fairly crude version of the first course of action, aimed solely at cheapness. It suited him, evidently, to employ W. V. Bowater and perhaps other agents in much the manner described in the *Paper Trade Review*. Bowater would know the market and would find Harmsworth the supplies he wanted at a price he was prepared to pay; hence the rather vinegary joke about sending for the paper agent and knocking off another 2½ per cent discount. If there were long-term contracts, it does not look as if Bowater negotiated them.

Edward Lloyd, in business long before the Harmsworths were born, took the other line, building his own mill. In his early days – the 1830s – he was a very sharp operator indeed, making his way by means of 'penny bloods', a shorthand textbook, 'imitations' – plagiarism – of Dickens and other authors, and evasion of the Newspaper Stamp Act, towards comparative respectability and a slightly spurious reputation for virtue as the highly successful owner of *Lloyd's Weekly News* and the worthily Liberal *Daily Chronicle*. With these two to provide for, 'Mr Lloyd came to the conclusion that he would find it of immense benefit to . . . render himself independent of the vagaries of the paper market by making his own paper.'[15]

The first site he chose, in 1861, was on the River Lea at Bow, in the East End of London, where he set up a mill with two machines of the conventional width of the day, about 90 inches or rather less. After he had taken over the *Daily Chronicle*, that mill was too small

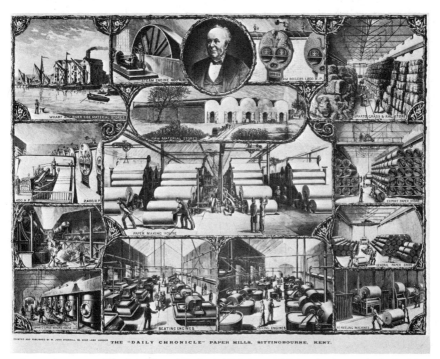

A supplement to *The British and Colonial Printer and Stationer* in 1889, depicting Edward Lloyd and the operations at his Sittingbourne mill.

and he moved to Sittingbourne in Kent, a place with a long tradition of papermaking, where ships could get access to the mill and the mill itself was about forty miles by rail from London for the delivery of finished products. There was also an excellent water supply and plenty of room. On this site, he and his sons – Edward Lloyd died in 1890 soon after forming a limited liability company to take over his business – built up the Daily Chronicle Mills, where, by 1902, eleven machines were running. The first really wide paper machine – 123 inches – was put up at Sittingbourne, at one time the largest paper works in the world, and No. 11 machine worked a wire 126 inches wide and 50 feet long at 550 feet per minute. The total output of the Old and New Mills, in 1902, was about 1,000 tons a week of newsprint and other grades of paper.[16]

Lloyd was determined not only to make paper but to control raw material supplies. He experimented with many fibres and having settled, as he thought, on esparto he leased land or grass-cutting rights (it is not clear which) covering 100,000 acres in Algeria and in Southern Spain. After Edward Lloyd's death, Edward Lloyd Ltd bought a site at Honefos in Norway and put up pulp mills and, a little later, bought mills already built at Vittingfos.

Lloyds' exuberant growth, sustained over many years, produced by the turn of the century the first British enterprise to have a stake in every stage of papermaking, printing and publishing, from making wood pulp to advertising and selling the finished newspaper. The mills at Sittingbourne, capable of producing a very wide range of paper, supplied by 1902 'an appreciable slice' of the world's newsprint and they handled 100,000 tons a year of other firms' products as well as their own, besides supplying 'every item . . . which is wanted in a printing works' from a rotary machine to cotton waste.[17] 'I buy my paper from Mr Frank Lloyd', said his newspaper-owning competitor, C. A. Pearson, just after he had launched the *Daily Express*. '[He is] the only paper-maker in the whole world who would enter into a contract to supply me with the quantity that I wanted at any price.'[18] That Lloyds' very large business should ever come into Bowaters' ownership would in 1900 have been inconceivable, yet in 1936 – still the larger business of the two – it did (Chapter 6.2 below).

Bowaters' 'first great agency', according to family tradition, was for Lloyds, though when or for what quantity or type of business is unknown. Presumably, such contracts as Pearson's would have been negotiated by Frank Lloyd, who followed his father as head of the firm. W. V. Bowater's method of working, as it has been described by one of his grandsons, hardly seems consistent with the largest or the highest class of business. He was a heavy drinker,

and if you wanted to do business in those days you had to agree to meet him at one of several inns in the City, ranging from Fleet Street to the other side of Lombard Street, and you sat at a table which he had reserved for him always and on it would be a decanter of port and you were expected to drink your share of that port if you wanted to do business with him. The effect of this was that he occasionally returned to his office the worse for wear.[19]

He would expect his sons to wait for him and, when he got back, he would dictate letters to them which Frank Bowater, much later, recalled taking to Euston to catch the night mail. Stories are also told of whist and drinking late at night at W. V. Bowater's house, Bury Hall, at Edmonton, however tired or unwilling the sons might be. On top of it all, the old man took a large share of the profits. Frank later claimed to have been paid only £200 a year.

Vansittart, the eldest son, was becoming a City figure in his own right, being elected a representative on the Court of Common Council in 1899. Whether for this reason or some other, he and his brothers decided, about 1900, that their father's behaviour was intolerable. They obliged him to sell out and took control of the business themselves, no doubt greatly to its benefit and their own.

In 1899 the firm had moved to larger offices at 159 Queen Victoria Street, but the space needed cannot have been very great

Fred Bowater, Eric's father, in his office at 159 Queen Victoria Street, 1908.

for in 1905 the brothers were only employing, besides themselves, six clerks, two 'lady typewriters' and a fifteen-year-old office boy. For transport they hired four horse-drawn vans. They must have been heavily dependent on the Harmsworth connection. They supplied paper for the first issue of the *Daily Mail* and, no doubt, for numerous other publications. When the *Daily Mirror* was launched in 1903, or perhaps when it was reorganised in 1904, the two younger brothers, Vansittart being much preoccupied in the City, scored a *coup*. Being agents to Peter Dixon & Co., papermakers of Grimsby, they persuaded the firm to put in a new machine – a

A Bowater advertisement, 1909.

serious capital investment – to supply the *Mirror*'s needs and, to the Harmsworths, they guaranteed Dixon's output. Bowaters' agreement with Dixon ran until 1915 when Dixons, feeling no need for agents in the sellers' market of that day, declined to renew it.[20] Bowaters were supplying paper also for *The Observer,* taken over at a low point in its fortunes by Harmsworth in 1905, for, at the end of 1908, Cornford, of *The Observer*, called for help from G. A. Sutton, one of Northcliffe's most trusted subordinates, saying 'Bowater are pressing me for three months' on account.' He got the money he sought, so presumably Bowaters got theirs.[21]

W. V. Bowater died in 1907 and in 1910 his sons formed a private company to replace the partnership. At last Bowaters' business begins to emerge from the colourful but imprecise half-light of reminiscence and anecdote into the colder but clearer illumination of accountants' figures, and for the first time it is possible to give something like an accurate impression of size and shape.

The nominal capital of the new company, at £125,000, suggests an enterprise still small by comparison with those of the large publishers or the large papermakers – Edward Lloyd Ltd went to the public in 1911 for £550,000 in Preference capital alone – but fairly large, by the standards of the day, to be in the hands of three individuals, though in 1911 it was still only employing fifteen people.[22] Ownership and control, naturally, remained with the former partners, who were each allotted 20,000 Ordinary shares of £1 each as payment for the assets transferred. There were no other Ordinary shareholders, though 15,000 shares remained unissued. Mrs Eliza J. Bowater, W. V. Bowater's widow, was provided for by the issue of 6,000 6 per cent Cumulative Preference shares and the brothers subscribed for 4,000 each. Of the remaining Preference shares issued, 500 were taken up by each of two women, probably relations, and 1,000 by each of two limited companies – James Killing Jr Ltd, of which nothing is known, and Peter Dixon & Son Ltd, papermakers – giving a capital structure as follows:[23]

Authorised capital	£125,000
Divided into:	
£1 Ordinary shares	75,000, £60,000 issued
£1 6 per cent Cumulative Preference shares	50,000, £21,000 issued

The new company, in its first year, made a profit of £9,402 before directors' fees and tax. The profit did not come entirely from the agency business. There were activities also in export packing, in lighterage and towing, in wharfing, and in trade in printers' waste,

off-cuts and ends of reels, all sold as wrapping paper to shop-
keepers. The goods for export, tightly packed in bales, were surplus
newspapers which found a ready market in the East both for
wrapping and for other purposes such as wall-covering and the
protection of young tea-plants.

The company had probably been formed with an eye to the
future, for the third generation, sons of the three brothers, were at
or just over the threshold of the business. The Board gave the export
trade a lot of attention: in 1911–12 Frank Bowater made a long
tour in India and the Far East, and in 1913 the Board were
considering laying down plant in New York 'for the Press Packing
of News, etc., similar to the businesses in London and Glasgow'.
Plant was duly laid down and an American connection thereby
established which was to have far-reaching consequences.[24]

In November 1913 Sir Thomas Vansittart Bowater (he had been
knighted in 1906) became Lord Mayor of London, leaving the
running of the business even more decisively with his two younger
brothers. Their minds were beginning to look a long way beyond
the established form of the business. Prosperous and varied though
no doubt it was, it offered no very great scope for expansion and as
a medium-sized firm in an industry populated by giants its future
might not be promising. On 2 January 1914, after a couple of
months' negotiations by Fred, the Board decided to buy freehold
land and buildings on the Thames at Northfleet near Gravesend,
and the purchase was completed in May. The price was £18,500.
The brothers were preparing to switch Bowaters from dealing in
paper to manufacturing it.

CHAPTER TWO

The expanding market and the urge to manufacture 1914–1923

2.1 THE EXPANDING MARKET

When the Bowater brothers decided to buy land at Northfleet they presumably hoped to take advantage of the still rising demand for mass-market newspapers and periodicals, but any plans they may have had for building a mill must have been overwhelmed by the outbreak of war. Construction did not start for ten years, which can hardly have been part of the original intention. In the meantime, however, the underlying assumption of rising demand remained sound and the newspaper and periodical industry went on growing and developing. By the time there was at last a mill at Northfleet ready for production, in 1926, its principal customers and prospective customers had carried their business organisation, their products and their competitive methods a long way beyond the stage they had reached in 1914.

The Great War was good for the newspapers. It interfered with the supply of newsprint and raised its price, but it sharpened people's appetite for news and raised their wages, so that more readers fell into the habit of buying a paper regularly. A. P. Wadsworth speaks of 'a boom in circulation and profits' and quotes circulation figures – admittedly not over-reliable – of between 500,000 and 750,000 during the war or soon after, for the *Daily News*, the *Daily Chronicle*, the *Daily Express*, and much more for the *Daily Mail*.[1] Northcliffe, early in 1916, wrote: 'What with the price of paper and the calling up of the married men, it looks as if we shall soon have nothing to print and no one to print it',[2] but really he had little to complain of. *Daily Mail* sales rose from about 800,000 a day pre-war to more than one million and although they dropped to 850,000 in 1917 when the price was doubled to a penny, they soon recovered.[3] In 1920 the *Mail*'s circulation was claimed to be 1.3 million – the world's largest – and still rising.[4]

To those who seek not only profit but power, newspaper

ownership is very risky but very attractive. Lord Rothermere, a profit-seeker with a taste for power, launched the *Sunday Pictorial* in 1915 undeterred by failures and near-failures among newly founded newspapers before the war. Lord Beaverbrook, a power-seeker with an eye to profit, bought control of the *Daily Express* at the end of 1916 and in December 1918 launched the *Sunday Express*. He could have found easier ways of making profit than putting money first into a sickly newspaper and then into a completely new one, but profit was not altogether what he was after. Nevertheless he did not underrate its importance and being new to the newspaper business he turned for advice – rather cheekily, it may be thought – to his most powerful competitors, Northcliffe and Rothermere.[5]

Rothermere responded with enthusiasm. It was not long before he joined Beaverbrook in buying out minority shareholders in the *Daily Express*. Then after Northcliffe died in 1922 Rothermere, not greatly to the liking of some of his numerous relations, arranged for Northcliffe's 400,000 shares in Associated Newspapers, which owned the *Daily Mail*, to be transferred to a new holding company, the Daily Mail Trust, in which Rothermere directly or indirectly owned or controlled nearly half the shares. The Daily Mail Trust proceeded to buy 49 per cent of Beaverbrook's holding in London Express Newspaper, paying him partly in cash and partly in shares.[6]

Thus the newcomer to newspapers, Beaverbrook, allied himself with the most powerful group in the business, though he never ceased entirely to compete with it. The alliance eventually broke up, but for several years in the twenties and early thirties Rothermere and Beaverbrook, two very dissimilar characters, were in close if somewhat uneasy partnership: a partnership, as we shall see (Chapter 4 below), which came to exert a powerful influence on Bowater.

Rothermere and Beaverbrook were two of the 'Press barons' who, controlling larger or small groups of newspapers and periodicals, became dominant in their industry between the wars. In the early twenties the Harmsworth group was the largest, and after Northcliffe died in 1922 Rothermere was at the head of it. In 1915 two other brothers, William and Gomer Berry (Lord Camrose (1929) and Lord Kemsley (1936)), moved from periodicals into newspapers by buying the *Sunday Times*. A sustained campaign of expansion during the twenties, largely in alliance with Lord Iliffe (1877–1960), carried the Berrys ahead of Rothermere, from whom in 1924 they bought a Manchester-based group of papers formed by Sir Edward Hulton (1869–1925). In 1926 the Berrys bought from Northcliffe's executors the Amalgamated Press, owner of the ancestral periodicals from which the Harmsworths had originally made their fortune.[7]

These great magnates, who had their peers in other publishing groups, were powerful personalities and many of their moves were made for personal reasons. There were sound commercial motives also, however, for forming their groups. They spread the very heavy risks of the business, they could command the large capital required, they kept the printing plant occupied and they generated sufficient activity to support the costs of mass production. Newspapers are part of the apparatus of politics and politics dictated arrangements made to take over the *Daily Chronicle* from Frank Lloyd (for £1m, it is said) in 1918[8] and to rescue the *Daily Herald* in 1929.[9]

2.2 THE URGE TO MANUFACTURE

This was the rapidly changing environment in which W. V. Bowater & Sons carried on the last phase of their business as paper merchants, before they became papermakers. In 1914 there were six Bowaters in the family firm: Sir Vansittart and his eldest son Rainald (1888–1945); Frank and his son Noel (b. 1892); Fred and his son Frederick (1895–1962), later universally known as Eric. Rainald was educated at Whitgift Grammar School and came into the business in 1905. Noel, reflecting perhaps the rising fortunes of the family, went to Rugby and, in 1912, started making out bills of lading in Bowaters' office for a sovereign a week. Eric, having left Charterhouse, was sent to Dixons to gain an acquaintance with their trade but he said later that he had no commercial experience before the war and hoped to be an army officer.[10]

He had his desire. In 1913 he and Noel were commissioned into Territorial units of the Royal Artillery. Frank was also a Territorial officer, so that when war broke out three of the family went on active service, followed in 1917 by Rainald, and the management was seriously depleted. All of them survived but, on 4 September 1915, a shell changed the course of Eric's life. It wrecked a dugout where he was resting, killed two other officers and trapped him for eighteen hours in the dark, unable to move, wondering whether anyone would find him.[11] For about three years he used crutches, but then he consulted a leading neurologist, E. Farquhar Buzzard (1871–1945), who, having decided that Eric's symptoms were physical manifestations of mental stress, boldly ordered him to cross the room, which he immediately did. Ever afterwards he considered that his ailment, having been shown to be psychological rather than physical, had been unreal and therefore shameful, and he was impelled by a strong desire to 'prove himself'.[12] The shell-burst wrecked his military ambitions and diverted the force of his imperious personality, against his earlier inclinations, into the family business.

Government control of business activities, even in wartime, was an heretical notion to those who governed England in 1914, brought up as they had been on over seventy years of marvellously successful Free Trade and *laissez-faire*. 'Business as usual' was their slogan, provided for them by Winston Churchill at Guildhall on 9 November 1914. Nevertheless, control came and it came to paper-making as to other industries. From February 1916 onward the import of papermakers' materials was more and more heavily restricted and, in March 1918, a Paper Controller was appointed. Straw was used; rags were collected; waste paper was re-pulped; English woods were cut down.[13] Production fell while quality grew worse and costs, prices and profits rose, although high rates of Excess Profits Duty, introduced in 1915 and made retrospective to the beginning of the war, snatched a good deal away – some of it from Bowaters.[14]

Profitable the business might be but it could hardly be progressive, especially with Frank, Noel, Eric and, finally, Rainald away at the war and Fred, in 1918, called to serve under Lord Beaverbrook at the Ministry of Information. Two suits against Bowaters for breach of contract, one brought by the *News of the World* in 1916 and one by D. C. Thomson & Co. in 1917, may be evidence of this wholesale disruption of the management. Both suits were settled out of court. The *News of the World* accepted £7,500 damages and costs, partly offset by £2,000 received by Bowaters from Peter Dixon in settlement of claims against them. D. C. Thomson, having claimed £12,000, settled for £4,170 including their costs, suggesting that their claim was somewhat exaggerated.[15] What the grounds for action were, in either case, are not revealed in the scanty records which survive.

These records do show, however, that Bowaters were not prevented by the Great War from setting up a business in the USA, modelled on their similar business in the United Kingdom, to export hydraulically baled surplus newspapers to India and the Far East. The pre-war origins of the project we have already seen in Chapter 1. Frank was in charge of it and, even after he went into the army, he did not lose touch for, in 1916, he was corresponding, presumably from France, with E. A. V. Capern, Bowaters' man on the spot. The business, set up in 1914 as the Hudson Packing & Paper Co., was incorporated in the state of New Jersey in September 1916, with $100,000 capital, eventually held as follows:

W. V. Bowater & Sons Ltd	9,500 $5 shares
Sir T. V. Bowater	2,500
Frank Bowater	2,500
Frederick Bowater	2,500
E. A. V. Capern	2,500
Harry Pickess	500

Capern was President; Pickess, Secretary, Treasurer and General Manager; the three brothers, directors.[16] In its first year of existence, the company paid a dividend of 15 per cent.[17] It was small, as all Bowater enterprises were in those days, but it established a base for transatlantic operations in the future on a scale which none of its founders is likely to have foreseen.

No complete picture of Bowaters' wartime finances has survived, nor sufficient figures to make even a guess at one, but there are indications that the firm was stronger, breach-of-contract actions notwithstanding, at the end of the war than at the beginning, though 1915 may have been rather unrewarding. The Ordinary dividend on £60,000 issued capital was 10 per cent, plus 10 per cent bonus, for 1914, 10 per cent for 1915, 15 per cent free of tax for 1916 and 1917 and 17½ per cent, free of tax, for 1918. Probably as much as £36,000 was invested in War Loan during the war and, at the end of 1918, the Board decided to subscribe for £15,000 5 per cent National War Bonds 'as funds were available'.[18] Most important of all, perhaps, because it established a solid platform for the firm's contemplated advance into manufacture, was the repayment in stages, completed on 13 July 1917, of the £18,500 borrowed from Lloyds Bank in 1914 to buy the Northfleet site.

The war against Germany ended, as suddenly and unexpectedly as it began, on 11 November 1918. Before the end of the month, Major Frank – he displayed his rank, as the custom used to be, for the rest of his life – was attending a Board meeting, though evidently still in the army. At that meeting, on 25 November, the younger generation of Bowaters, Rainald, Captain Noel Bowater MC, and Eric, were elected to the Board, though it was made very clear to them that they were junior in status to the three brothers, who were Managing Directors.

Eric had become acting Secretary in September 1917, when Rainald went into the army, but his war-shattered health gave way in the spring of 1918 and he had to give place to yet another acting Secretary, George Pickford. He apparently told a journalist, much later, that he joined the business in 1921, so perhaps it was not until then that he was physically fit for an executive position, though he was paid the same salary for 1918–19 – £1,000 free of tax – as the other junior directors and, when Rainald and Noel received a bonus of £1,000 each in June 1920 for extra services, the same sum was paid to Eric 'for extra services in connection with the organisation and carrying on [of] the Inland Wholesale Paper Department'.[19]

In the nation's mood of 1919 there was a good deal of hectic optimism, especially among businessmen, for whom making good the ravages of war and taking advantage of the opportunities of peace seemed to promise long-lasting prosperity. The Government hastily dismantled its control of the economy, by this time far-reaching, while a boom set in which was intense and short-lived. In the summer of 1920 the steam began to go out of it. Over a matter of months, unemployment shot up from 400,000 or rather more to $2\frac{1}{2}$ million, to the accompaniment of industrial action which some people feared and others, no doubt, hoped might lead to revolution.

The worst effects of this collapse were concentrated in industries – coal-mining, cotton textiles, shipbuilding and heavy engineering – which had supported the prosperity of late Victorian Britain. Other industries recovered fairly quickly but those did not and they were still depressed when the world ran into the economic troubles of the thirties. In 1921 the nation suffered a severe heart-attack and perhaps it has never since truly recovered.

The outlook in the twenties, however, once the worst was over, was by no means entirely gloomy. Unemployment remained intractably over the million mark but, even at that level, 90 per cent or more of the working population had jobs and, outside the heavily depressed areas, standards of living were rising rather than falling. The slump of 1921 punctured the wartime inflation and the purchasing power of wages and salaries improved, so that there was plenty of scope for marketing the products of consumer goods industries and the services needed to distribute, sell and maintain them. To balance depression in the coal-mines, cotton mills and heavy industry, therefore, there was prosperity and expansion in the food trades, the motor trade, the electrical and chemical industries – and the manufacture of newsprint. Newspapers were not the least of the consumer goods of which consumers were buying more.

Bowaters' experience on the post-war switchback shows up in profit figures published in a share-issue prospectus in 1926 (Table 1). Bowaters' profits at this level were small by comparison with those of their major suppliers and customers, the large paper mills and the newspaper groups. They were adequate, nevertheless, to

TABLE 1. *W. V. Bowater & Sons Ltd, profits, 1919–25*

	£	Index
1919	39,908	59
1920	67,679	100
1921	35,466	52
1922	22,038	33
1923	31,901	47
1924	43,112	64
1925	37,473	55

Accountants' note: 'These profits are arrived at before charging Income Tax and Corporation Profits Tax (but after charging Excess Profits Duty), and after excluding items which are subject to altered conditions in the future, namely, Charges for Depreciation, Directors' Fees and Remuneration, Interest on Bank Loans (proposed to be paid off out of the proceeds of the present issue) and Credits for Interest and Dividends on Investments other than to be acquired by your Company.'

Source: W. V. Bowater & Sons (1926) Ltd, Prospectus for issue of 200,000 8% Participating Preferred Ordinary shares, 23 January 1926.

provide the six members of the family who were directors with a satisfying standard of upper-middle-class comfort and to enable the head of the family to support the dignity of the Lord Mayor of London in 1913–14 and of MP for the City of London after 1924. The profits came from selling newsprint and other grades of paper at home and abroad; from the sale of 'sundries' – china clay, belting, machine wires and other papermakers' supplies; from trade in hydraulically packed waste carried on from London and Glasgow and from New York. A very important part of the firm's complete package was service: warehousing, wharfage, haulage, lighterage facilities were designed to get orders to customers as promptly as possible and to cope with sudden fluctuations in the demand for newsprint.

Figures from W. V. Bowater & Sons' Private Ledger suggest that home sales of paper and the trade in waste were of about equal importance, accounting together for approximately 80 per cent of Trading Account gross profits, with most of the rest coming from exports, though since the Australian profits are not included in the figures they must be understated (Table 2). Australia and New Zealand were much the biggest takers of British exports of newsprint and Bowaters had for years cultivated their markets.

Bowaters' post-war profits fluctuated, but the directors were convinced that the prospect before them, as the worst of the slump passed away, was encouraging. A survey of market conditions written in 1926, covering the years since 1919, pointed out that

TABLE 2. *W. V. Bowater & Sons Ltd, Trading Account gross profits, 1923–5*

Years ending 31 August	Percentage of total		
	1923	1924	1925
Waste	39.3	34.0	51.9
Export	17.0	15.3	3.8
Inland paper (news and general)	42.9	49.4	44.2
Commission	0.8	1.3	0.1

Source: W. V. Bowater & Sons Private Ledger No. 2.

Bowaters' main markets were the United Kingdom and Australia and went on:

The consumption of Newsprint has increased steadily throughout the world before and since the War; growth since the War has been phenomenal and is of an entirely steady nature and every indication points to a continuation of such growth, which has been brought about largely by increased circulations owing to the more widespread reading of Newspapers and the consequent steady and heavy increase in advertising.[20]

In support, the author of the paper quoted figures of newsprint consumption in the United Kingdom, though without saying how he arrived at them (Table 3). The figures for exports to Australia were even more appetising (Table 4).

TABLE 3. *Approximate record of newsprint consumption in the United Kingdom, 1919–26*

	Consumption (tons)	Increase/decrease* compared with	
		1919 (%)	Previous year (%)
1919	462,000		
1920	515,000	11.5	11.5
1921	500,000	8.2	−3.0
1922	516,000	11.7	3.2
1923	564,000	22.1	9.3
1924	660,000	42.8	17.0
1925	685,000	48.3	3.8
1926	700,000†	51.5	2.2

* Percentages calculated by present author.
† Estimated figure.

Source: As Table 4.

TABLE 4. *Exports of newsprint to Australia from the United Kingdom, 1921–5*

	Exports (tons)	Increase* over	
		1921 (%)	Previous year (%)
1921	6,000		
1922	17,600	193.3	193.3
1923	61,000	916.7	246.6
1924	72,300	1,105.0	18.5
1925	101,600	1,593.3	40.5

* Percentages calculated by present author.

Source: 'Note on newsprint market conditions', attached to letter to Sir Joseph Napier, 7 December 1926, BPM/Sec/9.

By 1923, even without foreknowledge of the figures for later years, the outlook was promising enough for the possibility of building a mill to begin to harden into certainty. Eric Bowater, the youngest director, was anxious not to dawdle. The firm, he thought, was not large enough to go on supporting six members of the family indefinitely. The merchant business had probably reached its zenith, from which a slow decline might follow, or a takeover by one of the exuberant Press barons.

He thought also that his uncles, though not his father, 'saw him as an impractical dreamer whose flights of fancy might well ruin a successful business'. He regarded them as over-cautious.[21] Sir Vansittart, in 1923, was sixty-one; Major Frank, fifty-seven; Sir Frederick (KBE 1920 for war work), a small, dapper man of considerable charm, with a small beard, fifty-six. Sir Vansittart presided with dignity over the affairs of the firm rather than actively managing them. He and his brothers shared an office, to which, at eleven o'clock every morning, Sergeant-Major Stapleton, blind in one eye from a Boer War wound, would bring port and whisky on a silver salver. One morning he tripped on a telephone lead and fell on his face. Sir Vansittart, puffing on a cigar, observed: 'The man's drunk.' No more was said.[22]

A mill would need far more capital than this small patriarchy could command. The Board would have to look outside the family for investors, and for technical support as well, for no Bowater was an engineer. At a Board meeting on 3 July 1923 'The matter of the suggested scheme for the floatation of a Company to construct a new paper mill on the Northfleet property Site was discussed, Mr E. V. Bowater reporting to the Board the tentative arrangements which had been made with Messrs Armstrong, Whitworth & Co. Limited.'[23]

CHAPTER THREE

Merchants into manufacturers
1923–1927

3.1 THE NEWSPRINT INDUSTRY IN THE TWENTIES

In the early twenties, when the Bowater brothers were considering whether to launch their family business into the manufacture of newsprint, the industry was dominated by newspaper owners. Indeed, it is almost true to say that no newsprint mill of any consequence was independent of newspaper interests. In most cases, newsprint mills belonged to newspaper groups but, in one case, a paper business – Inveresk – owned newspapers and other publications.

It is not difficult to see how this high degree of integration arose between the manufacture and use of newsprint. On the one hand, newsprint is a specialised product requiring specialised machinery to make it. The capital investment is heavy and, if newspaper owners are not buying, there is no immediate alternative use for plant or product. On the other hand, newspaper publishers are entirely dependent on large, uninterrupted supplies of the specialised paper they need and the purchase of it represents a high proportion – estimated in 1938 at 35 to 40 per cent – of their total costs. The advantage to the mills of a guaranteed market and to the newspapers of a guaranteed supply is evident. Both can be secured by common ownership.

Edward Lloyd set up the first big integrated enterprise of this kind (p. 12 above). His mills became the biggest in Europe and, even after his son, Frank, in 1918 sold the publishing side – United Newspapers – to a Liberal syndicate, the two branches of the business remained closely linked, because United Newspapers contracted to take all their supplies of newsprint from Lloyds' mills for thirty-one years, from the beginning of 1920 until the end of 1950.[1]

The Harmsworths followed Edward Lloyd's example on a wider and more varied scale. About 1905 they became nervous of a paper famine, caused by 'the rapidly increasing depletion of the forests of the United States, Canada and Scandinavia'. Accordingly, the Amalgamated Press and Associated Newspapers acquired about 3,000 square miles of forest in Newfoundland and set up the Anglo-Newfoundland Development Co. with a base at Grand Falls, where hydro-electric power could be generated. 'The land was a wilderness', said an Amalgamated Press publicity brochure in 1912, '. . . but to-day it is the home of a flourishing township and of one of the biggest pulp and paper mills in the whole world.' By then, it was sending 2,400 tons of paper and 2,000 tons of pulp to the United Kingdom every three weeks.[2]

The Amalgamated Press required a greater variety of paper than Grand Falls could supply. 'All grades of paper', wrote George Sutton to Northcliffe, 'are used by the A. P. from cheap news to the highest qualities of ordinary, pure sulphites, esparto and colours. No one mill in the world could make all our requirements, running into one hundred kinds, sizes and colours.'[3] One mill, nevertheless, could supply some of AP's requirements and, in 1910, the Harmsworths set up Imperial Paper Mills at Gravesend to do exactly that. By 1912, Imperial were producing paper for *Answers* and similar publications at a rate of 300 tons a week and machines were being built to supply finer grades for periodicals such as *The London Magazine* and *Home Chat*. A good deal of the pulp was coming from Grand Falls and in time, perhaps, all of it would.[4] Plans for expansion were held up by the war. 'The idea', said Sutton in 1919, 'always has been to increase the output to 2,000 tons a week. The plans are prepared for enlarging the mill and the machines are being made. Of course, during the War, building was held up and also the making of machinery.'[5]

Rothermere specialised in this side of the Harmsworth business. 'We both know', Sutton remarked to Northcliffe, 'that it would be hard to find anyone with his knowledge of paper and the paper-making industry.'[6] Those words were written in the heady days of 1919, when the post-war boom was running strong and Rothermere was very busy. He wanted to develop Grand Falls 'on a large scale' and he wanted a salary of £5,000 free of tax for doing it. His brother jibbed. '"Tax free"', he said, 'will begin a bad system in the business.' However, he could have £7,500 subject to tax. 'Harold', said Alfred, 'is the only person who properly understands Newfoundland.'[7]

It was not only Newfoundland, apparently, that Harold understood. In June 1919 he wrote to Sutton to say that he and Becker ('the biggest pulp man in this country') had bought 'a mill at Greenhithe belonging to the Wallpaper Company. It is a very modern mill. It was erected at a cost of something over £600,000 and has been purchased at much below cost.' It was called Ingress Abbey Mill but Rothermere had the name changed to Empire Mills. It needed conversion from wallpaper to newsprint. 'I am forming a company', Rothermere went on,

and it occurred to me that, as a fall back in case of fire or any other calamity, the Amalgamated Press would like to have an interest in it. If you think anything of this, I can [arrange] for the A.P. 100,000 7% Preference shares. You might let me know what you think. I wish to make it quite clear that this is an offer I am not making in the ordinary way of business but simply because of my association with the A.P.[8]

Sutton, evidently startled, went to see the mill – 'it is a magnificent mill' – and reported to Northcliffe. 'Our paper consumption is so important to us that, in view of a calamity at Gravesend at any time, we should accept this', he said, referring to the offer of Preference shares, and added: 'Of course, this in no way interferes with our extensions at Gravesend for the machines are ordered but, between us, then we shall have the two finest sites on the Thames.'[9]

Northcliffe grumbled about the rate of interest and about the size of the investment – '£100,000 is a very large sum and a serious responsibility' – but Sutton was insistent. 'The Greenhithe mill', he said, 'will fill a gap which is not covered by any mill in which we are interested.' Northcliffe gave way. 'Go ahead with the paper mills', he said, 'I am glad that we shall be on the Board and that all precautions will be taken. As long as Harold is alive we shall be all right in any case but we are all getting on in years and never know what may happen.'[10]

Rothermere made one more important move into papermaking in the early twenties. In 1920 the executors of Albert E. Reed offered Rothermere shares in the Reed business, one of the larger independents, and Rothermere, through Sunday Pictorial Newspapers and Daily Mirror Newspapers, took 52 per cent of the Ordinary shares, apparently under the impression that the holding would be sufficient to give him control, as in most companies it would have been. He or his advisers failed, until too late, to discover that in Reeds the Preference shareholders had voting rights which could defeat him. The Berrys, to whom he offered the shares, refused them and Sunday Pictorial/Daily Mirror Newspapers were left for many years with a large minority interest in Reed.[11]

With or without control of Reed, the Harmsworths' position in 1922 looked strong. They had Anglo-Newfoundland across the Atlantic, Imperial at Gravesend, Empire at Greenhithe. Then in the

mid-twenties the Berrys began to advance in newsprint as well as
publishing. When Rothermere sold the Amalgamated Press to the
Berrys in 1926 Imperial Paper Mills went with it. A much larger
acquisition followed. In May 1927, Frank Lloyd died and, following his wishes, the Lloyd mills at Sittingbourne and Kemsley were
offered to Allied Newspapers, the holding company of the Berry
group, and the Berrys without hesitation bought them. They thus
came into possession of the largest newsprint plant in the country; a
plant which, Sir William Berry told his shareholders, 'is . . . larger
than any in Canada or the United States'. Its output of newsprint
was over 200,000 tons a year.[12]

We are now in a position to survey the state of the British
newsprint industry in the early twenties, when the Bowater brothers
were reaching the point of deciding to enter it. Reliable figures of
output are hard to come by but it seems clear that the ownership of
mills was heavily concentrated and that after the sale of Edward
Lloyd the balance of power, in newsprint as in newspapers, swung
from Rothermere towards the Berrys. Apart from these two, no
other newspaper owners also owned newsprint mills but, by contrast, the Inveresk Paper Co., reputed to be one of the largest
paper-producing groups in the world, owned the *Illustrated
London News,* other well-known illustrated periodicals and the
Lancashire Daily Post. William Harrison, in control of Inveresk,
was looking for a way into London newspapers and, in 1928, he
found it by the purchase of United Newspapers.

British-owned mills independent of newspaper groups were not
numerous nor, after the sale of Reed shares to Rothermere and the
sale of Lloyds to the Berrys, did they include many of the larger
producers. Allied Newspapers, between 1921 and 1933, dealt with
Lloyds and at least ten other suppliers, of whom five were in
Norwegian, Finnish or Swedish ownership (Table 5), a figure which
emphasises the permanent threat to British newsprint makers of
Scandinavian competition.[13]

There were also the Canadians. Newsprint production in
Canada, insignificant before 1914 by comparison with production
in the USA, was growing very rapidly indeed in the early twenties,
chiefly to supply the market in the USA where consumption of
newsprint rose by 48 per cent between 1919 and 1924. By that year,
Canadian production was almost equal to production in the USA,
having grown by 70 per cent since 1919. As long as demand from
the United States kept up, the Canadians paid very little attention to
the United Kingdom or other markets. Their own home market,
however, was very small – less than 5 per cent of the United States

TABLE 5. *Newsprint suppliers to Allied Newspapers, 1921-33*

British		
	Edward Lloyd Ltd	1921-32
	Peter Dixon & Son	1923-33
	Darwen Paper Mill Co.	1924-33
	Sun Paper Mill Co.	1924-31
	Chadwick & Taylor	1923
	Star Paper Mill Co.*	1924-31
Finnish		
	Finnish Paper Mill Association	1921-2
	Kymmene AB	1921-3
	Worgans AB	1921
Norwegian		
	Union Paper Co.	1921-6
Swedish		
	Stora Kopparbergs AB	1923-5
		1929-30

* Taken over by Kymmene AB in 1930.

Source: S. L. Lewis, Thomson, Withy Grove Ltd.

figure in 1924 – and it was not difficult to surmise what might happen if United States demand should ever fail, though in the roaring twenties there is no evidence that anyone ever let such a thought enter his head.[14]

British newspaper owners without mills of their own thus had a choice between newsprint suppliers at home, who might be owned by their competitors, and abroad, meaning chiefly the Scandinavians, or they might draw on both sources as Allied Newspapers did. It was a position not without its advantages but the field of choice was narrow, especially if mills owned by competitors were excluded. Lord Beaverbrook began to be haunted by fears of a hostile price ring closing around him, though perhaps they did not become acute until after the Berrys bought Lloyds in 1927. Then, being unwilling to see his suppliers in the hands of competitors, he cancelled the contract between the *Daily Express* and Lloyd which had been running ever since the *Express* was founded and turned towards the Canadians.[15]

By 1927, as the next section of this chapter will show, the Bowater brothers had committed their firm to newsprint manufacture. The price of their product – newsprint – was falling, in spite of rising demand, but the price of their main raw material – wood pulp – was falling also and from 1927 onward it fell faster. The ratio between these prices was obviously of the highest importance to the newsprint manufacturer and until the late thirties it was highly favourable to the manufacturer in the United Kingdom, controlling no timber supplies and buying pulp from those who did. For the Canadians, producing wood pulp on a huge scale from their own timber, the case was otherwise as soon as demand in the United States began to fall, as it did from 1930 onward, but to that we shall return.

The Bowaters were going into an industry in which relations between buyers and sellers were remarkably close, probably for two main reasons. There were very few of them in the first place and, since contracts were of the highest importance to each side, negotiations were carried out at the highest level. Secondly, although the newspaper owners had the normal buyers' interest in getting newsprint as cheaply as they could, they also had an interest in keeping efficient suppliers in production, since there were so few of them. In consequence, they were sometimes inclined to treat suppliers rather as partners in a joint enterprise than as parties to a bargain. 'If a manufacturer gives good service', Beaverbrook wrote to A. R. Graustein of the International Paper Co., New York, 'he is never squeezed. The "Express" hopes never to be squeezed by the manufacturer.'[16]

3.2 ARMSTRONG, WHITWORTH, NEWFOUNDLAND AND NORTHFLEET

The firm of Sir W. E. Armstrong, Whitworth & Co. Ltd, with which Bowaters opened negotiations in 1923, was one of the great industrial names of the world before 1914, ranking with Krupps in Germany, Bethlehem Steel in the USA and Schneider in France. Some of the heaviest guns and the largest battleships of the Royal Navy were built by Armstrong, Whitworth and in many ways the firm could show everything that heavy industry in late Victorian Britain stood for: splendid craftsmanship and excellent quality; paternal management; hostility to trade unions; rugged self-confidence, not wholly justified. Lord Armstrong, before he died at the age of ninety in 1900, had become a national figure: remote, wealthy and powerful in the magician's castle he had built for himself at Cragside; suffused with a sinister glamour as an armaments manufacturer. Something of his personality lingered in the business he had created, of which the Chairman until 1920 was John Meade Falkner (1852–1932) whose interests 'were palaeography, liturgical studies and the history of music' and who wrote novels which 'reveal a man profoundly out of sympathy with the twentieth century'.[17]

In the early twenties, the predicament of Armstrong, Whitworth illustrated the disasters that had overtaken British heavy industry in 1921, particularly the collapse of shipbuilding. There was no longer a demand for battleships – that was not to be expected after the war – and the demand for merchant ships, at first brisk, had been killed in 1921. Moreover Armstrongs had greatly expanded during the war in many activities besides shipbuilding, and when the demand for war-like stores dried up there was urgent need to find as many ways as possible to keep plant and labour force employed. Motor-cars? Locomotives? Certainly, and something more as well: pulp and paper mills in Newfoundland.

By the time this plan was taking shape, Meade Falkner had been replaced by a man of very different stamp: Sir Glyn West (1877–1945). He had gone to the Ministry of Munitions from Armstrongs in 1915. He came back, having been Director General of Shell and Gun Manufacture, with a high reputation for efficiency and drive. 'Confident of his own abilities', says J. D. Scott, 'he was the kind of man who did not listen readily to advice, and he stepped into a position which was ready-made for dictatorship.'[18] He tackled the Newfoundland proposition with enthusiasm.

Among the inhabitants of Newfoundland the Reid family was wealthy, prominent and powerful. Reid Newfoundland Ltd owned the Newfoundland Products Corporation, founded in 1915, which had rights over water power from the Humber River in western Newfoundland, rights over 670 square miles of timberland chiefly along Deer Lake and Grand Lake in the same region and land suitable for factories, power plant, a port and housing.[19] The company had been set up to produce cyanamid, but its assets could readily be adapted to the requirements of the pulp and paper industry. It was that industry, by 1921, which the Newfoundland Products Corporation was preparing to enter, encouraged, no doubt, by rapidly rising demand for newsprint in the USA and the United Kingdom. In 1922 its name was changed to the Newfoundland Power & Paper Co. Ltd.[20]

The company's project, as it was eventually put in hand, provided for hydro-electricity from Deer Lake to drive pulp- and paper-making machinery at Corner Brook, on the left bank of the Humber River between Deer Lake and the sea. Timber could be rafted to Corner Brook on the river: pulp and paper could be carried away by sea and there was also a rail connection with St John's, some 300 miles away on the Atlantic coast. Corner Brook itself had 250 inhabitants and a sawmill:[21] as well as putting up the power-station and the mill, Reids would have to develop the town. It was an ambitious enterprise.

Reids needed finance and they needed a contractor. As to the finance, which does not concern us here but will concern us later, their arrangements included £2m First Debentures guaranteed by the British Government and £4m Second Debentures guaranteed by the Newfoundland Government,[22] each Government being represented on the Board of NP&P. As to the contractor, they went to the top of the trade: Armstrong, Whitworth, who as early as July 1921 had a holding in Newfoundland Products Corporation.[23]

For Armstrongs there would be heavy engineering work in plenty, such as turbines for the electrical plant. Ships would have to be built for the service of the paper mills. There would be the equipment of the mills themselves, to be manufactured by Charles Walmsley & Co., then an Armstrong subsidiary. In November 1921 William Adamson, Walmsleys' technical director, was proposing plant to produce 300–320 tons of air dry groundwood pulp and 100 tons of air dry sulphite pulp a day, as well as machinery for 400 tons of newsprint a day, giving 120,000 tons a year.[24] Adamson put the total cost of the pulp and paper plant at $5m (about £1.3m at contemporary rates of exchange). For the Newfoundland operations as a whole, Armstrongs issued £3m of debentures, backed by the Bank of England.[25] They were the biggest customer of the Bank's Newcastle branch, which at this stage was very happy to accommodate them.[26]

In 1923 Eric Bowater was on the Newfoundland Power & Paper Co.'s Board.[27] It was a surprising appointment. He was about twenty-seven, with very little business experience. He may have known something about paper mills but it is doubtful whether he knew anything at all, at first hand, about Newfoundland – not the easiest of countries for a stranger to get to know. From developments which soon followed his appointment, it is likely that he was nominated by Armstrongs but nothing is known for certain. It was perhaps the first indication that he was a rising man, not merely in his own firm but in the business world generally, and not only at home.

He worked hard at his directorship. A journey to Corner Brook, even from relatively near points in North America let alone the United Kingdom, was a matter of days', not hours', travelling and he said in 1945 that he made the trip three or four times between 1922 and 1925. Newfoundland, remote and bleak, made a deep impression on him and engaged his affections.

About the time when Eric took up the NP&P directorship, two negotiations were going on simultaneously. One was directed at getting Bowaters appointed selling agents for the paper to be pro-

Logging in Newfoundland, 1920s.

duced by NP&P when Armstrongs had built them their mill at
Corner Brook. The other was about Bowaters' projected mill at
Northfleet, for which, it seems, Armstrongs were seeking the construction contract. That there was a link between the two negotiations seems certain, though we have no positive knowledge. It may

be that Bowaters were unwilling to commit themselves to giving the construction contract to Armstrongs until they were sure of getting the sole agency for NP&P, which would bring them an assured income and a share, at one remove, in the largest market for newsprint in the world – the USA, where consumption of newsprint rose 30 per cent in five years from 2,197,000 short tons in 1920 to 2,847,000 short tons in 1924.[28] The Bowater directors watched the progress of construction in Newfoundland attentively, presumably mainly through the eyes of Eric, their man on the NP&P Board.

Sir Frederick and his son, Eric, were in charge of Bowaters' side of the negotiations. Sir Frederick was ailing. He attended only one Board meeting after 4 April 1923 and died on 16 May 1924. Force of circumstances as well as his own character were thus thrusting Eric into the leadership of his own generation on Bowaters' Board. During the spring and summer of 1923, Bowaters' directors agreed first to a draft and then to a preliminary agreement, but the binding contract was not signed until 11 July 1924.[29] It then took the form of an agreement between NP&P and the Bowater Paper Co. Inc. of New York, who became NP&P's 'sole agents throughout the world for the sale of all paper and pulp (of whatsoever kind or quality) manufactured or sold by the Company' at a commission of $2\frac{1}{2}$ per cent on the fob mill price received by NP&P.[30]

The Bowater Paper Co. Inc. was set up in September 1923, under Eric's supervision in New York, to take over the assets of the Hudson Packing & Paper Co. (p. 20 above). That company seems to have been almost inert and the Bowater Paper Co. must have been formed with the sales contract in mind. Its importance to Bowaters was proclaimed by Eric's assiduity in attending to its affairs as a Vice-President. Its President was Earle C. Duffin (d. 1949), a Canadian formerly in business for himself in Winnipeg, and its Sales Manager was August (Gus) B. Meyer (1892–1964), a graduate of Cornell University.[31] For both, Eric conceived a deep affection, and they also became close colleagues with him, in later years, in the Bowater business.

After the general principles of the NP&P sales agency had been agreed, but before the definitive contract, Bowaters, working closely with Armstrongs, set up a company to contract for building a paper mill at Northfleet and to run it when built. The first directors were the three elder Bowaters, Eric and Major Douglas C. Jennings, DSO (1892–1973). Jennings, three years older than Eric, had connections in the City and in Newfoundland, where he evidently acted as an intermediary between the Reid interests, Armstrongs and the Newfoundland government. Presumably it was in

Earle Duffin. *Robert Knight*

connection with NP&P's affairs that he and Eric became acquainted. He resigned in 1926. Eric, the only Bowater of his generation on the Board, was probably beginning to step into his father's
place. The company was called Bowater's Paper Mills Ltd and it
came into existence on 16 July 1923. For Bowaters, this was the
decisive step from trade into large-scale industry.[32]

3.3 THE BUILDING OF NORTHFLEET MILL

The plans for Northfleet mill were on an ample scale. They provided for 'a complete modern paper-making mill' at the heart of which would be two large buildings: a beater house, perhaps 250 feet long, for preparing the pulp, and a machine shop, some 450 feet long, for the paper machines themselves. There would be a boiler house, a mechanics' shop containing large machine tools, a reel store, a store for waste paper and other buildings. Roads would be built and railway sidings connected to the Southern Railway, and a river wall and embankment, with a barge bay, would provide for the landing of materials.[33]

Walmsleys were to build two papermaking machines, among the largest in the world, producing paper of a trimmed width of 221 inches on one machine and 228 inches on the other. The speed of newsprint machines was rising rapidly as machine-makers applied equipment installed during the Great War to peace-time purposes and the output mentioned in the contract was 'about 800 tons [a week] of newsprint paper of the highest quality working twenty-four hours a day, five and one-half days per week', giving roughly 50,000 tons of newsprint a year.

The capital required for these works, it was recognised from the beginning, would outrun the combined resources of the merchant business and of the owning family. It seems equally to have been recognised, if not right from the beginning, then very early on, that a great deal of the money needed would be found by Armstrongs. They needed the contract and were prepared to add to their existing commitments in Newfoundland and elsewhere, heavy though these were, to make sure they had it.

The capital structure of Bowater's Paper Mills Ltd was therefore designed to keep the ownership of the business in the family's hands but to admit other investors, principally Armstrongs and a syndicate called Power Securities Corporation Ltd as debenture holders. The share capital was £300,000 in £1 Ordinary shares, of which, by April 1924, £117,000 had been taken up at par by W. V. Bowater & Sons (95,693), the family and their friends. Table 6 shows how £300,000 6½ per cent First Mortgage Debenture stock had been subscribed at £90 per cent. BTH and Babcock & Wilcox were sub-contractors. Saxton Noble was Armstrongs' Managing Director.[34] The company also proposed to create £175,000 7 per cent Second Debentures to be taken up by Armstrongs under conditions laid down in the construction contract.

Six and a half per cent of £300,000 is £19,500; 7 per cent of

TABLE 6. *Bowater's Paper Mills Debenture holders, April 1924*

Armstrong, Whitworth	£100,000
Power Securities	£100,000
W. V. Bowater & Sons	£ 50,000
British Thomson Houston	£ 25,000
Babcock & Wilcox	£ 15,000
Saxton Noble and others	£ 10,000

Source: BPM 4.iv.24.

£175,000, £12,250. Bowater's Paper Mills therefore faced the prospect of having to earn £31,750 – 10.6 per cent of the authorised share capital – in interest alone, without providing for the redemption of the debentures, before the Ordinary shareholders would be entitled to anything. Someone, it seems, was optimistic about BPM's earning power and optimistic he continued to be throughout the twenties and thirties, for debenture borrowing on a steadily increasing scale became the characteristic method of financing the rapid expansion of the business.

The contract for the construction of the Northfleet mill, between Bowater's Paper Mills and Armstrongs, was sealed on 4 April 1924. Its essential terms were simple. Armstrongs undertook to build 'a complete modern paper mill' and to deliver it to Bowater's Paper Mills 'in a complete and uninjured state ready to commence operations on or before the first day of July, 1925'. The price was to be 'the lump sum of £481,926' and the money was to be provided, as to £273,926 from the proceeds of the issue of the £300,000 6½ per cent Debentures (though it is not clear how the issue price – £90 – was going to provide the sum specified), and as to £208,000 from the issue to Armstrongs of 33,000 £1 Ordinary shares and £175,000 7 per cent Debentures, both to be taken up and paid for progressively as the work went on, so that BPM could immediately pay the money back to Armstrongs.[35] It appears therefore that Armstrongs, taking their subscription of £90,000 for 6½ per cent Debentures together with the £208,000 they were proposing to put up for Ordinary shares and 7 per cent Debentures, were intending to lend Bowaters £298,000, or 62 per cent of the price they had set on the mill: £481,926. Since they were heavily in debt themselves, the success of Bowaters' venture was of more than ordinary importance to them; failure would be disastrous.

Outside the scope of the construction contract, BPM had bought the land from W. V. Bowater & Sons, paying for it with £60,000 raised by the issue of Ordinary shares. W. V. Bowater also gave an undertaking in certain eventualities to find £50,000 working capital, of which Walmsleys, the machine builders, were to provide half.[36] Finally, on the same day as the construction contract was sealed, BPM granted W. V. Bowater the sole agency for the output of the mill, at $2\frac{1}{2}$ per cent commission. The parent firm thus provided the marketing organisation needed by its new and much larger subsidiary.[37]

Nobody in Bowaters, in 1924, knew much about paper mill construction. For knowledge, the directors substituted a touching faith in Armstrongs' technical competence, presumably derived from Eric's observations in Newfoundland. 'We relied upon your special knowledge and experience in this class of work', wrote Sir Vansittart to Armstrongs in May 1925, 'and did not appoint an independent Engineer conversant with paper mill construction, as we otherwise would have done.'[38]

It was an omission which they began to regret almost as soon as work on the site began. The discovery of a fault in the hard chalk, leading to subsidence of five-eighths of an inch under 30 hundredweight to the square foot, caused them to call in Basil Mott, CB (1859–1938), an eminent consulting engineer, who recommended piling the foundations. C. O. Ridley, Armstrongs' man on the site, said piling would not delay completion of the mill 'in any way whatsoever', but so emphatic a claim may have seemed ominous. The question then arose of providing a jetty and Noel, by this time on BPM's Board, found himself deputed to seek information about the draft of vessels that might use it; hardly, it might be thought, a task for a director. The Board by this time – May 1924 – was evidently becoming disillusioned with Armstrongs' 'special knowledge and experience'. Eric was looking for an engineer.[39]

He found Arthur Baker (1881–1969), one of the foremost men in the paper industry though not, by early training, an engineer. He was originally a chemist, educated at Bury Grammar School and Manchester College of Science and Technology, who had spent nearly all his career with Wallpaper Manufacturers Ltd, formed in 1900 by combining thirty-one firms, about half of them in Lancashire.[40] He was many-sided, with a very lively mind, and he added engineering to chemistry to become one of the early British members of a rising profession, chemical engineering. As he rose in his firm, so also he rose in the industry generally. In 1919 he became a member of the Council of the British Paper and Board Manufacturers' Association and, in 1920, started the Association's Technical Section with the intention of bringing a scientific approach to bear on the technology of a somewhat reluctant industry.[41] He

MR. ARTHUR BAKER

His sacks with corn the harvest farmer fills,
The wheat into flour the miller mills ;
But the man we admire is A Baker,
For of paper he is a great maker ;
To us producing it means daily bread—
Drink to Arthur Baker, our worthy Head.

Arthur Baker, caricatured for *Bowater's News*, 18 December 1929.

directed the production of shell cases during the Great War but afterwards came back to Wallpaper Manufacturers. When Bowaters became interested in him, however, he was director and General Manager of their close neighbours, Empire Paper Mills of Greenhithe, Kent.

Empire had formerly been Ingress Abbey Paper Mills, one of three papermaking plants (the other two were in Darwen, Lancashire) belonging to Wallpaper Manufacturers. Baker had been at Ingress Abbey as Chief Chemist and then as Deputy Manager but, when he came back after the war, by this time in charge of all three of the Wallpaper Manufacturers' mills, he found Ingress Abbey in such a poor state that he recommended selling. He knew, he said, that the directors of Wallpaper Manufacturers had very little interest in paper manufacture.[42] Lord Rothermere, on the other hand, had a great deal. In 1919 he bought Ingress Abbey (p. 28 above), changed its name to Empire and put Baker in, as Director and General Manager, to convert the plant to the making of newsprint, which took two years. During his time with Empire, Baker went to Newfoundland to advise the Treasury on the affairs of the Newfoundland Power & Paper Co., presumably with the British Government's guarantee of the firm's debentures in mind. He was in Newfoundland in 1922–3 and there, if not elsewhere, he probably met Eric Bowater, adding yet one more strand to the web of connections between Newfoundland and Bowaters.

With this imposing background, Baker would be a great prize for a firm so new to papermaking as Bowaters. Moreover, he would be gambling with his own career if he joined them. He knew the strength of his position and, although there is no evidence that he was reluctant to come, he nevertheless made sure he came on his own stiff terms:

Mr Baker asks to be made Managing Director and to have a free hand in the management. He wishes all his recommendations regarding all purchases to be acted on by the Board. As he will be responsible for the quality and quantity of paper produced he particularly wishes to have his advice as to the quality of the pulp purchased accepted and acted on by the Board.

He further wishes to have a free hand in the appointment of the technical staff and . . . will wish to appoint an Engineer at an early date.

He is at present living in a house which is the property of the Empire Paper Mills Limited and, as he would like to remain in this house, he asks the Company to take over this house from the Empire Paper Mills.

He further asks for a three years agreement at a minimum Salary of £5000 per annum for the first two years and £4000 in the third year and at the expiration of the agreement he would like to have a substantial interest in the concern.[43]

He went on to say that he would be able to start, full time, on 1 October 1924 and that in the intervening three months or so he 'would give the Company the benefit of his advice on all matters concerning construction etc.' He added that there were 'a number of minor modifications in the layout' which he wished to make. 'Minor', as we shall see, turned out to be a decidedly elastic term.

The Board gave Baker nearly all he asked for, in a four-year agreement by which he was engaged from 1 December 1924 as resident director and General Manager of the mills at Northfleet. They did not make him Managing Director but they agreed that, during his period of management, no managing director should be appointed. His salary was to be £4,000 a year – a very high figure – and he was to have 3,000 fully paid Ordinary shares on appointment, with a right to take up 2,000 more after 30 November 1927, providing his agreement was not then terminated. He was entitled, so long as he remained Manager, to remain in his house free of rent, rates and taxes.[44]

On these extraordinarily generous terms – Bowaters must have wanted him very badly – Baker moved from Lord Rothermere's service into Bowaters', bringing with him, by arrangement, Douglas MacIvor, who became BPM's Chief Engineer, and several others.[45] Rothermere obviously wanted to see the new mills succeed and was ready to go to great lengths to make sure that they would, presumably in order to widen the choice of newsprint suppliers open to him for his publishing interests, even at the cost of encouraging competition with his own paper mills. His attitude, as will appear, was more than a passing whim.

As Baker came on the scene, there were already disturbing signs of bad planning and incompetent management. The piling recommended by Basil Mott was going forward but not smoothly. There was disagreement about what ought to be done, misunderstanding about costs, lack of information about the foundations of the boiler-house and power-house, regarding which there was talk of writing to Sir Glyn West 'requesting him to look into the matter and to supply a satisfactory explanation'.[46] All this was ominous and its delaying effect was compounded when Baker and MacIvor, as soon as they arrived, began making numerous small and smallish criticisms of the contractors' work generally. These, however, were not all.

The efficiency of the mill would depend very heavily on the

arrangements made for handling materials, especially pulp. One
look seems to have convinced Arthur Baker that Armstrongs' ideas
on the subject were thoroughly bad. He was still talking about it
thirty-six years later. 'The Contract they had with Armstrong Whit-
worths', he said in his retirement speech, 'would have provided a
very poor Mill.'

He reached this conclusion, after some hesitation, in the autumn
of 1924. The problem started at the wharfside, where materials
were to be landed. 'The first thing he had noted when looking at the
original layout of the Mill', he told the Board on 10 December
1924, 'was that the proposed pulp landing facilities were quite
inadequate and he had immediately taken the matter up with the
Contractors.' Armstrongs proposed to unload ships in the river into
barges, unload barges at the wharf and distribute pulp by 'Con-
veyors'. 'If it were impossible to bring steamers alongside', said
Baker, 'bargeing alone would cost approximately £12,000 per
annum', so he suggested going into the whole question of the
shipping side of the mill afresh and calling in expert advice. He
wanted to scrap the conveyor proposal and put in a jetty and a
railway system. There would have to be at least three cranes on the
wharf for unloading ships, and the placing of the china clay stores,
the oil tanks and the coal bunkers would have to be reconsidered,
along with the movement of cranes. He realised that any alterations
to shipping facilities would add to the capital cost of the mill 'but
. . . he felt he could not allow the Company to continue on the lines
as at present proposed as it was certain to involve a much heavier
expenditure if alterations had to be made . . . when the Mill was in
operation'.[47]

Baker was saying, in effect, that the layout of the mill, as designed
by Armstrongs, would have to be radically altered several months
after construction had begun. He and Eric were empowered by the
Board to decide on the necessity of alterations and Eric, still under
thirty and still with very little experience, had to confront Sir Glyn
West with Arthur Baker's unwelcome message in September 1924.
Apparently neither of Eric's uncles relished the task, or perhaps he
preferred to keep them out of the way. The upshot was a conference
between the company's engineers and the contractors 'and in nearly
all cases a definite decision [was] arrived at to fall in with the
Company's Engineer's views'. Armstrongs very soon afterwards
wrote asking Bowaters to confirm that they realised there was a
possibility that more time might be needed to complete the contract.
Sir Vansittart refused.[48]

Sir Vansittart might refuse to recognise the facts on paper, no doubt for good tactical reasons, but he must have been aware of two things: the completion of the mill was going to be seriously delayed and construction was going to cost more, probably much more, than the contract price. After several months of rather confused exchanges between the contractors and their clients, the matter came to a head at a conference on 2 April 1925 at which two key proposals were made. Eric Bowater suggested 'that the Mill should be paid for ab initio on the basis of cost plus an agreed percentage for establishment charges and an agreed profit'. Armstrongs, as a condition of acceptance, made a proposal of their own: 'that Mr Baker should take sole charge of the work from the present time including arrangements with the sub-contractors, so that the Mill can be finished rapidly in accordance with his views . . . Mr Baker will, of course, receive from our Staff every possible assistance.'

In the same letter, Armstrongs made a heartfelt plea to Bowaters to make up their minds about what they wanted done: 'They' – Armstrongs' directors – 'are impressed with the necessity, in our joint interest, of completing the Mill at the earliest possible date, but it seems impossible to concentrate attention on this aspect of the matter whilst discussions are taking place regarding suggested modifications or additions to the original scheme.'[49]

Baker had first begun to criticise Armstrongs' plans in the summer of 1924. It was now May 1925 and the contract date for completion – which was bound to be missed – was 1 July. Armstrongs' anxiety is understandable.

It was one thing for Armstrongs to agree to re-negotiate the contract price – quite another to get the basis of a new price settled, especially since Armstrongs had to re-negotiate not only with Bowaters but with their sub-contractors, especially the builders, James Byrom Ltd.[50] Discussions, as we shall see, dragged on for a year or more with increasingly serious financial consequences for Armstrongs and for Bowaters. Most firms would have gone to law with each other but these two remained remarkably amicable, probably because, in the first place, each needed the other too badly to contemplate breaking off relations and, in the second place, each was conscious of weakness. Armstrongs had discovered embarrassing deficiencies in their technical competence. Bowaters, by demanding far-reaching alterations in Armstrongs' plans, were going against a clause in the original contract which laid down that Baker had no right to overrule engineering decisions taken before he was appointed.[51]

Against this background Bowaters' first paper machine came into production on 8 February 1926; the second on 6 April, rather more

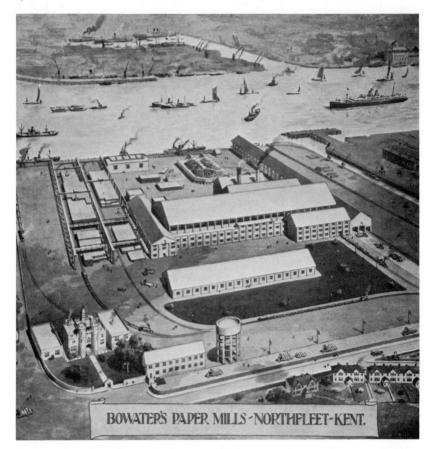

Northfleet mill, from a publicity pamphlet of 1926.

than nine months after the date set for opening a complete mill. Even with both machines working, completion was a long way off and Bowaters' troubles were far greater than the usual difficulties of starting up. Neither manufacture nor materials handling could yet be as efficient as had been planned and to meet what should have been the proudest moment in its history so far the firm was compelled to advance at a hobble.[52] Moreover, delay and the prospect of extra cost had done so much damage to Bowaters' finances that there was no certainty that the business would survive.

3.4 CRISIS AND RECOVERY

At the beginning of 1926, Bowaters' plans for their new manufacturing business lay in ruins. They were based on two major assumptions. The first was that the price of building the Northfleet mill would be fixed and unalterable and would be paid as laid down in the construction contract. The second was that the mill would be in production during July 1925, so that orders could be taken beforehand for forward delivery and cash would almost immediately start to flow when the machines began to turn. The first assumption was destroyed by the comprehensive re-planning of the mill, and the delay caused by re-planning destroyed the second. Sir Vansittart wrote in May 1925:.

Any delay will mean a considerable loss of revenue, which we had relied on obtaining for the sale of paper during the first year's operations. With the Mill in its present condition, we do not feel safe in accepting orders for substantial tonnage for forward delivery at the remunerative prices now offering, and it is very difficult to foresee how long the present situation of favourable conditions in the paper market is likely to continue.[53]

Armstrongs' situation, interlinked with Bowaters', was equally precarious. At the heart of it lay Newfoundland. Armstrongs' mismanagement there had been as bad as at Northfleet, with far worse consequences. When the mill at Corner Brook opened in August 1925, Armstrongs' total indebtedness was $45m (£9.3m) on which annual interest charges were running at $22.50 (£4. 13s. 9d.) a ton of newsprint when the price per ton in England was averaging £17. 10s. Armstrongs' debt to the Bank of England at the same time was at least £2.6m and the Governor, Montagu Norman, was preparing to have their affairs investigated.[54]

Investigation would lead straight towards Bowaters, for Bowaters owed Armstrongs money which they badly needed. But Armstrongs, like Bowaters, were caught by the breakdown of the construction contract. They had received £265,000 under the 'fixed price' clause but, as soon as it was abolished, they no more knew how much they ought to receive than Bowaters knew how much they ought to pay. The new basis of pricing – cost plus allowances for overheads and profit (quaintly called 'time and lime') – afforded scope for months of investigation and argument by Bowaters and their accountants, during which time Armstrongs received nothing although construction was still going on.

It may now be apparent why Bowaters and Armstrongs could not afford to quarrel with each other. Bowaters dared not provoke Armstrongs into stopping construction, for in the completion of the mill lay their only hope of survival. In Bowaters' survival, in turn, lay Armstrongs' only hope of getting the money they so badly needed, so they dared not drive Bowaters into liquidation. The construction contract between the two firms, as solicitors called in by the Bank of England to examine it observed, 'seems . . . to have been looked upon rather as a joint venture than as a Contract strictly between two separate entities',[55] and, indeed, between the autumn of 1924 and the spring of 1927 it is probably fair to say of Bowaters and Armstrongs that the collapse of one would have destroyed the other. It was extremely fortunate for Bowaters that Montagu Norman, taking an unconventional view of the Bank of England's place in the economy, considered it his duty to see that Armstrongs did not collapse.[56]

Bowater's directors started 1926 by deciding, on 13 January, that the company was seriously short of capital. With £250,000 unfunded debt, it would have to be reconstructed.[57] Over the next three months they took measures no doubt intended as preliminaries.

Of the greatest importance in the long run, perhaps, was their decision to change their auditors. Instead of Messrs Touche they appointed Blackburns, Barton, Mayhew & Co. and, by so doing, laid claim to the professional services of Sir Basil Mayhew (1883–1966).[58] Not the least of Eric Bowater's talents was his skill in choosing people, and many of the associations formed in these early days served him well and lastingly. As he came to rely on Arthur Baker on the technical side, so he came to rely on Sir Basil, though not on Sir Basil alone, in financial matters. His ambitions always outran his immediate resources and he needed the best advice he could get.

More in the nature of emergency aid, perhaps, was the service rendered by F. R. A. Shortis, elected to the Board on 22 February 1926. He enabled the company to negotiate a loan of £50,000, on the security of pulp stocks, from Kleinwort, Sons & Co.[59]

The mill company could also fall back on the resources of its parent. In the early months of 1926, a new company, W. V. Bowater & Sons (1926) Ltd,* was formed to take over the old merchant business by exchange of Ordinary shares, nearly all held within the family, and by cash purchase of the Preference shares. It was also intended to raise fresh Preferred capital on the market but, for a newly launched, rather obscure undertaking with a subsidiary – Bowater's Paper Mills – in rough water, that was far from easy. Eventually John Keeling (1895–1978) who, with two partners, had formed the London & Yorkshire Trust, agreed that the Trust should underwrite the issue: 200,000 8 per cent Participating Preferred Ordinary shares of £1 each. To make the issue go, the shares were entitled not only to an 8 per cent dividend but also, after an 8

---

* '(1926)' was dropped after 22 December 1926.

per cent Ordinary dividend had been paid, to another 2 per cent, making 10 per cent altogether. The Trust charged 2½ per cent underwriting commission, with an overriding commission of 1 per cent on the nominal value of the shares. With Bank Rate at 5 per cent, it was expensive borrowing.[60]

Arthur Baker and Douglas Jennings were not on W. V. Bowater's Board but otherwise the new company's directors and BPM's were the same and, apart from running a flourishing merchant business at home and abroad, including the Corner Brook agency, W. V. Bowater acted as a holding company for all the Bowater interests. In that capacity, almost as soon as the company was formed, it was repeatedly called upon for help by BPM. In February 1926, W. V. Bowater agreed to buy BPM's paper for cash. In March, the company guaranteed Kleinwort's loan to BPM. In April, W. V. Bowater was asked to buy three houses in Northfleet for £3,500 and to advance the £25,000 for working capital promised by the private company in 1924 (p. 40 above), and twelve days later BPM's state was so desperate that they were asking W. V. Bowater to advance £13,000, against paper invoiced, to pay the wage bill.[61]

In the midst of its embarrassments, the Northfleet mill was hit by the General Strike, which began at midnight on 3-4 May 1926. The Government, fairly well prepared, put emergency measures into force, including the publication of the *British Gazette*, printed under Winston Churchill's close and enthusiastic supervision on the presses belonging to the *Morning Post*. The *British Gazette* needed paper, which would have to come across picket lines, so the Government appointed a Controller of Paper Supplies, Eric Bowater. The choice was surprising; no doubt it reflects Eric's rapid rise within the industry. He was armed with considerable statutory powers and it appears that, on 5 May, he succeeded in running a convoy of lorries, laden with paper, driven by volunteers, protected by police, from Edward Lloyd's wharf to the *Morning Post*'s offices. The volunteer drivers, here as elsewhere, came mostly from the middle class, more confident then than later of its power, its position in society and the rightness of its views. In the course of a search for any supplies of paper that might be available, Eric deputed his cousin, Ian (b. 1905), who had recently joined the business, to collect paper from the *Sunday Times*, carrying a warrant in his pocket in case William Berry demurred. William Berry did not. Back at the *Morning Post*, Ian was able to announce the arrival of William Berry's paper to Churchill, smoking a huge cigar and greatly enjoying himself. Churchill later called a conference at which it was decided to commandeer a paper mill, and the mill chosen was Bowaters', because their machines would run without waste on the 74-inch reels required.

In the early hours of Sunday, 9 May, a detachment of Royal Engineers and sailors, under Captain C. G. Martin, VC, DSO, landed from barges on the river, took over the mill on behalf of His Majesty's Stationery Office, protected it with barbed wire, posted armed guards and ran up the Union Jack. Arthur Baker, armed with a pistol and dismayed by the striking propensities of his work force, ran the mill with volunteers who all lived in Army tents, on Army food, within the mill perimeter while the Royal Navy patrolled the river front. Paper went to London in barges provided by the Port of London Authority.

This stirring episode in Bowaters' history was short, for, on 12 May, the General Strike collapsed. The Government gave up control of the mill on 15 May, George Grossmith brought a concert party to the mill in the afternoon and, in the evening, there was a celebration dinner among the paper machines. On Tuesday, 18 May, the Union Jack was hauled down and the troops left. By the following Monday the mill was running normally again.[62]

The General Strike was less damaging to Bowaters, as to the nation generally, than the coal-miners' strike which set it off, lasted

15 May 1926: Royal Engineers at Northfleet, stood down after the collapse of the General Strike, have improvised a stage to accommodate the concert party. The legend over the proscenium reads 'By Permission of the Tea You See'. *Eric Baker*

for six months and was called by Sir Alfred Mond, in 1927, 'the longest and most devastating industrial dispute in the history of the country'.[63] It shot the price of coal up from its normal level of 16–18 shillings a ton to as much as £4; it delayed the completion of the mill still more; it brought about short-time working and it reduced the demand for newsprint – largely, in Bowaters' opinion, because spending power was down and advertisers were not taking so much space – so that, in September 1926, large quantities were being held in stock, another strain on Bowaters' inadequate working capital.[64]

At the time of the General Strike, the affairs of Bowater's Paper Mills were rapidly working up towards a crisis. Nearly a year after the 'time-and-lime' basis of payment had been suggested by Eric Bowater and accepted by Armstrongs, it had still not been put into effect.

Armstrongs, with reason, were becoming impatient and they suspected Bowaters of playing for time. BPM, for their part, mindful of the delay caused by Armstrongs' incompetence, were no nearer reconstruction and the injection of fresh capital than at the beginning of the year. They were existing on temporary expedients, chiefly the arrangements with Kleinworts and with W. V. Bowater & Sons.

On 19 May 1926, BPM's Board at last agreed to execute a Supplemental Agreement with Armstrongs modifying the terms of the construction contract. The text of the agreement is lost but its main terms are clear from other sources.[65] It started from the position that BPM had already paid Armstrongs £265,000 in cash and went on to provide for payment of the balance outstanding by the creation of various securities which, together with the cash, set the total cost of the mill at £823,000.

The question which the Agreement left unanswered was critical: What was the true cost of the mill? Armstrongs could render accounts giving their idea of it but Bowaters had a right, under the Agreement, to have the accounts examined by their accountants and their engineer and they could not be required to pay until the engineer had certified the amount due. Armstrongs tried, but failed, to tie Bowaters to a fixed period of days for the examination by accountants and for the delivery of the engineer's certificate. The best they could do was to get a provision 'that certification of the amounts found to be due should be made within a reasonable time of the delivery of the Accounts and payment was to follow within fourteen days of such certification'.

The possibilities of delay were boundless and accounts for more than £700,000, delivered by Armstrongs between 11 and 18 June

1926, were still incompletely certified by 22 September. 'Messrs Bowaters', said solicitors acting for the Bank of England, 'have been continuously pressed to complete the investigation of the Accounts and to provide that the Engineer should give Certificates.' Bowaters issued the shares required by the Agreement in June and the debentures on 19 August but they could not be induced to give bills for the balance claimed by Armstrongs. The solicitors drew the obvious conclusion: 'The reason for non-payment of Armstrongs Accounts . . . is we think largely due to the financial position in which Bowaters find themselves. They have had to raise money on the stocks of pulp at their Mills' – the Kleinwort loan – 'and it is evident that their working capital is exhausted.'[66]

Armstrongs, meanwhile, were in the hands of the Bank of England and, from June 1926 onward, largely under the direction of J. Frater Taylor (1874–1960), an Aberdonian with a reputation in Canada as a 'company doctor', and in Bowaters, later, for never going further in expressing approval for a project than to say 'I'm not against it'. He was put in by Governor Norman on the advice of Edward Peacock, first to report on Armstrongs' business and then to run it. He has been described as unassuming and rather insignificant but he was a match for Sir Glyn West and the part he played, now and later, in Bowaters' affairs was very far from insignificant. Sir Glyn was unceremoniously sacked – it is said he was refused the use of a company car to carry him away afterwards – and his place as Chairman was taken by Lord Southborough (1860–1947), a solicitor with a distinguished record of public service. The hand on the controls, however, appears to have been Frater Taylor's.[67]

Frater Taylor's views on Bowaters, frequently and variously expressed, were pessimistic. He and Sir Gilbert Garnsey (1883–1932), of Price Waterhouse, reported on Armstrongs in March 1926, dwelling at length on the Northfleet construction contract. They mentioned that Eric Bowater had said in February that BPM would have to be reconstructed and they questioned whether BPM would be able to keep up payment of interest, presumably on the debentures held by Armstrongs.[68] Nevertheless, Frater Taylor could no doubt see that the survival of BPM, if it could be contrived, was for Armstrongs a matter of the greatest importance.

It was also a matter of the greatest importance to W. V. Bowater & Sons. If BPM went down, could the rest of the Bowater group survive, financially sound though it was? In any case, W. V. Bowater was bound to be concerned in any rescue operation mounted for BPM, if only because other lenders to BPM would demand

W. V. Bowater's backing for its subsidiary. BPM's survival depended partly on the size of the sum they would finally have to find and partly on the manner in which they would find it; that is, how much in securities and how much in cash. Bowaters had already paid £265,000 under the original contract, as the Supplemental Agreement recognised, so they would have to find the sum required to fill the gap between £265,000 and whatever might be agreed as the final bill for the mill, and Bowaters' aim in negotiation was to persuade Armstrongs to make the gap as narrow as possible. As to the method of payment, since cash was what Bowaters were short of, securities were what they wished to offer but Armstrongs' interest lay in getting as much of the settlement in cash as possible. In June, Bowaters asked Sir Basil Mayhew to advise on settling the sum due to Armstrongs and on the financial reconstruction of BPM,[69] but much of the negotiation was carried on by Harold Brown, of Linklaters & Paines, for Bowaters and by Sir Gilbert Garnsey for Armstrongs.

After some further negotiations,[70] at an emergency meeting of the BPM Board on 4 August 1926 Brown reported 'that he had reason to believe' that Armstrongs would accept 'a lump sum offer of £600,000'. He said further that Frater Taylor was almost immediately going on holiday and 'if a figure were not agreed now, Armstrongs ... would in all probability not settle at ... £600,000'.

Eric Bowater, it seems, was no more inclined to tolerate delay than Frater Taylor. He told his uncle Frank and his cousin Noel, the only other directors present, that 'the alternatives before the Board were whether a lump sum offer ... be made now, or the matter be left in abeyance, when it would be doubtful for what figure Armstrongs would settle'. He further stated that 'in the interests of the Company it was desirous [sic] that a definite figure be ascertained now'. Sir Basil Mayhew was there and no doubt he supported Eric. After more discussion, doubtless gloomy, Frank and Noel authorised Eric to tell Harold Brown, who had left the meeting, that BPM were prepared to seek a settlement at £600,000, 'which sum the Company are prepared to accept in principal [sic]'.[71]

Fifteen days later the full Board met to consider a letter offering £600,000 in settlement of Armstrongs' claims, made up as follows:

Already paid	£265,000
Second Debentures already issued, to be redeemed or purchased at par	£175,000
Cash	£160,000
Total	£600,000

Armstrongs, for their part, were to agree to complete various major items of construction in the mill.

The offer thus required £335,000 in cash and, as the directors surveyed the possibilities of raising it, the bleak facts of their position one by one emerged. First, Garnsey would expect W. V. Bowater & Sons to be associated with the offer and would try to insist on its being made by them, not by BPM. But, if the offer were made and accepted, 'all parties present agreed that it would be necessary to dispose of the Company's Mill . . . In the present state of the financial market and the Company's immediate prospects, it was deemed inexpedient to attempt reorganisation and consequent flotation.' The directors of W. V. Bowater decided that they could no longer go on supporting BPM financially and, if no other arrangements could be made, 'there was no alternative to a firm offer to settle being written'.[72]

The offer was made and Frater Taylor agreed to recommend it to Armstrongs' Board, provided that Bowaters paid over the £160,000 three months after signature, not six as they had suggested, and on certain other conditions. 'It is most obvious', he wrote to Price Waterhouse, for onward transmission to Bowaters, '. . . that we are now compelled to impose a time limit . . . I feel convinced that, if the matter is not finally settled this month, there will be little chance of settlement on the basis indicated; on the contrary, Armstrongs will instruct their Solicitors to take immediate action.'[73]

In the first fortnight of September 1926, therefore, it looked very much as if Bowaters were going to lose their mill before it was properly completed, certainly before they had made any money from it. Various possible purchasers came forward, including William Harrison, Chairman of Inveresk and 'interests represented by Mr Stanley Cousins', which probably meant Reeds, in which Rothermere had a large holding (p. 29) though not control. Eric Bowater and Arthur Baker were empowered by the BPM Board, on 14 September 1926, to negotiate with Armstrongs and with possible purchasers.[74] Bowaters' position, however, was not quite so hopeless as it appeared. Salvation might lie in the interdependence of their business with Armstrongs'.

If Bowaters' independence were to be saved, it would have to be saved with the goodwill, perhaps the active intervention, of Frater Taylor and the Bank of England and of this Eric Bowater was well aware. His cousin Ian, many years later, had a memory of leaving Eric on the corner of Threadneedle Street, going to see Montagu Norman. Norman was powerfully influenced by intuitive judgment of character and, if Eric had made a bad impression, it is unlikely that BPM would have survived. In fact, by 14 September, Bowaters' situation had improved sufficiently for Eric to have withdrawn the offer of £600,000 which would have required the sale of the mill. Armstrongs must have consented and moves were afoot, then or soon after, to raise the extra capital which Bowaters so urgently needed.[75]

Frater Taylor commissioned two professional enquiries into what he called 'the Bowater affair'. Batten & Co., solicitors, looked into the contract and examined the processes open to Armstrongs to get their bills paid. The solicitors' findings, though far from flattering to Bowaters, went a long way towards ensuring their survival by showing Frater Taylor how empty was his threat of legal action against them and how heavily dependent Armstrongs were on the success of the mill they had built. What was the point of pursuing debtors who had no means to pay their debts? This, after all, was the root of the trouble.

It was not in Armstrongs' interest to attack Bowaters at all; indeed, very much the contrary.

It is inadvisable [wrote Battens] to at once stop work as the sub-contractors are already committed to pay for the machinery, etc., which they have to erect and it must be to the interest of Armstrongs to complete the works so far as is really necessary to enable the Mill to be efficiently worked as a going concern . . . Armstrongs have no power, at any rate at present, to apply to the Court to wind up Bowaters and we cannot think it would be to their interest to do so until at least it is seen that a reconstructed Company with a reasonable capitalisation cannot be formed to work the Mill.

While Battens were examining the contract, Price Waterhouse, also commissioned by Frater Taylor, were investigating Bowaters' finances. The lawyers' and the accountants' reports both came to hand in the latter part of September and each hammered home the same point: that Bowaters' survival was essential to Armstrongs' welfare.

'On the Bowater situation', Frater Taylor told Barings on 24 September,

we have just had Messrs Price Waterhouse & Co.'s preliminary report to the effect that a sum of at least £100,000 must be found to enable the Bowater Paper Mill Ltd to carry on and that our only chance to make something of a recovery of the serious debt due by Bowater Paper Mills to Armstrongs is to enable them to continue in operation.

He was not, he told Garnsey on the same day, 'sanguine', but he had nevertheless worked out a draft scheme of reconstruction. 'Needless to say', he added, 'it must be demonstrated that there is justification for carrying on the business from the point of view of making profits especially.' Of that he was doubtful. 'We are in a sorry plight', he remarked to Edward Peacock, sending him a copy of the letter to Garnsey, and, at a meeting with Peacock and Montagu Norman a month later, he said he thought Bowaters' ability to sell their paper was doubtful.[76]

In spite of Frater Taylor's carefully reiterated pessimism, probably more or less deliberately exaggerated in order to restrain false hopes, his utterances in September 1926 mark a turning-point in Bowaters' fortunes. Bowaters must be preserved because their preservation was necessary to the health of Armstrongs, themselves about to undergo drastic surgery leading up to the formation of Vickers-Armstrong in October 1927,[77] and in order to preserve Bowaters, fresh capital would have to be found. There was no more talk of selling the mill. Instead, every effort was directed to devising ways of financing BPM so that they could run the mill at a profit.

In the first suggestion of a plan, sketched by Frater Taylor after he had seen Price Waterhouse's report on BPM, working capital of £100,000 was to be found for BPM by W. V. Bowater and Armstrongs jointly, and the outstanding balance of Armstrongs' account was to be settled, not in cash, but in debentures and shares, giving Armstrongs control. This Frater Taylor intended to exercise quite strictly, with two Armstrong directors on BPM's Board, restriction on capital expenditure and information for Armstrongs about all agreements covering the sale of BPM's product, with a view to seeing whether they might be modified to ease the situation.[78] What Frater Taylor probably had in mind was a reduction of W. V. Bowater's agency commission.

The thought of control by Armstrongs must have been unwelcome to Eric Bowater, Arthur Baker and their colleagues. It soon began to give way to the idea of raising cash by a private placing or a public issue of Preference shares to provide working capital and to redeem the second Debentures held by Armstrongs under the Supplemental Agreement. In September, any kind of 'flotation' had been considered 'inexpedient' (p. 54) but, by November, it formed an essential part of an Agreement of Compromise and Settlement. That is the measure of the change in Bowaters' situation during the autumn of 1926.

Bowaters and Armstrongs executed the Agreement of Compromise and Settlement on 1 December 1926. Its main provision was a payment by BPM to Armstrongs of £175,000 which was to be accepted by Armstrongs in final settlement of the balance due to them under the construction contract.[79] This settlement, immensely favourable to BPM, stood or fell by their ability to issue Preference shares to raise the £175,000 due to Armstrongs and to provide themselves with working capital. A public issue was decided upon but, for reasons which will by now be sufficiently obvious, it was not very easy to arrange, though it was probably helped on its way by a breeze of optimism which began to blow through the British economy and the Stock Exchange late in 1926 and early in 1927.[80]

BPM went to the market on 6 April 1927 for 275,000 7½ per cent Cumulative Participating Preference shares of £1 each at par. The terms of the issue, like the terms of W. V. Bowaters' issue the year before, were onerous for the issuing company and they required massive support for the shares, also, from the holders of BPM's First Debentures – Armstrongs, Power Securities Corporation, W. V. Bowater – and from W. V. Bowater in its capacity as BPM's parent company.

Holders of the new shares, besides being entitled to a 7½ per cent cumulative dividend, also had a right to 25 per cent of distributed profits remaining after 7½ per cent had been paid on the Ordinary capital; altogether, surely, an extremely generous entitlement, making a severe dent in the rights of Ordinary shareholders.[81] Moreover, to make this arrangement possible, the holders of First Debentures agreed to cancel a clause in their Trust Deed requiring BPM, before paying any dividend at all on the share capital, to accumulate out of profits and carry to reserve a sum equal to the total amount applied in payment of interest on the debenture stock during the construction and equipment of the mills and one year thereafter. W. V. Bowater, as BPM's parent, unconditionally guaranteed the payment of the Preference dividend for three years and – perhaps most important of all – agreed to reduce the commission on sales of BPM's paper from 2½ per cent to 1¼ per cent, thus making a considerable contribution to BPM's prospective profits.[82]

The issue went well, being heavily over-subscribed.[83] Its proceeds at last cut Bowaters loose from the embarrassing and potentially very dangerous entanglement with Armstrongs. Moreover, it provided them with a cut-price mill. In December 1926 the mill buildings and plant were valued, as a going concern, at £867,110[84] but, on 14 June 1928, it was calculated that the final cost of the mill to Bowaters had been £422,170. 12s. 4d. (Table 7), against the original contract price of £481,926. No wonder Frater Taylor observed acidly: 'Much of my time has been taken up . . . with unsatisfactory contracts. If contracts had been properly drawn and carefully

TABLE 7. *The cost of the Northfleet mill*

	£	s	d
Armstrongs' cash	265,000.	0.	0.
Accounts for electricity, water, etc.	1,173.	1.	1.
Architects' fees and sundries	12,072.	2.	8.
Plant and machinery	10,758.	12.	0.
Office and laboratory fittings and technical instruments	1,576.	18.	1.
Armstrongs' Compromise and Settlement	175,000.	0.	0.
Completion cost:			
Wages – Byrom's men	196.	7.	2.
Walmsleys – supercalender and spare granite roll, etc.	1,393.	11.	4.
	467,170.	12.	4.
Deduct Walmsleys' loan for working capital included in Compromise and settlement	25,000.	0.	0.
	£442,170.	12.	4.
Mill site, 31 The Shore and Bungalow	£ 61,514.	11.	0.

Source: BPM/Sec/7.

carried out, much trouble and loss would have been avoided. The most glaring example is, of course, the Bowater Paper Mills Contract which has resulted in such serious loss to Armstrongs.'[85]

Bowaters launched themselves into the manufacture of newsprint with a clear view of the opportunity open to them in a rapidly expanding market but with no technical management and insufficient command of capital. Moreover, it is probable that the long illness and premature death of Sir Frederick Bowater deprived them of their most forceful and experienced director just at the time when they stood most in need of him.

Bowaters' deficiency in technical management was made good by the appointment of Arthur Baker and his subordinates, most of whom he brought from Empire Paper Mills. The alterations which he demanded to Armstrongs' plans, however essential they may have been for the future efficiency of the mill, disrupted such financial planning as there had been and brought on a cash crisis which almost destroyed the business and probably would have destroyed it but for the intervention of the Bank of England in the affairs of Armstrong, Whitworth.

Arthur Baker's presence, nevertheless, was no doubt crucial in restoring Bowaters' credit sufficiently for the eventual financial reconstruction to be put in hand. He and Eric Bowater carried the main weight of responsibility in the Bowater group throughout the prolonged period of crisis and they were evidently seen by Frater Taylor, Sir Basil Mayhew, John Keeling and others as the twin pillars of the business. In March 1927 they were appointed joint Managing Directors of Bowater's Paper Mills Ltd.[86]

Eric Bowater, it seems fair to assume, was thrust by his father's death into the leadership of the business before he was adequately prepared for it. It seems equally fair to assume that his obvious lack of experience was discounted in the minds of those who had dealings with him, from the Governor of the Bank of England downwards, by the force of his personality. As for himself, once he had taken charge something in his imperious nature drove him headlong towards expansion, pressing forward always to the extreme limits of prudence. Caution seems to have been unknown to him. Even when matters were approaching their worst, in April 1926, plans were being laid for two more paper machines to double the output of the mill.[87] As soon as the crisis was over, he launched Bowaters on to a career of growth, adventurously financed and extremely rapid, which has few parallels in the history of British business.

CHAPTER FOUR

Eric and the barons 1927–1932

4.1 INDEPENDENCE LOST

Eric Bowater never felt he had much help from his uncles. They regarded him, he thought, as a rash young man. Naturally, Eric did not agree and, once the future of Bowater's Paper Mills was reasonably secure, he was no longer prepared to put up with it. The uncles would have to go.

There was another difficulty: limits on the supply of capital. Two issues had been successful – W. V. Bowater's 8 per cent Participating Preferred Ordinary shares in January 1926 and BPM's 7½ per cent Cumulative Participating Preference shares in April 1927 – but that was as much as the market would be likely to take, on Bowaters' unsupported credit, until there was something to show in the way of performance and Eric Bowater had no mind to wait that long. He needed a backer with greater command of capital than his own.

The backer he found was Lord Rothermere, so that once again, as in the early days of the merchant firm, a Harmsworth (probably the same Harmsworth) provided the support that Bowaters needed. Whether the approach came from Rothermere or from Eric Bowater we have no means of knowing but there is a strong presumption that Rothermere had favoured the Northfleet venture from the start – would he otherwise have been so accommodating when Arthur Baker left Empire Mills with his train of supporters? – and he was presumably unwilling to see Bowaters' development delayed or stunted. Like the other Press barons, Beaverbrook in particular, he was very attentive to his newsprint supplies.

The first AGM of W. V. Bowater & Sons, as a public company, was held on 30 March 1927. Among those attending, along with a representative of the company's brokers, was John Cowley, a prominent member of Rothermere's management team who was on the Board of the *Daily Mirror*. In August, he reported to his colleagues on negotiations which for some months he had been carrying on with Eric Bowater for the purchase, at 35s. a share, of 90,000 Ordinary shares in W. V. Bowater.[1] The *Daily Mirror*'s offer was made on 25 August 1927 and, on 16 September, the shares were bought, in three equal parcels of 30,000 each, from Sir

Eric Bowater in the mid-1920s. *Robert Knight*

Vansittart Bowater, Major Frank and the trustees of Sir Frederick, Eric Bowater's father. It was a condition of the purchase that the brothers should resign from the Boards of their family companies and, on 30 November 1927, they did so. On the next day Eric Bowater, already a managing director of W. V. Bowater and of Bowater's Paper Mills, became Chairman of each company. He was now head of the Bowater business, a post he was to hold for the rest of his life.[2]

Eric Bowater thus attained one of his objectives – emancipation from avuncular surveillance. Emancipation, however, did not bring independence. Sixty per cent of W. V. Bowater's Ordinary shares – 90,000 out of 150,000 – passed from family ownership into the ownership of the *Daily Mirror* and so, effectively, into the hands of Lord Rothermere. Control of the Bowater business thus no longer rested with the Bowater family and the new 'principal share-holders', Eric soon discovered, were far more formidable than his uncles. It is a measure of his hunger for capital that he was prepared in this way to put the whole future of the Bowater business in pawn and submit his own imperious will to superior authority.

The Rothermere purchase did not put any money directly into the Bowater business. As a device for strengthening Bowaters' credit in the City, however, it seems to have been immediately successful. News of it became known on 28 September and the *Daily News* of 29 September reported a sudden demand for BPM's $7\frac{1}{2}$ per cent CPP shares. Here, no doubt, was the sign from heaven, or at least from the Stock Exchange, that Eric Bowater and his advisers were wait-ing for. They could now see their way towards the finance they would need for doubling the capacity of the Northfleet mill – a plan which had been in their minds as far back as the spring of 1926, perhaps earlier. Rothermere may also have given them solid grounds for expecting contracts to keep the doubled capacity busy. Certainly they had the *Daily Mail*, the *Sunday Pictorial* and the *Daily Mirror* on their books within a year of his buying the uncles' shares.[3]

About the beginning of August 1927, before even the formal offer had been made for the shares, Arthur Baker was asked to get an estimate from Walmsleys for two additional paper machines and a pulpwood grinding mill.[4] By that time it is likely that Bowaters were assured of a large order from another great Press baron, Beaver-brook, for, in a list of customers and their requirements made out in March 1928, much the largest entry is 17,725 tons of newsprint for the *Daily Express*.[5]

Before the machines could be ordered, finance had to be arranged. Before finance could be arranged, the principal shareholders had to be convinced of the soundness of the proposed arrangement. Before the principal shareholders could be convinced, an arrangement had to be devised which would carry conviction. By the end of May 1928, BPM's Board had a scheme which was acceptable to two finance houses, to Harold Brown of Linklaters & Paines and to Sir Basil Mayhew. Eric Bowater and A. E. Linforth were deputed to put it before the principal shareholders.[6]

Arthur Linforth, who had worked for Northcliffe, was one of Rothermere's nominees to the Boards of BPM and W. V. Bowater and perhaps his colleagues thought that, with his endorsement, the financial scheme and the scheme for extending the mill would quickly pass the scrutiny of John Cowley and the *Daily Mirror* Board. In fact, it took six weeks and at least two meetings between Eric Bowater, Linforth and Cowley before agreement, even in principle, was reached on 21 August 1928 and a provisional order for the two machines could be placed. The firm order was not given until 21 September. Such were the penalties, to Eric Bowater, of lost independence. The delay cannot have been to his liking but worse, as we shall see, was to come.[7]

The measures for financing the mill extension were put into effect during October 1928. The central feature, of a kind which became characteristic of Bowaters' financial technique as the business grew, was a plan for increasing the amount of debenture stock in issue and converting it to as low a rate of interest as the market would bear. As well as that, the share capital, Preferred and Ordinary, was brought up to its full authorised total.[8]

BPM created £750,000 6 per cent First Mortgage Debenture stock. Holders of the existing £295,000 6½ per cent Debentures were given the option of redemption in cash or exchanging into the new stock, and holders of £150,000 exchanged. The balance of £600,000 of the new stock was then placed privately, as Eric Bowater told the shareholders at the end of the year, 'on very satisfactory terms to the company', which evidently meant a price of £98 per cent with London & Yorkshire bearing certain costs and commission.[9]

As to the share capital, the London & Yorkshire Trust took up 25,000 7½ per cent Cumulative Participating Preference shares of £1 each at 21s. a share and the Ordinary shareholders, offered one new share for every two they already held, took them up readily at 22s. for a £1 share. The total gross amount of new capital raised, to meet the estimated cost of the extensions of £550,000, was £582,600, as follows:

£600,000 new Debentures at £98	£588,000
Less £145,000 Debentures	
redeemed for cash at £103	£149,350
Total	£438,650
25,000 new Preference shares at 21s.	£26,250
107,000 new Ordinary shares at 22s.	£117,700
Total	£582,600

The cost of the extensions, then, was to be more than £100,000 higher than the figure finally agreed for the cost of the original mill – another indication of how good a bargain Bowaters eventually struck. 'These extensions', Eric Bowater told BPM's shareholders in December 1929, 'entailed the installation of two three-roll high-speed newsprint machines complete with supercalenders and auxiliary equipment, the buildings to house them and the provision of the necessary additional power plant.'[10]

Firm orders for the two machines were placed in September 1928. No. 3 was to have a wire 246 inches wide, guaranteed to make a trim width of paper 230 inches, and No. 4 a 262-inch wire to make a trim width of 245 inches, both to run at a sustained speed of 1,250 feet per minute. They were to be ready on or before 7 August 1929 and they were to cost £148,000.[11] There were delays and the total cost of the project rose. It had reached £563,153 by 14 December, when the first of the new machines came into production, and there is no record of the final figure. The second machine did not start until January 1930. Nevertheless, Eric Bowater was very pleased. Papermaking plant on such a scale had never been built so quickly before and, with improvements to the two original machines raising their production by 15 per cent, the Northfleet mill would be capable of providing over 120,000 tons of newsprint a year.[12]

That so large a figure should have been so quickly attained – less than four years after the troubled start-up of the original machines – is a measure of the drive which Eric Bowater put behind his ambitions and of the energy which his leadership generated among those who worked under him. His pleasure in the achievement shows through his words to the shareholders in December 1929: 'Your company now possesses one of the finest newsprint mills in existence and the only mill where four wide machines are installed, each having its own supercalenders. These supercalenders are the largest in the world.'

They were very important, too, because they gave newsprint a surface of the quality needed for the half-tone illustrations which were more and more in demand as the newspaper owners competed fiercely with each other for circulation.

Eric Bowater, nevertheless, was never allowed to forget that the development of his business was conditional on Lord Rothermere's approval, delivered or denied through the mouth of John Cowley. Alongside the scheme for extending the Northfleet mills, Bowaters pursued a parallel scheme for putting up a paper mill in Tasmania to supply the Australian market, where they had a flourishing export trade. Probably they were responding to Australian pressure to establish industries in Australia instead of relying on imports and they certainly intended taking Australian partners, although Bowaters would put up 51 per cent of the Ordinary capital and thus keep control. In March 1929 a preliminary agreement was signed and, in April, it was sent to Cowley. Cowley decided, and Eric Bowater had no choice but to agree, 'that the scheme . . . was too ambitious for us to carry through on our own'. It was suggested 'as an alternative means of ensuring our continued participation in the Australasian market, [that] we might take a minority interest in the scheme, always providing that we do not take the leadership, or assume the responsibility for it being a commercial success'.[13] That, perhaps understandably, was turned down by the Australians and Bowaters' Tasmanian mill died unborn. The Rothermere connection killed it.

Then there was the curious affair of Empire Mills. These had belonged to Rothermere (p. 28), through Associated Newspapers, since 1919 and were largely the creation of Arthur Baker. The Chairman was A. E. Linforth. In March 1930, Associated Newspapers offered the entire Ordinary capital of Empire – £400,000 – to W. V. Bowater, as parent of the Bowater group, for £208,302. 16s. W. V. Bowater accepted, financing the purchase by a loan granted by Lloyds Bank on the understanding that it would be funded as soon as possible.[14] This unorthodox finance clearly disturbed at least one of the Bowater directors, probably Shortis, as carrying an element of risk 'should anything in the nature of a national financial crisis arise' – a sign of the times – but Linforth recommended it as less expensive than a capital issue and added soothingly 'that very many firms habitually assumed similar risks and had built up large businesses in this manner'.[15] Linforth played a prominent part in the transaction, presumably on instructions from Rothermere, and 'in recognition of [his] services . . . and having regard to his long association with and special knowledge of the Empire Paper Mills' he was asked 'to act in an advisory capacity in connection with the Mills' for five years at £1,000 per annum.[16]

The inducement held out to Bowaters, when the Empire shares were offered to them, was that a large part of Empire's business came from supplying the *Daily Mail* and that the *Daily Mail*'s order 'would continue on the same basis for at least one year, and thereafter on a gradually declining basis'. No other positive reason for the purchase is on record and it is difficult to believe that on Bowaters' side there was one, for their resources of capital and management, as we shall shortly see, were already fully extended.

Bowaters' purchase of Empire was completed on 31 March 1930. At a Board meeting on 3 June 'the Chairman stated that he regretted to have to put on record the disappointment we had met with in connection with Empire Paper Mills'. 'The *Daily Mail*'s order for newsprint', he said, 'was being reduced almost at once and would cease altogether after September.' The consequences for Empire would be grave. It would be difficult to dispose of 'the production thus thrown on our hands'. The mill might have to work short time or temporarily close down. Raw materials on order would continue to come in and would have to be paid for.[17] All this, in turn, would react on Empire's new owners, Bowaters, and, in fact, for over a year their position was thoroughly uncomfortable. They were reduced to borrowing from subsidiaries, including Empire itself, to keep down the cost of the loan from Lloyds Bank, which the Bank only grudgingly renewed, and at one time they were buying paper from Empire for re-sale at a loss. From this misery they were not released until September 1931 when Linforth, acting for Associated Newspapers, offered to buy back the Empire shares for the price Bowaters had given for them. The offer was not outstandingly generous but Bowaters had no option but to accept and the sale was completed on 30 September.[18]

Why did Rothermere sell Empire? Nothing certain can be said because nothing is certainly known. The most likely explanation seems to be that, early in 1930, Associated Newspapers ran short of cash and Rothermere decided to make use of Empire Mills and Bowaters to relieve Associated Newspapers' difficulties. If Bowaters were to raise the money by borrowing instead of issuing capital, that would be a great convenience, because it would be much quicker. It is charitable to assume, but difficult to believe, that Rothermere, at the time of the sale, knew of nothing in the *Daily Mail*'s affairs which would make it likely that the *Daily Mail* would so soon have to cancel the order to Empire. For Eric Bowater, the consequences of the *Daily Mail*'s cancellation, and indeed the whole long-drawn dance to Rothermere's tune, must have been most humiliating.

He would have been even more humiliated if he had known, as he almost certainly did not, that the purchase of Empire was by no means the worst of the dangers brought upon Bowaters by the surrender of control to Rothermere. During the summer of 1930, while Empire's difficulties were deepening, John Cowley and his colleagues on the *Daily Mirror* Board were considering whether to sell the *Daily Mirror*'s holding in Bowaters to Canada Power & Paper Corporation. In October they decided against the sale but only 'after very careful consideration and in view of many important developments . . . in the newsprint situation here and in Canada'.[19] It seems to have been the nearest of near things and, if the decision had gone the other way, control of the Bowater business might have passed permanently into Canadian hands, apparently without Bowaters' Board having been consulted in any way.

4.2 ROTHERMERE, BEAVERBROOK AND THE MERSEY MILL

Lord Rothermere was not the only newspaper owner in the late 1920s who took an interest in the rise of the new young man, Eric Bowater. Lord Beaverbrook, Rothermere's partner and rival – both at the same time – was interested too; the more so, probably, because unlike Rothermere he controlled no newsprint mills himself and seems to have been considerably shaken when the Berrys took over Lloyds, the largest newsprint firm in the United Kingdom, in 1927. He immediately cancelled the *Daily Express*'s long-standing contract with them but then found himself, he considered, at the mercy of 'rings'. To frustrate their knavish tricks, real or imagined, he began negotiating in Canada but he did not find the going easy. 'I may say', he told Rothermere in September 1927, 'that I tried to get newsprint at reasonable prices from every English mill before I turned to the Canadians. I had to use my personal influence in Canada to get the necessary concessions.'[20]

With or without 'necessary concessions', Beaverbrook made terms with the Montreal firm of Price Brothers and with the Canadian subsidiary of the International Paper Co. of New York, thus encouraging them to compete with the English newsprint makers, including Bowaters. In July 1929 he contracted with Canadian IPC for 75,000 tons of newsprint a year, during 1931, 1932 and 1933, for the *Daily Express* and the *Evening Standard*.[21] Beaverbrook, however, had no more intention of committing himself wholly to the Canadian suppliers than to the English and, at the time this contract was made, he was far advanced in negotiations with Rothermere and with Eric Bowater for the building of a completely new mill for making newsprint at Ellesmere Port in Cheshire.

The idea of setting up this mill probably came from Eric Bowater, although there is no contemporary evidence.[22] It would have been in keeping with his restless ambition and it was founded on sound judgment. Manchester was rapidly growing in importance as a newspaper production centre and Ellesmere Port, forty miles from Manchester, on the south bank of the Mersey and on the Ship Canal, was well placed both to receive seaborne supplies of wood pulp and for the despatch of newsprint to customers. The main purpose of the mill would be to supply paper for the northern edition of Beaverbrook's *Daily Express*.

There would no doubt be business from other proprietors printing in Manchester and, altogether, there were the makings of an attractive proposition.

Beaverbrook, in the summer of 1929, was also intending to buy newsprint from Bowaters at Northfleet. 'Dear Eric,' he wrote on 2 July, '. . . I have instructed the Evening Standard to sign a contract with you for their requirements for 1930.' He added: 'I understand that you will assist me in my intention to exploit the possibility of obtaining all our supplies of newsprint in England not only for the Evening Standard but also for the Daily Express', which may well be a reference to the Ellesmere Port plan. On the following day, 3 July, Eric Bowater wired to Beaverbrook: 'Have seen Rothermere and am in position to further discuss Mersey proposition.'[23]

The 'Mersey proposition' came formally before W. V. Bowater's Board a fortnight later. Eric said it was unnecessary for him to explain the proposals in detail because the directors were already 'fully acquainted with the facts'. He referred to 'the investment on equal partnership terms with the Daily Express'.[24]

The investment was in Bowater's Mersey Paper Mills Ltd, newly formed to build and run newsprint mills on a 55-acre site at Ellesmere Port between the Manchester Ship Canal to the north and a road connecting it with Birkenhead, Chester and Manchester to the south. Two machines, costing, with supercalenders and other equipment, £190,734, were ordered from Walmsleys on 28 August 1929, to be ready for commercial operation by 31 October 1930. They were each to be 216 inches wide and together capable of supplying 60,000 tons of newsprint a year.[25]

The rock on which the company's business was founded was a

twenty-year agreement, dated 19 July 1929, with the London Express Newspaper Ltd. It provided for the supply of 30,000 tons of newsprint a year, starting in 1931, plus as much more as the Express saw fit to order, up to one-third of the remaining capacity of the mills, to be delivered in Manchester or, at the buyers' option and expense, at any of their other printing offices. The price, to be agreed on 30 November every year for the following twelve months, was either to be the London price or the lowest price charged to other buyers for newsprint of similar quality and, in case the parties could not agree, arbitration was provided for.[26] Thus the mills were assured, before building began, of an order for at least half and possibly two-thirds of their output and Beaverbrook's sleep need no longer be disturbed by nightmares of papermakers' rings threatening supplies to the *Daily Express*.

Bowater's Mersey Paper Mills Ltd was capitalised at £1,050,000, raised as to £650,000 by a public issue at £96 per cent of 6½ per cent First Mortgage Debentures and as to £400,000 by the issue of £1 Ordinary shares. Instalments for the debentures, which were heavily over-subscribed, were timed to bring the proceeds in by 15 November 1929 but calls on the Ordinary shares, by contrast, were spread over two years, from July 1929 to 21 August 1931. The Ordinary capital was entirely taken up by W. V. Bowater and the two newspaper groups as shown in Table 8.[27]

It will be immediately obvious that the 'equal partnership' mentioned by Eric Bowater was much more equal for the two newspaper owners than for himself and most equal of all for Beaverbrook. Through his newspaper interests, Beaverbrook was effectively the largest shareholder in BMPM and, in alliance with Rothermere, he could at any time override Eric Bowater; a

TABLE 8. *Bowater's Mersey Paper Mills Ordinary shareholders, 1931*

W. V. Bowater & Sons Ltd	£100,000
Rothermere interests	
(Associated Newspapers; Daily Mirror	
Newspapers; Sunday Pictorial	
Newspapers (1920))	£100,000
Beaverbrook interests	
(London Express Newspaper; Sunday	
Express; Evening Standard)	£200,000

Note: This table ignores certain very small minority holdings by directors and others. It also ignores nominee arrangements made by the newspaper groups to suit their own convenience.

Mersey mill in 1930.

possibility, as we shall see, never far from the forefront of his mind. Rothermere controlled his newspaper companies and, through them, W. V. Bowater & Sons. The independent Bowater interest, in so far as there was one, was represented by the family's holding in W. V. Bowater, amounting to less than 40 per cent of the Ordinary capital. The Bowater investment in Bowater's Mersey Paper Mills was less a matter of finance than of character and will-power. Bowaters also provided technical skill in papermaking which London Express Newspaper lacked. Altogether, Beaverbrook was to find Bowaters formidable.

4.3 THE UNEASY ALLIANCE

Beaverbrook in 1929 was fifty, Rothermere eleven years older. Each was a national figure, each immensely wealthy, each immensely powerful, though probably not chiefly in the way – the political way – that either most desired. Each was self-made, each had been wealthy and powerful for many years. The contrast with their junior partner, Eric Bowater, still under thirty-five, still relatively inexperienced, by no means wealthy, far from securely established, could scarcely have been greater, and the position was full of peril for the younger man and his family business.

This was because a conflict of interests underlay the partnership. The Bowater companies, as papermakers and paper merchants, were concerned simply to sell their products on the best possible terms. For the newspaper companies, on the other hand, paper-making was a subsidiary activity and, although it suited them to have suppliers who were prosperous and stable, yet if in the end they had to sacrifice one activity or the other there was no doubt which would go. Rothermere had given a plain enough indication in his treatment of Empire Mills.

There was another twist to the tangle. The newspaper groups had a common interest as buyers of paper but they were in direct and bitter competition in their main business. 'I shall go back to New Brunswick and retire a failure', Beaverbrook told the Chairman of the Conservative Party in 1928, 'if I don't succeed in killing the *Daily Mail*.'[28] He did neither the one thing nor the other but his feelings are plain and it is doubtful whether his papermaking ally, Lord Rothermere, was any more charitably disposed towards the *Daily Express*.

The directors of BMPM were appointed equally by W. V. Bowater and by London Express Newspaper, meaning respectively, at one remove, Rothermere and Beaverbrook. W. V. Bowater appointed Eric Bowater, A. E. Linforth and Arthur Baker. Eric Bowater was Chairman and Managing Director; Arthur Baker Technical Adviser, with £2,000 a year and a fee of a thousand guineas for supervising the building and equipment of the company's mills.

The executive direction of the business was therefore firmly in Bowater hands but the appointments made from the Express side showed that Beaverbrook intended to install powerful guardians of his interests, and they quickly showed themselves to be far more than merely benevolent observers of Bowater in action. They were A. W. Rider, E. J. Robertson and Michael Wardell, all directors of London Express Newspaper. Rider, Vice-Chairman of London Express, was a powerful figure in the newspaper business. Wardell, London Express's Assistant Manager, became a close associate of Beaverbrook in the 1930s. Robertson, General Manager of London Express, 'a dark, tall, saturnine Scot', quickly showed himself active and bellicose in looking after what he considered to be his own company's interest in BMPM's affairs.[29]

The management of the business, below the level of the Board, was wholly a matter for Bowaters. H. J. Inston (1889–1956), the Secretary, who had joined Bowaters from Blackburns, Barton, Mayhew in 1927, was already Secretary and a director of W. V.

Bowater and influential in Bowaters' increasingly elaborate financial planning. He was a meticulous, quiet man belonging to the
small circle of advisers on whom Eric Bowater was accustomed to
rely for devising the means necessary to attain his ends.

The General Manager of the mills was Kenneth Linforth, son of
A. E. Linforth. Eric Bowater, as a young man, gave responsible
positions to other young men and Linforth was about twenty-six
when he was appointed. He had served under his father and Arthur
Baker at Empire Mills and had spent eighteen months in Canada
and Newfoundland before he joined BPM at Northfleet.[30] As a mill
manager he gained a reputation for steadiness and caution rather
than imagination and is described by one who knew him as 'perhaps
too kind', but he earned lasting respect and loyalty from other
young men at the Mersey mills in the 1930s.[31]

Eric Bowater treated Kenneth Linforth much as if he were dealing
with a younger brother, promising but occasionally in need of
correction. He watched the work of the mill through regular, detailed reports, commenting on them freely by letter and occasionally drawing comparisons, unflattering to Mersey, with Northfleet,
though he was by no means unvaryingly critical. Linforth must have
been able to judge what was coming by the style of the opening in
which, unusually for his class and period, Bowater normally called
Linforth by his Christian name. 'My dear Kenneth', which was
fairly frequent, was usually a purr of satisfaction, though it might
cover a warning: 'It is absolutely essential that from now [15
January 1931] onwards a concerted effort is made . . . to reduce
your costs of manufacture'; exhortation: 'I am not going to be
satisfied until you can convince me that the last possible ounce has
been got out of your present equipment' (9 October 1931); and
even exasperation: 'I am disappointed to see the serious reduction
in output for last week; according to the figures . . . it dropped to
1048 tons as against 1177 tons for the previous week. What is the
explanation, I do wish you would not leave me to enquire each time'
(21 June 1932). This letter is marked in pencil in the margin:
'Normal week as against one with one extra shift. Wire No. 1 first
thing Monday morning.'

The standard form was 'Dear Kenneth', but 'Dear Kenneth Linforth' was a storm signal and 'Dear Linforth' meant the storm was
about to burst. In April 1934 Percy Fitt, W. V. Bowater's highly
respected Sales Director, who had been with the business since
1905, 'brought back with him from Manchester and Liverpool
most distressing evidence of the rubbishy paper which has been
delivered . . . recently'. Eric Bowater's reaction was brief but devas-

tating and ended with an ultimatum: 'There is no excuse, with your equipment and the abundant means of supervision at your disposal, why a single faulty reel should ever reach any Newspaper Office with whom we deal. I object to having to waste my time dealing with matters of this kind and it should not be necessary.'[32] How Kenneth Linforth dealt with a broadside of this nature is nowhere recorded. Perhaps his composure ran deep enough to stand the strain.

BMPM came into existence just in time to feel the shock of the chain of economic disasters which afflicted the world, in the early 1930s, after the collapse of prices on the New York Stock Exchange in the autumn of 1929. The consequences of the depression were by no means so catastrophic in the United Kingdom, where real national income actually rose by about 6 per cent between 1929 and 1933, as they were in the United States, where it fell by almost 35 per cent,[33] but they imported another element of strain into the already uneasy relationship between the *Express* and Bowaters.

The underlying tension between them – mistrust is hardly too strong a word – showed itself early in 1930. In 1929 Odhams Press Ltd, under J. S. Elias, later Lord Southwood (1873–1946), had taken over control of the ailing *Daily Herald*. Early in 1930 W. V. Bowater, as paper merchants, made a contract to supply the *Herald* with at least 10,000 tons of newsprint a year for three years, prudently investigating the credit standing of the purchasers beforehand. Bowaters had had trouble with the *Herald* in the past but the change of ownership seems to have reassured them. The *Herald* was printed in Manchester as well as London and W. V. Bowater, as BMPM's agents, strongly advised BMPM to contract for the Manchester portion of the *Herald*'s tonnage. Pending a contract, they arranged for the Manchester tonnage to be supplied from Northfleet, at extra cost for carriage, until the Mersey mills came into operation.

Eric Bowater wanted to accept the agents' advice. 'Such a contract', he told BMPM's directors on 11 February 1930, 'should be very beneficial to the Company, this type of order being more desirable . . . than the smaller orders calling for constant changes in colour, quality and substance, which entail loss of production at each change.'[34]

Robertson and the other *Express* directors were immediately suspicious. They comprehensively disliked the arrangements by which W. V. Bowater were BMPM's agents and Eric Bowater, besides being Chairman of BMPM, was Chairman also of their

agents and of the other Bowater manufacturing company, Bowater's Paper Mills. Robertson therefore queried W. V. Bowater's
contract with Odhams, though on what grounds the BMPM Board
minutes do not make clear. The advantages to the Mersey mills of
supplying newsprint to the *Herald* in Manchester were clear and
Eric Bowater, admitting his double interest in the matter, held his
ground. 'Although he was also Chairman of W. V. Bowater & Sons,
Ltd', he said, 'he endeavoured to regard the matter from this Company's [BMPM's] point of view and was firmly of the opinion that it
was very desirable that this Company should accept the offer.' The
Board, including Robertson and the other *Express* directors, agreed
unanimously but that did not mean that their suspicions abated.[35]

The state of the newspaper business, as 1930 went on, was hardly
such as to lead them towards a more open state of mind. In September 1930 Beaverbrook wrote 'a terrible dirge' (his own phrase)
to A. R. Graustein of International Paper. There was only one
newspaper company in England, he thought, which was financially
strong – the company that owned the *Daily Mail*. 'Rothermere', he
said, 'tells me that Company has £1,000,000 of cash in hand' –
which, if true, sheds an even more curious light on the Empire Mills
episode. Beaverbrook said Rothermere was having troubles with
his provincial papers and that his own *Daily Express* was 'certainly
not sitting pretty'. All newspapers, he said, were carrying 'so much
less advertising than they did a year ago'.[36]

Beaverbrook's 'dirge' must be treated with some caution. His
letters are full of extravagant optimism and extravagant gloom. He
loved self-dramatisation and his view of the truth usually depended
on his state of mind, his view of his own interests and the effect he
wished to create in his correspondent's mind. We need not, however, entirely discount a remark in the letter just quoted that the
Evening Standard, in the first part of 1930, was making a loss, for
when, early in September, Eric Bowater enquired confidently about
the renewal of his contract for the supply of newsprint to the
Standard, Beaverbrook prevaricated, pleaded illness as a reason for
not seeing him, said he was taking no part in the direction of the
paper – and finally, in October, refused a renewal.[37] He had in any
case, as we have seen, committed himself in July 1929 to taking all
the newsprint the *Standard* needed, from 1931 to 1933, from
International Paper.

While Beaverbrook was thus spreading gloom about the finances
of newspapers in general and of his own in particular, the BMPM
Board was facing construction costs which, as is the way of costs,
were going well above the estimates. The original estimated figure

for the construction of the Mersey mill was £805,854. The actual cost was put at £880,000 in August 1930, £950,000 in January 1931 and £1,010,800, the final figure, in November 1933.[38] Eric Bowater came three times to the Board, between August 1930 and January 1931, saying as he did so that 'the mill would still be cheap and an economic producer'.[39] He may have been right but to be right is not always to be popular and the *Express* directors, presumably short of cash and no doubt nervous of Beaverbrook, looked long and hard at the rising costs. They suggested, apparently without much conviction, that calls for their contribution to the Ordinary capital might be postponed if BMPM raised an overdraft but, in the end, they had to accept them.

Along with rising costs and the accompanying demands for capital, other causes of friction developed. Eric Bowater was very anxious for the *Express* to start taking newsprint from Mersey mill – and paying for it – as soon as the mill was in production and, when it appeared certain that production was going to start unexpectedly early, he insisted that the *Express* was obliged by contract to take paper from 17 November 1930 onward. Robertson objected, saying that the *Express* had plenty of paper, would need no more until the New Year and was not obliged to take any.[40] The *Express* directors of BMPM, anxious as ever about the level of costs, objected to contracts for pulp and other supplies being made without consulting them. Eric Bowater explained that 'he had acted in a similar manner in connection with other Companies' – an explanation which his critics may not have found reassuring.[41] Robertson, acting presumably as a director of London Express Newspaper rather than of BMPM, objected to the price of £13. 10s. a ton charged to the *Express* for newsprint and refused to pay more than £13.[42] The *Express* directors greatly objected to a claim by W. V. Bowater, supported by Eric Bowater as Chairman of that company, for commission on a portion of the newsprint supplied by BMPM to the *Express* and to a proposal by W. V. Bowater, after a conference of their shareholders, to withdraw 'the offer made by them to the Mersey company of a portion of their "Daily Herald" contract and to retain this business exclusively for Northfleet mill'.[43]

These last complaints were fundamental, arising directly from the conflict of interests which underlay the partnership. The *Express* directors of BMPM did not trust Eric Bowater to be impartial in judging between the claims of the various companies of which he was Chairman, being well aware that the Bowater interest in W. V. Bowater and in Bowater's Paper Mills was greater than in BMPM. The point was made for them, without their knowledge, by Noel

Bowater, Eric Bowater's colleague as Managing Director of W. V. Bowater, when he said: 'Having regard to the shortage of tonnage available and the fact that our interest in Mersey was much smaller than in the other mills, he did not consider it to be in the best interests of this Company [W. V. Bowater] that Mersey should receive preferential treatment.'[44]

Eric Bowater deeply resented the *Express* directors' distrust and his indignation occasionally breaks through the bland phraseology of Board minutes. Nevertheless, he hardly gave his colleagues ground for greater confidence when, as Chairman and joint Managing Director of W. V. Bowater, he acquiesced in that company's proposal to take away from BMPM the *Herald* tonnage which, as Chairman and Managing Director of BMPM, he had a few months earlier strongly urged the Mersey company to accept.

Unrest on the Mersey Board communicated itself to those with whom the fate of the Mersey company rested: Beaverbrook on the one hand and, on the other, Rothermere, acting through John Cowley. 'I feel', wrote Cowley ominously to Beaverbrook about a week before Christmas 1930, 'that many of the points which have been raised in connection with the Mersey mill should never have been necessary, as they appear to have been matters such as could quite easily be settled by a harmonious Board of Directors.'[45]

Beaverbrook, in his excitable way, had meanwhile been evolving vast and probably unpractical schemes for a twenty-year contract with International Paper and for International Paper to take over Mersey. 'In the alternative', he went on, in a telegram to Graustein sent in November 1930,

I will join you now in buying at agreed prices Mersey Dixon Lloyd then making agreement for merger with Rothermere's including Bowater Empire and Reid [sic] STOP Price should take interest in this deal and both of you should agree that all your English capacity has been exhausted STOP I have no doubt Dixon can be purchased very cheaply and present is very best possible opportunity to deal with Lloyds.[46]

Graustein, unimpressed, replied: 'I am just concocting a long telegram on the subject of a long term contract. I will supplement it here by saying that we shall be very stupid if we are unable to protect the Express so that it will feel no need of making any investment in a newsprint conversion mill.' He then asked for details of the Mersey mill which International Paper was being invited to take over but added: 'Just to be honest, though, I ought to say that I am not at all enthusiastic about the acquisition of any

paper mill properties abroad at this time so I do not think we are
likely to go ahead.'[47]

Thus another attempt to sell the Bowater business, over Eric
Bowater's head, came to nothing. The danger, however, remained
and would remain as long as Beaverbrook and Rothermere had
substantial holdings in Bowater enterprises. Over Christmas 1930 a
moderate degree of seasonable goodwill prevailed – Eric Bowater
told Beaverbrook he was 'delighted at the happy outcome of our
partnership'[48] and contributed to Beaverbrook's 'Empire Crusade'
– but on 13 January Beaverbrook told Cowley, 'Eric Bowater
dropped another bomb', his latest revelation of the mounting cost
of the Mersey mill. 'I think something must be done about this
Company', Beaverbrook went on, 'along the lines of the discussion
between Lord Rothermere and me last November.'[49] Presumably
Beaverbrook intended to revive his grandiose plans for a merger
of the newsprint makers, with or without International Paper's
participation.

Cowley himself, no doubt as disturbed as Beaverbrook by the
rising costs, had already seen Eric Bowater. Eric explained them
chiefly by saying that the original estimate had been hurriedly made
and that afterwards the architect 'had been considerably over-
worked, having been working twelve to fourteen hours a day for
seven days a week' (no wonder the mill was ready ahead of time), so
that he had not properly compared costs with estimates as work
went on. Eric followed his explanation with a dramatic gesture. He
and Arthur Baker offered to resign.[50]

A tactical resignation is a risky ploy. This one succeeded. Cowley
went into conference with Rothermere and emerged with an offer to
sell the united Bowater–Rothermere interest in the Mersey company to the Express company 'in order that it may have the direction of the Mill entirely under its own control'.[51] Beaverbrook was
out-manoeuvred. He had no mind to try running a paper mill
without Eric Bowater and Arthur Baker to guide him. 'I have
consulted the Daily Express Directors', he told Cowley. 'The Board
is not equipped to deal with a newsprint enterprise and on that
account cannot consider acquiring any more Bowater shares.'[52]

Beaverbrook accompanied his refusal of Cowley's offer with a
typically grandiloquent and loosely phrased counter-offer to sell his
Mersey holding to Rothermere. It is doubtful whether he meant it
very seriously because nothing more seems to have been heard of it.
In making it, however, he put his finger firmly on the root of the
trouble: 'A great difficulty in the present situation is the confusion
of interests.'[53]

After this decisive engagement there seems to have been no more talk of one Press baron selling out to the other or of selling the Mersey mill to a third party. Confusion of interests remained, however, and with it disharmony on the Mersey Board. By the beginning of 1931 Eric Bowater seems to have dropped or modified his demand that the *Express* should begin to take deliveries as soon as the Mersey mill was in production and W. V. Bowater had agreed to forgo commission on *Express* business.[54] Their proposal to divert *Herald* tonnage from Mersey to Northfleet seems to have been discreetly dropped. Some of the more contentious issues were thus out of the way but others remained, in particular the dispute over the price which the *Express* should pay for newsprint in 1931.

The curious situation in which Robertson was refusing to pay the price asked by BMPM while remaining on the BMPM Board came to an end in January 1931 when both he and Michael Wardell resigned. The directors nominated to replace them[55] – W. H. Marriott and T. Marson Till – were no less zealous, however, in pursuing what they conceived to be the interests of London Express Newspaper and, as long as the partnership lasted, they kept a close watch on pulp contracts and on costs and remained unflaggingly suspicious of the selling agents, W. V. Bowater & Sons, and of their practice of making contracts in their own name rather than in the name of their principals, the Mersey company.[56]

The dispute with the *Express* reflected the dramatic change which came over the world market for newsprint during the time the Mersey mill was being set up and coming into production. It was caused by the collapse of newspapers in the United States, leading to a fall in newsprint consumption in that country of about 25 per cent between 1929 and 1933, with catastrophic results for Canadian producers who relied almost entirely on the USA for their market. Newsprint production in Canada fell by about 25 per cent between 1929 and 1933 and a great deal of plant stood idle.[57]

In the United Kingdom in the early thirties there was no over-capacity – indeed, the reverse – and newsprint consumption, in spite of the depression, in spite of Lord Beaverbrook's gloom and in spite of a temporary drop caused by a drop in advertising, was still tending to rise rather than fall. It was estimated at 41.2 lb a head in 1929 and 47.1 in 1932, against corresponding figures in the USA of 62 lb and 45.5.[58] Pressure on the market from countries where over-capacity did exist, nevertheless, was heavy. Eric Bowater repeatedly complained of it and, in December 1930, he told Bowater's Paper Mills' Annual Meeting that imports of newsprint were forcing short-time working in British mills, including

Bowater's, in spite of the fact that in the United Kingdom about a million tons of newsprint were consumed in a year and productive capacity was about 800,000.

In these circumstances the price of newsprint, like the price of many other commodities, was falling. The London market price, to which BMPM's price to the *Daily Express* was imprecisely related, dropped from £14 a ton in 1930 to £11. 15s. in 1933 and £9. 15s. in 1934.[59] Robertson, therefore, was strongly placed to hold out for a lower price than BMPM asked for 1931 and he did. From the moment deliveries began he paid £13 instead of the £13. 10s. at which the paper was invoiced. Months of argument ended with surrender by BMPM in September 1931. Rather than face the heavy expense and general undesirability of arbitration with their largest customer they agreed to accept £13 as the price for the year.[60] For 1932, the prospect was a London price of £12. 2s. 6d. for six months and then £11. 17s. 6d. but the price to the *Express* might well be lower.[61]

If, at the end of 1930, mills in the United Kingdom could produce about 800,000 tons of newsprint a year, then the two manufacturing companies of which Eric Bowater was Chairman could produce about 22 per cent of it – 120,000 tons from Northfleet and 55,000 tons (they had not yet reached 60,000 tons) from Mersey, making 175,000 tons in all. Moreover, although Mersey's financial results had so far been rather disappointing, Northfleet's had been good. Even in the grim year 1930–1, with Northfleet working at about 72 per cent of capacity, Bowater's Paper Mills generated enough profit to show a return of $14\frac{1}{2}$ per cent on the net assets employed.[62] This was altogether a remarkable position to have reached for a business which less than half-a-dozen years earlier had produced no newsprint at all.

Remarkable Bowaters' position might be but it was far from comfortable. At the Mersey mill the *Express* directors on the BMPM Board were constantly at odds with their Bowater colleagues and usually, it seems, able to have their own way. Rothermere's control over the business as a whole, exercised through Cowley, was a constraint on Bowaters' freedom of action. Worse, there was always the danger that Rothermere alone, or Rothermere and Beaverbrook acting together, might sell the Bowater group to other owners who might not even be British. The danger might become imminent if either newspaper baron should find his major companies short of cash.

The only remedy for this disagreeable state of affairs was for the

Bowater business to recover its independence from Rothermere and cut itself loose from Beaverbrook, but how? The prospect at the beginning of 1932 can hardly have seemed hopeful.

4.4 INDEPENDENCE REGAINED

Eric Bowater says he has purchased your shares in Mersey Mill STOP We went into this venture with you and trusting you STOP We regard with horror prospect of any other partner STOP Will you please instruct your companies not to dispose of these shares until you and I talk over situation STOP

This telegram, a fine specimen of agitated Beaverbrook, was sent to Rothermere, who was in the South of France, on 11 May 1932.
Rothermere replied the next day:

Cowleys companies must sell urgent need for more cash to meet probable liability Anglo Can[adian Pulp & Paper Mills Ltd] STOP He has no option but would I am quite sure prefer sell Daily Express STOP He advises me he insisted on similar offer to you STOP Strongly urge you to accept and concentrate at Price Brothers STOP[63]

From these telegrams it is clear that the troubles of the Canadian newsprint industry, by forcing a cash crisis upon Anglo-Canadian, faced Eric Bowater both with a danger and an opportunity. Anglo-Canadian owned middle-sized newsprint mills, with capacity rated in 1943 at 206,800 short tons a year,[64] in Quebec. The company was controlled by Daily Mirror Newspapers Ltd and hence ultimately by Rothermere and, when it ran short of cash, one obvious course of action open to him was to sell his holdings in W. V. Bowater and in BMPM to raise money to rescue Anglo-Canadian. The danger, from Eric Bowater's point of view, was that Rothermere might sell to a third party – Beaverbrook, perhaps. On the other hand, if he could somehow raise enough money, the opportunity presented itself of buying the shares himself and thus freeing the Bowater business from Rothermere's control.

There is nothing to show when Eric Bowater first heard of Rothermere's difficulties with Anglo-Canadian, nor whether he or Rothermere made the first move towards the sale of Rothermere's Bowater holdings. Family tradition suggests that Eric did. He would have had to work fast, because Anglo-Canadian's needs would have been urgent. He had no adequate resources at his disposal, either as an individual or through the Bowater companies, to pay for the shares and there was no time for a capital issue. He turned, as he had done in the past, to Lloyds Bank for an immediate loan and to the London & Yorkshire Trust for proposals for funding it. By 11 May – the day when Beaverbrook sent his agitated telegram – Eric Bowater's financial arrangements were made, Cowley had agreed to the transaction and all that was needed was formal sanction to proceed. Eric came to the Board of Bowater's Paper Mills to get it.

Lloyds Bank provided the indispensable loan – £300,000 at one per cent above Bank Rate, secured by a debenture on Bowater's Paper Mills Ltd and repayable on 15 June 1932. By that time, little more than a month after the Board meeting of 11 May, it would be necessary to get the shareholders' sanction to an increase of the authorised capital of Bowater's Paper Mills to make an issue of 500,000 £1 6½ per cent Cumulative Preference shares at par and to get sufficient of the proceeds in to cover most of the repayment of the loan.[65]

The shares to be purchased from Rothermere's companies – the Daily Mirror and Sunday Pictorial companies and Associated Newspapers – were 120,000 shares in W. V. Bowater & Sons, which would free all Bowater companies from Rothermere's control, and 100,000 shares in BMPM, which would put Bowater into Rothermere's place as an equal partner with Beaverbrook in the ownership of the Mersey company. Bowater's Paper Mills were to take over the shares in W. V. Bowater and both companies – BPM and W. V. Bowater – were to take over the shares in BMPM in equal proportions, so that BPM would become the parent company of the Bowater group. The price of the Mersey shares was fixed at par; the price to be paid for the shares in W. V. Bowater was 36s. 8d.[66]

As soon as Eric Bowater had got rid of Rothermere he intended to get rid of Beaverbrook as well. Therefore, as soon as he was sure of Cowley's agreement to the sale of the shares mentioned above and as soon as BPM's Board had ratified his purchase of them, he went to Beaverbrook, presented the transaction as an accomplished fact and, either then or very soon afterwards, offered to buy Beaverbrook out of Mersey. The report of the resulting explosion can still be heard in Beaverbrook's telegram to Rothermere. Evidently this was the first he had heard about the sale of the Rothermere holdings and his indignation is understandable. He felt that Rothermere had let him down and, no doubt, that young Bowater had outwitted him.

Rothermere unadmirably took cover behind Cowley, saying he was sure Cowley would prefer to sell to the Daily Express. Cowley, who presumably had Rothermere's agreement before he committed himself to Eric Bowater, told Beaverbrook firmly that he was 'quite unable to vary the agreements already entered into . . . The offers made for our interests . . . were so attractive that my co-directors and I . . . felt that we could not do anything but accept', and he added: 'The money that these transactions will realise will, I fear, owing to the plight of the newsprint industry in Canada, be needed for our Quebec Company.'[67]

Beaverbrook, unappeased, raged telegraphically from Canada at Bowaters' plans for a public issue: 'If Bowater buys Rothermere shares with public money and then conducts himself on same lines as heretofore with no restraining hand from Rothermere stalemate will result in court application for winding up STOP.' Evidently he felt that Eric was quite unfit to be trusted to run Mersey single-handed and he tried to associate Rothermere with himself in frustrating Eric's plans:

Rothermere and I will not permit an issue of securities involving public in this jam STOP Alternatively if Express sells out to Bowater danger of stalemate over Mersey disappears STOP It would be much better for us to buy Rothermere interests STOP Rothermere telegraphed me prefers sell to Express STOP I notified Cowley of our intention to purchase and Rothermere will certainly see me through STOP[68]

Rothermere did not see Beaverbrook through. On the contrary, Beaverbrook agreed to the sale of the *Express* holding in the Mersey company and it was paid for out of the proceeds of the public issue by Bowater's Paper Mills which Beaverbrook had been so anxious to stop. At about the same time, the Ordinary capital of Bowater's Paper Mills was increased by the creation of 200,000 new £1 shares, of which 120,000 were at once issued in exchange for 80,000 Ordinary shares in W. V. Bowater held by directors and a few other private individuals. Thus BPM was given 100 per cent ownership of the Ordinary capital of the original parent company of the Bowater group and, with it, unshakeable control of a business capable of manufacturing 175,000 tons of newsprint a year.

Between 1929 and 1932, Eric Bowater was a very lucky man. The gains he made were handsome but the risks he took were incalculable. By his association with Rothermere and Beaverbrook he was enabled to develop the Bowater business much faster than would otherwise have been possible but, against that, he took a risk which very nearly ended in the equivalent of having his horse killed under him – that is, the sale of the Bowater business, against his will, into other ownership. Moreover, he cannot have known how quickly, if ever, he would be able to buy back his independence. That was a chance result of the collapse of the Canadian newsprint industry in the depression. He cannot have foreseen his opportunity but he was very quick and very skilful in making use of it. He brought Beaverbrook to spluttering indignation, Rothermere to undignified defensiveness – and no wonder!

Independent once again, in the mid-thirties, he was able to give free play to his restless ambition for growth and to his talent for seizing opportunities. He could organise the Bowater companies without interference from Rothermere, expand the Mersey mill without hindrance from Beaverbrook and then, in 1936, when the chance arose, buy control of a larger business than his own, indeed the largest and most respected newsprint business in the United Kingdom, if not in Europe – Edward Lloyd Ltd of Kemsley and Sittingbourne in Kent.

The Bowater Group in the thirties

5.1 THE CUSTOMERS

Bowaters' business had been brought into existence chiefly to serve the owners of mass-circulation newspapers and periodicals in the United Kingdom. In the 1930s the Press barons were riding high. Neither the cinema nor 'the wireless' was in direct competition with them. Television was still a speck on the horizon, deceptively distant. In spite of the slump, living standards were rising and there were plenty of potential customers. Never again, except perhaps for a few years in the early fifties, would the Press barons have it quite so good.

During the twenties, as we saw in Chapter 2.1, large publishing groups were emerging. The number and composition of groups kept varying but, in 1938, Political and Economic Planning distinguished ten, of which the two largest – Harmsworth and Kemsley – owned ten morning, nineteen evening, eight Sunday and twelve weekly newspapers in Great Britain. Between them, the groups owned every kind of newspaper, national and provincial, and a range of periodicals from the ancestral *Answers, Tit-Bits* and *Pearson's Weekly* to the *Illustrated London News, Britannia and Eve, Feathered World* and *Debrett.* Few newspapers of importance were by 1938 independent of one or other of the groups but those that were included *The Times* and the *Daily Worker* on weekdays and *The Observer,* the *News of the World* and *Reynolds' News* on Sundays and a number of highly respected papers in the provinces.[1]

These groups of publications came into existence to serve a large, growing and highly competitive market. There was, in fact, only one larger market in mass publishing in the world, the United States, and that was very different. American papers were and still are aimed chiefly at a local rather than a national readership. There was and still is nothing in the USA or any other country quite like British 'national newspapers'; that is, papers intended to be

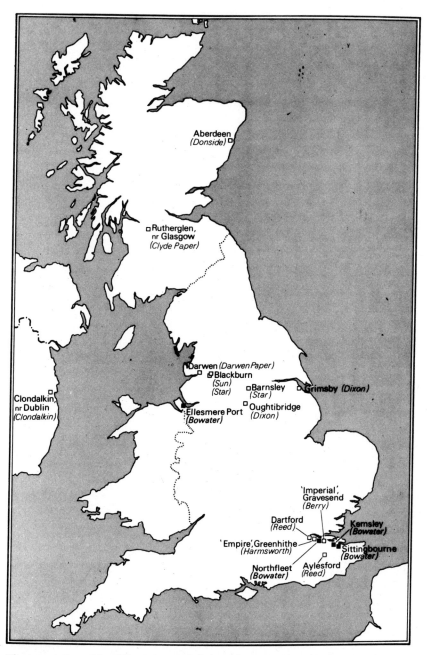

The newsprint mills of Bowaters and their main competitors in the United Kingdom, spring 1938. The main UK interests in newsprint manufacturing overseas were: Harmsworth – Anglo-Newfoundland Development Co. Ltd and Anglo-Canadian Pulp & Paper Mills Ltd; Berry – Gulf Pulp & Paper Co.; Bowater – Corner Brook, Newfoundland (acquired 1938). *Notes:* (1) The Harmsworth Group had a substantial interest in Reeds. (2) Star Paper Mills were controlled by Kymmene Aktiebolag, Finland.

available throughout the country on the day of issue and with circulation figures to match. American publishing groups may be large and American journalists influential but breadth of coverage comes from 'syndication' – simultaneous publication of the same item in many local papers – not from one national paper's widespread circulation.

Reliable circulation figures for the newspaper press in its entirety, as distinct from figures for some individual papers, seem impossible to come by for the twenties but it is certain they were growing, if only because imports of newsprint rose from 131,000 tons in 1913 to 346,000 tons in 1929.[2] Between 1930 and 1937 the circulation of national daily papers rose, according to one estimate, by 16 per cent; according to another, by 19 and both estimates put the increase in the circulation of Sunday papers between 7 and 8 per cent.[3] The absolute figures were very large; for 1930 not less than 8.5 million 'nationals' and 13.8 million 'Sundays'; for 1937 some 10 million and 15 million (Table 9). And, of course, there was a large periodical press as well.

TABLE 9. *Circulation of national daily and Sunday newspapers, 1930 and 1937*

		1930	1937	Percentage increase
RC on the Press, 1947–9	Dailies	8.6m	9.9m	16.0
	Sundays	14.6m	15.7m	7.5
PEP, *British Press*	Dailies	8.9m	10.7m	19.0
	Sundays	13.8m	14.9m	8.0

These bland figures mask ferocious competition. Between 1930 and 1937 the *Daily Mail* was beaten out of first place among the dailies, for the first time since its foundation, both by Beaverbrook's *Daily Express* and by Lord Southwood's *Daily Herald*. By 1937 each of these papers reported circulation figures above 2 million. Among the Sunday papers, the *News of the World* and *The People* each went over 3 million by 1937 and Lord Camrose, in 1947, considered the *News of the World*'s true figure was probably very much greater. In any case, no other newspaper in the world came near it. The *Sunday Express* was very successful, too, but the *Sunday Dispatch* and the *Sunday Pictorial* lost circulation heavily. In the provinces, the Harmsworths and the Berrys fought each other, especially at Bristol and Newcastle-on-Tyne. In London, the

Berrys bought the *Daily Telegraph* in 1927, and in 1930 halved its price and doubled its circulation. In 1937 they took over the *Morning Post*, merged it with the *Telegraph* and established themselves with an unprecedented circulation for the 'class' end of the market, some 600,000.[4]

In these barons' wars, the prize was advertising revenue. One result of the publishing revolution was that nobody, by the twenties, expected to pay more than a penny for a popular paper during the week or twopence on Sundays, but no paper could be sold at a profit for that price if it carried only news and features. There had to be advertising and the higher the circulation of the paper the more advertisers would pay for space in it, as they would also for space in periodicals, especially, as broadcasting took hold, the *Radio Times*.

Mass circulation could be earned by journalistic excellence or skill, not necessarily the same thing. It could also be bought. The large groups, between the wars, bid energetically against each other for it. They engaged armies of house-to-house canvassers and sent them into action with sets of Dickens' works, silk stockings, cameras, mangles, various kinds of insurance and much else which, offered free or cheap to householders and housewives, might induce them to place orders with newsagents and thus become 'registered readers' for a few weeks or months.

Readers thus won were easily lost. They failed to renew orders as they lapsed or they switched to other papers with more attractive offers. Costs mounted. Occasionally something approaching hysteria set in and rival campaigns threatened to get out of hand. Nevertheless, the penalties of giving up canvassing altogether seemed so dire that it never entirely ceased. There were other promotions such as the distribution of money prizes at seaside resorts and the election of beauty queens, eligibility for the one and votes for the others being dependent on buying copies of the papers concerned. Paper shortage in the Second World War put an end to these antics but not before they had played a large part in pushing up the circulation of the *Daily Express* and the *Daily Herald* to figures unapproached in any other country.[5]

In this way the British acquired the slightly spurious reputation of being the eagerest newspaper readers in the world, using newsprint in 1936 at a rate – 59.8 lb per head – rivalled only in Australasia (57.5 lb) and the USA (57 lb) and two-and-a-half times as great as the nearest Continental figure (22.8 lb in the Netherlands).[6] British imports of newsprint and the British newsprint industry grew very rapidly during the twenties and thirties. In 1921 it was estimated that there was capacity for producing 300,000 tons to meet consumption of 450,000.[7] In 1937, at the inter-war peak, 1,023,000 tons were produced towards a total consumption, including imports, of 1,496,000. At that figure more newsprint was being produced in the United Kingdom than in any other country of the world except Canada.[8]

5.2 THE GROUP

Eric Bowater emerged into independence, after extricating himself from Rothermere's control, at the head of a compact group of papermaking and paper-selling companies (Figure 1). From this base he launched a programme of expansion which included not only doubling the capacity of the Mersey mills but also a deter- mined attempt to establish Bowaters alongside their most powerful competitors in the Canadian newsprint industry. Before we ex- amine this expansion in detail it will be convenient to consider the organisation and policy of the group as it stood in the mid-thirties, when it was beginning to acquire many of the characteristics which would distinguish it for a quarter of a century or more, and when some of those who would direct its affairs in the fifties, sixties and seventies were coming into its service.

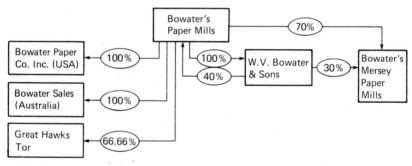

1   The Bowater Group in January 1935. Holdings and cross-holdings of Ordinary capital.

Emancipation from Rothermere made Bowater's Paper Mills, not W. V. Bowater & Sons, the parent company and the disengage- ment of Beaverbrook from Mersey brought that company fully within the group as a wholly-owned subsidiary. There were thus three Bowater companies in the United Kingdom: Bowater's Paper Mills, Bowater's Mersey Paper Mills and W. V. Bowater & Sons Ltd. In January 1935, the group extended activities into the supply of papermaker's materials by the purchase of a major interest in Great Hawk's Tor China Clays Ltd, intended as a protection against monopolistic pressure from English China Clays.[9] Overseas, the Bowater Paper Co. Inc., in the USA, was for the time being dormant but Eric Bowater fought a long battle to gain a position in Canada (Chapter 5.5 below), and in Australia a branch office opened in Sydney in 1919 was turned into Bowater's (Australia) Ltd, incorporated in 1928. It looked after newsprint imports from the United Kingdom. The export trade, in which Australia was the most important market, was managed by Eric Bowater's cousins, Noel and his brother, Ian.

Eric himself, free now both of his uncles and of Rothermere, stood unchallenged at the head of the business. With the small exception of Great Hawk's Tor, he was Chairman of all the companies, including the one in Australia which he never visited. He was sole Managing Director of one of the three principal companies, BMPM, and joint Managing Director of the other two, sharing the appointment at BPM with Arthur Baker and at W. V. Bowater with Noel. His authority, however, rested neither upon these appointments nor on a massive shareholding but on the force of his personality. It was not for that reason any the less absolute. It was projected, very consciously, by a commanding presence and manner: red hair, turning to white in middle age; a tall, soldierly figure and a carriage so erect that some observers, to his great annoyance, concluded that it could not be natural; a piercing stare, or glare, which he could use as a frightening weapon; a deep voice in which, when he wished to be affable, he would address an apprehensive subordinate as 'Dear boy'. In this, as in some other ways, he sometimes seems to step straight from the pages of Dornford Yates. 'I do not wish to be remembered as a popular Chairman', he is reported to have said, 'but I hope to be remembered as a just one.'

He is said by those who knew him well to have been a shy man, suffering perhaps from a sense of insecurity, and defending himself by the austerity of his manner. It certainly served to inspire respect, not to say awe, in many of those who dealt with him in business and few were allowed to catch a glimpse of the softer qualities which underlay it, including unadvertised kindliness to Bowater employees and others and a boyish playfulness. He kept up with affairs through the newspapers, which he read thoroughly, but he was not otherwise much given to reading and was in no sense an intellectual. He had a ready turn of phrase and could use it to great theatrical effect, as when, at an important dinner party at a famous London hotel, a cockroach emerged from under a dishcover. 'Delicious!' remarked Eric. 'We shall dine elsewhere'.

All who knew him agree upon his exceptional power of self-control. His temper, potentially violent, was very rarely lost, but terrifying if it was. 'If you lose your temper', he said, 'you lose face', and that he hated to do, finding it very difficult to laugh at himself or to come to terms with mistakes, preferring rather to quote the admonition: 'never explain, never apologise.' In the company of close friends he could be a relaxed and charming companion, dropping his public air of dignified aloofness. He greatly enjoyed the admiration of women, with several of whom and with one in particular his relations were extremely close. He was twice married and by his first wife Blanche Currie, née de Ville, whom he married very young in 1915, he had a daughter. By his second wife Margaret Perkins he had a daughter and a son.

In the direction of the business Eric acted very much as if he owned it. The directors and senior managers, apart from his two cousins, were his own men, chosen and advanced by him as he saw fit. His small circle of close advisers was by no means confined to members of the main Board or to full-time employees of the group. He valued professional advice highly, paid for the best he could find, and used it judiciously. There was little in the way of systematic recruitment or training for management, for although an able young man such as Robert Knight might join early in life and work his way to the top of the business, yet Eric Bowater, throughout his career, brought in from outside, sometimes at a high level and often with indeterminate duties, individuals who for a variety of reasons had caught his eye. Some came from the firm's professional advisers. One, after the war, was his personal doctor, Neville Whitehurst, who moved very successfully from medicine into general management (p. 242 below). He did not make appointments lightly and would watch a new associate or subordinate carefully for a matter of months before coming to a decision about his abilities and character. On the other hand his confidence, once given, was seldom withdrawn.

In this scheme of things the Board of the parent company had no very exalted place. It did not meet very often and its minutes record decisions and sometimes the reasons for them, but substantive discussion nearly always took place outside the Board Room, often over lunch. Eric's dominance was complete and he never concealed it. Even in public he sometimes went so far as to refer to 'my policy', omitting either accidentally or on purpose to clothe his naked autocracy in conventional phraseology acknowledging the collective authority of the Board.

Table 10 shows the management structure of the Bowater Group and the very high salaries paid as matters stood on 31 March 1934. All the levers of control came under Eric Bowater's hand but he had

TABLE 10. *Bowater Group directors and senior management, 31 March 1934*

	BPM	£	BMPM	£	WVB	£
E. V. Bowater	Chairman/MD		Chairman/MD		Chairman/MD	
N. V. Bowater	Director	1,000	Director	500	Joint MD	3,300
A. Baker	Joint MD	5,000	Tech. Director	2,000		
E. C. Duffin	Director	400	Director	250	Production and Sales Director	2,500
H. J. Inston	Director	400	Secretary	400	Director	
	Secretary(a)					
H. Rutherford	Res. Director	1,500	Director	250	Secretary	1,500
	Secretary(b)					
K. N. Linforth			Res. Director	1,500	Home Sales Director	1,400
P. R. J. Fitt					Director and Export Supervisor	1,250
I. F. Bowater					Director	300
A. E. Linforth	Director	400				
F. C. Symonds [Simmons]			Mill Supt.	1,250		
T. Killin	Mill Supt.	1,500				
G. W. Shaw	Supervising Engineer	650	Supervising Engineer	650		
W. T. Armstrong	Res. Engineer	1,000				
T. Tidbury			Res. Engineer	1,200		
A. R. W. Gillham					Services Manager	1,000

(a) From 31 March 1935.
(b) Until 31 March 1935.

Source: Deloitte, Plender, Griffiths & Co, Report, 16 May 1934. E. V. Bowater's remuneration is not given.

evidently provided himself with an inner cabinet for Noel Bowater and Earle C. Duffin each had a seat, like himself, on each of the three principal Boards. Inston, too, was near the throne. He was a director of two of the companies and from March 1935 onward, when he took over from H. Rutherford the Secretaryship of BPM, he was Secretary of all three. Rutherford and the older Linforth were also on two Boards out of the three but Linforth was ill and absent from March 1932 until July 1936 when he resigned. The remaining directors, with one seat each, were P. R. J. Fitt, Kenneth Linforth and Ian Bowater. They were all departmental managers and two, Linforth and Ian Bowater, were young men. Other senior managers with responsibilities in one or more of the major companies were the Mill Superintendents at Northfleet and Mersey, the Supervising Engineer at both mills, the Resident Engineer at Mersey and the Services Manager who ran W. V. Bowater's growing road transport fleet and the still important business in waste.

In any group of companies, the central management must strike a balance between controlling the group's resources for the good of all and allowing the constituent companies enough independence to be efficient. Companies very commonly feel that their particular interests are being sacrificed for the remote benefit of some other member of the group and we have seen that, as long as BMPM was jointly owned by Bowater and London Express, the Express directors were permanently suspicious of Bowaters' intentions. As soon as Bowaters had bought Beaverbrook out, they proceeded to carry out the measures, all tending towards greater central control, which his nominees had blocked.

'It is my policy', Eric Bowater nevertheless maintained in 1936, 'as Chairman of all the companies that, in so far as is practicable, each of them should rely upon its own resources, particularly in respect of its finances.'[10] Practicability evidently had fairly narrow limits, for the finances of the Bowater companies were interconnected by cross-holdings and by guarantees and, although these inter-connections altered as time went on, they became more intricate rather than less. One effect of the policy of financial self-reliance, no doubt intentional, was to perpetuate the issue of separate accounts for each company but no consolidated account, thus making it extremely difficult, as financial journalists sometimes complained, to form any true picture of the financial structure of the group as a whole. Within the business, from 1935 onwards, Inston, as Secretary of the three major companies, was building up in his office a highly centralised system which supplied Eric Bowater with all the financial information he called for.

The Chairman's letters to Kenneth Linforth show how closely he watched production and quality. Mill management nevertheless must by its nature be de-centralised but technical supervision and the co-ordination of labour relations lay with Arthur Baker. The key functions of Bowaters' commercial management – purchasing of pulp, selling of newsprint and the negotiation of selling prices – were kept firmly at the centre and it was Bowaters' insistence on control of pulp purchasing and, through the agency of W. V. Bowater, of selling which caused the worst of the disharmony on the Mersey Board during the period of joint ownership.

To Bowaters in the thirties, driven fast by Eric Bowater towards expansion with slender means, finance was important beyond all normal bounds. It needed great skill and, whatever Eric might say, co-ordination of the financial affairs of the group companies so that the resources of the stronger might be brought to the support of the weaker. We shall have plenty of occasion to observe the financial planning of Eric Bowater and his close associates inside and outside the company. In all these operations the anchor-man was Herbert Inston.

Pulp buying was directed by the Chairman and managed by Henry Rutherford. In July 1934, an agreement between BPM and BMPM demonstrated the advantages to be gained from central control of group resources. BPM would buy the pulp needed for both companies and hold stocks, getting the benefit of good terms for bulk buying and getting still further discounts by payment in cash. The Mersey company would pay only for pulp consumed.[11]

Selling was the function, as it always had been, of the merchant company, W. V. Bowater & Sons. Important customers were not numerous, personal relationships were unusually important and negotiations of consequence were carried out at a high level on both sides. Under the general supervision of Eric Bowater, Earle Duffin was responsible for major newsprint contracts at home; Percy Fitt for provincial newsprint contracts and miscellaneous grades of paper; Noel and Ian Bowater for exports. The importance of W. V. Bowater within the group was that sales policy could be framed in the interests of the group as a whole rather than of any single member of it, so that contracts might be split between Northfleet and Mersey or W. V. Bowater might accept contracts on their own responsibility and buy outside the group, if necessary, to fulfil them. On all their contracts, naturally, they earned commission.

None of W. V. Bowater's activities made much appeal to the Express directors of the Mersey company and some they resented as directing profitable business away from Mersey or attracting commission which they disliked having to pay. As long as the Mersey company was jointly owned, the Bowater insistence on appointing W. V. Bowater as agents to BMPM was a source of friction and the most important Mersey contract – with the *Express* – was kept out of the agents' hands. As soon as Bowaters gained control of BMPM, ambiguity ceased and W. V. Bowater took charge of sales from Mersey as they already had charge of sales from Northfleet.[12]

For the distribution of their products Bowaters, like many other companies, had to decide whether to rely on hired transport or to run their own fleet, with the extension of management responsibilities and capital expenditure which that decision would imply. For Bowaters, distribution has always been critically important and never more so than in the thirties when imported newsprint was being offered at attractively low prices. Getting and holding business might depend heavily on delivering newsprint quickly and reliably and on responding readily to sudden unforeseen surges of demand. Characteristically, Eric commissioned Barton, Mayhew to carry out an investigation designed to help him decide on transport policy. Equally characteristically, a few years later he took into Bowaters' service, though not directly from Barton, Mayhew, one of their investigators, Henry Chisholm (p. 146 below). To provide the services required, specialised road vehicles were needed, con-

Newsprint delivery by Foden steam wagon, 1932. *Barnaby's Picture Library*

stantly available, and during 1932–3 Bowaters began replacing
hired vehicles with vehicles of their own. By the end of 1932 they
had twenty-six petrol-driven lorries and four steam wagons.[13] The
fleet, as the servant of selling policy, was owned and run by W. V.
Bowater and, at that company's Annual Meeting in March 1933,
Eric Bowater said they would soon have a large enough fleet to deal
with almost all the production of newsprint from Northfleet and
Mersey. A little later that year, following the trend of the times, they
decided to switch to oil-fuelled vehicles.[14]

Newsprint delivery by AEC 'Mammoth', 1949.

Successful selling depended on the skilful negotiation of contracts
and, in particular, on the setting of prices. The importance of these
contracts to Bowaters needed no emphasis and their importance to
the newspaper owners is demonstrated by figures published in
1938, based partly on estimates made outside the newspaper industry in 1935 and partly on *Daily Express* figures made public by
Beaverbrook in 1937. These two sets of figures showed that, for a
mass-circulation paper such as the *Express*, the cost of newsprint
and ink together (they are not shown separately) was by far the
largest item in the newspaper's bill of costs, amounting to 36 per
cent of the total, with production wages in a rather distant second
place at 18 per cent.[15] It is immediately obvious why the price of

newsprint was of the highest importance to newspaper owners and why they took close personal interest in the terms of contracts, the more so since in the early thirties the price of newsprint was falling fast – the price on the London market fell by about 30 per cent between 1930 and 1935[16] – and competition between home and overseas suppliers, especially the Canadians, was keen.

Contract prices were usually agreed in the summer or autumn for the calendar year ahead. If the parties could not settle, the contract would provide for one or more of various ways of reaching a figure. It might be done by reference to the London market price, to the overseas market price or to Bowaters' costs of production, and the method of determining these standards, usually on the basis of a neutral accountant's report, would be laid down. Large buyers would usually insist that Bowaters should charge them no more than they charged other buyers, so that contracts with the major newspaper groups became interdependent, with the lowest price, which was not necessarily the London market price, setting the price for all.[17]

There were further refinements which the written contracts did not cover, such as the custom in the home trade of allowing over-weight and the practice of making cash rebates. Rebates were very confidential payments indeed, passed through a private account. When Beaverbrook, in 1929, agreed to a contract with Bowaters for the *Evening Standard*'s newsprint in 1930, it was also agreed that Eric Bowater would 'assist' him – Beaverbrook's own phraseology – 'to the extent of not less than £9,000 and not more than £10,000, which you will pay to me once every three months during the year 1930'.[18] This was a very large sum* and must indicate how greatly Bowaters needed the contract, or Beaverbrook's goodwill. In 1931, rebates were being paid to the *Morning Post*[19] and, from 1932 until February 1938 and possibly longer, to the *Daily Mirror*. The rate of rebate to the *Mirror* varied. In 1932 17s. 6d. per ton was being paid on the first $941\frac{2}{3}$ tons per month, representing about 7.2 per cent on the price of £12. 2s. 6d. In 1938 it had risen to 20s. a ton and the price by then, no doubt, was lower.[20]

Since newsprint mills have a great deal of capital employed in large machines which can only run profitably at or near their full output, mass production is of the essence of the industry and long-term contracts are attractive both to the producer and to the buyer, who has an interest in maintaining a secure source of supply. Contracts for periods up to a quarter of a century have long been a

* Beaverbrook must surely have meant £9,000 or £10,000 per year, payable in quarterly instalments. Even so, the total is very large.

feature of the newsprint business, though perhaps not quite so nearly universal as has sometimes been suggested.[21] Bowaters, during the thirties, made contracts for as long as twenty or twenty-five years but they also made spot contracts and contracts for a single year. Much of their business, as for instance with the *Herald*, the *Mirror*, Associated Newspapers and the *Manchester Guardian*, was done on contracts for three, four or five years.[22]

For Bowaters the early thirties were by no means so gloomy as for firms in cotton, coal, heavy engineering, shipbuilding or other industries heavily dependent on overseas trade. Bowaters' market, linked to the rising demand for consumer goods at home, was still growing. Between 1931 and 1933 the *Herald*, the *Mail* and the *Express* were fighting a spectacular battle for circulation in which newsprint was essential ammunition, extravagantly expended, and largely as a result the average daily circulation of morning papers in the British Isles rose, in the manner described earlier in this chapter.[23]

5.3 THE EXPANSION OF MERSEY MILL

Early in 1932, as heavy industry and the export trades of the United Kingdom sank into the depths of the slump, the Board of BMPM were considering an estimate for doubling the capacity of their mills.[24] From the outset of the Mersey project in 1929 the intention had been to double, if not triple, the mills' capacity as soon as possible after the first two machines were working but, as the depression set in, there were signs of a decline in enthusiasm on the Beaverbrook side, though Eric Bowater characteristically saw nothing in the surrounding gloom to make him slow down. He often claimed, in later life, that a period of depression was the right moment for expansion.

The effects of the slump on Bowaters, though delayed and indirect, were severe but they had not become apparent when the breaking of the Beaverbrook connection left the way clear to go ahead with the installation of two new machines which would bring the total capacity of the Bowater group to about 250,000 tons a year at an estimated cost of £850,000. To raise that sum, the BMPM directors drew on the company's own resources for about £200,000 and raised £100,000 within the group by the issue of 100,000 £1 Ordinary shares at par to BPM. BPM paid for them from the proceeds of an issue of 80,000 of their own Ordinary shares to their shareholders at 25s. For the remaining £650,000 BMPM went to the market. In December 1932, they issued 500,000

£1 5½ per cent Cumulative Preference shares at par and, in April
1933, they redeemed £650,000 6½ per cent Debentures and replaced
them with £800,000 4½ per cent Debentures at £99, gaining
£89,000 new money by the conversion. It says a great deal for the
confidence which the Bowater name by this time inspired, unsupported by the newspaper baronage, that both issues, slump notwithstanding, were heavily over-subscribed: the Preference shares,
Eric Bowater told BPM's shareholders, three-and-three-quarter
times within half an hour of the lists being opened.[25]

That confidence, in the short run, may not have been entirely
justified. The new machines at Mersey, built like all previous Bowater machines by Walmsleys, came into action in a remarkably
short time, by November and December 1933, but, by that time, the
Bowater Group as a whole was running into the full effects of the
Canadian and Newfoundland competition discussed below (see
Chapter 5.4). The difficulty was not to find business – Eric Bowater
never complained of short-time working – but to find it at profitable
prices. In 1934, low selling prices were bearing down on unyielding
costs of Scandinavian pulp. It was a bad year for the newsprint
industry in general and for Mersey in particular.

Mersey's results in the first quarter of 1934 were so extremely
poor as to shake Eric Bowater out of his habitual optimism into
almost panicky demands for economy: perhaps unnecessary at
Mersey where a penny was never spent if a halfpenny would do and
the content of expensive chemical pulp in the newsprint was kept
very low, though even at 12 per cent a good sheet of paper was
produced. Eric pointed out to the Mersey Board

> that we had for some years enjoyed a period of prosperity at a time when
> others were suffering from the prevailing depressed state of trade, and
> consequently had not put into practice any drastic economies, but the time
> had now arrived . . . when such economies were essential and the sooner
> the staff and workpeople realised this the better.

He commissioned Deloitte, Plender, Griffiths to make 'an independent investigation of the Bowater organisation as a whole with a
view to effecting economies generally', and he brought up the
subject of economies of scale: 'The question of co-operation with
the staffs of our associated Mills in such directions as buying, and
effecting comparisons in costs and expenses, was also raised and
discussed, and the desirability of a free interchange of information
and views on such matters was emphasised.'[26]

'The Directors anticipate', says the prospectus for the Preference
issue of 1932, 'as a result of their experience in the operation of

Bowater's Paper Mills at Northfleet, that the trading profits of the Company, when the Mills are operating to their full increased capacity, will approximate to £180,000 per annum.' In the thirties, they never did. In 1934, after paying debenture interest of £36,000, the company could barely afford to pay the Preference dividend at all and then only by providing nothing but 'a nominal amount' for depreciation.[27] Profits rose in 1935 but not enough to justify an Ordinary dividend and the highest figure they reached before the war – £170,471 in 1936 – was the only one on which an Ordinary dividend – 5 per cent – was paid.[28]

When 1936 began, Eric Bowater said that BMPM, with £100,000 still owing to contractors, was not financially ready for further development and, for that reason, he turned aside a suggestion by Baker to convert one newsprint machine, at a cost of £170,000, to making kraft* in order to reduce losses in the export trade.[29] Soon, however, he demonstrated his natural ebullience once again. In February 1936 the authorised capital of the Mersey company was doubled to £2m, with large but unspecified extensions in mind, and 150,000 new Ordinary shares were immediately issued at par to W. V. Bowater & Sons to provide cash to pay off contractors who had been constructing a wharf for the Mersey mill on the Manchester Ship Canal.[30]

5.4 THE CANADIAN INVASION

Mersey's troubles in the mid-thirties were caused by competition from overseas, especially from Canada and Newfoundland, and by the Government's refusal to protect the home newsprint industry. The newsprint makers felt particularly ill-used because, in 1932, when the National Government abandoned the hallowed Victorian principle of Free Trade and put a tariff on a wide range of imports, newsprint was among the goods specifically exempted. Imports could still come in duty-free. The Government's argument, supported by Labour members and Liberals but opposed in a division on 24 March 1932 by sixty-nine Conservatives, was that imports of foreign newsprint, chiefly from Scandinavia, did not amount to more than a small fraction of British consumption, but that fraction prevented British makers from charging excessive prices and that this was particularly important because so much of the British newsprint industry was controlled by three great newspaper barons: Beaverbrook, Camrose, Rothermere. By allowing duty-free

---

* A very strong paper, light brown in colour, made from unbleached sulphate wood pulp.

imports, the Government maintained, they were protecting news-papers independent of the great groups. Neville Chamberlain, Chancellor of the Exchequer, admitted that the home mills were working below capacity and could probably supply 'the whole of what now came from abroad' but 'this was one of those cases where other considerations came in besides the economic one'.[31] Eric Bowater could hardly be expected to agree. 'It is difficult to under-stand', he told W. V. Bowater's shareholders, 'why Newsprint . . . should be the only manufactured article included in the brief list of commodities which may enter the country free of duty.'[32]

TABLE 11. *British imports of newsprint, 1929 and 1935–7*

Country of origin	1929 (%)	1935 (%)	1936 (%)	1937 (%)
Canada	45	29	31	29
Newfoundland	26	43	42	45
Finland	13	19	18	18
Sweden	4	3	4	3
Norway	10	7	4	5
Others	2	*	*	*
Total tonnage (000 short tons)	387	410	460	527
Index	100	106	119	136

* Under one per cent.

Source: PEP, *British Press*, p. 307, Table VIII (adapted).

Imports from Scandinavia might threaten the price of British newsprint, as Chamberlain hoped and Eric Bowater feared, but a far more serious threat developed from across the Atlantic, because the quantities on offer were much larger and the sellers, suffering from the collapse of their accustomed market in the USA, were desperate for business.

Demand for newsprint in the United States had been growing rapidly in the prosperous twenties and the Canadian makers had been expanding their plant to match. Then the slump set in. Be-tween 1930 and 1933 shipments of Canadian newsprint to the United States fell by nearly 25 per cent. Plans for the expansion of plant could not rapidly be cancelled and building went on, so that productive capacity raced ahead of demand. In 1951 it was calcu-lated that between 1930 and 1939 North American newsprint capacity, of which far the greater part was in Canada and New-foundland, averaged 5,754,000 short tons a year, but average yearly production was 3,926,000: an operating rate of 68 per cent.

These were the years when Eric Bowater was rapidly expanding Bowaters' business, being helped to do so by the price of pulp which fell, until 1937, faster than the price of newsprint, thus adding to the troubles of the Canadians, most of whom produced pulp as well as paper, whereas Bowaters did not.

Newsprint manufacturers in Canada and Newfoundland, in a severe state of shock which persisted long after the cause had disappeared, turned for relief to the export trade, especially to the United Kingdom and Australia. Imports from Canada into the United Kingdom during the thirties were large, though lower than in 1929. Imports from Newfoundland rose by 137 per cent between 1929 and 1937, from 100,000 to 237,000 short tons.

The most troublesome competition came from International Paper Co. of New York, represented in Great Britain from 1932 onward by George Goyder, then aged twenty-four. Three years later he became Chairman and Managing Director of British International Paper, IPC's subsidiary. Beaverbrook, and probably other newspaper magnates as well, played International Paper and Bowaters off against each other. The *Express* made contracts with each and, in the mid-thirties, about half its requirements were probably coming from BIP; that is, from Canada and Newfoundland.

They were coming in at prices £1 per ton or so below the British makers' equivalent. In 1934, according to information reaching the Bank of England, the price of newsprint in the United Kingdom was forced down to £9. 15s. a ton, largely by Canadian competition. In 1936, Goyder was making contracts, running to 1939 and 1940, with Beaverbrook for £9 rising to £9. 15s. and with the owners of the *News Chronicle* and the *News of the World* for prices not higher than £9. 10s. Goyder said he thought it was good business to hold the English market at any price 'because the Bowaters position then appeared to be so strong and aggressive to the extent that they were aiming at shutting out I.P. newsprint altogether'.[33] Aggression is often in the eye of the beholder. At BPM's Annual General Meeting of 1934, Eric Bowater had been complaining of 'ruinous competition from abroad, and, I am sorry to say, from one of the Dominions'.[34]

Canadian competition in the Australian trade was even more serious than in the United Kingdom. During the years of depression the tonnage of newsprint sent from Canada to Australia grew rapidly until it was greater than the tonnage sent to the United Kingdom and greater than the tonnage sent from the United Kingdom to Australia, whereas formerly it had been smaller (Table 12). This development was particularly serious for Bowaters. Much the

TABLE 12. *Canadian exports of newsprint, 1929–39 (in thousand short tons)*

	To USA	To UK	To Australia	To other countries	Total
1929	2,173	174	63	105	2,515
1930	2,008	135	45	145	2,333
1931	1,753	104	30	121	2,008
1932	1,520	87	39	131	1,777
1933	1,520	107	58	153	1,838
1934	1,960	79	100	275	2,414
1935	2,052	115	108	300	2,575
1936	2,399	94	179	321	2,993
1937	2,899	148	118	290	3,455
1938	1,938	172	178	137	2,425
1939	2,207	177	131	144	2,659

Source: Kellogg, *Newsprint paper in North America*, p. 69 (adapted). Figures for Newfoundland are not included.

greater part of their export trade went to Australia and at one time the mills could not do without it.[35]

Prices in Australia in the thirties, forced down by Canadian competition, are reported to have been even lower than at home and, even with freight charges as low as 30s. a ton from the Thames to Sydney, with 3s. a ton rebate every six months, the trade was not profitable, though it helped to keep machines running.[36] In January 1936, as we have seen, Baker suggested modifying a machine at Mersey to manufacture kraft for the home market rather than newsprint for export, at a cost of about £170,000, and, although Eric Bowater said that the Mersey company was 'not ready financially',[37] he commissioned an enquiry by Barton, Mayhew into the profitability of the export trade. They found that the trade was run at a loss, which seemed to them 'to involve the choice of fostering the export trade at a loss in the hope of better times or of turning to some other type of paper to fill the gap'.[38] The seeds were being laid of a policy of diversification.

5.5 COUNTER-ATTACK

Eric Bowater's reaction to Canadian competition was characteristically bold or, as some might have said and probably did say, rash. Between 1933 and 1936, with Bowaters' resources already under strain and conditions of trade, as we have seen, by no means easy, he carried on a determined campaign to establish Bowaters in Canada by gaining control, either on their own or in partnership, of Price Brothers of Quebec, which went bankrupt in April 1933.

Price Brothers, with a capacity of some 225,000 short tons of newsprint a year, was nearly as large as the entire Bowater Group when Eric Bowater began trying to take it over. Moreover, his ex-partners, Beaverbrook and Rothermere, and the American Mellon interests were all concerned about Price Brothers' future with no very friendly disposition towards Bowaters. Beaverbrook, thinking of newsprint for the *Express* and *Standard* and constantly intent to play suppliers off against each other, had no mind to see Price pass under the control of another newsprint maker. Rothermere had Anglo-Canadian's troubles on his mind. Mellon wished to preserve a supply contract with Price for the Duke-Price Power Co. On top of all this, the conflicting interests of Price's bondholders, share-holders of various classes and creditors would make it difficult to frame an agreement which one group or another would not block. None of these considerations seems to have deterred Eric Bowater in the least but the same could not be said of all his colleagues, whose nerves were not as strong as their Chairman's.

The first plan, negotiated in Canada in the autumn of 1933 by Eric Bowater, J. H. Keeling and A. G. Allen, of Allen & Overy, provided for Bowater's Paper Mills to finance a new company formed to take over Price Brothers' assets from the Trustee in Bankruptcy. At the core of the scheme, which altered in detail as the negotiations went on, was an offer by Bowaters to find cash capital in the form of $5m debentures in the new company, which in 1933 would have required about £1.09m sterling. Bowaters were to be responsible for finding at least three-fifths of the money but associ-ates – R. O. Sweezey & Co. and John Stadler – agreed to subscribe $1,010,000 and there were various conditional arrangements for raising the balance.[39] Quite how Bowaters were to raise their share of the cash does not emerge from surviving records.

Price Brothers' Bondholders' Protective Committee accepted the plan, though they could not bind individual bondholders. BPM's directors had no alternative but to accept, having given Eric Bowater power to make an offer on behalf of the company,[40] but they were anxious about it and B. W. Young, a non-executive director with Harmsworth connections, resigned. Beaverbrook, Rothermere and the Duke-Price Power Co. were all in opposition and, by the beginning of 1934, were allied against a group con-sisting of Bowaters and about fifteen Canadians with minority interests in competition for the Price assets.[41]

Offer and counter-offer followed until, in March 1934, there was deadlock, with each side blocked by one group or another of interested parties. By this time, even Eric Bowater's nerves may have been feeling the strain. He began trying to make a partnership agreement with Rothermere and Beaverbrook 'under which we might be largely, if not entirely, relieved of our financial obligations and might also recover part, if not all, of our expenses'. These expenses were worrying him. The negotiations with the two Lords were held up by difficulties within their own group and, on 24 April 1934, he told the BPM Board 'that every effort was being made by himself and those assisting him in these negotiations as it was realised that in the event of our being forced to withdraw ... it might cost us a very considerable sum'.[42]

The partnership scheme, when it was agreed, provided for subscription to $5m 6½ per cent Mortgage Debentures in the proportions:

Duke-Price	40 per cent
Lord Rothermere	10
London Express Newspaper	25
Bowater's Paper Mills	25

and as a consideration for their subscription Bowaters were to have 16¾ per cent (72,656.14 shares) of the total equity of 433,768 shares of no par value. They were also to have the right to appoint two directors. London Express would also appoint two and the other partners, jointly, four.[43]

Eric Bowater was thus proposing to ally himself again, in Canada, with partners from whom, in the United Kingdom, he had very recently parted company with great relief and in circumstances of some acrimony. In addition there would be an American-controlled partner, Duke-Price Power, with a much larger holding than Bowaters'. It was perhaps just as well, in the interests of all concerned, that on 28 and 29 June 1934 the Preferred shareholders of Price Brothers refused to accept the scheme.[44]

Price Brothers thus remained untaken-over, with none of their problems solved. The idea of taking them over, dormant but far from dead, remained in Eric Bowater's mind awaiting revival. Meanwhile, at Liverpool, Nova Scotia, another Canadian possibility emerged: Mersey Paper Company Ltd.

The Mersey company was smaller than Price Brothers and newer. It came into production at about the time of the Wall Street crash in October 1929, having been set up by Izaak Walton Killam (1885–1955). He was a Montreal financier once employed by Beaverbrook, whom he greatly admired, and from whom he bought Royal

Securities Corporation in 1919. He died worth $150m, reputedly the richest man in Canada. He was a hard, shy man who made a chilling impression, being described by one who knew him in later years as having 'steely cold grey eyes and they just fixed you – and very little warmth'.[45]

In the autumn of 1934, when Bowaters first became interested, Mersey owned two newsprint machines producing upwards of 90,000 short tons a year.

There were plans for putting in another machine – almost un-heard of in Canada at that date – which, with improvements to the existing machinery, was expected to raise production to 150,000 short tons to take advantage of rising prices, recently announced, in the United States. 'Substantial profits', said Eric Bowater, 'should be earned . . . estimated at the equivalent of upwards of £380,000 a year, subject to interest and depreciation.'[46]

Eric never lacked optimism. During the thirties the surplus earned by Mersey met the sum needed for depreciation, but no more, and no Ordinary dividend was paid until 1948. On the other hand, simply earning a surplus gave Mersey distinction among Canadian mills of the day. The site had been well chosen, being the only one in Eastern Canada that gave a newsprint mill open navigation throughout the year and access by sea to all important markets. As a result, Colonel C. H. L. Jones, the President, could undercut competitors by $2 a ton and still keep Mersey solvent, if not popular.[47]

About 90 per cent of Mersey's capital – 50,000 $100 $6\frac{1}{2}$ per cent Cumulative Preference shares and 150,000 Common shares of no par value – was in Killam's hands. He was prepared to part with it at $90 per Preference share and $5 per Common share, which, if the minority holders also sold at the same prices, would require an outlay, at Can.$4.984 to the pound sterling, of just over £1m. There would also be the cost of the additional machine and equipment, which Eric Bowater estimated at about $4,750,000, to be met after the takeover.[48]

After Arthur Baker and George Shaw, Bowaters' Chief Engineer, had inspected and reported on the Mersey property which, besides mills, included wharves, warehouses, steamers, dwelling houses, timber limits and cutting rights, Eric Bowater was eager to have it, being, as usual, not at all dismayed by the scale of the financing required. 'The total cost of the complete unit', he told BPM's Board, 'would compare favourably with the cost of erecting and equipping a new mill of the same capacity and also with the known cost of other Canadian Newsprint Mills of similar capacity.'

He outlined a typically ambitious plan for providing cash both for the purchase and for discharging certain mortgages and bank advances. It involved forming 'a new Holding Company (Bowater's Dominion Newsprint Corporation Limited or other suitable name)' with Preference capital, publicly held, of £1.5m, on which BPM and W. V. Bowater would jointly guarantee the dividend for three to five years, and Ordinary capital of £750,000 provided to the extent of £200,000 to £250,000 by the two Bowater companies, the remainder apparently coming – he was not very specific – from an allotment to the London & Yorkshire Trust. 'Funds for the purpose of installing and equipping the additional machine', said Eric confidently, 'would be provided by a Bond Issue by the Mersey Company in due course.'

'Due course' never arrived. Bowaters, it is said, offered too little for the capital. 'Gentlemen', said Killam, appearing briefly at a meeting in Montreal, 'I am not going to sell.'[49] Mersey did not pass into Bowater hands for another twenty-two years.

Eric Bowater turned his attention once more towards Price Brothers. Throughout 1935 and 1936 negotiations between Bowaters and others and the Trustee in Bankruptcy were going spasmodically on but every time a scheme was put forward it was blocked by one group of interested parties or another. Among the interested parties, indirectly, was the Bank of England through its holding in the Preference capital of the mill at Corner Brook in Newfoundland.

Bowaters' last effort to gain control, or a share in control, of Price Brothers required a public issue in London of £2m Price Brothers bonds, so as to pay off the existing bondholders and clear the way for a reorganisation of the share capital. In June 1936, J. H. Keeling wrote to the Treasury to ask whether there would be any objection to such an issue, pointing out that, in his view, it provided the only means of ensuring that Price Brothers would remain a British concern .rather than passing under American control. From the Treasury the letter was passed to the Bank of England. 'I think', said a Treasury official, 'that the Bank of England know more about the paper industry than most people.'[50]

The proposal came to Frater Taylor (p. 52 above). Neither he nor anyone else in the Bank seems to have been greatly impressed by Keeling's patriotic argument. Their main concern was to see the Canadian newsprint industry rationalised and profitable, if possible through Canadian agency, and Frater Taylor was not at all sure that Bowaters' proposal would help bring prices up to a profitable level.

'Bowaters', he wrote on 7 July 1936,

are the ones on whom the arrangements would be focussed on this side. If, as I gathered, two outstanding Newspaper Peers [Beaverbrook and Rothermere, no doubt] are likely to be interested with them (and, after all, Bowaters must be sure of a sale of the Newsprint) are we not warranted in assuming that just as, say, Hearst, would *aim* at keeping U.S. Newsprint price down, the British Newspaper magnates may have the same idea in so far as the British price is concerned . . . I am not at all sure that a purchase by Americans of Price Bros. would not result in the maintenance of a higher relative price.

He recommended a 'negative answer on exchange grounds' and Keeling's proposal sank without trace.

The battle for control of Price Brothers was one of the few battles Eric Bowater lost, but it was a beginning, not an end. Transatlantic expansion, from the late thirties onward, was to become a dominant theme in Bowater policy. In the meantime Eric Bowater took the opportunity, unexpectedly offered to him by Lord Camrose, of buying control of Edward Lloyd Ltd.

CHAPTER SIX

The fall of the House of Lloyd
1918–1936

6.1 LLOYDS BEFORE BOWATERS

Frank Lloyd, at the head of Edward Lloyd Ltd from 1890 until 1927, when he died, seems to have inherited all his father's vigour and added to it a touch of liberal respectability which no doubt came more easily to him, as the heir to an assured position, than to his father, who had clawed his way upwards through the murk of Victorian popular journalism (p. 11 above). Frank's vigour showed in the growth and repeated modernisation of the business under his chairmanship; his liberalism in plans for the housing and general welfare of his people which recall the activities of W. H. Lever at Port Sunlight and the Cadburys at Bournville.

In 1918, Frank Lloyd sold United Newspapers (p. 19 above). He thus broke up the integrated newspaper and newsprint business, the first of its kind in Great Britain, which his father had set up, and he also cut his personal links with the origins of the family fortune. For the last seven years of his life he concentrated his energies on the newsprint mills, which still had a contract to supply United Newspapers with all their newsprint from 1 January 1920 to 31 December 1950.[1] Between the ages of sixty-five and seventy-two Frank Lloyd presided over the most ambitious extensions and improvements ever undertaken while Edward Lloyd Ltd was still in the hands of the founder's family.

They were undertaken, moreover, very largely on the strength of the company's own resources. In January 1927, five months before Frank Lloyd died, he told an Extraordinary General Meeting that extensions then in hand would cost £2m of which about £1½m would be found internally. The meeting was called to approve the issue of 7 per cent Preference shares to raise the remaining £525,000.[2] The contrast between this broad-based affluence and the crisis-ridden state of Bowaters' finances at about the same time needs no emphasis. It cannot have entered the mind of anyone present at Lloyds' meeting that, within ten years, Lloyds would have been taken over by Bowaters. The idea would have seemed absurd.

The centre-piece of the expansion programme was an entirely new mill at Kemsley, mid-way between the existing mill at Sittingbourne and the company's dock at Ridham. The start may have been delayed by the 1921 slump but, for Lloyds, its effects were short-lived and, in May 1923, Frank Lloyd told his shareholders that the company was putting in hand 'two wide and fast-running paper machines with the most up-to-date preparatory plant embodying all the latest improvements'.[3] These machines were at full output in the last quarter of 1924 and a third machine, apparently, was completed in 1927 but Frank did not live to see it in full working order in 1928.[4] A new power-house, started in 1926, was finished the following year.[5]

The mill at Sittingbourne was not neglected. During the mid-twenties, three narrow machines and two ranges of steam boilers were scrapped, a new power-house and a new boiler-house were built and the machines which were kept were brought elaborately up to date.[6] At the same time, the company developed its transport system,[7] serving both mills, no doubt for the same reasons as Bowaters, a little later, developed theirs (p. 94 above).

Frank Lloyd was prepared not only for conventional developments but for experiments also. During 1925, plant for grinding imported timber was put in at Kemsley. 'This experiment', said Frank, 'is the first of its kind to be made in this country.' It turned out expensive because steam power at Kemsley cost more than water power in other countries but, in 1926, Frank Lloyd claimed that the experiment had been justified. 'The grinding of our own pulp', he said, 'has turned out very well, as it has improved the running of our machines and is yielding a fair return on the capital invested.' He may also have felt that it added to Lloyds' bargaining power in dealing with Scandinavian suppliers.[8]

By 1927, Lloyds employed about 2,000 people. Frank Lloyd had elaborate plans prepared for a housing estate, on rolling land near Kemsley mill, to accommodate a population of 3,500. One hundred and eighty-eight houses were built by the summer of 1927 and altogether there were to be about 750, of

four grades adapted to the requirements of the different classes of tenants. The accommodation in the first three grades includes a kitchen–living room, scullery, parlour and three bedrooms, with an upstairs bathroom and the usual offices, while the fourth grade has in addition a separate kitchen and an additional bedroom. Great care has been taken to secure a

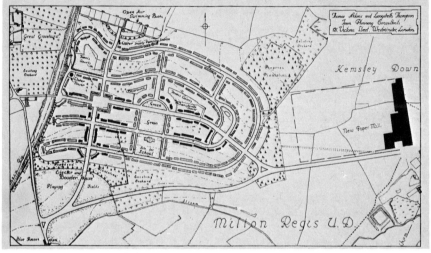

SITE.   **KEMSLEY VILLAGE.**

The Village, designed to provide comfortable and attractive homes for the staff operating the new paper mill, occupies a healthy, open site upon the top and south slope of Kemsley Down—conveniently near the mill, yet sufficiently removed from it to keep the industrial and residential portions of the scheme quite distinct. Additional emphasis has been given to this important feature of the scheme by taking advantage of the natural lie of the land to plan the roads and arrange the houses so that from the Village there is no direct view of the mill, which will be still more completely screened from the houses when the spruce plantation, indicated on the plan, has grown up.

Plan of Kemsley village, from a publicity pamphlet of 1927.

maximum amount of sunlight in all the houses and the convenience of the housewife has been a paramount consideration in the selection and arrangement of all the fittings. The houses are of several different designs and are grouped in pairs and blocks of 3, 4, 8 and 9; they are carried out both in brick and rough cast with tiled roofs. Sites have been reserved in the Square ... for an Inn, a Club, and a number of shops.[9]

In Sittingbourne a large club-house was built, with a ladies' lounge, a gentlemen's lounge, a billiard room, a library and reading room, a concert hall. At Tunstall, nearby, the company provided a sports ground. 'The late Mr Frank Lloyd's solicitous regard for his employees', says a brochure prepared for visiting journalists in July 1927, 'was marked in many ways.'[10]

Starting forty years earlier, W. H. Lever at Port Sunlight had built houses of varying grades, in varying architectural styles, disposed in groups and pairs around open spaces. He had provided his employees with club rooms, meeting halls, bowling greens, a church, a school, a hospital (Frank Lloyd did not run to these last three) and an inn (temperance). He had explained to them that this was his form of profit-sharing. He could, he said in 1903, give everyone a Christmas bonus of £8 but it will not do you much good if you send it down your throats in the form of bottles of whisky, bags of sweets, or fat geese for Christmas. On the other hand, if you leave this money with me, I shall use it to provide for you everything which makes life pleasant – viz. nice houses, comfortable homes and healthy recreation. Besides, I am disposed to allow profit sharing under no other than that form.[11]

Although less disposed to talk about it, Frank Lloyd acted in just this tradition of muscular paternalism which was widespread among the larger Victorian employers. It inspired Sir Alfred Mond in framing labour policy for the newly founded ICI as late as 1926 but by that time – Frank Lloyd's time – it was already obsolescent, weakened by changing attitudes among employees and by the ever-increasing public provision of housing and social services generally. The houses that Frank Lloyd caused to be built were a monument to his benevolence which was already old-fashioned and his full plans for the village were never carried out.

In the early part of 1927 Frank Lloyd was not well. He attended no Board meetings after the beginning of April and on 20 May he died. The business as he left it was capable of producing about 200,000 tons of newsprint a year[12] and his plans for expansion were still incomplete.

Frank Lloyd, as is not uncommon with powerful businessmen, had designated no successor but, as is less common, there was no unseemly struggle for his vacant Chair. No one in the family seems to have come forward and, within the business, there was no other candidate. Instead, the prosperous and powerful business was sold to new owners. Frank Lloyd, not long before he died, had let Sir William Berry know that, if the business were to be sold after he died, he would like Sir William and his brother Gomer, through Allied Newspapers, to be given the first refusal.[13] There was no opposition and the Berrys moved in.

Thus, after nine years of independence, the largest newsprint firm in Europe became a unit in a combine whose owners' chief interest lay in newspapers. It could safely be predicted, as it could be predicted when Bowaters about the same time were placed in the same position, that, in any conflict within the group between newsprint and newspaper interests, the newspapers would prevail.

Sir William and his brother were newspaper owners on a very large scale indeed. They had built up their group very rapidly, chiefly by purchase from other owners, until by 1927 they were at least level with Rothermere, perhaps ahead of him (p. 18 above). Among national papers they controlled the *Sunday Times*, the

Financial Times, the *Daily Sketch*, the *Sunday Graphic* and the *Daily Telegraph*, which they bought in 1927 itself, and they had a widespread list of provincial titles. In the field of periodicals they were allied with Sir Edward Iliffe and, in 1926, they had bought from Rothermere control of the Amalgamated Press, the biggest of all periodical publishing houses. Control of Amalgamated brought with it control of Imperial Paper Mills Ltd of Gravesend, Kent, manufacturers of newsprint.[14]

Sir William Berry, on taking a business over, was not the kind of man to change its policy and dismiss half the staff overnight. His methods were gradual and humane, as he showed when he took over the *Telegraph*[15] and, when he told the shareholders of Allied Newspapers that he and his brother would 'endeavour to carry on the business on the same lines as those on which it was carried on by the late Mr Frank Lloyd', no doubt he meant it. There were two reasons, he said, for acquiring the Lloyd shares, both related to the general soundness of the undertaking. 'The first was that they looked upon the shares as a desirable purchase on purely economic grounds. The other was that it gave them an opportunity of acquiring an extensive interest in the business of news paper-making, and thereby securing an effective safeguard in regard to the supply of raw material.' At the same time, he left no one in any doubt that the interests of newspapers, the Berrys' own and other people's, came first. 'If a time of crisis should arise', Sir William said, 'we shall regard other newspaper proprietors who purchase their paper from Edward Lloyd, Ltd, as partners more than customers and entitled to equally proportioned rights with ourselves. [Applause.]' He went further. 'When we decided to buy I may claim that we had in mind the desirability that this huge news paper-making business should be in the hands of the newspaper business itself.'[16] That was more comforting news, perhaps, for the owners of newspapers than for the employees of Edward Lloyd.

The price paid by the Berrys for control, through Allied Newspapers, of Edward Lloyd Ltd was £3.2m for the 1.6m Lloyd Ordinary shares, almost all held within the Lloyd family. 1.2m £1 7 per cent Cumulative Preference shares were left with the public. A holding company, Edward Lloyd Investment Co. Ltd, was set up and issued 994,993 £1 Ordinary shares to Allied Newspapers in exchange for the Lloyd Ordinary shares, having previously created £3.5m 5½ per cent First Mortgage Guaranteed Debenture stock. Of that stock £2m was issued to the former holders of Lloyds Ordinary capital in part payment for their shares. £1.2m was paid to them in cash, raised by issuing the balance of the Debenture stock (£1.5m) to Messrs Myers & Co. of Throgmorton Street at £95 per cent. The Debenture stock was unconditionally guaranteed, as to principal and interest, by Allied Newspapers.[17]

The Berrys bought themselves a solidly prosperous business. Cash reserves were ample, as Frank Lloyd had demonstrated by the way his extensions were financed, and profits for the years immediately before the takeover* were certified by Price Waterhouse as:

1923	£310,407
1924	£305,272
1925	£390,073
1926	£255,975

The calamitous drop – 34 per cent – in 1926 was attributed to the combined effects of the miners' strike and the General Strike. For some time the mills were closed and the company paid at least £100,000 more for coal than in 1925.[18]

The basis of Lloyds' prosperity was an order-book well filled with long-running contracts. As soon as the Berrys took over, Beaverbrook withdrew the *Express* contract which Lloyds had had since the paper started – evidently Beaverbrook took Sir William Berry's promise to treat his newspaper competitors as partners at something less than face value – but there was plenty left. Allied Newspapers had presumably been good customers before the takeover and, by 1932, they were buying about 30 per cent of Lloyds' weekly production. As well as that there were contracts with the *Daily News* and the *News Chronicle* – amended in 1928 and 1930 – and twenty-five-year contracts with the *News of the World*, C. Arthur Pearson and George Newnes. Other long contracts no doubt existed of which the records have disappeared and there were short contracts also, such as yearly contracts with Southern Newspapers.[19] A newcomer to the company in the early thirties was impressed to find Lloyds so secure that they could afford to hand over tonnage to competitors, especially Peter Dixon.[20]

After the takeover the two Berry brothers, William and Gomer, joined Lloyds' Board. So did their close associate, Sir Edward Iliffe, and Stanley Cousins, a senior figure in the newsprint industry who habitually wore a top hat and carried a silver-headed cane. Members of the Lloyd family all resigned but the three remaining directors, all professional managers who had been with Lloyds for many years, were not disturbed. The senior of them was Percy Denson,

---

*1923–6, after depreciation and interest but before directors' fees and tax.

who had been on the Board certainly since 1911, and probably longer, and whose father, T. E. Denson, had come to Sittingbourne with Edward Lloyd in 1873. He was joint Managing Director with E. H. Raynham, who had been a director since 1916, and the two of them were very highly paid: Denson at £6,000 and Raynham at £5,000 a year. Their junior colleague was the Mill Manager, R. B. Miller, who, before that appointment which he took up along with a directorship in 1921, had been Secretary at least as far back as 1911. He was followed as Secretary by another Denson – Gerald – who in March 1928 also came on to the Board.[21]

The Berrys' touch on Lloyds' helm was light and, as Sir William Berry indicated, they kept the company on the course Frank Lloyd had set. At Kemsley, a fourth machine was needed to complete 'the first unit of this mill' and it was ready by March 1930. A fifth – 'the largest and fastest paper machine in the world' – was in production at the beginning of 1936. To support the increasing production two new turbo-generators were put into an enlarged power-house, Ridham Dock was extended, transport and storage facilities were developed and up-to-date groundwood plant was installed. All the mechanical pulp needed at Kemsley – a very large tonnage – was henceforward made on the spot, so that Kemsley became an integrated mill like those which competed with it in Canada and Scandinavia. Logs went in at one end and newsprint came out at the other. Ensuring the supply of logs for Kemsley became a very important consideration, later on, in forming Bowaters' raw material policy.

The groundwood mill provided material from which wallboard could be made, and in 1934 Edward Lloyd Wallboards was set up to work a Swiss process under licence. It was the forerunner of Bowaters' business in building products. Developments at Sittingbourne were intended not for newsprint but for other grades of paper, and those too had their effect on the future spread of Bowaters' activities.

All this expansion, carrying Edward Lloyd's productive capacity to 320,000 tons a year of all grades of paper, including 275,000 tons of newsprint, required skilful finance and heavy investment. In the twelve years of Lloyds' drive for expansion, between 1924 and 1936, they spent about £4m on extensions, of which £2.5m came from their own resources and the balance from the issue of share capital.[22]

Such free spending had to be justified by high and rising profits, which in the happy years of the late twenties seemed to be assured. Even in the generally evil days of the early thirties, Lloyds' profits were excellent – they had never been so high as in 1931 – but, at length, the slump caught up with Lloyds in the same way as it caught up with Bowaters and Canadian competition prompted the switch of capacity at Sittingbourne from newsprint towards other grades of paper. To the directors of Lloyds, as to the directors of Bowaters, it seemed that the virtue had gone out of newsprint and they would be ill-advised, for the future, to rely upon it so heavily as in the past.[23] Profits began to fall disastrously until, in 1934, they were less than 58 per cent of the 1931 figure and the Ordinary dividend, at 7 per cent, was less than half the 15 per cent which had been paid in 1929, 1930 and 1932. After 1934, as Table 13 shows, the profits picked up again but the experience no doubt helped to disenchant the Berrys with newsprint. Certainly by 1936 they were turning their minds towards exclusive concentration on newspapers and periodicals.

One evening in 1936, Ian Bowater was dining with his father-in-law, Lord Dawson of Penn. Sir William Berry – Lord Camrose since 1929 – was there too. Sir Ian Bowater recalls that, after dinner, with a wave of the hand, Camrose said to him: 'I can't think what you fellows are doing with that paper mill of yours. Why don't you buy ours? We are not newsprint manufacturers, we are journalists. We don't want a whacking great paper mill at Sittingbourne or Kemsley – that is your job.' The remark was made lightly but Ian Bowater

TABLE 13. *Edward Lloyd Ltd: profits, 1927–36, after expenses and directors' fees but before depreciation, contingencies and tax*

	£	Ordinary dividend (free of tax except as shown) %
1927	486,507	
1928	637,389	
1929	625,597	15
1930	618,188	15
1931	673,200	$13\frac{3}{4}$
1932	615,573	15
1933	558,459	$12\frac{1}{2}$
1934	388,142	7
1935	424,617	7
1936	525,570	10*

* Plus cash bonus of 1s. 3d. per share, all less tax.

Sources: 1927–35 from BPM Prospectus of 21 July 1936. 1936 from Edward Lloyd ledger.

thought there might be weight behind it. There was. Once again, a newspaper owner was preparing to be rid of newsprint mills which no longer suited his purpose.

6.2 BOWATER-LLOYD ESTABLISHED

Camrose's suggestion to Ian Bowater must surely have come as a surprise. Lloyds' results for several years had been disappointing but times had been hard for all in the newsprint industry and, by 1936, they seemed to be on the mend. Moreover, if the Berrys did not intend to hold Lloyds, why had they put so much money into it and why did Gomer Berry, in 1936, take the title Lord Kemsley unless he wanted it purely as a souvenir? Finally, and for Bowaters most important, Lloyds' business was larger and more diverse than their own. Edward Lloyd Ltd's assets at 31 December 1935 were valued at £6.9m; the assets of all the Bowater companies at 31 March 1936, on the eve of the takeover, at £4.9m.[24] It is not very often that a company sets out to buy control of another with assets valued at 40 per cent more than its own.

Of the negotiations which followed from the dinner-party conversation we know only what Eric Bowater told his shareholders – that they 'were lengthy and necessarily of a confidential character', that they were conducted personally between Camrose and Eric Bowater and that they were concluded on 9 July 1936.[25] We may surmise that they presented Eric Bowater and his financial advisers with a problem which even by their adventurous standards was formidable, because the sum they had to raise was £4,187,500 plus expenses, equivalent to more than 85 per cent of the published value of the assets of the entire Bowater Group. To make the purchase tidy they had also to buy from Allied Northern Newspapers, at a cost of £75,346, a 46 per cent interest in Edward Lloyd Wallboards Ltd,[26] although that transaction did not form part of the main bargain. It was fortunate that Camrose's proposal came at a time when Bowaters' affairs seemed prosperous; when the Mersey company, seven years after its formation, was able for the only time in the thirties to pay an Ordinary dividend (5 per cent); and when the quoted stocks and shares of all Bowater companies stood at a premium, a premium which increased when the news of the Lloyd takeover became known.[27]

What Camrose had chiefly to offer to Bowater was Allied Newspapers' holding of 830,890 Ordinary shares* in Edward Lloyd

* The figures in this paragraph ignore a few small holdings by individuals.

Investment Co. Ltd. The balance – 169,110 – of the Investment
Company's 1m Ordinary shares were held by other newspapers,
presumably as part of the Berrys' declared policy of treating their
competitors as partners and, although some of the minority holders
were eventually bought by Bowaters for cash at par,[29] requiring
World, the Co-operative Press and the News Chronicle, were not.[28]
All these shares, whether belonging to Allied Newspapers or not,
were eventually bought by Bowaters for cash at par,[29] requiring
£1m and giving undivided control of the operating company,
Edward Lloyd Ltd, whose 1.6m Ordinary shares the Investment
Company had been set up to hold.

The really onerous part of the bargain was not the purchase of the
Investment Company's shares but the condition upon which the
Berrys agreed to let them be sold.[30] Bowaters had to agree to relieve
Allied Newspapers of their guarantee of the Investment Company's
£3m of Debenture stock. To discharge their undertaking they proposed to arrange the redemption of the stock at £104 per cent plus
£2.5s. per cent accrued interest,[31] requiring in all £3,187,500 in
cash and securities.

It would have been in keeping with Bowaters' previous financial
policy, and it might have been cheaper, if they had created debentures but 'it was felt', said Eric Bowater, 'that as the money was required for the purpose of acquiring Ordinary shares it was sounder
finance to raise it by means of the issue of shares rather than by
increasing the Debenture debt of your company'.[32] Accordingly, the
authorised capital of Bowater's Paper Mills was raised to £3m in
July 1936 by the creation of 500,000 new £1 Ordinary shares,
700,000 new £1 7½ per cent Cumulative Participating Preference
shares and 500,000 new £1 6½ per cent Cumulative Preference
shares.

The 500,000 Ordinary shares at 30s. raised £750,000 and the
700,000 7½ per cent Preference shares, also at 30s., £1,050,000.
Both issues were made during the summer of 1936. Of the Ordinary
shares, 11,537 were left with the underwriters but the Preference
issue was heavily over-subscribed.[33] To raise £427,500 to complete
the various transactions entered into, another issue of Preference
shares was made – 300,000 £1 6½ per cent Preference shares at
28s. 6d. The issue was over-subscribed.[34]

From the proceeds of these issues Bowaters applied £1m to the
purchase at par of the Ordinary shares in the Investment Company
held by Allied Newspapers and others. They also took up, at 24s.
6d. a share, the whole of a new issue of 1m £1 Ordinary shares, thus
providing £1,225,000 in cash to cover the premium and interest

required to redeem the Investment Company's debentures and relieve Allied of their guarantee. For the £3m stock itself, holders were
offered 2m £1 5 per cent Redeemable Cumulative Preference shares
in the Investment Company, created for the purpose. 'The debenture holders', Eric Bowater told BPM's shareholders on 1 December
1936, 'exercised their rights to exchange to the extent that the
whole 2,000,000 shares were required for this purpose.' Thus
Bowaters discharged their undertaking to Allied Newspapers and
entered into control of Edward Lloyd Ltd.

A little more than ten years after they had first produced newsprint,
Bowaters stood at the head of a group with an annual output of
about half-a-million tons of newsprint a year, as well as 45,000 tons
of kraft liner board, printing and wrapping papers produced at
Sittingbourne.[35] Moreover, the position of the Bowater-Lloyd
Group, as it came to be known, was extremely strong because it had
been a condition of the takeover that Allied Newspapers and their
associates, except for those, including the *Daily Telegraph*, which
were supplied by Imperial, should enter into twenty-year contracts
for newsprint.[36]

Bowaters claimed that, at the time of the takeover, Bowaters and
Lloyds were making 60 per cent of all newsprint manufactured in
Great Britain.[37] The figure may not be precise but there can be no
question that the Bowater-Lloyd Group was the largest newsprint
enterprise in Europe. In Canada two or three may have been larger –
Canadian International Paper certainly, Abitibi and Consolidated
perhaps – but, apart from these, no newsprint business in the world
was larger than Bowater-Lloyd.

The productive capacity of the Bowater-Lloyd Group was imposing but the speed and daring with which it had been put together
carried a penalty in the nature of the capital structure which Eric
Bowater and his advisers had erected. Being determined to grow
fast, and having little in the way of retained profits to draw on, they
had relied very heavily on debentures and on Preference shares with
attractively high rates of dividend and, in some cases, rights of
participation in the residuary profits.

The result, as some commentators at the time did not fail to point
out, was a capital structure which imperatively required high
profitability if the companies in the group were to meet their obligations to the suppliers of capital and at the same time build up
reserves to meet the cost of growth. By the end of 1936, as Table 14
shows, the ratio of prior-charge capital to issued Ordinary capital
was eight-and-a-half to one, requiring £472,500 before anything

TABLE 14. *Capital structure of the Bowater-Lloyd Group, December 1936, excluding inter-company holdings*

	£	£	Annual charge £
Loan capital			
3½ per cent Debentures			
Bowater's Paper Mills	1,000,000		
Bowater's Mersey Paper Mills	800,000		
		1,800,000	63,000
Preference shares			
Bowater's Paper Mills			
6½ per cent Cumulative	800,000		52,000
7½ per cent Cumulative Participating	1,000,000		75,000
Bowater's Mersey Paper Mills			
5½ per cent Cumulative	500,000		27,500
W. V. Bowater & Sons			
8 per cent Participating	200,000		16,000*
Edward Lloyd			
7 per cent Cumulative	1,200,000		84,000
5½ per cent Cumulative	1,000,000		55,000
Edward Lloyd Investment Co.			
5 per cent Redeemable Cumulative	2,000,000		100,000
		6,700,000	
Total, Loan and Preference capital		8,500,000	472,500
Ordinary shares			
Bowater's Paper Mills	1,000,000		
		1,000,000	
Total issued capital (nominal)		9,500,000	

* These shares carried a 2 per cent participating dividend which had to be paid before the parent could receive 10 per cent or more on the WVB Ordinary capital. This charge, within the group, was regarded as 'fixed', making the total annual charge £20,000, adding £4,000 to the total fixed charge of £472,500 shown in the table.

Source: Reports and Accounts of Bowater companies.

could go to the Ordinary shareholders. In good times, with rising profits, the Ordinary shareholders might do very well indeed but, if times were bad and profits fell, what then? Eric Bowater was an optimist and it shows.

The formation of Bowater-Lloyd was not the outcome of a long-term plan. Rather, it was accidental, becoming possible only through the coincidence of the Berry brothers deciding to disembarrass themselves of Lloyds, in order to concentrate on their newspapers, at a time when Eric Bowater could seize the opportunity they offered him. His own business, a few years earlier, had very nearly suffered a similar fate at the hands of Lord Rothermere (p. 67 above).

At Kemsley and Sittingbourne they found it hard to believe that Bowaters had taken over. Some thought that Lloyds had taken over Bowaters. But the news was true and almost as soon as Bowaters had taken charge – long before they had assimilated Lloyds into their system – they found themselves facing a crisis of raw material supply; the worst crisis so far in their short but tumultuous history as manufacturers.

CHAPTER SEVEN

The raw materials crisis
1937–1938

Bowaters did well in 1936. The Mersey company paid an Ordinary dividend for the first time and BPM's dividend, at 9 per cent, was higher than ever before. Eric Bowater, addressing BPM's shareholders in December 1936, spoke cheerfully of growing demand, especially in the United States, and the consequent prospect of slightly higher prices; of the acquisition of Edward Lloyd; of the Bowater companies' high earnings; of 'certain important extensions' contemplated by the Mersey directors. 'From my . . . remarks', he said,

you will have gathered that the financial and trading position of your associated companies . . . may be regarded as entirely satisfactory . . . The entire estimated production of all the mills now controlled by your company has been disposed of for the coming year at prices substantially similar to those now prevailing.

Over this bright scene fell the shadow of the suppliers of wood pulp asking for higher prices, which would affect the prices Bowaters could profitably charge for newsprint. In 1936, in order to meet overseas competition, Bowaters had come to a compromise with customers hoping for a reduction in 1937 by which prices were agreed for two years – 1937 and 1938 – instead of one. The price for 1937 and 1938 was fixed at £10 a ton and this was embodied in July 1936 in contracts with newspapers from whom Bowaters acquired minority holdings in the Edward Lloyd Investment Co. (p. 117 above). It may well have been a concession to induce them to part with their shares.

Under the system by which the agreement of a price for one contract in effect fixed the price for all (p. 96 above), Bowaters were tied to a price for all their customers of £10 for both 1937 and 1938.[1] The assumption underlying this figure was that pulp prices would rise a little because the price of wood was rising but not very much because 'the productive capacity of the pulp mills of the supplying countries is still considerably in excess of consumption'.

If that assumption should turn out wrong, Bowaters would be in trouble. For 1937, Eric Bowater professed himself unworried, saying 'we had purchased an important part of our total requirements for raw materials . . . at prices substantially similar to those we have paid in respect of the current year [1936]'.[2] Requirements for 1938, however, were partly uncovered and they would be large. In 1937 Eric Bowater claimed that Bowaters were the largest buyers of newsprint raw materials in the world[3] and, early in 1938, he estimated the group's requirements at 262,000 tons air dry of mechanical pulp and 107,000 tons air dry of sulphite pulp, as well as 160,000 cords of wood, for the pulp mill at Kemsley.[4]

The assumption did turn out wrong. Perhaps the pulp exporters did have too much productive capacity but, like other producers similarly placed in the 1930s, they very sensibly, and much to Eric Bowater's annoyance, formed cartels to regulate their output and support their prices. One was the Mechanical Pulp Suppliers Association, formed at the end of 1935, with members in Sweden, Norway and Finland. Another, said to have 'tightened up discipline' in July 1936, was the Sulphite Pulp Suppliers Association, which had members in Germany, Czechoslovakia, Austria and Memel as well as in the three Scandinavian countries.[5]

On the way these cartels worked we have very little inside information but the pressure they brought to bear on the newsprint makers in 1937 is evident from the record of prices charged during the year. The price for moist mechanical pulp rose about 77 per cent above the average for 1936 and the price for strong sulphite pulp almost doubled (Table 15).

The cartels were able to force these dramatic rises because, for a few months in 1936–7, all the influences in the market were running in their favour. Eric Bowater, as we have seen, remarked in December 1936 on the recovery in demand for newsprint in the United States. Early in 1937, the British Government announced an expanded rearmament programme which, in Eric Bowater's words, caused 'a great upswing in the prices of all commodities'. At the BPM Annual General Meeting in December 1937 he mentioned rises in the prices of mechanical and sulphite pulp which agree in tendency with the figures quoted in Table 15, adding that prices of pulpwood rose by over 100 per cent and 'seafreights in some cases by as much as 200 per cent'.[6]

The price rises of 1937, alarming though they were and far-reaching, as we shall see (Chapter 8 below), in their effects on

TABLE 15. *Pulp prices, 1936–7**

| | Average price (dry weight) per ton | | | |
| | Moist mechanical pulp | | Strong sulphite | |
	£	Index	£	Index
1936	4. 12. 6.	100	8. 10. 0.	100
1937				
1st quarter				
from	5. 5. 0.	113	10. 5. 0.	121
to	6. 15. 0.	146	13. 17. 6.	163
2nd quarter				
from	6. 15. 0.		13. 17. 6.	
to	7. 10. 0.	162	15. 10. 0.	182
3rd quarter				
from	7. 10. 0.		15. 10. 0.	
to	8. 4. 0.	177	16. 10. 0.	194
4th quarter				
from	8. 4. 0.		16. 10. 0.	
to	7. 10. 0.		15. 0. 0.	176

* Basis c.i.f. East Coast ports, three months' bill.

Source: Letter from E. A. Holmes to J. A. Colvin 21 June 1961, in Bowater Papers for the Royal Commission on the Press 1961–2. Holmes, of Price & Pierce Ltd, says: 'It is always difficult to give reasonable prices for the period 1930 onwards – people bought at different times, contracts were averaged and so forth – but the range we show is taken from our books here.'

Bowaters' policy, were temporary, being induced chiefly by influences which did not last. More important in the long run, probably, was the steadily rising demand in the world for wood and wood pulp for purposes other than papermaking, especially the spinning of rayon. It has been calculated that, between 1933 and 1938, the world output of rayon was growing by 25 per cent or more a year,[7] and there must have been a corresponding rise in the demand for wood pulp as a source of cellulose – demand which the newsprint firms would find hard to compete with because there is greater value added to cellulose in the making of rayon than in the making of newsprint, so that the rayon firms would be better able to afford higher prices for their raw material.

The speed and magnitude of the rise in raw material prices in the first three quarters of 1937 took Bowaters completely by surprise, as the Chairman admitted to his shareholders at the end of the year. 'We were overtaken', he said, 'by market factors which were all but unforeseeable.'[8] As early as 3 December 1936 he had some inkling of what was coming, for he wrote on that day to Arthur Baker discussing the rising trend of prices and reminding him that 'one of the decisions we came to when we all last met here was that we would eliminate waste of paper by re-pulping everything'.[9] He did not realise quite how serious matters were going to be until much later.

Early in 1937 Eric Bowater was away from business, ill. In February, at a Board Meeting postponed until he could attend it, he remarked that the upward trend of prices for all grades of wood pulp and wood 'had been sharply accentuated during December and January' and reviewed Bowaters' recent buying policy. The problem lay not in 1937, for which they had substantially covered their needs, but in 1938, for which they had covered about 75 per cent. 'In respect of the balance of our requirements', he said, 'it was proposed to follow our usual procedure of making purchases when in our judgment favourable opportunities presented themselves. Having regard to market conditions the present time was not considered favourable for effecting further purchases.'[10]

With prices rising strongly, this was a controversial judgment and the minutes betray uneasiness. The Chairman mentioned that the price of newsprint had been fixed for 1938 as well as for 1937 (p. 121 above) and reminded the Board that 'the agreement of a price under one contract fixed the price for all'. 'Suggestions had been made', he went on to say, 'that it might be necessary to approach our customers and obtain their agreement to some modification in respect of the price for 1938 but it was considered desirable to avoid this course if at all possible and in any case it was too early yet to formulate any definite policy in this regard.'[11]

The idea of having to ask customers a favour of this kind would be distasteful to any businessman and to none more so than Eric Bowater, a proud man and a bold one who, in the recent past, had not shown any exaggerated sense of awe in his dealings with the barons of the Press. The months of 1937 passed, however, and the break in prices which Bowaters must have been hoping for when they held off buying in February did not appear. On the contrary, as Table 15 shows, prices soared. On the Stock Exchange, so important to Bowaters with their constant hunger for capital, confidence was shaken and the price of Bowater securities fell. *The Economist*, in August 1937, commented obliquely on the absence of consolidated accounts and less obliquely on the consequences of the group's high gearing: 'If the group were a consolidated unit, a total of £472,500 would be needed for all prior charges, before anything would be available for the Ordinary shares of Bowater's Paper Mills, the only equity of the group in which the public has an interest.'[12]

In this atmosphere, Eric Bowater began negotiating with the

newspaper owners in the spring or early summer of 1937, just as pulp prices were reaching their peak. He conducted the negotiations personally and no detailed record of them has survived but there is no doubt he found them long-drawn, humiliating and unpleasant. He began by trying for an increase of £2 a ton (20 per cent) for 1938 to which the newspaper owners responded by offering an 'advance' of £1 a ton, refundable. Eventually they split the difference but, throughout the negotiations, the newspaper owners made plain that they regarded any increase as a temporary rescue operation which they were not prepared to continue indefinitely or to grant unconditionally and which should preferably at some time be repaid.[13]

Eric Bowater seems to have bargained individually with the owners of London papers but collectively, through the Newspaper Society, with provincial owners. On 28 July 1937 he addressed a meeting of the Society's members who had Bowater contracts for 1938. They resolved unanimously, no doubt greatly to his relief, 'That this meeting . . . considers it to be in the best interest of all parties that contractors should make some concession to enable the manufacturers to carry on their contracts.' They made clear, however, that they were conferring a favour by resolving also 'That any additional payment made on 1938 contracts should be treated as an advance to meet exceptional costs rather than as an addition to the contract price'.[14]

For the provincial papers that settled the matter in principle, though no price seems to have been named. That seems to have been left to the London owners. They agreed amongst themselves, at about the same time as the members of the Newspaper Society were being addressed by Eric Bowater, that the London market price for 1938, which set the level for all contracts, should be £11. 10s. a ton, representing a rise above the 1937 price of £1. 10s. or 15 per cent.[15]

This offer, ten shillings below Bowaters' asking price, was neither made nor accepted without conditions. Bowaters, for their part, insisted on tight credit during 1938 and that payment should be made on the seventh day of the month following the month of delivery, whereas the usual terms were that payment should be made at the end of the month following the month of delivery. The newspaper owners required two undertakings. The first was that Bowaters should go on with investigations already started, which are dealt with in the next chapter, into the possibility of developing new sources of supply of wood pulp from Newfoundland, 'but if the result of the investigations were unsatisfactory, or if it was found impracticable to finance the development of the properties, we' –

Bowaters – 'would at once consult the chief customers as to the steps to be taken'. Bowaters also agreed 'to consult their' – the chief customers' – 'representatives in regard to major decisions involving substantial capital expenditure or in regard to policy in relation to forward contracts for materials'.[16]

Addressing BPM's shareholders in December 1937, Eric Bowater described the negotiations and their outcome. Only one country newspaper, he said, had refused the increase, and he made much of the friendly spirit Bowaters' customers had shown, though he also said: 'it was not to be expected, and must not be assumed, that our proposals, involving as they did a substantial increase in the cost of what is to a newspaper its principal raw material, received a ready welcome and naturally they were subjected to the most critical examination'.[17] It is evident that the newspaper owners, in the provinces and in London alike, drove a hard bargain. Probably, however, the hardest thing for Eric Bowater to accept, which he did not mention to the shareholders, was that he had been obliged to concede to his 'chief customers' contingent rights of control over Bowaters' conduct of their own affairs.

It is difficult to be precise about the effect on Bowaters' business of the raw material crisis of 1937. In the most direct sense, indeed, it was a non-event, for Bowaters had covered their needs for 1937 and 75 per cent of their needs for 1938 before the really steep price-rise set in (Table 15) and, during the autumn of 1937, prices, as Table 16 shows, began to fall rapidly back towards their former levels. It is impossible, now, to follow Bowaters' buying while these movements were going on and, no doubt, contracts were made at inflated prices. In June 1938, however, a contract for 100,000 tons of Finnish mechanical pulp at c.i.f. prices of 77s. 6d. per wet ton for Northfleet and 79s. 6d. per wet ton for Mersey was cancelled and was replaced by a contract for 250,000 tons at 57s. 6d. per wet ton, to be delivered during the second half of 1938 and the first half of 1939, and, at about the same time, a contract was made for the delivery in 1939 of 10,500 tons of Chandler sulphite pulp from Canada at £8 a ton (c.i.f.).[18] These transactions suggest that a substantial part of any damage that may have been threatened by high prices was avoided. In May 1938 Eric Bowater, in a memorandum for the Bank of England, claimed 'that the aggregate cost of raw materials purchased [by the Bowater Group] for the manufacture of newsprint during 1938 amounts to some £1,200,000 more than would have been the case if the raw material prices ruling in recent years had continued unchanged',[19] but the statement is too

TABLE 16. *Pulp prices, 1937–8*

| | Average Price (dry weight) per ton | | | |
| | Moist mechanical pulp | | Strong sulphite | |
	£	Index	£	Index
1936				
Average	4. 12. 6.	100	8. 10. 0.	100
1937				
Highest				
(3rd quarter)	8. 4. 0.	177	16. 10. 0.	194
1938				
1st half	5. 15. 0.	124		
2nd half	5. 5. 0.	113		
January			13. 10. 0.	159
March			11. 0. 0.	129
April			9. 0. 0.	106
May			8. 10. 0.	100
June			8. 5. 0.	97
July			8. 0. 0.	94

* Basis c.i.f. East Coast ports, three months' bill.

Source: As for Table 15, and see note to that table.

imprecise to carry much weight. During 1938, in any case, the situation was rapidly changing and the chief problem facing the newsprint industry was no longer the level of raw material prices but a failure in demand.

The weakness of Bowaters' position arose not so much from the rising level of prices which they had to pay for pulp as from the inflexibility of the price which they could charge for newsprint. If Bowaters made a serious error of judgment it was the decision, taken in 1936 in response to their customers' pressure, to fix newsprint prices at the very low figure of £10 a ton for two years ahead instead of one. If, in 1937, Bowaters had been free to negotiate in the ordinary way, without having to seek a special dispensation, they might have been able to allow for the higher prices they would have to pay for pulp and still keep newsprint prices relatively low.

To a generation unused to inflation the unexpected upheaval in pulp prices in 1937 came like an earthquake. The shock-waves were far-reaching and severe. Gossip about Bowaters' buying policy – unjustified, for as we have seen it defended their position quite successfully – undermined investors' confidence. In December 1936, following what had become the accustomed pattern of Bowater finance, an offer was made to Mersey debenture holders to convert £800,000 4½ per cent stock, then due for redemption, into £800,000 stock bearing interest at 3½ per cent. Of the new stock

£206,934 was left with the underwriters.[20] The Board blamed the 'constitutional crisis' – King Edward VIII abdicated while the sub- scription lists were open – but there was certainly gossip going around then or very soon after, for it was bearing down on BPM share prices in the early weeks of 1937.[21] By April, BPM Ordinary, which at their highest point in 1936 had stood at 42s. 9d. were being quoted at 20s., a fall of 53 per cent.[22]

Within the business also, lately so buoyant, confidence wavered. There was a call for economy, reinforced by the appointment of a Budgetary Control Committee to administer a system devised with the advice of Barton, Mayhew.[23] At about the same time, the ambitious developments planned for Mersey (Chapter 5.3) seem to have been quietly dropped and an order placed with Walmsleys for a sixth paper machine at Kemsley was postponed.[24] In April 1937, the sales company agreed to make a familiar gesture in times of trouble: the reduction of commission rates within the group, by $\frac{1}{2}$ per cent, for 1937 and 1938.[25]

When BPM's accounts were discussed early in December 1937, the Board allocated £20,000 from the Contingencies Reserves to meet increased manufacturing costs attributable to the rise in raw material prices and £55,000, for the same purpose, from £264,067 available in the profit-and-loss account. As a direct consequence, no Ordinary dividend was paid.[26] There could be no more convincing evidence of lasting uneasiness.

Much more lasting, and far more important for Bowaters' busi- ness, was the effect of the price-rise on Eric Bowater's mind. He felt himself out-manoeuvred by the Scandinavian cartels, developed a deep suspicion of them and, like other businessmen in a similar situation, notably W. H. Lever in the market for soap-makers' oils and fats before 1914,[27] he was determined never to be caught in the same way again. Early in 1937, he launched measures to put Bowaters in control of sources of supply of wood pulp. That policy might lead to problems of its own as conditions in the market for wood pulp altered, as policies of a similar sort had led to problems for Lever in the market for oils and fats, but if this consideration entered Eric Bowater's mind he evidently decided that the balance of advantage lay with control of his own supplies. He set in motion a train of events which, during the twenty-five years of life remain- ing to him, would expand Bowaters' business from an exclusive concern with the manufacture of newsprint in England to control of all the phases of the newsprint industry, from the management of forests to the delivery of the finished goods, on both sides of the Atlantic.

CHAPTER EIGHT

The road to Corner Brook
1937–1939

In May 1938 Eric Bowater told the authorities of the Bank of England that, as far back as 1933, the Bowater Group had tried to 'protect its raw material position' by gaining control of 'certain properties in Canada', meaning presumably Price Brothers.[1] Evidently, therefore, the idea had been in his mind for some years before prices started to rise sharply at the beginning of 1937 and, when that happened, he moved very fast, though at first in the direction of Scandinavia rather than across the Atlantic.

By the middle of March 1937, Bowaters had come to an 'agreement in principle' with Hjalmar, Erik and Arne Unander-Scharin, who owned mills in Sweden which had been investigated by Baker and George Shaw, who later became a director of Bowaters. They were accompanied by Cecil Unthank, a partner in Barton, Mayhew. Negotiations evidently went smoothly and, on 27 May, the parties executed an agreement by which, for a consideration of about Kr.4,400,000 (£220,000), Bowaters became the owners of mills at Sofiehem and Umea on the Swedish coast of the Gulf of Bothnia and of the tugs, tenement houses, timber inspectors' houses and other assets that went with them.[2]

Bowaters agreed to pay the consideration money in cash, to be provided by a Swedish company, AB Umea Traemassefabriker, newly formed to own the mills. This company created Kr.1.5m $3\frac{1}{2}$ per cent twenty-year First Mortgage Bonds and Kr.2m $4\frac{1}{2}$ per cent Notes guaranteed by Bowater's Paper Mills. These securities were all placed in Sweden through the Stockholm Enskilda Bank at a discount of 3 per cent on the bonds and $3\frac{1}{2}$ per cent on the notes. The new company's Ordinary capital of Kr.2m was subscribed equally at par by the Bowater companies and by Lloyds.[3] The total cost of the acquisition to the Bowater Group was therefore BPM's guarantee of Umea's notes and about £100,000 (Kr.2m) in cash.

Bowater Svenska's groundwood pulp mill at Umea, photographed in 1977.

For their money Bowaters gained control of two mills – at Umea and Sofiehem – with combined productive capacity of 135,000 tons of mechanical pulp a year. They were also granted first refusal, for ten years, of 25,000 tons a year from Scharin & Sons' mill at Skelleftea, about seventy miles north of Umea, which was not included in the sale. The advantage of controlling Scharins, at the time of the purchase, was very much a theoretical consideration. Scharins belonged to the Mechanical Pulp Suppliers' Association, one of the cartels so much disliked by Eric Bowater, and Umea and Sofiehem were not released from its restrictions either by the change of ownership or by the formation of the new company. The MPSA allowed them a quota of 119,000 tons (88.15 per cent of capacity) for 1937 and 121,000 tons (89.63 per cent) for 1938[4] and presumably also fixed their prices.

Bowaters' penetration into the MPSA had nevertheless a degree of flamboyant aggressiveness about it, probably not unappreciated by Eric Bowater, which delighted the British Press. 'The appearance of Messrs Bowaters within the precincts of the cartel', said the *News Chronicle* on 20 April 1937, 'may be expected to exert a wholly salutary influence on its price and production policy.' A couple of days later, *World's Press News* ran the headline: 'Bowater's Purchase Seen as Threat to Pulp Cartel'.

In Bowaters' Board minutes there is no trace of this kind of euphoria. Eric Bowater certainly discussed the possibility of increasing Sofiehem's capacity by 50 per cent[5] and he may have intended to resign from the MPSA when the current cartel agreement ran out at the end of 1938. These measures, however, were for the future. For the time being, the new company was set up with a purely Swedish Board, the mills were left under Arne Scharin's management[6] and Bowaters gained no immediate relief from the pressure of high prices, except in so far as they might hope to share in profiting from them by way of dividends from the Umea company.

A smaller Scandinavian transaction, completed in June 1939, may have been intended as a more direct threat to the MPSA. At Risor, on the Norwegian coast about a hundred miles south-west of Oslo, there was a mill with an output capacity of 75,000 tons of mechanical pulp a year. For an outlay of £80,000 Bowaters gained control of the owning company, Risor Traemassefabriker A/S. No sooner was the agreement signed than the Risor company gave a year's notice to resign from MPSA,[7] but any plans which Bowaters may have had for following up the resignation would have been stultified by the invasion of Norway about the time the resignation was due to take effect.

8.2 DEAD END AT GANDER

While Bowaters were negotiating to take over the mills at Umea and Sofiehem they were also seeking assured supplies of pulpwood for their own mill at Kemsley. During 1937, they intended to put in six additional grinders and Kamyr presses. Thus equipped, Eric Bowater told Edward Lloyd's Board in March 1937, it would produce an estimated 60,000 tons of moist pulp for Sittingbourne during 1938.[8] He reported also

that Mr W. Bishop had been engaged on our behalf during the past few months in exploring various possibilities of securing supplies of logwood from North America and had just arrived back in this country to report on the result of his investigations, including an option . . . from the Newfoundland Government over 1,550 square miles of timber limits in Labrador; if it was decided to take up this option, between 100,000 and 200,000 cords of pulpwood would be available for export to England annually.

Eric Bowater's attention was thus swinging back, in 1937, towards Newfoundland, where in the early twenties he had been closely concerned with the building of the newsprint mill at Corner Brook (p. 34).

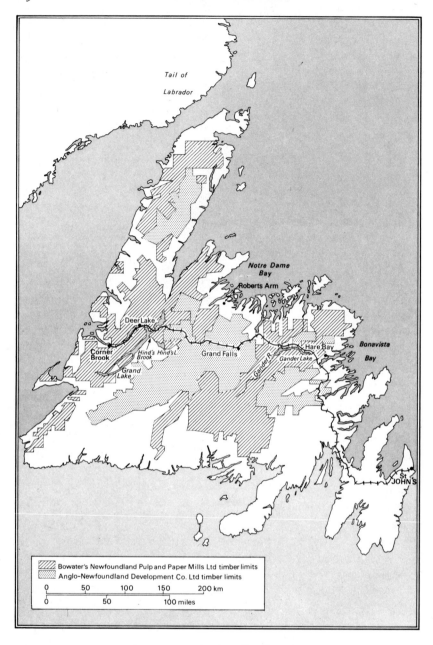

Bowater in Newfoundland, 1940.

Newfoundland, including Labrador, had in the twenties a population of about 260,000. The inhabitants' claim to self-government was well established in fact, if ill-defined in law, and in the Statute of Westminster, 1931, Newfoundland was recognised as a Dominion. For a few years before and during the First World War the country was unprecedently prosperous but, during the twenties, it slid towards economic disaster. The population was small, the sources of wealth few and one of the most important of them, the fisheries, out-of-date and increasingly uncompetitive. Public expenditure, on the other hand, was high and greatly dependent on external loans, creating a heavy burden of debt. By 1929, the public debt of Newfoundland was $87.7m with revenue of $11.5m a year to service it. The value of exported codfish, $25m a year during the war, had fallen to $12m.[9]

Then came the general world crisis. Newfoundland, with a small population excessively dependent on primary production, would have been hard hit even if the fisheries and public finances had been in good order. As matters were, the supply of loans from abroad dried up and, in 1931, when efforts to raise $8m totally failed, the Newfoundland Government called on the Government of the United Kingdom to come to the rescue.

The upshot, after a Royal Commission had reported unflatteringly on Newfoundlanders' conduct of their own affairs,[10] was that Newfoundland, at the request of the Legislature but without a plebiscite, passed in 1933 under the United Kingdom Government's direct authority, exercised through a constitutional device known as the Governor-in-Commission. Apart from the Governor, the Commission of Government had six members, three from Newfoundland and three from elsewhere – in practice, the United Kingdom. On their advice, the Governor was empowered to legislate. In certain matters he had to seek the authority of the Dominions Secretary before giving his assent and any law enacted by him might be disallowed by the Sovereign within a year but, although he and his Commissioners were liable to uninhibited public criticism, they were not obliged to seek consent for their legislation from the people of Newfoundland through any form of representative assembly. This was the curious form of government – unrepresentative and dictatorial, yet installed by due process of law through two elected legislatures, at St John's and Westminster – with which Bowaters had to deal as they developed their activities in Newfoundland from 1937 onwards.

The Commission of Government, eager to encourage any possibility of new employment, granted the Labrador option which

Bishop put before Bowaters in the spring of 1937. While they were considering it more news from Newfoundland arrived, brought by V. S. Bennett, Receiver of the Reid Newfoundland Co. The company, founded in 1901 by R. G. Reid (1842–1908), a forceful Scot who founded a commercial dynasty, had as its principal assets some 3,910 square miles of land, granted to Reid as contractor for building the Newfoundland Railway, and licences to cut timber on 3,632 square miles of Crown land.[11] The 'Reid Limits', as the company's property was called, lay along the Gander River valley some 130 miles north of St John's, reasonably accessible to the Newfoundland Railway but uninhabited and undeveloped. The virgin forest lay untouched. Bennett was seeking some company with the resources and the will to make something of it, preferably by putting up a paper mill like those already existing at Corner Brook and Grand Falls, a pioneering operation which would require the building of a town with all its services and a branch railway line. Among the few possible candidates for this heroic endeavour, Bowaters were the most promising.

Bowaters were more concerned to find timber for their pulp mill at Kemsley and perhaps for one which they had some thought of putting up at Mersey than to face the task of building a mill – and town – in Newfoundland. They were certainly not prepared to contemplate a paper mill, though they might be persuaded to consider a mill for making sulphite pulp if the conditions were attractive enough. The Commission of Government, seeing that uses for sulphite pulp outside the newsprint industry were growing and considering that 'it is perhaps well that the economic welfare of this country should not too exclusively depend on the price of newsprint', decided to accept the idea of a sulphite mill, though not on such favourable terms as had previously been granted for the paper mill at Corner Brook. There was thus the basis for a bargain but the negotiating stance of the parties to it was made quite clear in a speech broadcast by R. B. Ewbank (1883–1967), Commissioner for Natural Resources, an ex-Indian Civil Servant who might sometimes be seen reading Horace at breakfast in the Newfoundland Hotel, St John's. 'We made it clear, he said,

that in the general interests of this country we should prefer a mill which would carry on the complete processes of manufacturing paper here to one which would produce sulphite pulp only for the United Kingdom. We pointed out that there was a keen demand for pulpwood for export and that we should regard this part of the scheme more as a concession in order to secure the establishment of a mill here than as an advantage in itself.[12]

In June 1937 Bowaters took up an option on the Reid properties, expiring on 11 November, and sent Arthur Baker to inspect them, accompanied by A. G. Allen of Allen & Overy, solicitors to the company. Allen, who had had previous professional connections with the Corner Brook company, was at this time one of Eric Bowater's closest advisers. He had to go back to England after a couple of months and his place was taken by a much younger member of his firm, G. W. R. Morley (b. 1909), whose association with Bowaters was to last until he retired from the Board of the Corporation in 1979. Baker and Allen reached Newfoundland on 1 July and within a few days made Bowaters' main interest very plain by applying for a permit, which was granted, to export, during 1938 only, 100,000 cords of wood from Reid land and 20,000 cords from Robert's Arm on the coast of Notre Dame Bay, about forty miles north of the Gander. They 'undertook to go into the operation on a permanent basis and to spend a minimum of $65,000 on roads, camps and river improvements'[13] and in the summer of 1937 they set up Bowater-Lloyd Ltd at St John's, with a nominal capital of $100,000, to conduct the logging operations.[14]

At Robert's Arm, Bowaters ran swiftly into trouble; trouble of a kind which revealed the violence latent beneath the surface of labour relations in the logging camps. Bowaters, through their

A warning sign in Newfoundland, 1930s.

contractor, Hewlett, were paying the minimum wage allowable under their permit, which, with extras, came to about $2.25 a cord. On 16 October, Hewlett's men struck for $2.50 and elected Sir Richard Squires (1880–1940), a former Prime Minister of Newfoundland, to negotiate for them. Bowaters' representative was H. M. S. Lewin (1900–71), an accountant of Welsh extraction who was a partner in Macdonald Currie & Co. of Montreal.

When negotiations on the spot broke down, Squires and Lewin went by sea to Robert's Arm, arriving on 26 October to find the men angry and hungry, Hewlett having closed the camp and paid off the cooks. On 27 October, Lewin refused the men's demands, quarrelled with Squires, tried unsuccessfully to get him off the ship and ordered the master to put to sea. Strikers came aboard and prevented the anchor being raised. 'If word had gone out that I had been ejected', said Squires, 'Lewin would never have returned alive.' Lewin eventually agreed to a settlement at $2.50 but only, he said, to avoid bloodshed.[15]

Lewin then closed Hewlett's operations down and sent for the police, fifty of whom arrived on 30 October to protect the property.[16] A couple of days later, delegates from four logging settlements guaranteed no recurrence of what had just happened and asked to be allowed to go on cutting at $2 a cord, which appears to have settled the matter in spite of Lewin's earlier agreement to a rate of $2.50.[17] The men's resentment seems to have been directed at Hewlett, who gave them bad accommodation and overcharged for it, far more than at Bowaters, and Lewin told Ewbank that Bowaters appreciated the men's attitude and would be glad to go on with the operations.[18]

Lewin, as this episode suggests, was a bold man. He was stocky of build, dictatorial in temperament, not refined in his phraseology, prone to make enemies as well as friends. Sir Richard Squires, speaking on 30 October when feeling, no doubt, was still inflamed, said that 'Lewin is a liar and double-dealer, offensive, with no knowledge of human nature and devoid of tact. He angers men with his small discourtesies.'[19] Eric Bowater highly approved of Lewin's conduct at Robert's Arm. Recognising, no doubt, another autocrat when he saw one, he engaged Lewin to run Bowaters' business in Newfoundland, thereby setting him on the threshold of a career which was to carry him, in 1955, to a seat on the Corporation Board.

Whilst logging went ahead at Robert's Arm and elsewhere under the terms of the temporary permit, Bowaters and the Commission of Government, with the Dominions Office never far in the background, set about devising a permanent agreement on the basis that

Bowaters would put up a sulphite mill, which they did not really want to do, in return for rights to export timber which the Government did not really want to grant. There was very little common ground between the parties except, apparently, a disinclination to see the negotiations fail and, accordingly, the possibilities of argument over details were endless. Nevertheless, by the beginning of November, an agreement had been drafted which Ewbank, as Commissioner for Natural Resources, announced rather nervously in a broadcast to an audience which he clearly expected to be highly critical if not downright hostile.

Bowaters, he said, would put up, by 31 December 1940, a mill capable of producing 70,000 tons of sulphite pulp from 154,000 cords of wood in a working year of 310 days. He made great play with the cost ($6m plus $1.25m for a wharf); with the 'modern town' which Bowaters were going to build ('equipped with streets, lighting, water supply, fire prevention, school, church, hospital, etc.') and with the employment to be generated (300 permanent employees with a payroll of $350,000 plus a varying number, up to 3,000, employed on cutting timber with a payroll of $575,000). Bowaters had also undertaken to spend not less than half-a-million dollars in Newfoundland in the years 1938 and 1939 in addition to the cost of anything they imported.

The Government undertook to put up twenty miles of single-track branch line, or more if the company would pay for it, to connect the mill, the precise site of which had evidently not been fixed, to the main line. The Government would also operate the line but, if its gross receipts ran less than 7 per cent of the capital cost of construction, the company – Bowaters – would pay the difference.

The price to Bowaters, then, of securing some part of their supplies of raw materials was to be a sulphite mill costing $6m (£1,213,838 at the average 1937 exchange rate) plus a township with services for which no figure was mentioned, and this at a time when Bowaters' finances were under such strain that they were paying no Ordinary dividend. What, apart from the branch line, were they to get for their outlay?

'I now come', said Ewbank, 'to the difficult and debatable point of the export of raw wood from Newfoundland.' This was the most sensitive part of the agreement because exports of raw wood from Newfoundland would not provide so much or so lucrative employment as products manufactured from raw wood in Newfoundland. However, as Ewbank pointed out, exports helped to support prices and 'it is not in the interests either of the forests or the people that mature trees should be left to decay unused'. Moreover, 'it is a stark fact that the Gander properties have been awaiting development for years but . . . no company with the necessary resources has come forward and, even now when the demand for wood is more active than of recent years, there is still no other interested party in sight'. This was Ewbank's most compelling point: if they failed to come to terms with Bowater, when would another chance arise?[20]

There seemed, now, to be comparatively little in dispute between the two sides. In December, after the period of Bowaters' option had been extended, two members of the Commission of Government – Sir Wilfred Woods and Edward Emerson (the Legal Member) – went to London at the request of the Dominions Secretary and joined a third, John C. Puddister, who was already there. The strength of this party is evidence of the Newfoundland Government's anxiety to get the matter settled. Public opinion in Newfoundland was afraid of a breakdown and the Governor badly wanted an end to uncertainty. Bowaters, on the other hand, showed a maddening tendency to procrastinate.[21]

Christmas came and went: 1937 passed into 1938. Bowaters again asked for postponement of the option date, saying they needed time to arrange finance. Woods and Emerson put off their sailing date from 6 to 14 January. 'On the 12 January a new factor in the Company's plans was made known to the Newfoundland representatives through the Dominions Office. They were informed that the Company was investigating alternatives to certain parts of its project.' Woods and Emerson put off their departure to 28 January, 'the Company being informed that there could be no further postponement in any case'.[22]

It was becoming more and more evident to the Commissioners that, behind the negotiations which had taken them to England and kept them there far longer than they expected, something was going on of which they knew nothing, even though it vitally affected the interests of Newfoundland, of whose Government they were members. On 20 January 1938 'Mr. Eric Bowater gave them certain information orally' and then went on to explain why the information was incomplete 'and could not, therefore, be taken into account for purposes of negotiation'. He asked them, nevertheless, 'to settle the text of a draft agreement on the lines already followed' but to postpone a formal and binding execution of it until 31 May.

In this humiliating position the most dignified course would have been to break off negotiations but

it did not appear that anything was to be gained for Newfoundland by the adoption of that course. The company's representatives gave the most explicit assurances that they had in no way changed their intention to embark on operations on a large scale in Newfoundland and stated repeatedly that the alternatives they had in mind were entirely compatible with that intention.

Woods and Emerson accordingly went on negotiating and, on 26 January 1938, they and representatives of Bowaters (Arthur Baker and A. G. Allen) initialled an agreement, in the form of a draft Act (the Bowater-Lloyd Act 1938) of the Newfoundland Government, to come into force not later than 31 May 1938 if both parties gave notice of desiring it.[23]

8.3 TO CORNER BROOK BY WAY OF THREADNEEDLE STREET

Two or three days after Woods and Emerson arrived in London from Newfoundland, Eric Bowater received a secret cablegram from New York. It started: 'Urgent personal most confidential party prepared discuss sale equity roundly seven hundred thousand pounds STOP They will not name price but invite offer.' It went on to say that the 'party' insisted on absolute secrecy as to the negotiations and it ended:

Now that I have got so far it seems to me that you should come to New York as quickly as possible so as to conduct negotiations direct . . . In any event extension your present options would appear to be necessary doubtless you could arrange but without disclosure New York position this very important STOP Is there any reason why I should not now in confidence bring your name into my discussions here . . . Please cable Waldorf Frater Taylor.[24]

The 'party' was International Paper and the sale of equity they were prepared to discuss was the sale of the equity of International Power & Paper Co. of Newfoundland – the Corner Brook company, which International Paper had owned since 1927. Frater Taylor was representing the Bank of England and he sent a copy of his cablegram to E. H. D. Skinner, the Governor's Secretary, who passed it to Montagu Norman with the comment: 'I have not mentioned anything of this to Wilson-Smith because he would be obliged to mention it to the Dominions Office who in turn would mention it to the Newfoundland Commissioners. It looks promising.'

This, then, was the reason why, to the mystification of the Newfoundland Commissioners, Bowaters were so dilatory in their negotiations from mid-December onward. It may also have been the reason why they had previously been in no great hurry for some time because, before Frater Taylor left for New York on 1 December, he took the precaution of asking Eric Bowater whether he would be interested in acquiring the business based at Corner Brook,[25] and even Eric's ambition would hardly allow him to contemplate that as well as building a sulphite mill in the Gander area. In any case, he had never really wanted to build that mill and he wanted to do so less and less as the probable cost became plainer to him and the price of sulphite pulp began to fall.

The Gander project was never popular either at the Bank of England or at the British Treasury. Each was concerned in the Corner Brook company, the Bank through owning the Preference capital (on which no dividends had ever been paid) and the Treasury through its guarantee of the 'A' Debenture stock, and each feared that, if Bowaters put up a sulphite mill, they might later extend it into newsprint in competition with Corner Brook. On the other hand, they could not openly oppose the project because it had obvious advantages for Newfoundland.[26] Frater Taylor, who represented the Bank on the Corner Brook Board, had been pressing for years for drastic rationalization in the Canadian newsprint industry to get rid of surplus capacity and the last thing he wanted was new capacity in Newfoundland. He was critical, besides, of International Paper's control of Corner Brook's affairs. In October 1937, he was complaining to Skinner that capital expenditure was being dealt with too lightly; that there was a risk of Corner Brook becoming too heavily indebted to International Paper; that he doubted the value of Corner Brook's export trade to the United Kingdom.[27] This last matter particularly worried him, especially since International Paper was pursuing an aggressive policy towards Bowaters in the United Kingdom (p. 101 above).

Towards the end of 1937 the short-lived economic recovery in the United States, which, among its indirect consequences, had set off the dramatic rise in wood pulp prices and hence Bowaters' interest in the Gander project, began to peter out. The results at Corner Brook were immediate. The working week was cut, first to five days and then to four.[28] At about this time, Frater Taylor arrived in New York with his suggestion that International Paper should sell their interest in Corner Brook to Bowaters.

From International Paper's point of view there were obvious advantages. Corner Brook was isolated from their main operations and the investment there had never been an outstanding success. 'For the last five years', Arthur Baker told Ewbank in September 1938, 'it [Corner Brook] has incurred a continuous loss for its owners who have never received anything whatever by way of dividend on their investment in it.' Competition in the United Kingdom was severe and might be regulated if Bowaters took over. There may also have been the thought that, if International Paper got rid of Corner Brook, they would no longer have to bear with representatives of the Bank of England, the Treasury and the Newfoundland Government. They were prepared to sell but not to sell cheaply. They would not name a price but waited to see what Bowaters would offer.

For Bowaters, the possibility of buying the mill at Corner Brook created a completely new situation and a more attractive one. Eric Bowater, eager for an entry into North America and ready as usual for any opportunity that offered, seems to have decided at once that Frater Taylor's suggestion should be followed up and, by the time Frater Taylor came back from the United States on 11 January 1938, Eric had worked out detailed reasons for preferring the new project to the Gander River project on which Bowaters and the Newfoundland Government had been negotiating for so long.

Eric Bowater's case for buying Corner Brook, as disclosed in papers by himself and others in the archives of the Bank of England, had two main themes. On the one hand, as the Bank told the

Corner Brook, 1947. Note the log booms lying in harbour. *Canadian Pacific Air Lines Limited*

Treasury, there would be 'constructive possibilities including a large measure of rationalization of the British Newsprint Industry and the elimination of the unprofitable and unhealthy competition and price-cutting which has taken place between the International Paper Company and Bowaters in particular'.[29] On the other hand, as Eric told the Bank, the Bowater Group would gain 'a raw material insurance policy',[30] which was, after all, the purpose for which they had originally gone to Newfoundland.

'The Bowater Group at all times', said Eric Bowater, discussing the control of competition, '. . . is vulnerable to Canadian competition, the U.K. selling price of Canadian newsprint being in recent years about £1 per ton below the price of newsprint manufactured and sold in England.' The IP Group at that moment, he pointed out, were supplying newsprint at prices as low as £9. 5s. a ton against the British price of £11. 10s. and American price of more than £11. 'The acquisition, by the Bowater Group', he said, 'of the control of a low cost newsprint mill at Corner Brook, particularly favourably located to serve the U.S.A. as well as the British market, gives it a weapon with which to retaliate in the U.S.A. market should the Canadian mills continue to raid the U.K. market.'

It was intended, in any case,

that Corner Brook, after its sale to the Bowater Group, should be procured to co-operate with the Canadian newsprint industry and conform to U.S.A. prices and to the percentage of capacity to which the Canadian industry mutually agrees to work and that, in return, the I.P. Group should accept the principle that the I.P. organisation and the Canadian newsprint industry will not be allowed, so far as the I.P. Group can exercise control, to undercut the Corner Brook newsprint price in the U.K.

In other words, just as there was a Swedish pulp cartel, or rather two cartels, so there was to be a Canadian newsprint cartel, an arrangement typical of world trade in the thirties, though since forbidden by increasingly strict legislation in many countries.

Finally, and perhaps most important, Corner Brook would remain a party to the Sales Allocation Agreement within the International Paper Group, by which contracts, profitable and unprofitable alike, were shared on an equitable basis among the group's member mills. Frater Taylor was particularly anxious to see the system continue. 'I am very much interested', he told J. H. Keeling,

and, indeed, anxious to know about the Sales Allocation because, after a great deal of wrangling, we [the independent directors of the Corner Brook company] were able to develop the Sales Allocation which gave all of the mills in the I.P. Group their proper proportion of tonnage and of quality (their fair ratio of less profitable foreign contracts as opposed to domestic business).[31]

To make good their undertaking to the Newfoundland Government, Bowaters' new proposition was to build a sulphite mill at Corner Brook instead of building one in the Gander area. The suggestion was not very welcome to the Newfoundland Government, who had great hopes that the Gander project would provide employment where none had existed before. Bowaters, however, worked out the costs of the two mills and the case in favour of Corner Brook and against Gander was unanswerable.

First, there would be the capital outlay. Even assuming that Bowaters had to pay $6m for the equity of the Corner Brook company, Eric Bowater told the Bank before the price was settled, the proposition would still be better for Bowaters than the development of the Reid Newfoundland properties. That proposition, he said,

is a pioneering one and, in addition to its calling for the purchase and development of timber limits, it entails the erection of a sulphite mill, wharves, power plant and a town site in wholly undeveloped territory and involves an expenditure, on fixed assets, to an estimated cost of $8,000,000 [£1,627,008], excluding the cost of the timber limits and without taking into account working capital requirements and interest on capital during construction. The cost of a sulphite mill of similar capacity at Corner Brook . . . is estimated at $3,000,000 [£610,128] with little expenditure on a town site, which is already in existence, and where the necessary transport, power and other facilities, including an ample supply of labour, already exist.[32]

In other words, for an outlay of about $9m Bowaters could have a paper mill *and* a sulphite mill at Corner Brook whereas a sulphite mill alone in the Gander area would cost more than $8m.* Nor was this all. The mill at Corner Brook would be ready much more quickly – 'erected and in operation in little more than a year, whereas on the East Coast two-and-a-half years would be required' – and production costs would be over 10 per cent lower. In the Gander area, the only suitable site for a mill was at Hare Bay on Bonavista Bay, where transport and capital costs would push production costs to £11. 10s. ($56.50) a ton. The market price of sulphite, by May 1938, had fallen from the previous year's highest figure of £16. 10s. a ton to £8. 10s. and Eric Bowater made it quite clear that, with prices at that level, he could never go back to the Gander scheme even if the purchase of Corner Brook fell through.[33]

---

* Another source (see n. 33) puts the figure at $14m.

The price of sulphite pulp (£8 a ton in July) had now fallen below the level prevailing before the crisis of 1937. The average price for the nine years 1928–36, in the United Kingdom, was £9.22,[34] over £1 less than the expected cost of production ($50.50; £10.27) at Corner Brook. Looked at this way, Eric Bowater had to admit to the Bank of England that the Corner Brook transaction 'might be regarded as an uneconomical one'.

He cheered himself up, and evidently expected to cheer the Bank also, by regarding the purchase as 'a raw material insurance policy in that not only will reasonable prices be assured but supplies as well' and working out the premium, as follows:

Interest on purchase price, say $6m	$300,000
Cumulative Sinking Fund of 1 per cent per annum to amortise cost of investment in thirty-seven years	$60,000
Total	$360,000

'The Bowater Group's output of paper in England', he went on,

is 600,000 tons per annum, so that the above cost of $360,000 per annum is equivalent to less than 2/5d. per ton, an added cost which cannot be regarded as a large one for the advantages which it is believed will accrue to the Bowater Group from the acquisition of the control of I.P. & P. Co. of Newfoundland Ltd.

When his mind was set upon a course of action, Eric Bowater could be ingeniously persuasive – to himself, no doubt, not least.

The negotiations for the Ordinary capital of International Power & Paper Co. of Newfoundland were long, difficult and conducted in the utmost secrecy. Eric Bowater had to satisfy not only International Paper but also the Bank of England, the Treasury and, to a lesser degree, the Dominions Office and the Government of Newfoundland. The goodwill of the Bank, meaning in practice the personal goodwill of the Governor, Montagu Norman, was indispensable and Montagu Norman went to considerable lengths to satisfy himself both of Eric Bowater's character and abilities and of the soundness of the purchase.

Eric Bowater was in the States for several weeks between January and mid-March, or perhaps later, being joined early in March by J. H. Keeling. He was at home in April and May, accompanied by representatives of International Paper who, by the middle of the month, were anxious to get away.[35] It was not until the third week in May, at the earliest, that he was sure of Montagu Norman's agreement to the terms he wanted and, as late as 14 May, Frater

Taylor, who was prominent in the negotiations throughout, reported to E. G. D. Skinner at the Bank that Eric was 'in a very pessimistic mood'.

Eric's pessimism arose from Montagu Norman's attitude to the Bank's holding of £2,080,000 5 per cent Cumulative Preference shares in the Corner Brook company. The Governor wanted the Bank to be rid of the shares but it was beyond Bowaters' resources to buy them at the same time as they bought the Ordinary shares. The Bank had agreed to forego the accumulation of dividends to the end of 1938 but after that, if dividends were not paid, voting rights would come into effect which would give the Bank control of the company. If that were thought to be likely to happen, it would be most difficult for Bowaters to raise the finance they would need for the purchase and Eric Bowater was most anxious to get the Bank to ease matters for him. Norman was obstinate but eventually he consented to an agreement to extend what Frater Taylor called 'the non-cumulative feature' until the end of 1940, thus removing a serious obstacle from Bowaters' path.

The terms of purchase of International Power & Paper Co. of Newfoundland's Ordinary shares were finally agreed in time for Eric Bowater to report them personally to Bowater Paper Mills' Board on 31 May 1938. Broadly, the agreement provided for the purchase by Bowaters of the Corner Brook company's Ordinary capital – £700,000 in Common shares of £1 each – for $5,500,000 (£1,118,568). This was half a million dollars less than Eric Bowater had at one time contemplated paying but, on the other hand, Frater Taylor, at the outset, apparently expected him to get them at par or not much above.[36] Besides buying the issued shares, Bowaters agreed to subscribe for £100,000 new Common shares at par.[37]

Along with the purchase agreement went an agreement allowing Corner Brook the benefit of International Paper's Sales Allocation Agreement until the end of 1940. During that time, International Paper's sales company would act for Corner Brook but Bowaters would revive the dormant Bowater Paper Co. in New York (p. 36 above) to provide a sales organisation in the United States against the time when the Sales Allocation Agreement ran out. While it lasted, orders secured by Bowaters in North America would go into the pool and form part of the controlled tonnage to be allocated between Corner Brook and the subsidiaries of International Paper. So would contracts secured by Bowaters for Corner Brook with 'certain specified customers (understood to be English)'. Otherwise, Bowaters would be free to allocate contracts to Corner Brook without bringing them into the pool, the object being 'to enable

Bowaters to build up an independent business for the Newfoundland Company so that when the Allocation Agreement comes to an
end the Corner Brook mill may be well supplied with orders'.[38]

Arrangements for financing the acquisition went swiftly ahead,
being announced confidentially to newspaper proprietors in a circular letter of 14 July 1938. Bowaters formed a new subsidiary,
Bowater-Lloyd Newfoundland Ltd, with share capital, subscribed
by Bowater's Paper Mills, of £500,000 (3s. 6d. paid). The new
company would make a public issue (to which the newspaper
proprietors were invited to subscribe) of £1,250,000 4½ per cent
guaranteed First Debenture stock at £98 per cent and, with the
proceeds, would buy from BPM all 800,000 £1 Common shares in
International Power & Paper Co. of Newfoundland, the name of
which was changed on 18 August 1938 to Bowater's Newfoundland Pulp & Paper Mills Ltd.[39]

The new company's debentures issued on 21 July 1938 were
unconditionally guaranteed as to principal, interest and sinking
fund by Bowater's Paper Mills, Bowater's Mersey Paper Mills and
Edward Lloyd Ltd. In case it might be thought that this was rather a
heavy burden for companies whose 1938 profits, as the Advance
Particulars of the debenture issue made clear, had suffered from
'abnormally high prices of raw materials', the directors of BPM
were careful to record their opinion 'that as a result of the acquisition of the . . . Common Shares of the Newfoundland Company
the position of the Company [i.e. BPM] in relation to acquiring
supplies of raw materials and marketing its newsprint would be
greatly strengthened'.[40] Nevertheless, the obligation was a heavy
one, the more so since for several years the guarantor companies
were called upon to honour their guarantee.

Even before the finance of Corner Brook had been arranged,
Bowaters had made an offer for the Reid Timber Limits which had
originally attracted them to Newfoundland. It required an immediate payment of about $1,113,000 (£226,357), then payments of
$150,000 a year for two years and $90,000 a year for forty years
after that.[41] It was conditional on agreement with the Newfoundland Government on export of wood and other matters and it was
linked with an undertaking to extend the sulphite mill at Corner
Brook. The negotiations took time but, at BPM's AGM on 22
December 1938, Eric Bowater could say that they were complete.

The negotiators for Bowaters were Arthur Baker, Godfrey Morley and Henry Chisholm (p. 94 above) whom Eric Bowater had
recently engaged. 'You will act as my personal representative', Eric
told him, 'Write to me every day, and watch Arthur Baker to see

that he doesn't go too far.' Not unnaturally, Chisholm fell foul of Baker, partly through claiming precedence at the formal receptions they all attended, and Baker eventually engineered Chisholm's recall, expecting his dismissal, but he remained with Bowaters until 1944.

Bowaters had to persuade the Commission of Government to accept considerably less ambitious extensions at Corner Brook than the Commissioners had been hoping for: 30,000 extra tons of sulphite in place of 45,000 – a figure itself scaled down from 70,000 tons proposed in the original plan for a mill in the Gander Valley – and 30,000 extra tons of paper, plus any extra tonnage of sulphite which the increased output of paper might require. The new sulphite capacity was to be brought into operation by the end of 1941 and the new paper capacity 'so soon after the 31st December 1940 as the Government and the Company shall agree that it is practicable to do so'.

Against these undertakings the Government granted Bowaters the rights they sought to ensure supplies of timber for the groundwood mill at Kemsley. They were given permission to cut 50,000 cords of wood for export every year for ninety-nine years, plus 70,000 cords a year from 1939 to 1945, and after 1945 two cords of wood for every ton of sulphite exported during the previous year and half a cord for every ton of paper manufactured above the mill's rated capacity. The Government also granted tax concessions so generously that when Newfoundland entered the Canadian federation in 1949 the Canadian Government refused to honour them. To gain their ends Bowaters committed themselves to expenditure widely thought to be excessive in times of great and growing uncertainty. The risk was heavy.

The agreement, initialled on 30 September, was still awaiting legislative sanction at the end of the year. The extensions at Corner Brook which it provided for were by no means an equivalent for a completely new mill on the Gander. The final abandonment of that project came as a bitter disappointment in Newfoundland and Ewbank's broadcast announcing it was even more defensive in tone than his broadcast of the previous year (p. 137 above). He painted a bleak picture of the world economy, of the Newfoundland economy, of the state of the market for newsprint and sulphite pulp, with Canadian newsprint mills working below capacity, the sulphite mill at Grand Falls idle and depression in America and Europe. Above all, he made clear that, for Newfoundland, there was no question of a choice between an agreement with Bowaters and an agreement with some other firm. 'Since the great depression began in 1930', he said, 'the efforts of the Reid representatives to interest capital in the Gander have brought no other firm into the field but Bowaters.'[42] For Newfoundland, if the Gander area were to be developed at all, there was no alternative to Bowaters but Ewbank made no pretence of enthusiasm.

Bowaters, after a year or more of negotiations, found themselves with a result quite different from the one they had set out to obtain. Instead of a sulphite mill in the Gander area and a supply of timber for export from the Reid Limits they had the supply of timber but with it a very large newsprint mill, and much else besides, on the opposite coast of Newfoundland. The Corner Brook mill was the most important industrial undertaking in Newfoundland and therefore, as Bowaters had already discovered, inevitably a centre of attention in Newfoundland politics.

Corner Brook's newsprint capacity was about 200,000 tons a year and, to support that, there were 7,000 square miles of timber limits bearing about 14,000,000 cords of wood. The company owned the township of Corner Brook, including its port, and two steamships 'specially designed and constructed for the transport of its products'. There was electrical generating plant capable of developing 156,000 h.p., sufficient for the company's entire requirements, so that unlike many mills it was independent of outside suppliers. 'Geographically', Eric Bowater told his stockholders in his letter announcing the acquisition of Corner Brook, 'it is most favourably situated to enable it to furnish the requirements not only of the Bowater-Lloyd Group but also the newsprint requirements of newspaper publishers in the United Kingdom and the United States of America.'[43]

In time to come, the American connection was to be the most important outcome of the long, tortuous negotiations set in motion by the raw material crisis of 1937. It was unsought when the negotiations started and, by the time they ended, the crisis had long passed away. Quite unexpectedly, its effect had been to launch Bowaters into the North American newsprint industry.

8.4 THE GREATER GROUP 1938-9

Some of Eric Bowater's critics said he was a gambler, perhaps because of his fairly frequent visits to the casino at Le Touquet. Those who held that opinion in 1938 no doubt held it even more strongly after Bowaters moved into Corner Brook, which in some quarters was regarded as a highly speculative step.[44] Speculation, however, is closely related to enterprise and perhaps that is what they called it at the Bank of England, where they hoped Bowaters would speedily relieve them of their entanglement in transatlantic paper.

Certainly the buying of Corner Brook, along with the smaller purchases in Scandinavia, drastically altered the structure and functions of the Bowater-Lloyd Group. It had been concerned solely with buying materials from abroad to convert them into newsprint and a few other products which it sold in the United Kingdom or exported. In just over a year it was transformed into a vertically integrated combine active in every phase of newsprint production from the tree in the forest to the paper on the reel, operating not in the United Kingdom only but in Scandinavia and North America as well.

A transformation on this scale can hardly have been in Eric Bowater's mind early in 1937 when he set out to defend his business against the assaults of continental cartels. Nevertheless he was a brilliant opportunist and a very good judge of a situation, which he would discuss very carefully with his expert advisers before he decided what to do. When the chance of buying Corner Brook was put in his way, he took it, being never averse to seizing an opportunity, however unexpected, for furthering his long-term plans, in this case his plans for establishing Bowaters in North America. What kind of bargain were Bowaters getting when they committed themselves at the end of May 1938, to paying $5.5m for the new acquisition?

There is a good deal to be learned from the structure and ownership of the Corner Brook company's capital (Table 17), which displays the company's Anglo-Canadian–US associations, its troubled history, its importance to the economy both in Newfoundland and in the United Kingdom. The capital was held partly in dollars, partly in sterling. The ratio of Loan and Preference stock to Common stock was high – about 9:1 – leading to fixed interest charges, in 1938, of nearly £330,000. Since the company's earning power had always – with good reason – been suspect, two governments, in Newfoundland and the United Kingdom, had seen fit to guarantee loans and the Bank of England had taken up the whole of the Preference capital, though it had had to go without dividends. The consequence of this exalted concern with the company's fortunes was that all the interested parties had representatives on the company's Board – one each for the Bank and the UK Treasury, two for the Newfoundland Government – and they were zealous in promoting the interests of those whom they represented. One of them – Frater Taylor, the Bank's representative – had set the Bowater purchase in train (p. 139 above).

TABLE 17. *Capitalisation of the Corner Brook company at time of acquisition*

Authorised	Issued	Description	Outstanding	Remarks
		LOAN CAPITAL		
£4,000,000 or equivalent in dollars	(a)$4,866,000	5 per cent First Mortgage Gold Bonds, 1928 series	$4,866,000 ⎱	Held by public in US and Canada
	(b)£1,500,000	4½ per cent First Mortgage Sinking Fund Gold Bonds, 1936 series	$1,484,000 ⎰	
£1,877,600	£1,877,600	3 per cent Guarantee 'A' Mortgage Debenture stock	£1,818,100	Guaranteed by HM Treasury and held by public in UK
£154,300	£154,300	3 per cent Second 'A' Mortgage Debenture stock	£149,800	Held by Treasury
£2,000,000	£2,000,000	5½ per cent 'B' Mortgage Debenture stock	£1,851,100	Guaranteed by Newfoundland Government and held by public in UK
£8,031,900				
		SHARE CAPITAL		
£2,080,000	£2,080,000	5 per cent Cumulative Preference Shares of £1 each (non-cumulative to end of 1938)		Held by Bank of England Nominees
£700,000	£700,000	Common shares of £1 each		To be acquired by Bowaters
£2,220,000	Nil	Shares of £1 each		Unissued
£5,000,000				

Source: BPM Board minutes, 31 May 1938.

Bowater-Lloyd's control of Corner Brook was thus far from absolute and the financial responsibilities which the group was assuming were heavy. Bowater's Newfoundland Pulp & Paper Mills – the Corner Brook company – had to meet fixed interest charges which in total were about two-thirds of the seven-year average – £494,143 – of the profits of the whole group, before the acquisition, as disclosed in the prospectus for Bowater-Lloyd Newfoundland's debenture issue.* Moreover, the failure, year after

* The average is calculated from figures given for 'Profits after depreciation and debenture interest'.

year, to pay Preference dividends shows how heavily loaded with debt the Corner Brook company was.

The effects of this indebtedness were transmitted at once to Bowater-Lloyd by the method chosen, no doubt because it was the only method possible in the circumstances, of financing the purchase of Corner Brook's Common stock: that is, by debentures. The debenture issue ensured that the capital cost of the acquisition would be met by the public. Inseparable, however, from raising a loan rather than issuing shares there was another cost: the cost of servicing the debentures.

The company that issued the debentures, Bowater-Lloyd Newfoundland, was a holding company with no source of income except dividends on the Common stock of the Corner Brook company, but that company had never paid a dividend on the Common stock and there was no near prospect of its doing so after Bowater-Lloyd took over. The holding company had no hope, for several years, of servicing its debentures and this was the reason for the guarantee given by the Bowater-Lloyd Group's three manufacturing subsidiaries: Bowater's Paper Mills, Bowater's Mersey Paper Mills and Lloyds.

They guaranteed principal, interest and sinking fund and, for eight years, they paid an annual charge averaging about £28,000 or rather more in the proportions BPM twenty-five : BMPM twenty-five : Lloyds fifty.[45] Against the three companies' total revenue £28,000 was no great sum but it added to the burden of fixed charges, already heavy, on the highly geared capital of the Bowater-Lloyd Group and, as long as the guarantee had to be honoured, it gave notice that the investment at Corner Brook was yielding a negative return.

The responsibilities, direct and indirect, arising from the Corner Brook company's indebtedness were not all that Bowater-Lloyd had taken on. They were committed also to capital expenditure at Corner Brook, whether or not the business was profitable, during the years immediately after the take-over. Their commitments, given statutory force by the Bowater's Newfoundland Act 1938 (an Act of the Commission of Government), arose from promises given to the Government in return for export rights and other concessions, as discussed in Chapter 8.3 above. The concessions were valuable but the commitment to capital expenditure on a considerable scale, to be undertaken for the benefit of the Newfoundland economy rather than for Bowaters' own purposes, would have been a heavy one at any time and was particularly onerous in the conditions of 1938, with the newsprint industry in North

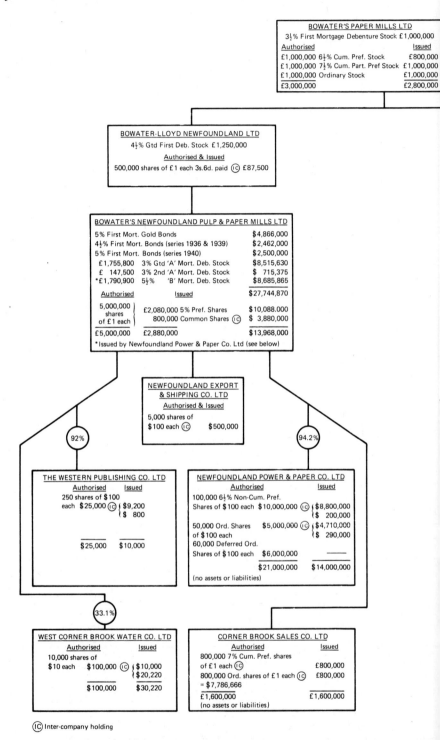

2 The Bowater-Lloyd Group in 1939.

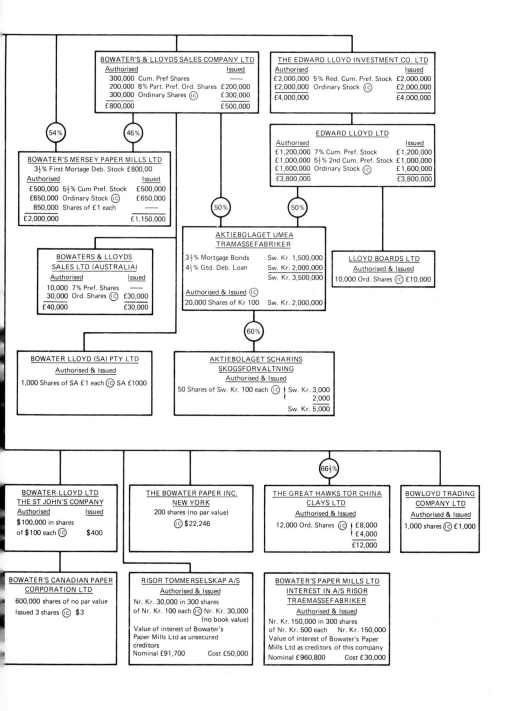

BOWATER'S & LLOYDS SALES COMPANY LTD

Authorised		Issued
300,000	Cum. Pref Shares	——
200,000	8% Part. Pref. Ord. Shares	£200,000
300,000	Ordinary Shares (IC)	£300,000
£800,000		£500,000

THE EDWARD LLOYD INVESTMENT CO. LTD

Authorised		Issued
£2,000,000	5% Red. Cum. Pref. Stock	£2,000,000
£2,000,000	Ordinary Stock (IC)	£2,000,000
£4,000,000		£4,000,000

54%   46%

BOWATER'S MERSEY PAPER MILLS LTD

3½% First Mortage Deb. Stock £800,00

Authorised		Issued
£500,000	5½% Cum Pref. Stock	£500,000
£650,000	Ordinary Stock (IC)	£650,000
850,000	Shares of £1 each	——
£2,000,000		£1,150,000

EDWARD LLOYD LTD

Authorised		Issued
£1,200,000	7% Cum. Pref. Stock	£1,200,000
£1,000,000	5½% 2nd Cum. Pref. Stock	£1,000,000
£1,600,000	Ordinary Stock (IC)	£1,600,000
£3,800,000		£3,800,000

50%   50%

AKTIEBOLAGET UMEA TRAMASSEFABRIKER

3½% Mortgage Bonds	Sw. Kr. 1,500,000
4½% Gtd. Deb. Loan	Sw. Kr. 2,000,000
	Sw. Kr. 3,500,000

Authorised & Issued (IC)
20,000 Shares of Kr 100   Sw. Kr. 2,000,000

LLOYD BOARDS LTD
Authorised & Issued
10,000 Ord. Shares (IC) £10,000

BOWATERS & LLOYDS SALES LTD (AUSTRALIA)

Authorised		Issued
10,000	7% Pref. Shares	——
30,000	Ord. Shares (IC)	£30,000
£40,000		£30,000

60%

BOWATER LLOYD (SA) PTY LTD
Authorised & Issued
1,000 Shares of SA £1 each (IC) SA £1000

AKTIEBOLAGET SCHARINS SKOGSFORVALTNING
Authorised & Issued
50 Shares of Sw. Kr. 100 each (IC) { Sw. Kr. 3,000 / 2,000
Sw. Kr. 5,000

66⅔%

BOWATER-LLOYD LTD THE ST JOHN'S COMPANY

Authorised	Issued
$100,000 in shares of $100 each (IC)	$400

THE BOWATER PAPER INC. NEW YORK
200 shares (no par value)
(IC) $22,246

THE GREAT HAWKS TOR CHINA CLAYS LTD
Authorised & Issued
12,000 Ord. Shares (IC) { £8,000 / £4,000
£12,000

BOWLOYD TRADING COMPANY LTD
Authorised & Issued
1,000 shares (IC) £1,000

BOWATER'S CANADIAN PAPER CORPORATION LTD
600,000 shares of no par value
Issued 3 shares (IC) $3

RISOR TOMMERSELSKAP A/S
Authorised & Issued
Nr. Kr. 30,000 in 300 shares
of Nr. Kr. 100 each (IC) Nr. Kr. 30,000
(no book value)
Value of interest of Bowater's
Paper Mills Ltd as unsecured
creditors
Nominal £91,700   Cost £50,000

BOWATER'S PAPER MILLS LTD INTEREST IN A/S RISOR TRAEMASSEFABRIKER
Authorised & Issued
Nr. Kr. 150,000 in 300 shares
of Nr. Kr. 500 each   Nr. Kr. 150,000
Value of interest of Bowater's Paper
Mills Ltd as creditors of this company
Nominal £960,800   Cost £30,000

America depressed and war in Europe only too plain on the near horizon.

Eric Bowater had no illusions about the unprosperous state of Corner Brook when Bowaters took over, nor did he hide it from public view. At BPM's Annual Meeting in 1938 he explained that the Corner Brook company, like others in the pulp and paper business in North America, was suffering from renewed depression in its main market, the United States, and Bowaters had no immediate hope of a return on their investment. He was looking entirely towards the future. The company, he said, owned 'one of the most efficient and lowest cost producing mills in North America'. It would give Bowaters 'a means of obtaining . . . an important footing in the United States market, which should prove of great value in the future'. At the same time he repeated his original reason for going to Newfoundland. 'The primary purpose of this acquisition', he said, 'was to provide a means of assuring to all our mills and their customers a permanent source of supplies at reasonable costs.'[46]

The result of this search for security was as dramatic as it was unplanned. A little more than twelve years after the first Bowater newsprint came off the machines at Northfleet, Eric Bowater was able to claim: 'we are now the largest newsprint manufacturers in the world, the total productive capacity of the mills of your company [Bowater's Paper Mills] and its associated mill companies being approximately 800,000 tons per annum'.

The organisation of this business, with mills in Scandinavia, the United Kingdom and Newfoundland, and with an important export trade, especially to Australia, remained rudimentary. Eric Bowater, like many founders of large businesses – the first Lord Leverhulme and Sir Robert Barlow are two who come readily to mind – paid little attention to corporate structure or to what came later to be called 'corporate planning'. He was capable of directing affairs himself, with the help of a small group of advisers, and he preferred to do so, without even the guidance of consolidated accounts. Nevertheless, by the time he addressed BPM's Annual Meeting in 1938, reorganisation of the capital structure of the group was probably under discussion and the substance of the Bowater Paper Corporation was in being, though neither the new capital structure nor the Corporation's organisational framework were created until nine years later.

It is evident that, in covering Bowaters against the risk of being over-charged for raw materials, Eric Bowater ran risks, at least as great, of another kind altogether; the risks inherent in the indebtedness of the Corner Brook company, the uncertain outlook before it and the commitment to capital expenditure at its mills. Since Corner Brook, as soon as it was acquired, became the largest centre of pulp and newsprint production in the Bowater-Lloyd Group these risks were very grave. Risk, nevertheless, is another face of opportunity and the ability to balance one against the other and, if the balance seems favourable, to accept the risk and make the opportunity pay is what distinguishes a creative businessman from a competent manager. Eric Bowater, as he explained at the 1938 General Meeting, struck the balance and took the risk but, before Bowaters had a chance to develop the opportunity, the situation was entirely changed by the outbreak of war.

CHAPTER NINE

War and paper control
1939–1945

The outbreak of war in 1939 took no one by surprise. Moreover, at the upper levels of politics, the civil service and business the experience of organising war production was fresh in many minds, so that the mistake was not made, as it had been in 1914, of assuming that Great Britain could fight Germany abroad while, at home, people carried on 'business as usual'. On the contrary, during the last five years or so of peace, preparations were made for bringing the productive resources of the country under central control, with the ironic result that, during the first months of the war, Neville Chamberlain's National Government, in which Conservative influence was predominant, presided over the early stages of building a full-sized working model of the controlled economy of a socialist state, designed not for socialist purposes but for military victory. The framework thus set up turned out to be well-built, durable and adaptable, much more so than anyone at the beginning can have imagined. Many of the wartime controls, including the control of newsprint, lasted well into the 1950s. Exchange Control, perhaps the most imposing edifice of them all, was not torn down until the autumn of 1979, forty years after it had been set up.

Edith Summerskill is reported to have said: 'Priorities are the language of socialism.' She might equally have applied the phrase to the planning of war production, for the central problem was to arrange demands on a descending scale of urgency, especially where shipping space was required for meeting them. Many products, such as ice cream, silk stockings and motor cars for civilians, disappeared altogether from the market but, since news and its discussion were almost as essential to the war effort as weapons and munitions, newsprint or the materials for making it had to be brought into the country in whatever quantities the general scheme of priorities would allow.

For Bowaters, with their prosperity dependent on papermaking machines which could only operate profitably at or near their full capacity, it was of the greatest importance that pulp for making newsprint should be imported rather than newsprint itself. Moreover, on national grounds, a good case could be made out, as Sir Andrew Duncan, Minister of Supply, explained to Oliver Lyttelton, Minister of Production, in 1942, when a proposal for reduced imports was being discussed: 'it is most desirable that the reduced imports should come entirely in the form of wood pulp and not newsprint. With the addition of home produced materials, the same tonnage of imported pulp can be made to go half as far again as imported newsprint.'[1]

The newspaper owners in Great Britain, however, did not see matters in this light, nor did the Canadian newsprint producers. The newspaper owners had no wish to see the British makers of newsprint in the monopoly position which the policy of importing pulp in preference to newsprint would give them and the Canadian newsprint firms, naturally, were reluctant to lose business. Neither of these arguments touched on the economics of shipping space, which was the central matter in issue, but their proponents were too powerful politically to be ignored.

Control of paper came into effect on 2 September 1939, the day before Great Britain declared war on Germany. As with all branches of industrial control, administrators were appointed from the businesses affected and the regulations were enforced so far as possible by persuasion rather than compulsion. The Paper Controller was A. Ralph Reed (1884–1954, knighted 1945), Chairman of Albert E. Reed Ltd, and the Director of Newsprint, initially, was Earle C. Duffin of Bowaters. Reed certainly and Duffin probably had worked with officials of the Board of Trade, before the war, in planning the machinery of control. 'The plan of operation', wrote H. J. Gray of the Board of Trade, 'envisaged an immediate control of raw materials, particularly where these were imported, to be followed by a rationalised control of paper production and ultimately a detailed control of the delivery of paper for all purposes.'[2]

By May 1940 the system of control was fully developed. Manufacturers of newsprint and other grades of paper were licensed, for periods of four months at a time, to supply their products in quantities expressed as percentages of the quantities used for the same purposes in a basic period which, for newsprint, was the twelve months ending 21 August 1939.[3] When licensing started, the quantity permitted was 60 per cent of the 1939 figure.

Control had no sooner been established, in the autumn of 1939, than dissension broke out over the question of importing pulp or paper. Eric Bowater, at BPM's Annual Meeting in 1939, complained of 'the unrestricted import of newsprint' and, in February 1940, he explained his views to Frater Taylor who, in turn, reported them to E. H. D. Skinner at the Bank of England.[4] Bowater put the import of newsprint in normal times at 400,000 tons out of a total consumption of about 1.3m and he said that, although consumption had been cut, since war had broken out, to a rate of about 650,000 tons, the owners of newspapers – he mentioned especially the *Express,* the *Mail* and the *Chronicle* – were still seeking to import 300,000 tons, which would cut the total output of mills in the United Kingdom to 350,000 tons, or about 40 per cent of their capacity. 'A more uneconomic operation', Frater Taylor observed, 'could hardly be conceived.' As a matter of fact it could be and very shortly was, but that was not apparent in the unreal atmosphere of early 1940. Eric Bowater considered that the lowest figure for economic operation of newsprint mills would be 70 per cent of capacity but, by way of insurance 'in case anything should happen to the English newsprint mills', he was willing to countenance the import of 140,000 tons or one-fifth of total requirements. From the point of view of the public interest, as distinct from his private interest as a newsprint manufacturer, the core of his case was: 'not only are [imported raw materials] less costly involving substantially less foreign exchange but as opposed to newsprint they are space saving when it comes to the use of ships'.

Eric Bowater was evidently repeating the official policy of the Paper Control authorities for, at a meeting with the newspapers on 10 January 1940, Earle Duffin proposed to limit newsprint imports in 1940 to 150,000 tons in order to help the mills in the United Kingdom. Of that total, 80,000 tons were to come from the mills at Grand Falls in Newfoundland, leaving 70,000 tons for Canada and Scandinavia between them, a most unwelcome prospect for Canadian mills which were still only working at about 70 per cent of their capacity. Someone – Beaverbrook? – reported the proposal to Vincent Massey, the Canadian High Commissioner in London. He wrote twice within ten days to the Dominions Secretary, Anthony Eden, saying: 'The proposed restrictions would limit Canadian imports to less than 50,000 tons and might, I fear, eliminate them altogether . . . Indeed, the suggestion now made by the Newsprint Controller would, in effect, go far towards eliminating Canada from the newsprint business in the United Kingdom.'[5]

This was probably the first time during the war that the Canadian High Commissioner intervened in the affairs of the Paper Control on behalf of the Canadian newsprint mills. It was not the last.[6]

Always behind the newspaper owners, demanding imports of newsprint rather than pulp, stood the representative of the Government of Canada, and Canadian goodwill was vastly valuable to the Government of the United Kingdom. Against political pressure so powerful, those who wanted to import pulp rather than newsprint could make little headway, no matter how strong their case.

Suddenly, in April 1940, the arguments about newsprint supplies were interrupted by events. The Germans conquered Norway and blocked all trade between Scandinavia and Great Britain. There would be neither wood pulp nor newsprint from that direction until Germany was beaten. British newsprint makers were denied their most important supplies of raw materials; British newspapers, comparatively small but useful supplies of newsprint. All future imports of both commodities would have to make the long, dangerous passage across the North Atlantic and the competition for shipping space, both between pulp and newsprint and between these and other imports, would be intense.

The newspaper owners understood very well what the defeat of Norway meant to them. Their response was remarkable. On the initiative of Lord Kemsley and Lord Beaverbrook they proposed to the Government that they should take the rationing of newsprint into their own hands. Such was their weight in public affairs that the Government, partly no doubt through preoccupation with the disastrous turn of events in the war, readily accepted their proposal. To put it into effect, the Newsprint Supply Co., a private company which did not seek to make profits, was incorporated in May 1940, a few weeks only after Kemsley and Beaverbrook had launched their scheme.

Lord Camrose, in 1947, was very positive about the objects of the Newsprint Supply Co. 'They were two in number: (i) to secure as large a supply of newsprint as war conditions permitted; (ii) to distribute that supply on a fair and orderly basis to all the newspapers of the country.' Lord Layton and F. P. Bishop, giving evidence to the Royal Commission on the Press in 1948, added: 'the proprietors of the larger newspaper companies and the representatives of the newspaper societies decided . . . to act upon the principle that no single newspaper, however small, should be permitted to perish through inability to secure its fair share of the limited supplies of newsprint'.[7]

There were two ways of serving these purposes: to import wood pulp for conversion at mills in the United Kingdom and to import newsprint. The NSC was wholly dedicated to the second. 'The company', said Layton and Bishop, 'became directly responsible

only for imports of newsprint. Home manufacture continued under
the control of the Government.' The company bought the output of
the British mills but its preferred source of supply was in North
America and it entered at once into a close relationship with the
International Paper Co. Probably at Beaverbrook's instance, International Paper lent George Goyder (p. 101 above) to the NSC for
the duration of the war and paid his salary. It can hardly be
supposed that the newsprint makers of the United Kingdom took
kindly to the appointment of an employee of their most powerful
competitor to such an influential position and it may not be a matter
of chance that, in October 1940, E. C. Duffin left his appointment
with the Paper Control and went back to Bowaters.[8]

No attempt was made, in founding, staffing, or running the NSC,
to allow for the interests of the home newsprint manufacturers.
Apart from Goyder, the most energetic of the senior members of the
staff of the Newsprint Supply Co. was Stanley Bell, who held his
appointment in parallel with his normal duties as General Manager
of Associated Newspapers. The company's policy towards the
home manufacturers, indeed, amounted almost to open hostility, or
so it appeared to Eric Bowater. Speaking to the BPM Board in
October 1940 of the newspaper proprietors' 'considerable pressure
on the Government' in favour of their demands for imported newsprint he said: 'Having regard to the existing stocks of newsprint
. . . and the available production of Mills in the United Kingdom,
this quantity [325,000 tons during the remainder of 1940] must
be considered excessive in relation to consumption and an unwar-
ranted employment of Dollar exchange.' Later he referred to 'the
exclusion of home produced paper', adding 'ships and dollars have
been and are being made available to a greater extent than would be
necessary if corresponding facilities were granted to the Mills in this
country to import pulpwood and other raw materials, thus enabling
the increase of their operations.'[9] As the war went on his attitude did
not change. He frequently commented bitterly on the policy of
importing newsprint and cutting the production of British mills,
which he saw as a sacrifice of the home newsprint industry to the
interests of the newspaper proprietors and their Canadian suppliers.[10]

The newspaper proprietors' attitude to the newsprint makers
had long been equivocal. They wanted to be sure that there would
be suppliers in the United Kingdom, strong but not too strong and
preferably under their own control; they wanted to be able to play
suppliers off against each other, particularly in the United Kingdom
and North America; they feared any supplier or group of suppliers
gaining a monopoly. This fear was a strong motive in forming NSC

policy. In 1945 Rothermere said as much when, in addressing a meeting of ministers in the caretaker Government, he said: 'if . . . a large dependence were placed on home production of newsprint the newspaper proprietors might . . . be faced by a monopolistic squeeze by suppliers, since 85% of the production in this country was in the hands of two mills only'.[11]

He did not say which mills he meant but one must have belonged to Bowaters. Certainly the growth of Bowaters in 1938 had given grounds for fearing monopoly, which would scarcely have been calmed by Eric Bowater's claim at that time that the group was the largest newsprint firm in the world, with 800,000 tons' productive capacity. He hardly saw himself, however, as threatening his customers – rather, as threatened by them – and his wartime experience played a part in hardening his determination, already forming before the war, to make sure that Bowaters in the future would not be so heavily dependent on newsprint manufacture as they had been in the past.[12]

The long-drawn Battle of the Atlantic, almost lost in 1942, combined with the convoys to Russia to strain British shipping to the uttermost. For the newsprint makers the growing strain was reflected in the falling quantities of paper they were permitted to supply for newspapers which shrank from about half their peacetime size in the early months of war to six pages (for the mass-circulation penny papers) in July 1940, to four in the spring of 1941 and, in March 1942, to the lowest point they reached. For about eighteen months the number of copies printed, as well as the number of pages, was severely restricted and newsprint was being used at about one-fifth of its peace-time rate.[13] Consumption of newsprint per head, 56.3 lb in 1939 – the highest figure in the world – fell in 1942–3 to 11.3 lb.

The quantity of newsprint that Bowaters and other makers were allowed to produce fell even further, proportionately, than the total quantity consumed. From 60 per cent of pre-war production it was cut to 30 per cent, then from 1 June 1940 to 20 per cent and later to $17\frac{1}{2}$.[14] By September 1942 the official view, strongly expressed in October in a Treasury brief to the Chancellor of the Exchequer, was that shipping space was so short that all imports of newsprint should cease at least until the summer of 1943, thus releasing four ships belonging to the Newsprint Supply Co. for other uses. Any imports that were to be permitted should take the form of pulp.[15]

This was a threat to the policy of the Newsprint Supply Co. On its behalf Stanley Bell called on ministers; a deputation of newspaper proprietors met Sir Kingsley Wood, Chancellor of the Exchequer;

Vincent Massey entered into correspondence with C. R. Attlee, Deputy Prime Minister. The final decision showed once again the strength of the NSC–Canadian alliance. Sixteen thousand tons of newsprint were to be imported and home production was to be cut by another 10 per cent, even though Attlee told Massey that it was almost impossible to cut the activity of the home industry any further 'if it is to be kept alive at all'.[16] Nevertheless the cut was made in December 1942, bringing permitted output from news-print mills down to the lowest point it reached – about 15 per cent of output in the 'reference year', that is, the twelve months ending 21 August 1939. At that level it remained until 1 November 1943, when it was raised to $18\frac{1}{2}$ per cent. Bowaters' output in the reference year was 466,643 tons. Fifteen per cent of that figure is 69,996 tons; $18\frac{1}{2}$ per cent, 86,328 tons. The output of most other grades of paper was reduced, also.[17]

Drastic reduction of output, applied to newsprint machines de-signed specifically for mass production, played havoc with costings. Official policy, applied to all industries similarly placed, aimed at concentration into as few production units as possible – a policy understandably unpopular with firms which might be concentrated out of existence or whose post-war prosperity would be endangered.[18] Bowaters, with thirteen machines, could quite easily have provided all the newsprint used in the United Kingdom be-tween 1940 and 1945. Instead, in agreement with Government, they shut down the machines at Northfleet in June 1940 and concentrated such production as was permitted at Mersey and Kemsley, both of which were better placed than Northfleet to receive raw materials from North America.[19] By 1945 only three Bowater machines were making newsprint. 'It is a heart-breaking sight', said Eric Bowater, 'to see so much magnificent machinery – before the war the most up-to-date of its kind to be installed anywhere – standing idle for such a long period of time.'[20]

Throughout the war, Eric Bowater grumbled about price control. Wages, fuel and other costs, he said, were continually rising. The price and quality of raw materials, being under Government con-trol, were not open to negotiation. Above all, output was severely restricted. None of these considerations, he thought, was given due weight in arriving at controlled prices and he was particularly aggrieved by the authorities' reluctance to allow adequately (in his view) for depreciation, particularly the depreciation of idle machin-ery, and deferred repairs. 'One is reluctantly driven to the conclu-sion', he said in 1943, 'that newsprint as such is treated differently by the Government from practically any other commodity.'[21]

Controlled prices, until the end of 1941, were calculated to encourage the concentration of production.[22] 'As production declined prices were calculated for a time as if the mill overheads were limited to those which would have existed if production had been concentrated in a limited number of mills.' A formula was devised by which overheads were calculated as if a mill were running at 50 per cent of capacity when, in fact, it was running at 25 per cent or less. 'This', as one of the officials concerned admitted, 'imposed a very severe restriction upon paper prices which was the subject of much protest from the Industry' – not least, from Eric Bowater.

The policy of concentration was 'virtually given up' in 1942 and overheads were somewhat more generously calculated but no allowance was ever made for the depreciation of idle plant, which in the official view would have sent prices far too high. Profits in wartime were suspect, with the gross profiteering of 1914–18 in recent memory, and prices were calculated accordingly, with an eye to what the man from the Ministry rather than the businessman, such as Eric Bowater, considered reasonable. Even so, prices for home-produced newsprint were consistently higher than for imports from North America – the difference was averaged out, to the buyers, by a system operated by the Newsprint Supply Co.[23] – and at the end of the war the controlled price was three times as high as at the beginning, when even in the Ministry's opinion it had returned too little profit to the makers.

The small quantity of paper they were allowed to make and the prices they were allowed to charge were not the newsprint makers' only wartime complaints. They were obliged to work with unsatisfactory materials. Only 322,917 tons of wood pulp were imported, all from Canada and Newfoundland, in the four years 1941–4, whereas one year's imports, from all sources, in 1939 had amounted to nearly twice as much – 637,878 tons.[24] Imports of pulpwood, for which Bowaters had negotiated so hard in Newfoundland in 1937–8, almost ceased because pulpwood, unlike wood pulp, was an uneconomically bulky cargo and, in any case, such logs as shipping could be found for were required for pit-props. In place of imported materials, newsprint makers had to make do with waste paper and pulp from home-grown timber which needed more preparation than imported timber and yielded less pulp.[25]

The result was poor and the newsprint makers' customers did not like it. They compared it with the paper brought in from North America, by the Newsprint Supply Co., which was still up to peace-time standards. The Chairman of the Newsprint Section of the Paper Makers' Association complained to the Paper Controller:

The quality of the Paper being supplied and the services in the maintenance and assurance of supplies by the Newsprint Supply Company unfortunately form a striking contrast with those which the U.K. Mills are allowed by Government regulation to provide. The position is gravely detrimental to the U.K. mills and will create a severe handicap when normal trading conditions are resumed.

The Paper Controller, himself a maker of newsprint, was sympathetic. In forwarding the complaint to the Ministry of Supply, he elaborated on it. He remarked that George Goyder, of International Paper, managed the NSC's affairs and went on:

The N.S.C. set up has provided Mr Goyder with the entree into every Newspaper establishment in the country where his Company appears as a provider . . . of better paper and cheaper paper than the home mills can provide . . . As a war-time gift to the overseas competitor at the expense of the home producer, this case is probably unique.[26]

The case of the newsprint industry illustrates how thoroughly, ruthlessly and efficiently the British economy was organised for war between 1939 and 1945. It illustrates, too, the degree to which wartime controls relied on goodwill and active help from within the industries controlled. The regulations governing the paper trade were intricate and minutely detailed. They required expert knowledge in their drafting and administration and it was supplied by staff drawn from paper-making firms, just as regulations for other industries were drafted and administered by staff drawn from the firms affected.

The newsprint makers' goodwill was severely strained by the sponsorship activities of the Newsprint Supply Co., which seemed to them to be heavily biased in favour of their customers and their competitors. No doubt, under appallingly difficult conditions, the NSC was 'of inestimable value to the newspapers of the country'. That was Lord Camrose's opinion.[27] Eric Bowater might have agreed but not in the same tone of voice.

In 1939, Bowaters in the United Kingdom had a newsprint business or they had nothing. In the twelve months ending 21 August 1939 they made 99,070 tons of other grades of paper but that only amounted to 17.5 per cent of their output in the United Kingdom, and all but 12,000 tons of mechanical printing paper was made at Sittingbourne, which could have been closed down without doing much damage, if any, to the group as a whole. With newsprint gone, by contrast, what else was there to do?

Principally, the making of containers for war stores, chiefly gun ammunition, from kraft liner board produced at Sittingbourne. The first contract, for containers for 4.5-inch shells, was made in the summer of 1938 and, by the summer of 1945, Bowaters had made 10,542,577 containers and other items from kraft liner board, including 982,270 containers for 3.7-inch anti-aircraft shells, 8,324,612 for 40 mm Bofors ammunition and 42,599 'Jettison Fuel Tanks'.[28]

These tanks, holding forty-five or ninety gallons, represented an entirely new use for paper in which it was required to stand a strain of 9G. They were fitted chiefly to American fighter aircraft escorting bombers and they were jettisoned when they were empty. Most of the development work was done by Bowaters but the tanks were built by Bowaters and nine other firms, on contracts handled by Bowaters & Lloyds Sales Co., and altogether 7,995 forty-five-gallon tanks and 253,432 ninety-gallon tanks were supplied.

In the first months of the war, with the agreement of the authorities, Bowaters began preparing to increase their output of kraft by modifying No. 4 machine at Mersey to make it. After the invasion of Norway, the same authorities decided that they could import similar material almost as cheaply and that the import of the pulp required for making kraft was a wasteful use of shipping space. They therefore decided not to import so much, with the effect, said Eric Bowater, of denying Bowaters the means of operating plant which they had been encouraged to install. Bowaters adapted No. 4 machine to make a product 'in line with our Long-Term plans', toilet tissue,[29] which it did until 1949.

At all Bowaters' paper mills there were well-equipped engineering shops and highly skilled maintenance men. At Northfleet, where papermaking ceased entirely and, to a smaller extent, in other mills, maintenance staff and their machine-tools were diverted to work on gun-carriages and mountings, on gun barrels, on other parts of guns and on an assortment of other military hardware. The work had nothing to do with the firm's peace-time business but it helped to make good the missing newsprint profits and, perhaps more important, it kept the maintenance staff together.[30]

Such was the fear of aerial bombardment in 1939, and so shattering were its effects expected to be, that in Bowaters and other large businesses it was assumed that, in wartime, control from London would be unworkable and plans were made for decentralisation and setting up temporary head offices elsewhere. In Bowaters' case, startled secretaries and clerical staff found themselves directed not only to work but to live at very close quarters with members of the

Northfleet in wartime. Production line of gun-carriages between two idle paper machines.

Board and the Chairman himself at the Chairman's house, Dene Place, at West Horsley in Surrey.

London did not become uninhabitable and the carrier pigeons which were intended to maintain communications between Dene Place, Northfleet and Sittingbourne never flew in earnest. Nevertheless, unlike many businesses, Bowaters did not move their head office back to London during the war. Until 1945 most of it remained at Horsley, congestion at Dene Place being relieved, after a few months, by the purchase of other property nearby.[31]

War, as will by now be apparent, distorted Bowaters' business almost beyond recognition. While the war lasted, the group was the helpless prisoner of Government, with its position as the major supplier of newsprint to the British Press gravely threatened and Eric Bowater's plans for building a self-sufficient combine, bridging the Atlantic, indefinitely delayed. Eric Bowater himself was summoned into the Ministry of Aircraft Production by Beaverbrook in 1940 and did not emerge until 1945, having been knighted for his services in 1944. He remained Chairman of Bowater's Paper Mills and the fact that he could thus divide his energies between his business and the Government service indicates the low level of activity to which Bowaters in wartime were reduced.

The effect of the war on Bowaters' profits (Appendix II, Table 1) was less disastrous than might have been expected. There was even a spectacular leap in 1940, thanks to Lloyds' earnings from paper, other than newsprint, which was required for the war effort and for which, early on, prices were favourable. Profits dropped when restrictions were at their tightest, but by 1946 they had been rising strongly for three years.

Dividend policy, between 1937 and the formation of the Bowater Paper Corporation in 1947, was extremely cautious, the whole emphasis being on the need to build reserves against the uncertainties of the times. During the whole period Bowater's Paper Mills, the holding company of the group, paid no Ordinary dividend, no doubt largely as a result of the heavy fixed charges for which BPM were directly or indirectly responsible and which were rising rather than falling as time went on. Nor was it only the Ordinary dividends that were passed. For three-and-a-half years – that is, for the second half of 1939 and for the whole of 1940, 1941 and 1942 – no dividends were paid on any of the various classes of Preference shares issued by the Bowater-Lloyd companies in the United Kingdom, as shown in Table 18.

The reason for not paying these dividends as they fell due was not lack of money. On the contrary, in each year when the dividends were not paid, equivalent sums were credited to a dividend reserve

TABLE 18. *Bowater-Lloyd UK companies Preference capital, 1939–42*

Company	Preference shares	Sum required for dividend before tax £
Bowater's Paper Mills	£800,000 in 6½ per cent £1 Cum. Pref. shares	52,000
	£1,000,000 in 7½ per cent £1 Cum. Part. Pref. shares	75,000
Bowater's Mersey Paper Mills	£500,000 in 5½ per cent £1 Cum. Pref. shares	27,500
Edward Lloyd Ltd	£1,200,000 in 7 per cent £1 Cum. Pref. shares	84,000
	£1,000,000 in 5½ per cent £1 Cum. Pref. shares	55,000
Edward Lloyd Investment Co. Ltd	£2,000,000 in 5 per cent £1 Red. Cum. Pref. shares	100,000
Total		393,500
Bowater & Lloyds Sales Co. Ltd	£200,000 in 8 per cent £1 Part. Pref. Ord. shares	16,000[a]

[a] This dividend was always paid.

or carried forward, so that payment was deferred. The reason for deferment, Eric Bowater explained at BPM's Annual Meeting in 1939, was

to provide the substantial additional amounts of cash required to meet the greatly enhanced and rising cost of freights, insurances, raw materials, and of the many other commodities we use, and the further demands upon our resources in the form of contingencies that may be brought about by war conditions and that will almost certainly arise from time to time.

To that rather ponderous exposition he added, in the following year, the necessity of keeping 'the liquid resources of the business . . . intact' so that the directors might be 'in a position, upon the resumption of normal trading conditions, to take proper advantage of the opportunities that should then present themselves'.

The decision to defer payment of Preference dividends, when first announced, had a good press. 'What is abundantly clear', said *The Times*, 'is that the directors . . . were only acting with common sense prudence . . . when it came to deciding dividend policy.' *The Financial Times* and *The Economist* both broadly agreed.[32] What the shareholders thought is nowhere recorded. They seem to have been remarkably patient, even though Eric Bowater admitted that 'in some cases even hardship . . . might arise' but, by the end of 1942, 'he was aware that there was a feeling in some quarters that the time had arrived when steps should be taken to deal with the situation'.[33]

It took a long time. Proposals for funding the arrears ran into difficulties and perhaps into opposition.[34] Payment in cash began in September 1943 and for most of the companies took three years, until September 1946, to complete. For one, Edward Lloyd Investment, it was still not complete – indeed, not begun – until the shares were redeemed in June 1947, when seven-and-a-half years' arrears fell due for settlement. 'As you know', wrote Inston to Eric Bowater in 1946, 'correspondence from E.L.I. Preference Shareholders has made it abundantly clear that quite a considerable number of them do not understand even the present position . . . '[35]

What they did not understand seems to have been complicated terms for payment. Payment of the other deferred dividends was simpler and quicker, but those to whom it was due nevertheless had no choice but to stand out of the whole or part of their money, which may have been a greater or less part of their income, for six-and-a-half years. When all allowances have been made for Bowaters' wartime difficulties, which were considerable, this method of dealing with them seems both high-handed and long-drawn-out, showing Eric Bowater at his most arbitrarily autocratic. The original decision in the uncertainties of 1939 was no doubt justifiable, and perhaps its continuance when the heavens seemed to be falling in 1940, but was it necessary to go on building up the reserves in this way for two more years after that? The suspicion is not easily dispelled that a measure which began as a prudent precaution against unforeseeable contingencies became all too easily a cheap and convenient way of providing cash for the current needs of the business.

Bowaters' wartime experience at home was part of the experience of wartime England – England in its last phase, as it now seems though it was not obvious at the time, as a great imperial power. Bombs fell on Northfleet; on Kemsley mill and village; on the tug *Sirdar* which was lost with her crew of three; on Bowaters' wharves and offices in London. Men went away to the war and labour became extremely scarce. Women came to the mills, especially Sittingbourne, in unprecedentedly large numbers. All kinds of stores and replacements became difficult or impossible to come by. Black-out, make-do-and-mend, rationing, fire-watching, ARP, the Home Guard, became part of the pattern of everyday life. The national spirit reached a high point of exaltation and unity in 1940, then fell into increasing dreariness and strain until news of victories began to come through: victory in North Africa, in Italy, in Western Europe, in Burma; victory, in the spring and summer of 1945, on all fronts and in all theatres of war. Then, with a new Government, the nation turned with relief and with high expectation from the bleakness of the thirties and the violence of the early forties to the construction, it was hoped, of a new order of welfare and equal opportunity for all.

CHAPTER TEN

The wider outlook
1938–1947

10.1 THE WESTERN HORIZON

By taking over the mill at Corner Brook in 1938, Bowaters linked themselves as firmly to the United States' economy as to the economy of the United Kingdom and, in 1945, the contrast between the two was profound. The United States were stronger at the end of the war than at the beginning; the United Kingdom, weaker. Moreover, the contrast was psychological as well as material.

The American nation – that is, the inhabitants of the United States – emerged from the Second World War not only physically unscathed, apart from relatively minor casualties, but psychologically exalted, bursting with power, pride and self-confidence. They could justifiably claim to have propelled the Western allies to victory and perhaps the Russians, too. They had no doubt that 'the American way of life' was the most desirable in the world, morally as well as materially, and they zealously propagated its blessings amongst those nations not yet fortunate enough to enjoy them, notably in Japan and Western Europe. In Western Europe, the United States were regarded with mingled envy and admiration. American power and plenty, in the bleakness of the late forties, seemed fabulous and American political dominance and military protection, in the face of the growing threat from the East, were readily accepted.

The United Kingdom, on the other hand, suffered wartime damage and losses, and the population suffered privation and nervous strain which, though slight in comparison with parallel damage, losses and hardship in Germany, Japan, Russia and the countries of occupied Europe, were nevertheless far more severe than anything the Americans, as a nation, were required to undergo. Moreover, there were practically no reserves left, either of material supplies or of money – especially dollars – with which to buy supplies from abroad, for post-war reconstruction. The incoming Labour Government, therefore, faced with massive demands for imports of all kinds, including food, was immediately bedevilled with the intractable problem of the balance of payments. Ministers, whether they liked it or not (and some uncharitable people thought some ministers did rather like it), found themselves obliged to prolong and even intensify wartime regulations for far longer than anyone expected. The rationing of food, for instance, went on for nine years after the war had ended.

The years of austerity brought no real hardship and, indeed, with full employment and relatively high wages many people were better off than before the war. On the other hand, there was a marked absence of red meat and other desirable foods, most goods of high quality seemed to be made for export only and such goods as did appear on the home market were apt to be of 'utility' design – serviceable but plain – or to be labelled 'sub-standard' or 'export reject'. Rationing, regulations, restrictions, controls and exhortations from ministers to export or die seemed to penetrate every nook and cranny of the national life. This was hardly what the nation had looked forward to as the fruit of victory. It felt far more like the aftermath of defeat, as also did the mounting evidence of the collapse of British power in the world. Just at the time, therefore, when American self-confidence was flowing strongly, British self-confidence was running away into the sand.

The Anglo-American contrast showed up starkly in the differing conditions of business in the newsprint industry on either side of the Atlantic. On one side, the bounding exuberance of the American mood showed itself in a galloping demand for more and larger newspapers and there was nothing to stop the newspaper owners from buying as much paper as they needed from producers at home or abroad. On the other side, in the United Kingdom, there was likewise a rising demand for newspapers but supply of newsprint was frustrated by the weakness of the economy. There was no adequate source of raw materials at home and lack of dollars prevented the import either of raw materials or of newsprint in peace-time as effectively as imports had been prevented in war by lack of ships. In 1950 the consumption of newsprint in the United States was 69 per cent greater than in 1939. In the United Kingdom it was 46 per cent less.[1]

Wartime and post-war conditions in the United Kingdom, where Eric Bowater bitterly resented the restrictions imposed on the newsprint industry, added force to his resolve to bring into Bowaters' business some counter-weight to newsprint. The first steps in that direction were taken in 1944 (Chapter 10.2). For newsprint, much the most brilliant prospects in the world lay in the United States: enormously attractive to Eric Bowater's adventurous temperament, though to those of his colleagues who did not share it the glitter of the opportunity was dimmed by the shadow of the attendant risks, which were heavy. We must trace the gathering momentum of Bowaters' assault on the American market, from their base at Corner Brook, through the years of war and just afterwards.

As soon as Bowaters were established at Corner Brook, they began to build a North American organisation in parallel with their organisation in the United Kingdom but separate from it. The two sides of the Bowater business were joined, administratively, only at the head, through Eric Bowater and his close advisers. The key move in setting up the new organisation, after control of Corner Brook passed to Bowaters, was the revival in 1938 of the dormant New York company, Bowater Paper Co. Inc., to provide a selling organisation for Corner Brook and to build on the Sales Allocation Agreement with the International Paper group (p. 142 above) which ran out at the end of 1940.

In the later development of Bowaters' business, it would be difficult to exaggerate the importance of the revived New York company. It was three-fold. First, there was the primary function of selling Corner Brook's output and getting it firmly established on the American market. Secondly, the New York company lay at the heart of things, financially and commercially, whereas Corner Brook was remote, and in consequence, as Earle Duffin wrote after visiting New York in 1943, the New York company 'really act as Mill Executives in a great many matters' and he instanced a recent occasion when BPC had 'borrowed from the Chase National Bank a substantial sum to loan Corner Brook in order that their bank loan should not exceed the then prescribed limit'.[2] Thirdly, the New York office quickly became a policy-making centre for Bowaters in North America, thus profoundly influencing Bowaters' policy as a whole.

No doubt this second development arose partly from the fact that New York was the obvious place from which to direct the expansion of Bowaters' business in North America. It arose also from the character of August B. Meyer, President of Bowater Paper Co. His association with Bowaters went back to the days when Bowater Paper Co. was the sole selling agent for Corner Brook (p. 36 above). When Corner Brook was taken over by International Paper and the sole agency ceased, Meyer and Duffin tried for a time, at reduced salaries, to build up a business as agents and merchants but, within a couple of years, Duffin went to Bowaters in England,

Meyer to other employment, with the St Maurice Valley Paper Co., and the Bowater Paper Co. became dormant.[3] When it was revived, Meyer came back, took charge[4] and rapidly joined the select band of Eric's close advisers. Perhaps he had never entirely left it.

Just as New York was the gateway to the American newsprint market, so Montreal stood at the centre of the Canadian pulp and paper industry – the world's largest – and gave access to high-grade financial and professional services of the kind which Eric Bowater relied on heavily for the planning and, to some extent, the execution of his business activities. In Montreal, as in London, he had associates of high independent standing who were nevertheless prepared to concern themselves closely with Bowaters' affairs and he greatly valued their judgment and advice. The most distinguished of them, very highly regarded by Eric, was George S. Currie, CMG, DSO, MC (1889–1970), senior partner in the accountancy firm of Mac-Donald Currie & Co. and, from 1942 to 1944, Deputy Minister of National Defence (Army) in the Canadian Government. He was associated with Corner Brook and other Bowater enterprises from 1938 until the mid-sixties.

As travel became easier in the years after the war, Eric Bowater developed a style of management, suited to the Anglo-American nature of the Bowater business as it was then developing, which is reminiscent of nothing so much as the style of government of earlier autocrats: the Norman and Angevin kings of England. Just as they had widely separated dominions, so had he (and both, it might be added, needed to keep an eye on princes of the blood). Just as they were peripatetic, so was he, for he made frequent progresses, usually in spring and autumn, in North America. Just as they had castles for occasional occupation, so had he, for the North American companies provided residences for his use and the use of other distinguished guests in Newfoundland, in Montreal and later in Tennessee and Nova Scotia. Just as where the king went, the government of the country went with him, so where Eric Bowater went, the direction of Bowaters' affairs went with him, acting on one side of the Atlantic as Chairman of Bowaters' parent company in the United Kingdom and on the other as President of the appropriate North American company. Communication was by a constant two-way traffic of cablegrams, the writing of which Eric developed into a highly personal branch of the literary art. He scotched a direct challenge to his authority – the only one of which there is any record – by cablegram from North America (pp. 219–20 below). No doubt King Henry II would have applauded.

Eric Bowater's feelings towards North America were ambivalent.

In private, especially in moments of tension or depression, he would express vehement dislike. On the other hand he had a clear perception of the immense opportunities – and difficulties – of the North American market, and probably the greatest ambition of his life was to overcome the difficulties in order to seize the opportunities.

For Newfoundland, he showed a certain affection. A great deal of work was done on his regular September visits there, but he would entertain friends and the visits had traces of holiday atmosphere – the more so, perhaps, after a house was built at Strawberry Hill, in the early 1950s, which enabled him to withdraw some eight miles from the concentrated attention of the small and isolated community at Corner Brook, entirely dependent for its welfare on Bowaters' mill. He did not enjoy the numerous parties: still less the duty, self-imposed, of making very frank and sometimes severe addresses to the assembled employees. 'I feel so alone', he once wrote from Corner Brook, 'and so utterly frustrated. I am "Sir", I am the *President*, I am a creature apart. The red carpet appears, I must smile, I must utter the "bon mot", I must recall the family. I must Behave!!'[5]

In North America, following the custom of the country, he dropped something of the austerity of manner which overawed subordinates in England. He used Christian names and was altogether less formal than at home, not greatly to the liking of some of those who had to deal with him on both sides of the Atlantic. Why, they felt, should Newfoundlanders, Canadians and Americans be thus favoured?

In the early days of its development, then, from 1938 until the early fifties, Bowaters' North American business rested upon a tripod with one leg planted in the United States, one in Canada and one in Newfoundland. Selling was directed from New York. Financial and other services were provided in Montreal and the Corner Brook Board usually met there. The productive muscle of the enterprise was developed at Corner Brook.

Production at Corner Brook had three main aspects: the cutting of pulpwood, the manufacture of sulphite pulp and the manufacture of newsprint. The cutting of pulpwood was provided for by acquiring rights, in agreement with the Newfoundland Government, over large areas of forest (pp. 146–8 above). The same agreement, given force in Bowater's Newfoundland Act 1938, required Bowaters to increase the productive capacity of the Corner Brook sulphite mill by 30,000 air dry short tons a year.[6] Finance for the extensions, for the construction of No. 6 machine to dry pulp for export, and for working capital were provided partly by a loan from the Bank of Montreal, partly by the issue to Dominion Securities Trust, at $94 per cent, of $2.5m 5 per cent First Mortgage Bonds, and the enlarged mill was complete by the end of March 1941.[7] The Act also contemplated an extra 30,000 tons of newsprint capacity at Corner Brook but, before that could be provided, the USA was pitchforked into war by the Japanese attack on Pearl Harbor in December 1941.

In the United States the effect of the war on newspapers and the newsprint industry, as on consumer goods industries generally, was trifling by comparison with its effects on similar industries in the United Kingdom. American consumption of newsprint had been rising strongly since 1938 and in 1941 it reached the record figure, up to that time, of 3.9 million short tons. Then it dropped by 17 per cent to 3.2 million tons in 1944.[8] That was its lowest point, at which the average American Sunday paper had only about seventy pages and daily papers were making do with less than thirty,[9] against a comparable British figure of four. Nevertheless, price control and shipping regulations both interfered disconcertingly with Corner Brook's established pattern of business.

This pattern was very different from the pattern of Bowaters' business in the United Kingdom, dominated by contracts with a few large customers based on two main centres, London and Manchester. Contracts with owners of local newspapers, scattered about the country, were considerably less important. The USA, on the contrary, was – and is – a country of local newspapers, without mass-circulation 'nationals', so that Corner Brook and other North American newsprint makers relied less on large contracts with a few customers, geographically concentrated, and more on small or smallish contracts with a great many customers, widely dispersed. Thus in 1941, under the Sales Allocation Agreement with International Paper, Corner Brook had sixty-four contracts for 70,374 short tons of newsprint, averaging 1,099 tons each and running from 12,000 tons for the New York *World Telegram* down to 5 for *New Smyrna Beach News*. International Paper, with 435 contracts for 336,338 tons, showed an even lower average – 773 – because 381 of the contracts were for less than 1,000 tons each, though there were four contracts for more than 20,000 tons each and the largest, with the News Syndicate Co. Inc. of New York, was for 45,000 tons.[10]

After Pearl Harbor the newsprint industry in the USA, like the newsprint industry in the United Kingdom, was brought under Government control. The Corner Brook company found its business squeezed between the activities of the Office of Price

Administration, which fixed the price of newsprint, and those of the War Shipping Administration, which determined the cargoes that might be carried and the rates charged for carrying them. Corner Brook was totally dependent on sea transport and a good deal of its output went to ports south of New York. Before the war, 'ocean freights from Newfoundland to all port cities along the Atlantic and even into the Gulf of Mexico, were about the same, and . . . a uniform price for all so-called port cities . . . resulted in a mill net . . . equal to the mill net on shipments to New York City and other northern ports'. During the war, the War Shipping Administration forbade the shipping of newsprint to any United States ports except those on the Northern Atlantic and the Great Lakes.[11]

In 1957, Meyer described the result to a Senate committee:

During the war period . . ., under O.P.A. regulations, the price of news-print in Florida was held down to, I believe, $42 a ton . . . We had to get ships from the War Shipping Administration who charged us prices that were simply incredible. In other words, before the war it cost us $2 a ton to ship to Florida, ocean freight. And suddenly when we got ships from the War Shipping Administration it cost us $35 a ton to ship paper to New York and we couldn't go south of New York. We had to rail that paper to Florida.

So we were selling paper in Florida at less than the freight rate from Newfoundland to Florida.[12]

In March 1943, Meyer was expecting Corner Brook to ship about 110,000 tons of newsprint to the USA during the year, of which 65,000 tons would go to the South. He contemplated sending it partly by way of the Great Lakes, partly by way of ports on the North Atlantic seaboard. With production, at that time, at 60 per cent of the mill's capacity, he estimated the cost at $31.99 a ton, giving a loss of $2.01 on a mill net price of $29.98. How much, if any, was actually shipped in this way is uncertain, since negotia-tions were going on at the time for transferring the orders to mills in Canada in exchange for groundwood to be manufactured at Corner Brook, on the Canadian mills' account, on orders from the Ministry of Supply in England.[13] Such were the convolutions introduced into the North American newsprint industry as a side-effect of Government control in the United States and the United Kingdom.

Some on either side of the Atlantic, including Noel Bowater, doubted whether it was worth while holding the Southern business at a loss, or at all. Exports to Australia and New Zealand, said Noel, would always be more profitable.[14] Meyer defended his policy passionately. When the question of withdrawing from the South was raised in 1943,

> Mr Meyer pointed out vigorously the dire results to the future business of the company should we lose our business in the south. In peace-time these contracts are very valuable and, if the business were lost now, it would be taken away from us by other mills on long-term contracts which would be most difficult to recover.

He hung on. As he put it to the Senate committee in 1957: 'We could have cancelled those contracts or refused to renew them, but those people had stuck with us for years and we gave our paper away and lost money on our freight for years in order to take care of those people.'[15] In such opinions so strongly held by one of Eric Bowater's closest advisers there were the makings of controversy over the direction to be taken by Bowaters' post-war expansion.

The figures in Table 19 summarise Corner Brook's wartime

TABLE 19. *Bowater's Newfoundland Pulp & Paper Mills, shipments, sales and income, 1938–45*

Year to 31 Dec.	Tonnage shipped			Net sales $Can.000	Net income[b] $Can.000	Sterling equivalent[c] £000
	Newsprint	Sulphite pulp	Misc. products[a]			
1938	113,200			4,997	−483	−98
1939	151,800	2,341		7,191	342	74
1940	202,800	7,870	1,053	12,150	1,010	227
1941	197,200	25,143	8,111	12,615	942	212
1942	175,100	43,849	6,241	12,254	436	98
1943	138,400	26,976	20,661	9,822	249	56
1944	161,000	12,411	21,463	10,727	712	160
1945[d]	153,252	11,154	3,540	11,839	1,030	231

[a] Groundwood and sulphite tailings, offcuts, groundwood pulp, mechanical pulp, 'specialities'.

[b] 'Net income' = operating profit plus other income, less depreciation and depletion, bond interest and taxes.

[c] Calculated at the following rates:

$Can. to £1

1938	4.917
1939	4.608
1940–4	4.450

Source: *The British Economy – Key Statistics 1900–1966*, Times Newspapers n.d., Table L.

[d] Nine months to 30 September.

Source: Coverdale & Colpitts, 'Report on Bowaters Southern Paper Corporation', 1 October 1951, Exhibit 1 (adapted).

experience. Like many other mills in North America, it was driven
into low production and losses in 1938 but, by the time the USA was
brought into the war, sales and profitability were both responding
to the rising American consumption of newsprint. Then during the
war demand for newsprint dropped, prices were controlled, costs
rose, particularly in Bowaters' Southern trade, and profits ran low.
Pulpwood was short because woods labour was scarce and the
output of sulphite pulp was cut back by shutting a machine down
for the last quarter of 1943 and, in 1944, producing no more than
was required to satisfy a Ministry of Supply contract for about
12,300 short tons.[16]

Throughout the period, as Table 20 shows, interest charges bore
heavily on profits. They arose partly from mortgage bonds and
debentures, partly from the loan arranged with the Bank of
Montreal when the extension to the sulphite mill was being planned
(pp. 174–5 above). As profits sank and the loan mounted, Eric
Bowater became anxious. In February 1943, when the Corner Brook
Board was meeting, as it usually did, in Montreal (this time, at the Ritz-
Carlton Hotel), he wrote to G. S. Currie, then Chairman, and had
the text of the letter cabled to Lewin so that Currie could read it to
the directors. 'Although', said Eric,

the company has continued hitherto to operate on a profitable basis there
has nevertheless during the past year been a substantial increase in the
bank loan from $1½m. at 31st December 1941 to over $2m. at 31st
December 1942 although it had been expected that profits during the past
two years would have by now enabled its reduction to smaller proportions. It may be that during the coming period the company's operations

TABLE 20. *Bowater's Newfoundland Pulp & Paper Mills, income
and interest charges, 1938–44 ($Can.000)*

	Operating profit	Other income	Depreciation and depletion	Interest	Tax	Net income
1938	1,424	1	634	1,124	150	−483
1939	2,061	262	701	1,130	150	342
1940	3,099	50	730	1,259	150	1,010
1941	2,897	362	879	1,288	150	942
1942	1,930	827	884	1,287	150	436
1943	1,676	711	848	1,140	150	249
1944	1,908	823	843	1,026	150	712

Source: Coverdale & Colpitts, 'Report on Bowaters Southern Paper Corporation',
1 October 1951, Exhibit 1 (adapted).

will be less profitable and in my view it is highly undesirable that the bank loan should approach any further towards its limit of $3½m.'[17]

In this way Eric Bowater, through his appointment as President of the Corner Brook company, governed his empire from afar.

His rule, so far as Corner Brook was concerned, was less than absolute, for he had to take account of the outside interests represented on the Board, namely the Government of Newfoundland, HM Treasury and, from 1938 to 1942, the Bank of England. During those years the Bank, not Bowaters, was the largest shareholder in the Corner Brook company, since it held the entire Preference capital (£2,080,000 nominal), against the £800,000 Ordinary capital held by Bowaters.

It was an uneasy arrangement. The Bank's holding was a relic of the rescue of Armstrong, Whitworth (Chapter 3.4 above), and Montagu Norman would have been very glad to see Bowaters take it off the Bank's hands when they bought the Corner Brook Common stock in 1938. At that time it was impossible, so the Bank reluctantly held on, the Governor complaining of the lack of dividends. In August or September 1941, he began to look again at the possibility of selling the shares to Bowaters.[18]

The idea would scarcely have been unwelcome to Eric Bowater. Frater Taylor, the Bank's principal representative on the Corner Brook Board, watched Bowaters' policy closely and made his views known, even to the point of pressing for a vote, whenever he disagreed with it, which was often. He was very free with advice, too, on organisation and management, usually with the aim of limiting control from London. Eric Bowater did not welcome independent advice unless he personally had chosen the adviser. He had not chosen Frater Taylor.

In March 1940, apparently at the Bank's suggestion rather than his own, Frater Taylor went to live in Canada. His principal function, barely concealed, was to watch the Bank's interest at Corner Brook and the interests of the Treasury and the Newfoundland Government also, although they both had their own representative directors on the Corner Brook Board.[19] He began to work in concert with the Treasury Director, A. A. Ritchie, who was based in New York, and became, in effect, the Leader of the Opposition, corresponding copiously with the Bank and raising grievance after grievance, including the non-payment of a Preference dividend in 1940 although it had been fully earned. Evidently Eric Bowater was extending to Corner Brook – and to the Bank of England – the dividend policy already in force with the other Bowater companies,

and the Bank's representative did not like it. Taylor and Ritchie
consulted Freshfields, the Bank's London solicitors, who sympath-
ised, saying that, although they did not feel that Ritchie and Taylor
were strongly enough placed to go to law, yet 'we do emphatically
agree' that 'declining to declare a dividend when profits were
available . . . is in direct contravention of the spirit of the arrangement made in 1938 for the extension of the period during which the
preference dividend was to be non-cumulative'.[20] Eric Bowater
remained unmoved. The Bank got no dividend until 1941.

Frater Taylor did not always get the support he may have felt he
deserved. A Treasury official, writing in 1941 of J. H. Penson who
had just left the Corner Brook Board, said: 'Penson's attitude is, I
think, that Bowater's have put so much effort and vitality into this
Company that they should receive the maximum encouragement.'[21]
If that was Frater Taylor's attitude he concealed it quite effectively.
His popularity among the Bowater directors was not high.

Eric Bowater believed in the essential soundness of Corner
Brook. Frater Taylor, Alfred Ritchie and Montagu Norman, it
seems, did not. Frater Taylor, in March 1942, thought Corner
Brook was 'weak owing to heavy fixed charges and a probable
slump in newsprint, especially after the war,' and by June he
thought transport difficulties had made matters worse and that lost
orders would be difficult to make up after the war. If Bowaters, who
by then had been talking to the Bank, made any reasonable offer, he
advised the Governor to accept it. Ritchie observed in May 1942
that in ten years there had been losses at Corner Brook in six years
and profits only in four, of which three had been war years when
everything was abnormal, and that the prospects for 1942 were
anything but bright. The Bank, he thought, should get rid of its
Preference shares. Montagu Norman himself wanted to sell and
even told Frater Taylor that he would be prepared to meet Bowaters
if they could not find the money, presumably meaning that he
would help to find it for them. The Bank, he recalled, had had an
investment in Corner Brook for about twenty years and a dividend
only in one – 1941.[22]

In their judgment on Corner Brook's prospects the eminent
gentlemen at the Bank and the Treasury turned out in the long run
to be wrong and Eric Bowater right. In 1942, however, pessimism in
high places suited Eric very well, for it improved his bargaining
position. In July 1942 Frater Taylor, in the 'Gents' on Waterloo
Station, said to Henry Chisholm, apropos of nothing in particular, 'I
believe Mr Norman would take fifteen shillings.' Chisholm quickly
replied: 'I fear Bowaters would not go beyond twelve-and-six'

and reported this conversation to Eric Bowater and his 'cabinet' (at that time J. H. Keeling, A. G. Allen and W. R. T. ('Boss') Whatmore of Peat, Marwick). Keeling, on Bowaters' behalf, offered the Bank 12s. 6d. a share[23] and a couple of months' 'difficult negotiations' – Skinner's phrase – began.

They ended with a deal in which, apparently as an added inducement to Bowaters, the sale of the shares, for 13s. 9d., was linked with the conversion of £1,750,000 'B' Debentures, guaranteed by the Newfoundland Government, from an interest rate of $5\frac{1}{2}$ per cent to one of $3\frac{1}{2}$ per cent: a conversion which had long been desired by the Treasury and had obvious attractions for the Newfoundland Government also. The reasons why the conversion had never been attempted before are obscure. They seem to have turned on the political undesirability of making it too plain that, as long as government by commission lasted, the United Kingdom would have to stand behind the Government of Newfoundland if it had to honour its guarantee.[24]

The sum required to buy the Bank's Preference shares was £1,430,000. Lloyds Bank was prepared to provide an overdraft but it was not needed. The Bowater companies in the United Kingdom drew the whole amount from their own resources: a remarkable comment on the success of Bowaters' wartime financial policy including the suspension of the Preference dividends. To redeem the $5\frac{1}{2}$ per cent Debenture stock at 105, £1,777,520 was to be provided by the creation and issue of a like amount of new $3\frac{1}{2}$ per cent stock. As an essential part of the agreement for the sale of the Preference shares, the Bank of England undertook to subscribe for £84,600 of the new debenture stock and to underwrite the issue of £1,225,400, using the cash received from the sale of the shares. The Newfoundland Government agreed to underwrite £217,200; Bowaters, £250,000.[25]

When the debenture issue was made, little more than half the stock was taken up, suggesting that the Bank's view of Corner Brook's prospects was more widely shared than Eric Bowater's. By the terms of the underwriting agreement, the Bank was required, in December 1942, to take up about £634,000 stock, Bowaters about £112,000 and the Newfoundland Government about £97,000.[26] On these terms, Bowaters entered into full possession of the Preference share capital of the Corner Brook company and they were well pleased. Mr Governor Norman, on the other hand, seems to have been left with a feeling of slightly puzzled resentment. 'Personally', he told Frater Taylor, 'I think they' – Bowaters – 'could not avoid trying to be sharp – perhaps it's in the blood or in the business

TABLE 21. *Bowater's Newfoundland Pulp & Paper Mills, ship-ments, sales and income, 1946–50*

Year to 30 Dec.	Tonnage shipped			Net sales $Can.000	Net income[b] $Can.000	Sterling equivalent[c] £000
	Newsprint	Sulphite pulp	Misc. products[a]			
1946	195,525	13,704		17,627	1,778	419
1947	193,315	18,130		20,784	3,318	823
1948	202,276	48,628	2,708	25,653	3,617	897
1949	248,178	39,774	421	30,166	3,086	821
1950	276,768	27,700		33,175	2,978	980

[a] *and* [b] As Table 19.
[c] Calculated at the following rates:

$Can. to £1
1946   4.24
1947–8 4.03
1949   3.76
1950   3.04

Sources: as Table 19.

— but I do not count it to them for righteousness much as we all wish to escape from the Newfoundland Company.'[27]

Eighteen months or so after the Bank's escape, Corner Brook's fortunes turned decisively upward. The underlying cause was the consumption of newsprint in the United States, which after its low point in 1944 increased by 1950 by 83 per cent.[28] The full consequences for Bowaters of this strongly rising demand were momentous. They will be discussed in Chapter 11. Here it is only necessary to observe that, from late 1944 onwards, at Eric Bowater's bidding, the General Purposes Committee (p. 189 below) of the BPM Board in London was intermittently considering the possibility of putting in a new machine – No. 7 – at Corner Brook. If a three-roll machine were built, it would add 60,000 tons to Corner Brook's newsprint capacity. A machine of four rolls' width would add 75,000 tons.[29]

The members of the GPC were not enthusiastic but Eric Bowater was and he propelled them unceremoniously in the direction he meant them to go. He founded his optimism, no doubt, on advice from A. B. Meyer and others on the far side of the Atlantic, and particularly, perhaps, on Meyer's confidence, expressed to the Board of the Corner Brook company in 1946, that he could get ten-year contracts for the output of a new machine from 'a few of the largest publishers in the vicinity of New York and Philadelphia'.[30]

The Corner Brook Board, with the cabled encouragement of Eric Bowater, decided on 20 May 1946 to put in a four-roll machine for a total expenditure of not more than $7m.[31] By this time Eric Bowater's mind was turning more and more towards newsprint for Bowaters in North America, further and further from newsprint for Bowaters in the United Kingdom. 'It may well be', he observed to the Comptroller in 1945, 'that, in future, it would be more beneficial from the Group's point of view as a whole to make newsprint at Corner Brook rather than in England.'[32] As time went on, and demand in the United States continued to grow, his ambitions began to run even further and larger than Corner Brook.

By 1946, the Corner Brook company was well set for post-war prosperity. Eric Bowater decided that the opportunity had arrived – 'much sooner than had been anticipated at one time' – of realising part of Bowaters' investment in Corner Brook 'at a substantial profit'. What he had in mind was to sell the shares which in 1946 represented the Preference shares bought from the Bank of England in 1942.[33]

The Bank's shares, in September 1945, had been converted into Common shares and included with the rest of Corner Brook's equity capital, which in total in 1946 had a nominal value of £3m. When the sale was decided upon, £1.5m Common shares were converted into 4½ per cent Cumulative Preference shares which were 'placed' by the London & Yorkshire Trust and Bowaters' brokers at 20s. 6d.

The sale was a vindication of Eric Bowater's confidence in the soundness of the business at Corner Brook. What Montagu Norman said on this occasion is not on record.

10.2 THE ORIGINS OF DIVERSIFICATION AND THE ESTABLISHMENT OF THE BOWATER PAPER CORPORATION

Ten years' growth within the United Kingdom, ten years' growth outside it – that, briefly, is the history of Bowaters' first twenty years as manufacturers. Put another way, the business grew from a merchant firm of moderate size to an international organisation with about £30m of capital employed, in a series of enormous leaps – first, between 1926 and 1936, from Northfleet by way of Mersey to Kemsley and Sittingbourne; then, between 1937 and 1947, from the United Kingdom by way of Scandinavia to Newfoundland and the United States. In 1947, with the publication of consolidated accounts for 1946 (before they were required by law), accurate measurements of the size and spread of the Bowater Organisation were publicly displayed for the first time.

They showed how the geographical spread and balance of the business had altered since the first adventures abroad in 1937–8 for, by 1946, when the net assets were valued at £32.6m, rather more than half – 52 per cent – lay overseas.[34] The Corner Brook company, with about £13.5m capital employed, was described by Eric Bowater as 'the largest and by far the most important of our subsidiary companies'.[35] The second largest concentration of overseas assets would have been at the groundwood pulp mills at Umea in Sweden and a comparatively small proportion at Risor in Norway. There were marketing companies, but no mills, in Australia, South Africa and the United States, and the importance of the Bowater Paper Co.'s marketing effort – 'a remarkable achievement and one I [Eric Bowater] believe to be without precedent in the United States'[36] – needs no emphasis.

The Bowater Organisation was still overwhelmingly in newsprint. Speaking of the time, not far distant, when 'certain extensions now in hand are completed', Eric Bowater gave the total productive capacity of the Organisation as 'almost nine hundred thousand tons of paper, of which some three-quarters of a million tons will be newsprint'. To support that production, Bowaters would be able to provide themselves with 360,000 tons of wood pulp above the quantity consumed at Corner Brook. The only other product he referred to was 20 million square feet of building boards, produced at Kemsley from 'tailings' from the groundwood mill and later from home-grown timber.[37]

He gave the plainest indication, nevertheless, that this pattern of production would be changing, at least in the United Kingdom, where the quantity of newsprint that might be produced (at the time he spoke, equivalent to about 35 per cent of the rated capacity of the newsprint industry) and the price at which it might be sold were still controlled at levels which he considered unreasonably low. In public and in private he complained of the activities of the Paper Control and the Newsprint Supply Co., both of which he accused of bias against Bowaters, and the conviction deepened in his mind that a future in which Bowaters were totally dependent on newsprint was no future for Bowaters.

He was coming to this conclusion in the later thirties, in reaction against the strength of his principal customers' bargaining position.

They, for their part, feared a Bowater monopoly. Bowaters, in taking over Lloyds, acquired the wallboard business and plant for manufacturing kraft, both of which provided them, more or less by accident, with a starting-point for a policy of diversification. No doubt it would have been carried further but for the raw materials crisis of 1937–8 and then the outbreak of war.

In 1942 Bowaters, like a good many other companies, began to pay some attention to post-war planning. Eric Bowater urged his directors to consider, amongst other things, enlarging the production of kraft, kraft liner and wallboards. They might also, he suggested, look at the possibility of making grades of paper, pulp and other products which Bowaters did not then make and they might consider going in for the manufacture of containers and boxes, using plastics either on their own or together with paper and board.[38]

To start with, Eric Bowater did not press his diversification policy on anything like the grand scale of his assaults on the newsprint industry on each side of the Atlantic. There were no negotiations with powerful partners, the Bank of England, Government departments. No ambitious and ingenious financial plans were laid. Instead, an air of caution and secrecy lay about the whole proceeding, quite unlike the flamboyant daring which Eric so often displayed.

Almost certainly this was because Bowaters' early forays away from newsprint were in the direction of box-making for which they already supplied kraft liner and they were nervous of being seen to go into competition with their customers.[39] They therefore preferred to keep their early moves as inconspicuous as possible. Between 1944 and 1947 they equipped themselves in the United Kingdom with three companies, none of more than moderate size, which besides giving them a base for expansion also assured them, under the Paper Control regulations, of being able to carry on operations at whatever level of output was from time to time permitted.

The first of these companies was Acme Corrugated Paper & Box Co. Ltd, a title which accurately indicated how it earned its living. Between 1935 and 1940 Acme had a contract with Edward Lloyd for 75 per cent of its supplies of kraft liner and the firm dealt with W. V. Bowater also, thus illustrating the kind of situation which made Bowaters coy about publicising their entry into box-making. When Bowaters took the business over, for £100,000 in the summer of 1944, they referred to it as 'Boxone' (i.e. Box One) and 'the Chairman . . . explained that for the time being the acquisition . . . is to remain undisclosed for business reasons'.[40]

Acme had a factory on the edge of Croydon Airport. The Ministry of Aircraft Production took it over in 1942 and handed it back in July 1945. Acme's machinery was moved back and something like normal production started. At the end of the year E. Howard and A. H. Davies, who had founded the business on £3,000 capital in 1923, retired. Their successors worked for three or four weeks with the incoming Bowater management and then resigned, though 'they agreed to give every assistance in handing over the business for such a period as was considered necessary'. After that, Acme was steadily assimilated into Bowaters under the name Bowater Fibre Containers Ltd.[41]

In the summer of 1947 Bowaters added two more packaging firms to their collection. One was a small Manchester firm, the Three-Ply Barrel Co., which in spite of its name did not make barrels of three-ply wood but fibre packaging drums, in factories at Coventry and New Mills. Its issued capital of £2,478 in £1 shares cost Bowaters £49,560.[42] R. P. Peters, who had been Chairman since the company was set up in 1934, joined Bowaters and contributed his experience to the development of their packaging activities. The other acquisition, W. J. Maine (1939) Ltd of Bolton, specialised in the manufacture of paper bags and 99 per cent of its 540,000 2s. shares were bought for about £240,000.[43]

To own and supervise the packaging companies in the Bowater Organisation, Associated Bowater Industries was set up in 1947 with A. R. W. Gillham and Weimar Cross as joint General Managers. Day-to-day management, covering production and sales, remained with the operating units but in 1951 a separate division for packaging sales was set up under Weimar Cross.

Another indication of Bowaters' post-war intentions was the setting-up, in 1948, of a company formed to undertake the functions formerly undertaken by the Planning and Development Department and the Research and Technical Division. The new company combined, perhaps a trifle uneasily, the functions usually associated with research and development with the investigation of possible new acquisitions, on which a good deal of its time was spent. Its costs were levied on the operating companies, who for that reason were inclined to watch its activities with close and not over-charitable attention. This is the common lot of central service departments in large organisations and it is a measure of the post-war growth and complexity of Bowaters' business.

Bowaters, like other British companies, were keen to buy technical and marketing knowledge from America: an arrangement which often suited American firms hoping to expand overseas

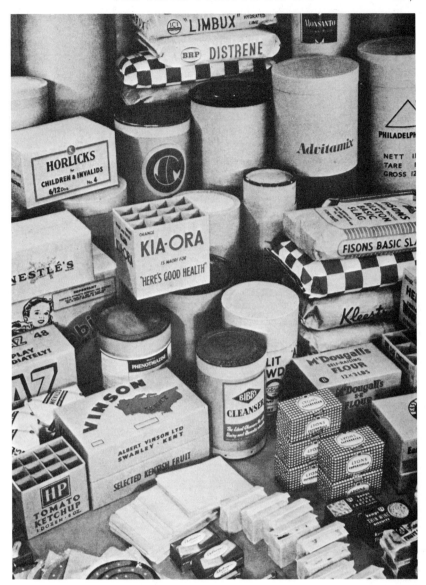

A range of Bowaters packaging products in 1954: corrugated containers from Croydon, multiwall sacks from Ellesmere Port, fibre drums from Disley, waxed and greaseproof papers from Sittingbourne and paper bags from Bolton.

without having to commit themselves to the risk and heavy capital expenditure required for setting up on their own in markets strange to them. Bowaters' first venture in this direction was represented by the Bowater-Riegel Corporation, formed in 1949 to sell 'glassine' and greaseproof papers to be made from materials produced at Sittingbourne in partnership with the Riegel Paper Corporation who would supply some of the plant and technical knowledge required.

Without this arrangement, in Eric Bowater's opinion, there was a danger of unemployment at Sittingbourne with consequent damage to Bowaters' local goodwill. Moreover, although the manufacture of the base paper might not do more than break even, he expected good profits from conversion.[44] His colleagues do not seem to have been wholly convinced and, whether for that reason or some other, the agreement with Riegel was not finally signed until 1951.[45] Production then started but, by that time, competition from plastic film was becoming severe. Both sides became disenchanted with the partnership and it was dissolved in 1956, by which time a far more promising Anglo-American proposition was in view: Bowater-Scott (Chapter 12.4 below). Bowater-Riegel's legacy to Bowaters was the Waxwrap Department at Sittingbourne and ultimately Flexible Packaging, both of which are discussed in Chapter 13.5.

The diversification policy was explained by Eric Bowater to his shareholders in March 1948. It was based partly on pre-war experience but it was immensely strengthened by Eric's angry reaction to the 'austerity' forced upon the British newsprint industry by the Labour Government, beset by the problem of the balance of payments. 'It had been decided by the Cabinet', Hugh Dalton and Stafford Cripps told a meeting of newspaper proprietors in September 1945, '. . . that the maintenance of the four-page newspaper was not a hardship which could not be borne when . . . it might be all we could do to maintain the food supplies to this country.'[46]

This was no doubt a reasonable view in 1945 but it was not a view which, in 1948, Eric Bowater was prepared to accept. The quantity of newsprint which United Kingdom mills were allowed to produce was brought down from 35 per cent of pre-war output in July 1946 to 20 per cent in January 1947, where it stayed until March 1948, so that nearly three years after the end of the war the production of newsprint was almost as severely restricted as in the war's worst days. For a short time, in the bitter winter months of 1947, restriction grew even tighter, for coal ran short and the quantity allocated to Bowaters was only enough to run the machines at a little more than $11\frac{1}{2}$ per cent of their rated capacity. Eric, who did not like the Government's politics, put the worst construction on the facts. 'The Government', he said, 'appear . . . to be thinking only in terms of a continuance of four-page newspapers; this is indeed a shocking and an alarming thought.' His political views he summarised by complaining 'I do not like automatically to be labelled a Conservative', and he was highly critical of Sir Winston Churchill, whom he disliked. On the other hand he abhorred socialism. In his view of world affairs, by contrast with his view of his business, he was in later life pessimistic, contemplating sombrely the apparently unstoppable advance of Marxism and the rise of black power in Africa.[47]

Shock and alarm at the Government's imputed wickedness played their part in hastening Bowaters along the road which, in any case, the Chairman wished them to travel – away from news-print and towards a diversity of products. 'We have in recent times', he said in 1948, 'acquired concerns engaged in the processing of various descriptions of paper and boards produced by the mills of the Organisation, and in the future we shall look increasingly in this direction for our revenues in this country.'[48]

Bowaters, with about £30m of capital employed in the United Kingdom, North America and Scandinavia, was by 1947 well up the list of large British businesses. The largest of all were very much larger – ICI, for example, had about £115m capital employed and Bowaters ranked roughly with one of ICI's larger divisions. On the other hand, Metal Box, built up like Bowaters by a single outstand-ing autocrat – Sir Robert Barlow – but over a period about four years shorter, was much smaller, with barely £6m capital employed.[49]

In spite of the size of Bowaters' business (the hyphenation Bowater-Lloyd gradually dropped out of use), the organisation in the late forties remained rudimentary. In this, also, Bowaters re-sembled Metal Box and for the same reason: each company had a Chairman who neither shared nor delegated power. In March 1944 Eric set up an Advisory Committee of Directors and then, in Sep-tember, a General Purposes Committee which might include senior managers who were not on the Board. Both bodies had the assis-tance of a Planning and Development Department set up at the same time as the Advisory Committee. Until the Advisory Commit-tee was abolished, in November 1945, the membership of the two committees overlapped and, on one occasion, Eric pointed out sardonically that members of the GPC had contradicted advice which they had given as members of the Advisory Committee.[50]

The General Purposes Committee became permanent but as the document establishing it said: 'The Committee will be a consulta-tive as distinct from an executive body.' Eric Bowater kept power in his own hands and, although the GPC was required to review capital expenditure proposals and co-ordinate the progress of 'adopted plans', it remained nevertheless essentially a deliberative and advisory body. Its attention was directed almost entirely to matters in the United Kingdom, the export trade and, later, Europe. In North America there was no parallel body until 1960. The GPC's recommendations were conveyed to the Chairman, sometimes trenchantly, in writing. He wrote back, usually through an intermediary, with equal trenchancy. In any disagreement, there was no doubt whose views would prevail.

In 1945 Stanley Bell (1899–1961) joined Bowaters, was at once appointed to the GPC and served for many years as its principal spokesman. Bell had joined Anglo-Newfoundland Development Co. in 1915 and worked his way up through Rothermere's interests until he was Managing Director of Associated Newspapers. In 1944 he quarrelled with Rothermere and left him.[51] Eric Bowater, being willing, it appears, to disregard Bell's activities during the war in the service of the arch-enemy, the Newsprint Supply Co., brought him directly on to the Board of BPM. He was given a varied assortment of duties, among which public relations were prominent, but as time went on he came to concentrate on sales and on the procurement of materials, eventually with the title 'Director in charge of Supplies and Marketing'.[52] It is said that Duffin, on seeing Bell's original list of 'principal activities and responsibilities', enquired plaintively what was left for him – Duffin – to do.

Below the level of the Board, the most powerful official in Bowaters was the Comptroller. 'I decided on the creation of the post of Comptroller', the Chairman wrote, naturally in the first person, 'as the senior Official in the organisation directly responsible to me for dealing with all matters not directly and solely concerned with the manufacturing, operating, buying, selling and distributive activities of the business and in particular all administration matters and the general control of day to day finance.'[53]

For the first holder of this position, in May 1944, Eric Bowater chose H. J. Inston, already a director. C. G. Rye (1909–73), of whom we shall hear much more, replaced him as Secretary of BPM and its principal subsidiaries. The Comptroller's appointment, though new, had roots running back to Bowaters' earliest days and strong links with the Secretary's department. With these associations, and through control of a centralised accounting system, the Comptroller accumulated power and the standing of his department within the Bowater Organisation may perhaps be compared to the standing of the Treasury in the United Kingdom. In 1948 the Chairman set up a standing Finance Committee – himself, Keeling and Inston – to attend to the procurement of finance, thus emphasising the central importance, in the Bowater Organisation, of Inston and his department.

Trusted advisers: 'Boss' Whatmore of Peat, Marwick (left), K. N. Linforth, Cecil Unthank of Barton, Mayhew and Herbert Inston, on a visit to Tennessee, mid-1950s. *Robert Knight*

Although the administrative structure of the Bowater Organisation, as it stood just after the Second World War, was simple, the financial structure was not. It had come into being, piecemeal, during the hectic years of growth between 1926 and 1938 and it was already recognised to be overdue for simplification and rationalisation before war broke out. As Figure 3 shows, the parent company, Bowater's Paper Mills Ltd, both operated the paper mills at Northfleet and held the shares of subsidiaries, with the effect in practice that the company provided both the seat of management for the Bowater business as a whole and a head office for one – not the largest – of Bowaters' manufacturing companies. At the next

Sir John Keeling, 1958. *J. A. B. Keeling*

level down, Bowaters & Lloyds Sales Co. was chiefly a marketing
company yet, for reasons which had ceased to have any validity, it
held 46 per cent of the Mersey Company's capital though it took no
part in running the Mersey mills. The two companies alongside it –
Edward Lloyd Investment and Bowater-Lloyd Newfoundland –
had now no function but to hold shares and were redundant.

Over several months in 1946 and 1947 a scheme was worked out
between Bowaters' management and their professional advisers for
drastically pruning this luxuriant growth and bringing it into simpler and more practical shape. Bowater's Paper Mills ceased to be
an operating company and became solely a holding company in
which the higher direction of the entire enterprise was lodged. The
operation of the Northfleet mills and all that went with it was
handed to a newly created company: Bowater's Thames Paper Mills
Ltd. The Edward Lloyd Investment Co. and Bowater-Lloyd Newfoundland Ltd were both eliminated and the Sales Company
became what its name implied, not a holding company any more.

Before the new scheme of things (see Figure 4) could come into
effect, the capital structure of the group had to be reorganised – a
difficult task because the issue, over the years, of various classes of
Debenture stock and of the Preference capital of the Edward Lloyd
Investment Co. had created rights which, in some cases, impeded

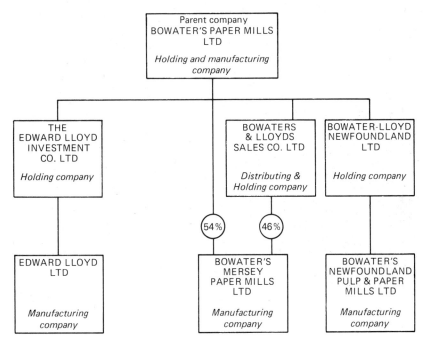

3 The Bowater Group before reorganisation. Only those companies directly affected by the reorganisation are included. From pamphlet, 'Capital reorganisation, 1947', March 1947, RK.

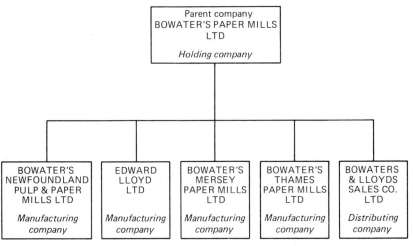

4 The Bowater Organisation. From pamphlet, 'Capital reorganisation, 1947', March 1947, RK.

the process of reorganisation. The mills at Northfleet, for instance, formed the major part of the security for £921,096 3½ per cent Debenture stock of Bowater's Paper Mills, so that the consent of the Debenture holders was needed, or the Debenture stock would have to be repaid, before the mills could be transferred to the proposed new company, Bowater's Thames Paper Mills Ltd. Rather similarly, it was necessary to repay the Debenture stock of Bowater-Lloyd Newfoundland before that company could be liquidated and, before the Edward Lloyd Investment Co. could be liquidated, £2m 5 per cent Redeemable Cumulative Preference stock, on which arrears of dividend were payable, had to be redeemed.[54]

The details of the capital reorganisation scheme were complicated, chiefly because new Debenture stocks had to be created to finance necessary repayments but the effect which it achieved was simple. Bowater's Paper Mills became entirely a holding company which directly owned all the issued Ordinary capital of the five main operating companies of the Organisation:[55]

Bowater's Thames Paper Mills
Bowater's Mersey Paper Mills
Bowater's Newfoundland Pulp & Paper Mills, Corner Brook
Edward Lloyd
Bowaters & Lloyds Sales Co.

The capital of Bowater's Paper Mills, as well as most of the fixed interest securities of the subsidiaries, were publicly held and the capital structure of the group took the form shown in Table 22.

At an Extraordinary General Meeting of members of Bowater's Paper Mills, held on 13 June 1947, a resolution was passed to change the company's name to the Bowater Paper Corporation Ltd. This resolution signalled the completion of the first phase in the

TABLE 22. *The Bowater Paper Corporation Ltd, capital structure, 1947*

CAPITAL OF THE CORPORATION (HOLDING COMPANY)

Share capital

Authorised	Shares and stock units	Issued
£1,500,000 £1	6½% Cumulative Preference	£1,000,000
2,000,000 £1	7½% Cumulative Participating Preference	1,500,000
2,000,000 £1	Ordinary	1,500,000
5,500,000		4,000,000

Loan capital

£4,000,000 3¼% First Debenture stock 1951/97	£3,250,000

TABLE 22. *Contd.*

CAPITAL OF THE SUBSIDIARIES

Bowater's Mersey Paper Mills Ltd
Share capital

Authorised	Stock units and shares	Issued
£ 500,000	£1 5½% Cumulative Preference	£ 500,000
650,000	£1 Ordinary	650,000
850,000	£1 Shares	——
2,000,000		1,150,000

Loan capital

£ 750,000	3¼% First Mortgage Debenture stock	£ 750,000

Edward Lloyd Ltd
Share capital

Authorised	Stock units and shares	Issued
£1,200,000	£1 7% Cumulative Preference	£1,200,000
1,000,000	£1 5½% Second Cumulative Preference	1,000,000
1,600,000	£1 Ordinary	1,600,000
3,800,000		3,800,000

Bowater's Newfoundland Pulp & Paper Mills Ltd
Share capital

Authorised	Stock units and shares	Issued
£1,500,000	£1 4½% Cumulative Preference	£1,500,000
1,500,000	£1 Common Stock	1,500,000
2,000,000	£1 Shares	——
5,000,000		3,000,000

Funded debt

3½% First Mortgage Bonds	£14,183,500
3% Guaranteed 'A' Mortgage Debenture	£ 1,556,200
3% Second Guaranteed 'A' Mortgage Debenture	£ 128,800
3½% 'B' Mortgage Debenture Stock	£ 1,651,100

Bowater's Thames Paper Mills Ltd
Share capital

Authorised		Issued
£1,250,000	£1 Ordinary shares	£1,250,000

Loan capital

£ 750,000	3¼% First Mortgage Debenture stock	£ 750,000

Bowaters & Lloyds Sales Co.
Share capital

Authorised	Shares	Issued
£ 300,000	£1 Cumulative Preferred	——
200,000	£1 8% Participating Preferred Ordinary	£ 200,000
300,000	£1 Ordinary	300,000
800,000		500,000

Source: Pamphlet, 'Capital Reorganisation, 1947', March 1947, RK.

development of the Bowater Organisation. In 1926, the old family firm had given birth to Bowater's Paper Mills. Twenty-one years later Bowater's Paper Mills in turn gave birth to the Corporation – an appropriate embodiment for the multi-purpose, multi-national business which Bowaters in twenty-one years had become. Sir Eric Bowater, ambitious as he had always been for Bowater's Paper Mills, had even larger plans in mind for the Corporation.

CHAPTER ELEVEN

The Tennessee venture
1944–1954

11.1 THE POST-WAR PROSPECT

With the establishment of the Corporation Bowaters' business came to maturity. From 1945 until 1960 profits rose rapidly, though not without interruption, to levels many times higher than before the war (Figure 5) and corporate wealth rose with them, so that when new capital was needed Bowaters could come to the market, on either side of the Atlantic, from a position vastly stronger than in the days when neither their earning power nor their financial soundness were beyond question (p. 60 above). In the late forties and in the fifties new capital was needed frequently and massively, for Sir Eric and his advisers pushed rapidly ahead with developments at home and in North America, carried on simultaneously but along divergent paths which this and succeeding chapters will explore, taking the American expansion first.

In public and in private Eric Bowater made clear his opinion that in the United Kingdom the outlook for the newsprint industry was not promising, partly because of the Government restrictions which he so greatly deplored but more importantly, in the long run, because of the natural advantages enjoyed by mills in Canada and Newfoundland, including Corner Brook. Those advantages had been neutralised to some extent for a few years in the thirties but the circumstances of the thirties were unlikely to return and Sir Eric was determined that Bowaters in the United Kingdom should develop with less emphasis on newsprint and more on paper and allied products for packaging and other purposes.

In North America, by contrast, demand for newsprint was outrunning supply and Eric Bowater intended Bowaters to take advantage of the trend, as, thanks to his foresight, they were well placed to do. No. 7 machine at Corner Brook came into full production, after a very uncertain start, in December 1949, giving the mill total capacity of about 300,000 tons of newsprint a year.[1] Eric, in a letter

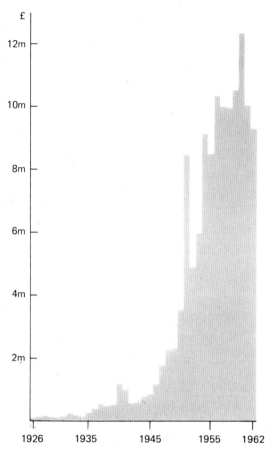

5 Bowater consolidated profits, 1926–62. Profits shown after depreciation and interest on loan capital but before taxation. 1926 – sixteen months; 1928 – nine months; 1954 – fifteen months. 1926–45 compiled by Robert Knight; 1946–62 from published accounts.

to Mrs Reay-Mackey, expressed his delight: 'The new mill which I inspected today is a positive *Marvel*. I love it. I love the super modern in machinery.' It was unfortunate that for some time this machine gave almost incessant trouble.

Corner Brook's output was all contracted for – Meyer and Charles T. Hicks in New York saw to that – and Corner Brook, vindicating Eric Bowater and confounding Montagu Norman (p. 180 above), became a major profit earner. With six machines making newsprint and one making sulphite pulp it had about reached its economic limits. Characteristically, Eric Bowater was not content. He intended, as soon as a good site for a new paper mill could be found, to expand Bowaters' production of newsprint in North America still further and, at the same time, to put in plant for

Charles T. Hicks (left) and A. B. Meyer in New York, 1960.

supplying sulphate pulp to Bowaters in the United Kingdom for the packaging business which he intended them to develop there.

The pattern of Bowaters' capital issues during the Corporation's early years displays not only the geographical spread and growing diversity of its activities but also its vitality at a time when its prosperity was rising and hopes for the future were high. It also had moments of tension, as when in 1948 the costs associated with the building of No. 7 machine at Corner Brook were found to be running about 43 per cent higher than the original estimate. The Bank of Montreal had already lent $5m for the project and when Eric Bowater and Jack Keeling asked for more they were unsympathetically received – an unique experience for them. Officials of the Bank suggested that Bowaters should 'find ways and means of obtaining permanent finances for these additional requirements'. The upshot was an issue, requiring lengthy negotiations by Inston and Keeling at the Treasury and the Bank of England, of 1,000,000 £1 4½ per cent Cumulative Participating Preference shares in the Corner Brook company at 21s.[2]

Episodes like this one brought heavy pressure to bear on everyone concerned, especially Eric, with whom the final responsibility lay.

He hoped, he said, that people whom he met socially were 'deceived by my exterior and poker face', but in private he revealed the continuing strain. 'It's 4am', he wrote from Montreal in October 1949, 'and today I met my bankers to whom I owe $8,000,000 . . . I detest being here and resent comments by these Canadians – "What's the trouble?" "Why can't you enjoy yourself?" "What do we lack?" I wanted to get out of Corner Brook. I have and here it's worse'. In September 1950, with the investment at Corner Brook beginning to show a return, matters were very different. 'Yesterday I lunched with the Bank. Amusing. Two years ago we owed them $12 million. Today we have $2 million to our credit and they were very polite.'[3]

In September 1950 an issue of 300,000 £1 7½ per cent Cumulative Participating Preference shares of the Corporation at 30s. and 300,000 Ordinary shares at 37s. 6d. produced £980,000 for new plant at Kemsley, Sittingbourne and Mersey, all intended for 'diversification', not newsprint.[4] Altogether, in the five years ending 30 September 1951, Bowaters spent about £9m on 'plant, machinery and development generally', of which about £3.2m was new money raised on the market.[5] The balance – nearly £6m – Sir Eric told BPC shareholders in March 1952, was 'found out of the Organisation's own resources and from profits ploughed back into the business'. What a remarkable contrast, he might have added, to the state of the business when he had had to sell control of it to Rothermere before his credit was good enough to allow him to raise capital on the market.

All this was preliminary, for in 1952 the period of really large expansion, at home and in North America, was just about to open. At home the worst effects of wartime and post-war restrictions were over – 'we are now back in our full stride', said Sir Eric – and in America the advance into manufacturing, as well as selling, in the United States was under way.

11.2 FINDING A SITE

At least as early as 1944, perhaps much earlier, Eric Bowater's mind was turning towards the idea of putting up another North American mill, perhaps representing an initial investment of nine to ten million dollars. A newspaper proprietor in Tennessee, knowing something of Eric's leanings, contrived two meetings, in June and August 1944, between representatives of the Tennessee Valley Authority and of the Bowater Paper Co. At the end of the second meeting A. B. Meyer was polite but non-committal[6] but, by the time the search for a site seriously began in 1947, he was already in favour of looking in the same direction for a new mill as he had already looked for new customers – towards the South.

This, at the time, might have been considered eccentric, for the Southern states were not greatly favoured in the newsprint industry. They had plenty of timber but the only trees suitable for paper-making were varieties of pine which, on account of their high resin content, were considered vastly inferior to the trees available in Canada and Newfoundland. Southern pine matures in twenty-five years rather than the seventy-five years or more needed for the Northern spruce and balsam fir but, even with that advantage, newsprint makers were not greatly attracted to it, although a mill at Lufkin, Texas, had been using it since 1940 and another was being planned for Coosa River, Alabama, in 1947.[7]

Certainly Arthur Baker was not at first in favour of the South and his influence with Eric Bowater was probably at least as great as Meyer's. In 1947 he took charge of a 'task force', drawn from Bowaters' staff on both sides of the Atlantic, which travelled widely and energetically in Canada and the United States, including the South, inspecting possible sites for mills to manufacture both news-print and the kraft pulp which the policy of diversification in the United Kingdom demanded. Pulp was evidently regarded as at least equal in importance to newsprint and, in 1948, the GPC considered a proposal for putting up a pulp mill only.[8] Baker's report has disappeared but, in 1950, he reminded Eric Bowater that in it he 'came down unhesitatingly in favour of development in B.C. [British Columbia]'.[9]

Although the attractiveness of the South, for reasons which we shall examine in detail later, seems to have been the most consistent theme in Meyer's plentiful advice to Eric Bowater and in his discus-sions with H. M. S. Lewin and Earle Duffin, yet surviving letters show that Meyer's extremely lively mind was open to proposals of many kinds in many parts of the United States and Canada, some requiring partnership with other interests, some directed at buying existing mills rather than building new ones.[10] The one proposition which he and his allies took for granted – the bedrock on which all others were founded – was that outside the United Kingdom Bowaters' major expansion should be in North America.

This was not a notion greatly to the liking of Noel and Ian Bowater on the export side of the business. Their main connections did not lie with North America but with traditional British markets elsewhere, especially in Australia and South Africa. They were in a weak position. They were on the Board but not in the circle of their cousin's close advisers and the Export Sales Division, as is common in British business, was underprivileged. Ian, put in charge of it in 1945, was severely snubbed at the end of 1948 when his proposal that the Division should be represented on the General Purposes Committee was turned down on the grounds that it was part of the Sales Organisation which was represented by Duffin. Duffin, a Canadian, belonged to what might be called the North American party in the highest circles of the business and, unlike Ian, he had the ear of the Chairman. Ian was also rebuffed at about the same time by the Comptroller, almost with contempt, when he suggested that he – Ian – as Director in charge of Exports, should direct investigations and receive reports on all projects in Australia, New Zealand and Africa.[11]

There was worse to come. Ian, with reservations, brought a proposal before the GPC for manufacturing wallboard in South Africa, probably requiring an investment between £800,000 and £1m. The GPC recommended against it in November 1948 and the Chairman confirmed the recommendation.[12] Then in April and May 1949 Eric Bowater, in North America, had talks with a New Zealand delegation which about a year later resulted in Ian going to New Zealand to investigate an ambitious plan, backed by the New Zealand Government, for setting up pulp and paper mills at Murupara. Again an investment of about £1m seems to have been contemplated and it was generally accepted that if Bowaters did not undertake the enterprise someone else would, with an obvious threat to export contracts which Bowater held for 48,000 to 50,000 tons of newsprint. Ian, after initial scepticism, a great deal of discussion and investigation in New Zealand and at home and conversations with Sidney Holland, Prime Minister of New Zealand, gave the scheme his backing.

His cousin, after 'prolonged and careful thought', turned it down in September as being 'a pioneering venture' which 'is not a practicable economic proposition at the present time', adding:

Beyond all this, but by no means secondary, is the prospect of the opportunity occurring . . . of constructing a newsprint plant in the Southern United States – an infinitely more attractive proposition than any of those recently brought to notice either in New Zealand, Australia, South Africa or elsewhere. There, there is an assured market, immense and relatively readily available financial resources and the undoubted backing of the U.S. publishers which will assure real success.[13]

From this pronouncement it is clear that by the early autumn of 1950 Eric's mind was made up, and had probably been made up for some time, in favour of a venture in the Southern States and, consequently, closed to possibilities elsewhere.

Ian found himself with the embarrassing task of informing the Prime Minister of New Zealand that Bowaters were not, after all, going forward at Murupara. He had also, about the same time, to contrive withdrawal from negotiations, which had also gone a long way, for a co-operative venture in newsprint in South Africa. The Chairman's decision was conveyed to him at second hand, evidently with some feeling of awkwardness, by J. H. Keeling in a letter of 25 September 1950 from Corner Brook where Keeling and Eric Bowater were in residence.

Apart from the commercial merits or demerits of any project that might be recommended in South Africa, the Chairman had strong views, which he 'dwelt and enlarged upon . . . from time to time', on the economy of South Africa and the political situation there. 'Briefly', he said at the end of 1950,

they are that, as its whole economy continues to be based on gold and as the country is being unrealistically governed, South Africa is sitting on a gunpowder barrel which may go up at any time. In short, the Chairman prefers to keep out of South Africa on the manufacturing side, other than in a very small way, though he is not averse to entering the converting side in that country.

With the essential soundness of these opinions few people, at thirty years' distance, would quarrel but in 1950 they were not fashionable among British businessmen. Many, attracted by the glittering surface of the expanding economy, newly industrialised, of South Africa, preferred to ignore or play down the underlying, still distant, danger. It was therefore not surprising that Ian Bowater and others should have been attracted by a South African proposition but it is surprising that Sir Eric, holding the views he did, allowed Ian's negotiations to go so far. Moreover, he then went out of his way to write to Stanley Bell, for the benefit of the GPC, saying that he disagreed with a letter with which Ian proposed to withdraw from his uncomfortable situation, saying that it 'would give a wholly wrong impression'. If he was not actually seeking a quarrel with his cousin he was scarcely taking much trouble to avoid one.[14]

In the spring of 1950, while the New Zealand and South African negotiations were in train, Charles T. Hicks was in British Columbia reconnoitring the Pacific Coast 'and apparently', Meyer told Eric Bowater, 'it is a fabulous place. The indications are that from a sales angle' – Hicks was predominantly a salesman – 'there is going to be no problem at all particularly if we are prepared to handle a large Hearst contract.'[15]

Meyer, however, foresaw a different problem: cost. The most promising site available in British Columbia was in the valley of the Fraser River, 'but a mill in that area is going to be another Corner Brook and we will have to think in terms of $60/$70,000,000 rather than $35/$36,000,000 unless, of course, the Province will build the hydro-electric plant, but even then we would be stuck with the necessity of having to build a town and house the employees'. He concluded:

I think it may be advisable for us to forget about British Columbia and again consider the South. There should be no real sales problem with a new Southern mill and certainly every U.S. publisher would welcome the building of another mill in the United States. The South, with its cheaper wood, natural gas and plenty of labor already housed, would, I think, be preferable to the headaches of a Fraser River development. I realize the financing in the South creates a greater problem, but I do believe that much pressure would be brought upon the R.F.C. [Reconstruction Finance Corporation] by publishers to assist us in the financing, and it occurs to me that even the British Treasury might consider the permission of a dollar investment by a British firm if there are prospects of healthy dollar dividends on the investment.

He went on to urge that Arthur Baker should 'come over as soon as possible so that we can look over the available sites again and be prepared to act if it seems advisable'. If Arthur Baker came promptly, he added, 'we ought to have an up-to-date mass of information when you arrive in New York this Fall'.

Meyer, like Ian Bowater, was pushing for a decision but unlike Ian he was pushing at a door already three-quarters open. During the summer of 1950, apparently, Eric Bowater made up his mind that the Southern States, rather than British Columbia, would be the best place to build Bowaters' new North American mill.

The Southern States may be taken to mean ten south-eastern states – Alabama, Florida, Georgia, Kentucky, Mississippi, North and South Carolina, Tennessee, Virginia, West Virginia – and six – Arizona, Arkansas, Louisiana, New Mexico, Oklahoma, Texas – in the south-west. The region included all the states of the Confederacy, ruined in the Civil War, and had long been poor and backward by comparison with the rest of the USA. By 1950, however, great changes were coming over the South and it was at last beginning to catch up.

The consumption of newsprint in particular, though still much lower than in the USA as a whole, was rising much faster. Figures collected by the American Newspaper Publishers Association, admittedly incomplete, suggest that in 1950 consumption in the USA was 68.4 lb a head, in the south-eastern states: 33.7, and in the south-western: 42.9, but that since 1939 consumption had risen by 131 per cent in the south-eastern states and 107 per cent in the south-western, against 70 per cent in the United States as a whole. These figures probably represented consumption just short of a million tons in 1950 in the sixteen Southern states taken together,[16] which was nearly 350,000 tons more than consumption in Great Britain.[17]

In twelve months or so, during the final phase of reconnaissance, Bowater representatives looked at about thirty-five sites in North America. A team under Arthur Baker inspected twenty-two in five Southern states, making repeated visits to the Tennessee Valley, and by the middle of May 1951 they had reduced the possibilities to two: one at Naheola, Alabama, and another at Calhoun,* Tennessee. Arthur Baker, it is said, having visited twenty-one of the twenty-two Southern sites, arrived at Calhoun, walked briskly up a low hill, looked around, and announced emphatically that this was the place. His colleagues were not disposed to disagree and the choice was made, though not before Bowaters had satisfied themselves that they would be able to get up to 300,000 cords of wood a year without over-cutting and without interfering with other firms' supplies. Meyer's letter confirming the choice of the Calhoun site was sent on 27 July 1951.[18]

Calhoun lies on the Hiwassee River, a tributary of the Tennessee, in rolling, wooded countryside with no large towns nearer than Knoxville, seventy-three miles to the north-east, and Chattanooga, forty-two miles to the south-west. The surroundings are thoroughly rural. 'The towns of Cleveland, Athens, Charleston and Calhoun, with an aggregate population of 22,000' – American usage eschews the word 'village' – 'lie within a radius of fifteen miles of the proposed site', says a document prepared by Morgan Stanley & Co., bankers, 'and afford a good labor supply, predominantly Anglo-Saxon.'[19] The labour supply was attractive, no doubt, not least because labour unions were less powerful than in the North, but the site had other advantages, too. It was well placed not only for labour but for wood, water, fuel and power, and transport, both for supplies arriving at the mill and for finished goods going to market.

Bowaters expected to draw their pulpwood from thirty-four

* Some documents place the site at Charleston, another small town on the opposite bank of the Hiwassee River. Calhoun is more accurate.

contiguous counties in Tennessee, northern Georgia and northern
Alabama and, if necessary, from a block of twelve counties in North
Carolina and Virginia. Precisely how much timber these areas could
provide was a matter of sharp controversy between the Forestry
Division of the Tennessee Valley Authority and the federal Forestry
Service but Bowaters, advised independently of either, were confident that supplies would be ample. Twenty-five million gallons of
water a day would be needed; that and more the Hiwassee would
provide and it would also provide storage ponds for timber, lagoons
for waste disposal and a highway for barges. Natural gas would
come from a pipe-line already laid across the site and electricity
from the TVA, whose officials enthusiastically supported the whole
project and fought its battles when they could . US Highway 11 and
the Southern Railway both served the site. The site itself, of about
1,800 acres, presented no great difficulties to the builders.[20]

On this site Bowaters intended to put up a mill with two machines
designed for the production of 125,000 tons of newsprint a year
and 50,000 tons of commercial unbleached sulphate (kraft) pulp.
The market for the newsprint would be among newspaper publishers in the south-eastern and south-western States; for the pulp,
with the Bowater Paper Corporation in the United Kingdom.
Bowaters intended also to buy, over a period of years, 150,000 to
200,000 acres of forest which they would manage and develop for
continuous production, so that they would eventually control a
substantial proportion of their pulpwood supplies, endlessly
renewable.[21]

The cost of building the mill was estimated by J. E. Sirrine
Co., engineers, at $42,685,000 and Bowaters themselves added
$7,745,000 chiefly for timberlands and working capital, giving a
total proposed investment of $55m, as shown in Table 23. These
estimates, with a sterling equivalent of nearly £20m – and estimates
have a habit of increasing – displayed Eric Bowater's ambitions at
their boldest, especially since he had simultaneous plans, on a large
scale, for the business in the United Kingdom (Chapter 12 below).
The United States market was and remains notoriously difficult for
foreign firms to break into and the Tennessee project required
strong nerves. That it was welcome in the locality there was no
doubt.

There would be jobs at the mill, variously estimated at 750 or
900, but that was not the only nor perhaps the most important
consideration. There would also be a buyer for the timber which so
many of the farmers in the neighbourhood wanted to sell. The
Chamber of Commerce of Calhoun and Charleston had long

TABLE 23. *Initial estimates for Calhoun mill, 1951*

	$
Construction and equipment	42,685,000
Mill site	250,000
Spare parts	500,000
Interest during construction	1,750,000
Expenses during construction	2,070,000
Total for the mill	47,255,000
Timberlands	3,000,000
Woods equipment	995,000
Working capital	3,500,000
Other expenses	250,000
Total	55,000,000

Source: Coverdale & Colpitts, 'Report on Bowaters Southern Paper Corporation',
1 October 1951, p. 3.

sought industrial development and, in August 1951, the 'Twin Cities Chamber' arranged a mass meeting at which the people of the two small towns and the surrounding area issued a formal invitation to Bowaters 'to establish . . . plant for the manufacture of paper on the considered site in this area', pledged 'our resources, our labor and our unwavering support' and asserted 'the truth of the presence of pine wood within economic hauling distance in ample quantity'. This was a hit at the US Forest Service, who wanted Bowaters to get most of their wood from twenty-nine counties in Virginia and North Carolina.

The invitation was backed by 10,000 signatures and it was given wide circulation in the neighbourhood. Doubt has been cast on its genuineness, implying presumably that it was engineered by or on behalf of Bowaters, but it was followed in the early part of 1952 by a resolution of McMinn County Council granting tax concessions and it seems eminently reasonable that the development should have been welcome to the majority of the local population.[22]

There remained the task of arranging the finance of the project and of piloting it along a formidable obstacle course – it had enemies as well as friends – before construction could begin.

11.3 FINANCING THE MILL

In the United States

Bowaters, always adventurous in their financial planning, devised a scheme for financing the mill at Calhoun which was far bolder than anything they had previously attempted. There was not the remotest possibility of the Bank of England permitting them to acquire the whole of the dollars they needed – $55m – and therefore they proposed to borrow a very high proportion – their first thought was 80 per cent – from financial institutions in the United States. They were determined, nevertheless, to keep control of the business by keeping the equity capital – less than 20 per cent of the whole – in their own hands.

From the point of view of HM Treasury, this was a truly beautiful scheme. The loan capital would, in time, be paid off and Bowaters would enter into unencumbered possession of very valuable dollar assets. Moreover, as soon as they were able to pay dividends, a dollar income – a large one, it was hoped – would flow in the right direction across the Atlantic. There was another advantage, too, namely that Corner Brook's Southern trade, not very profitable because of transport charges, could be transferred to the new mill in Tennessee, leaving Corner Brook with 60,000 tons of newsprint which could be sold either in the United Kingdom, elsewhere in the Commonwealth, or – for even more dollars – in other parts of the United States. What could be better? Bowaters had no difficulty at all, in April–May 1951, in getting permission from the Bank of England to acquire the $10m which was all, at that time, that they thought they were going to have to subscribe for equity capital.[23]

The scheme might be beautiful but it was also audacious, as American critics did not fail to point out. Not only did Bowaters propose to raise most of the money they needed by borrowing in the USA while keeping control in their own hands but they also intended to make full use of tax concessions and other privileges available under American emergency legislation.

The emergency arose from the outbreak of war in Korea in June 1950, bringing with it the threat of a wider war which Eric Bowater, among others, took very seriously. Both the American and the British Governments launched into rearmament and, in the USA, one result was a provision in the Internal Revenue Act 1950 which allowed a proportion of investment for defence purposes to be written off against Federal income tax at an accelerated rate for five years. With Federal tax at 52 per cent, this concession was very valuable, especially in the raising of capital.

To gain this concession Bowaters needed a Certificate of Necessity – that is, a certificate issued by an appropriate agency of the American Government that the plant Bowaters proposed to build was necessary for defence purposes. Without that certificate, capital would be difficult and more expensive to raise. There might also be difficulty in getting materials and equipment brought under Government control by the Defense Production Act 1950. With the certificate, Bowaters would be in a position of privilege which would lay them open to criticism.[24]

'This certificate', says an *aide-memoire* prepared in November 1951,

is essential to the financing of the scheme, as it enables the high debt to be refunded in a very short time out of profits, more than half of which would, without the Certificate, be absorbed by taxes. There has, in consequence, been considerable criticism of the propriety of granting a Certificate to a wholly-owned British Corporation as, in effect, this enables a project such as ours to be largely financed by American capital, such American capital being repaid out of the cash made available by the accelerated amortisation [writing-off], leaving the small British-owned equity holding very valuable assets standing in the books at greatly reduced figures.[25]

Precisely. The financial plan was not calculated to make Bowaters popular. However, the Certificate of Necessity was indispensable and on 25 May 1951 Bowaters set out on the long, plentifully obstructed road towards it before either they had finally made up their minds about the site or the Defense Production Administration had decided that newsprint was essential to the defence of the United States. By the time the *aide-memoire* was written, this latter decision had just been made. The grant of a certificate, however, was still far from certain.

Meanwhile, other preparations were in hand for the financing. First, prospective lenders had to have hard evidence that newsprint from the new mill could be sold. Meyer, aided by Charlie Hicks, set out to provide the hardest evidence of all: firm contracts, for a long period of time, to take all that the mill could produce.

Meyer never doubted that the contracts could be made. World demand for newsprint, of which about four-fifths was American demand, was above world capacity to supply and still rising. In contrast with the conditions of the thirties, the Canadian mills were working above their rated capacity, not below it, and American newspaper publishers, not always on the most cordial terms with Canadian suppliers, were anxious to see new mills in the United States, where in 1950 only about a million tons of newsprint were produced against more than five-and-a-quarter million tons in Canada, which by this time included Newfoundland.[26]

Whether the new mills were to be American-owned or not does not seem to have mattered very much to the publishers, so long as the owners were competent, and they were not disposed to quibble about the finance. Meyer's controversial policy of looking after Southern publishers during the war (pp. 176–7 above), however, began to yield dividends. They were well-disposed towards Bowaters when Bowaters' representatives came seeking orders for the new mill before it was built.

The first and, as it happened, the largest contract for supplies from the new mill was made on 23 May 1951, with Atlanta Newspapers Inc. of Atlanta, Georgia, for 24,000 tons a year for fifteen years. By the end of October the figure of 130,000* tons – the mill's designated output – had been passed but contracts continued to be made at least until April 1952, by which time eighty-two publishers had contracted for 147,680 tons a year, about 14 per cent more than the mill was designed to produce. How the excess was to be provided is not clear.

Only one of these contracts was made outside the South but that was a big one: 10,000 tons for Scripps-Howard, New York. None was large by the standards of English national papers. One contract was for 60 tons, another for 90, many were below 1,000 and the average was 1,801. The Calhoun mill's business, like the mill itself, was to lie chiefly in small towns below the Mason and Dixon line.[27]

As the signing of these contracts and the pursuit of the Certificate of Necessity went ahead, so did negotiations for the financing. Bowaters' advisers in London were the London & Yorkshire Trust; in New York, Morgan Stanley & Co., with whom lay the responsibility for finding American banks and insurance companies ready to put up the money required. The capital structure proposed, at first, was:[28]

First Mortgage Bonds	$37,500,000
Serial Notes	$7,500,000
Equity capital, supplied by	
Bowaters from the UK	$10,000,000
Total	$55,000,000

The application for the Certificate of Necessity was held up, first, by a mistake in procedure by Bowaters and then, more seriously, by a dispute between the TVA and the US Forest Service over the adequacy or otherwise of wood supplies available to the mill. Bowaters themselves made up their corporate mind in July, being fortified by advice from the consultants C. D. Shy of Memphis, Tennessee, and A. W. Bentley, late of Corner Brook but by this time

* Some documents say 125,000.

an independent consultant forester with an international reputation. On 20 July 1951, Bowaters Southern Paper Corporation was incorporated in Delaware and, a week later, A. B. Meyer notified the Defense Production Administration of Bowaters' intention to take the Calhoun site.[29]

About this time, one of the insurance companies approached by Morgan Stanley, in principle willing to lend, nevertheless asked for an independent enquiry into the soundness of the whole Calhoun proposition. It was undertaken by Coverdale & Colpitts, consulting engineers, of New York, who reported on 1 October 1951. 'The Bowaters Southern project', they said, 'is soundly conceived and constructive, and derives great benefit from the experience and long record of successful operation and growth of its parent and associated companies in the Bowater Organisation.'[30]

The engineers' report had a sting in its tail. They thought 'additional funds of $4,000,000 to $5,000,000 should be available if needed for the completion of the project and for adequate working capital'. Worse, 'The proposed capital structure of the Company involves an exceptionally high initial debt, both in amount and in ratio to total assets.'[31] No doubt others had noticed the high level of 'gearing', too. It would scarcely have surprised anyone familiar with Bowaters' favoured methods of financing. Nevertheless, combined with difficulties in the way of getting the Certificate of Necessity, it nearly wrecked the whole proposal.

The struggle for the project reached a climax during the latter part of 1951. The battlefield was in Washington. Bowaters employed a Washington lawyer, Arthur J. Swanick, to promote their interests and detached Victor J. Sutton to work with him. Sutton, a Canadian, formerly mill manager at Corner Brook and now a Director of Bowaters Development and Research Co. in London, had been one of the team which chose the site. During the latter part of 1951 and the first two months of 1952 these two watched over the progress – or, at times, lack of progress – of the application for the Certificate of Necessity. They had support from the TVA and from newspaper publishers but two paper firms – Champion Paper & Fiber Co. of Canton, North Carolina, and the Mead Corporation of Rome, Georgia – would have been glad to see the application fail. In the end it succeeded but not until February 1952. 'Sutton and Swanick', says an American commentator, 'formed a very effective spearhead for the Bowater attack', but he also shows that their unresting persistence was apt to exasperate those at whom it was aimed.[32]

Much of the detailed financial negotiation was entrusted to

John Kirwan-Taylor, recruited into Bowaters from the London &
Yorkshire Trust.

Eric Bowater himself was in America for ten weeks until mid-
November 1951. By the time he got back he must have been under
great strain, for negotiations for the Certificate of Necessity were
maddeningly slow and objections to Southern's proposed capital
structure were mounting. In private he was vituperative. 'The ob-
stacles American bureaucracy is putting in our way', he wrote in
October 1951, 'is quite incredible to say nothing of those in industry. The approach of their financiers . . . and their insurance companies who are to participate financially is that everyone, including
ourselves, are fools, rogues, rascals and thieves. England for me,
and this incidentally I say a dozen times a day in one connection or
another.'[33] When *Queen Mary* reached Southampton he gave an
interview which was widely reported:

I offered to put over $50,000,000 into the establishment of a paper-
producing mill in eastern Tennessee. It would have produced 130,000 tons
of newsprint a year. It would have helped the world newsprint shortage.
Americans have been crying out for greater production within their own
country. I went along and told them a British firm was willing to take the
risk and put up the cash. All they would say [was he aiming at the officials
in charge of the application for the Certificate of Necessity?] was the offer
must come through the proper channels. In America, there has been a lot
of Congressional ballyhoo and committees screaming for more production. But vested interests [Champion and Mead, presumably] have done
their best to oppose my project – and that is an English understatement.

He went on to attack the Washington officials again: 'I am not sure I
really understand the bureaucratic mind.'[34]

This despondently aggressive outburst – it gives the impression,
despite its pugnacity, that Eric thought he was beaten – was surely
unwise. First, it was hardly tactful to say that he had been offering
to put up $50m when, in fact, he had been seeking to borrow the
greater part of it in the United States. Secondly, it gave great offence,
understandably, to officials in Washington whose goodwill was
vital to Bowaters' success. 'That boy', said one of them, 'is going to
have to learn to keep his mouth shut. The industry men who are
now working in the U.S. defense agencies are not going to be
swayed by pressure, and the pressure from Bowater has been enormous. I myself am frankly sick of it.'[35] Did this official and his
colleagues take their revenge for Eric Bowater's uncharacteristic
display of ill-temper by working even more tenaciously to rule?

By the time Eric Bowater came home, it seemed only too likely
that the project would founder, not because of delays or obstruction

in Washington but because the capital could not be raised. Metropolitan Life, the largest insurance company in the United States, had agreed to subscribe up to $15m for bonds and J. P. Morgan had agreed to subscribe $2.5m for serial notes and to head a syndicate of bankers to subscribe the balance of $7.5m, but other insurance companies had declined to subscribe at all. The reason was 'the relatively small equity capital in relation to the amount of the proposed First Mortgage Bonds and Serial Notes'. By 30 November Morgan Stanley had given up hope. The project, they told Bowater, could not now be financed on the original basis.[36]

If Bowaters could put up $15m instead of $10m, said Morgan Stanley, the project might yet be saved, provided always that the Certificate of Necessity were granted, but they must hurry, otherwise investors who had provisionally committed themselves might be lost. Bowaters did hurry, and so did the Exchange Control authorities. Between 20 December 1951 and 3 January 1952 permission was sought and granted for Bowaters to acquire the extra dollars.[37]

That removed one major obstacle to raising capital. The other, the granting of a Certificate of Necessity, disappeared on 19 February 1952 when a certificate was issued allowing 45 per cent 'of the cost of construction, erection, installation, or acquisition' of the proposed plant to be written off over five years as 'accelerated depreciation' because it was 'attributable to defense purposes'.[38] Bowaters had hoped, perhaps without much conviction, for 60 per cent, but 45 per cent satisfied potential lenders.

Morgan Stanley's revised proposals for the capital structure of Bowaters Southern Paper Corporation were:

4¾ per cent twenty-year First Mortgage Bonds	$34,000,000
4¼ per cent five-year Serial Notes	$ 6,000,000
Equity capital	$15,000,000
Total	$55,000,000

There was also provision for issuing $3.5m Bonds and $1.5m Serial Notes if more money were required, as it eventually was, to complete the mill and provide $3.5m working capital.[39]

The long-dated bonds were intended for insurance companies, the Serial Notes for banks and the entire equity capital was to be provided by Bowaters, either by subscribing for shares or for 'convertible subordinated debentures' (i.e. debentures ranking after all the other loan capital, to be converted eventually into Common stock) which were alleged, rather doubtfully, to confer tax advantages. No dividends were to be paid unless, after payment, there

would be not less than $3.5m working capital and unless the total of
the share capital and reserves would be at least equal to the total
loan capital. It was forecast that the first dividends might be paid
about five years after the mill went into production.[40]

For potential lenders, one of the main attractions of Bowaters
Southern was that for fifteen years its business was as secure as it is
possible for business to be, since its whole output of paper was sold
and its whole output of kraft pulp also. Bowaters in England had
been obliged to agree, before the lending agreements were completed, to take all pulp apart from any that might be required for
Calhoun and it was estimated that 50,000 tons would cross the
Atlantic every year.

The kraft pulp mill at Calhoun, in Eric Bowater's eyes, was
almost as important as the newsprint mill. Bowaters in the United
Kingdom were building a diversified business which would need
large quantities of kraft pulp and Eric intended to make sure there
was a secure supply base under Bowaters' own control. The Scandinavian machinations of 1937 were still a lively memory and he
was determined never to be caught like that again. So determined
was he that he willingly accepted a form of contract, acceptable to
the bondholders, which guaranteed that the price paid to Southern
should never be less than $125 f.o.b. cars seaboard. The ruling price
when the financing was being arranged was $157.50 and the risk of
the floor collapsing under it did not then seem great.[41]

Rather late in the proceedings, the insurance companies demanded a guarantee from Bowaters that the mill would be completed not later than 1 July 1960.[42] The date was a long way off and,
in any case, Bowaters were intending to complete in 1954 but they
were irritated. Morgan Stanley, however, assured them that the
companies were bound by their rules of business to require the
guarantee and a theatrical gesture by Eric Bowater disposed of the
difficulty. At a meeting with the insurance companies he strode to
the front and pledged his personal honour, no doubt to a somewhat startled audience, that the mill would be completed as
promised.[43]

The insurance companies' agreement to purchase Southern's
bonds was dated 17 June 1952.[44] It was signed on behalf of twelve
companies, subscribing sums varying from $1m to $13m. Seven
were based in New England, three in New York, one each in New
Jersey and North Carolina, thus demonstrating, presumably, confidence outside the South in the South's revival. The agreement
demonstrated also, after all viscissitudes, the confidence of established American financial institutions in Bowaters and, with the

loan capital assured, the construction of the Calhoun mill could go ahead.

In the United Kingdom

Bowater Southern's equity capital of $15m had to be provided from money raised in the United Kingdom. It was only part, and not the largest part, of the capital sum which Bowaters in 1952 were seeking. In the United Kingdom they intended at last to put in No. 6 newsprint machine at Kemsley, planned but repeatedly postponed since the mid-thirties, estimated cost, £1.5m. Kemsley and North-fleet were each to have new power plant, estimate £2.8m. Completion of projects already in hand would need £800,000 and other items unspecified would bring the UK total to £6m. At Corner Brook, improvements over several years were expected to cost the equivalent in Canadian dollars of about £2.5m and two new ships, for carrying newsprint to the United States, the equivalent of £1.5m. Altogether, Bowaters' plans for their business on both sides of the Atlantic in the early fifties called for over £15m, nearly all for the newsprint side of the business – diversification was not yet calling for heavy investment – and split geographically as follows:[45]

United Kingdom	£ 6,000,000	39 per cent
United States	£ 5,360,000	35
Newfoundland	£ 4,000,000	26
Total	£15,360,000	100

The motive power behind all this proposed activity was Eric Bowater's optimism, which appears to have been shared by J. H. Keeling, whose financial planning was designed to give it full scope. It seems to have been scarcely, if at all, damped by the menacing aspect of world affairs after war broke out in Korea in June 1950. The war set off a world-wide scramble for raw materials of all kinds and, in 1951, the price of pulp shot up as dramatically – and as briefly – as in 1937. Newsprint prices rose also and Bowaters' profits in 1951 were so high as to be embarrassing. A recession followed, just about the time when Bowaters needed to raise money for Southern's equity capital. Throughout this switchback of events, Eric remained sanguine. 'The outstanding uncertainty prevailing in industry', he remarked to Stanley Bell in December 1950, 'is in my belief that which relates to war; subject to this I should have thought that the prospects for industry in general were brighter than perhaps at any time in previous history.' Recession did nothing to change his views. 'Short of a depression of a first magnitude which no-one anticipates', he cabled across the Atlantic to Keeling in September 1952, 'the future to me looks good.'[46]

With the Chairman, supported by his chief financial adviser, in this ebullient mood, Bowaters' financial tactics went forward. In the spring of 1951, £900,000 was capitalised from the reserves of the Bowater Paper Corporation and applied to paying up in full 900,000 new Ordinary shares, allotted equally to Ordinary shareholders and holders of 7½ per cent Cumulative Participating Preference shares. In return for this allotment the Preference shareholders agreed to give up their right to participate in the profits after payment of the 7½ per cent Preference dividend and to make certain other concessions.

The details of this bargain displeased certain insurance companies who were major shareholders, both Ordinary and Preferred. Eric, in the States, rose to considerable heights of telegraphic eloquence. In a message to J. H. Keeling, he said:

I am as opposed as ever to permitting the institutions or other in any way to influence our decisions, or indeed in any way to insinuate themselves into the position of interfering in the conduct of our business and I say this almost, repeat almost, regardless of the consequences . . . In brief [it was a very long cable], I am resentful of this unwarrantable attempt by outside interests to interfere in our affairs. I will now have a dry Martini and drink your blessing, regards as ever. Postscript: I have no ambition to aid in building up the prestige and authority of Association of Trust and Insurance Companies; do not let us forget that finance is the servant of industry and that industry is not the servant of finance – platitudinous but true. Post Postscript: Together we have enjoyed many a good battle, should this develop into a battle let us also enjoy this one. ERIC[47]

Concessions were made, under Keeling's influence, and no battle developed, but Eric's attitude towards financial institutions, as displayed in this cablegram, no doubt accounts for the view of him, amounting to something less than enthusiasm, taken in some quarters in the City. 'It has been a hectic day', Keeling cabled after the decision had been taken, 'and your colleagues, who enjoyed your PRESLON 222' – quoted above – 'have already departed in search of dry Martinis. Inston and I can hardly wait. JACK.'[48] The exchange of cables gives a glimpse of an aspect of Eric Bowater – high-spirited and boyish – which in business he rarely displayed.

He needed all his authority and all his powers of persuasion during the months when the inflationary effect of the Korean war was making its impact. In April 1951, Stanley Bell 'drew attention to the very substantial items of capital expenditure which the [General Purposes] Committee had recommended and which the

Chairman had approved in recent times . . . It was obvious that this expenditure, together with the continuing upwards spiral in raw material prices will impose a serious strain on the financial resources of the Organisation.'[49] The Chairman emphatically did not agree and gave his reasons. Nevertheless, the records of the GPC and the Board suggest a running undercurrent of uneasiness which he could not quite dispel.[50]

Early in 1952, another £900,000 from the reserves of BPC was capitalised as Ordinary stock, the authorised Ordinary capital was doubled to £8m and the dividend, notwithstanding the capitalisation issue, was kept at 15 per cent as in previous years. 'It is considered to be essential', runs the application to the Capital Issues Committee for permission to carry out the capitalisation, '. . . to bring the issued Ordinary Share capital more nearly into line with the capital actually employed in the business in order to facilitate the raising of additional capital for cash in due course.'[51]

This 'additional capital to be raised for cash' was part of the sum of £15.36m required to cover the numerous projects outlined above including the equity capital for Calhoun. About £8m was to come from Bowaters' own resources, and that included the whole of the money for Corner Brook and the two new ships, all of which the Corner Brook company would provide – a remarkable demonstration of the flourishing state of the Bowater business, especially in Newfoundland, in the early 1950s. About £7m remained to be raised on the market and, by the beginning of 1952, preparations were in hand for raising it.[52]

On 10 January 1952 Bowaters asked the Capital Issues Committee for permission to raise about £2.5m in Ordinary shares and the rest in loan stock. The CIC quickly agreed but even Eric Bowater felt the chill of the shadow which the post-Korean recession had cast on the money market. 'As you know', he told the directors, 'I was not over sanguine having regard to current circumstances and was fearful that consent would be obtained only to that part of the proposition relating to the issue of Ordinary shares.'[53]

The CIC's consent opened the road for an issue but it turned out far from smooth. A proposal to issue 3.6m £1 Ordinary shares at 21s. was frustrated, late in May, by a leakage of information which briefly halted dealings in Bowaters' shares.[54] After that, there was an uneasy pause while Bowaters's shares, in a generally depressed market, stagnated at a level some 30 per cent lower than at the time when an issue was first contemplated and misgivings began to come to the surface about the wisdom of the Tennessee venture as a whole.

At a Board meeting on 22 May 1952 'a personal opinion' –
almost certainly Ian Bowater's – 'was voiced that the risks which
would be accepted by going forward outweighed the present prospects of success'. This was a direct challenge to Eric Bowater's
judgment and authority, opening up the prospect of a humiliating
withdrawal from Tennessee just at the moment when Metropolitan
Life and the other American insurance companies were poised to
lend $34m to make the venture possible. Eric responded with a
detailed defence of his policy, especially the pulp contract which,
with its guaranteed 'floor price', was particularly under attack. The
opposition was overborne, but not extinguished, for it flared up
again at a Board meeting on 12 June, concentrating once again on
the pulp contract. 'One of the objects behind this contract', said
Eric, '. . . from the point of view of the United States financiers was
to get as near as they could to an unconditional guarantee [of
Bowater Southern's debt] on the part of the parent Corporation
which, except for exchange control reasons, would obviously have
been sought', and once again he defended it in detail.[55]

At the same time as Eric Bowater was fighting doubt amongst
members of his own Board, he found himself obliged to go to the
Prudential and Pearl insurance companies for their view on the
form of a new issue and on the desirability of making one in the
prevailing state of the money market. This may have been an even
more painful blow to Eric's pride, especially when he had to tell his
Board that 'he could not pretend that the idea had been enthusiastically received'.[56]

The idea of an issue was accordingly put to sleep for the time
being and Bowaters fell back upon Rothschilds, who had a standing
arrangement to provide working capital by means of a revolving
credit, and Lloyds Bank who, as so often in the past, were making a
bridging loan to cover the gap between assuming responsibilities
and raising permanent capital. Lloyds seem to have been exceptional, at this moment of difficulty, in their unqualified support for
the Tennessee venture. The Chief General Manager 'expressed the
view that the project in the southern United States was so important
nationally, as well as to the Corporation, that the transaction must
be completed, and recognised that the question of permanent
finance could only be dealt with when a favourable opportunity
presented itself'.[57] For Eric Bowater such a forthright declaration, at
that moment, must have come both as a relief and as a tonic.

During the late summer of 1952 the possibility was briefly ex-
plored, but rejected, of raising Southern's equity capital in North
America through the agency of the Corner Brook company. After

the proposal had been turned down, the Chairman 'indicated that he personally had a preference for raising the money here as he did not consider it would be a good thing for it to be said that we could not raise money in this country and had had to go abroad'.[58] By that time plans for an issue at home were once more in hand. It looked as if the 'favourable opportunity' had at last presented itself and, when Eric left for his autumn visit to Canada and the USA, a circular announcing the terms of the issue was in draft.

Even at this late stage, the issue had to weather another storm. Bowaters' profits for 1950–1 had been carried up to a record level on the wave of alarm caused by the Korean war. By the time the issue was made it was clear that the profits for 1951–2 were going to be carried down again as the wave receded, for the price of sulphate pulp was falling rapidly in the recession caused by the post-Korean drop in demand for commodities generally. The circular announcing the issue was to contain a forecast of profits and it would have to be phrased even more carefully than such statements usually are.

The figure that Keeling (by now Sir John Keeling), Inston and Rye proposed to publish, as a forecast of the Corporation's consolidated profits for 1951–2, after depreciation but before loan interest and tax, was £6m. The comparable figure for 1950–1 was £8.825m. The Chairman, by then in Newfoundland, accepted his advisers' estimate with some misgiving. 'You well know', he told Sir John, 'my strong liking for understatement and I would not care in any circumstances to put in a profit figure that in the final accounts would not be substantially exceeded.'[59]

This figure and the text of the paragraph in which it was to appear were accepted informally by a number of the directors on Friday, 12 September 1952, and the draft circular was issued to the underwriters. Then over the weekend Ian Bowater had second thoughts. He accepted the figure of £6m but thought two or three sentences should be inserted in the circular warning shareholders that profits might be lower again in 1953. He was not prepared to sign unless some such qualification were inserted.

This, said Sir John Keeling, the London & Yorkshire Trust would not accept and they would have to call off underwriting operations unless the Corporation would authorise them to go ahead on the basis of the existing proof of the circular. When Keeling spoke to Eric Bowater on the transatlantic telephone Eric reacted with great vehemence and could hardly be restrained from going straight back to London. His private comments are unprintable, but he cabled a version, no doubt suitably edited, of his words on the telephone. 'I am in entire agreement', he said,

that having very properly made circular available to underwriting institutions, it would be suicidal now to attempt to make any substantial alterations to its contents or any material alterations such as are now suggested.
I know of no grounds for apprehension in regard to the future, on the
contrary, I have complete confidence in the future for the Organisation
including next year.[60]

At a formal Board meeting held the day after the telephone call
Ian Bowater found himself a lonely rebel, faced with the displeasure
of his cousin and of Keeling, and with a solid array of professional
advisers. He gave way and the text went out as originally drafted.

The breach between Ian Bowater and his cousin, with Sir John
Keeling in support, was now complete. Over a period of two years
or so – possibly longer – Ian had seen his recommendations on
matters of major policy consistently disregarded, not always in the
most courteous possible manner. He had then moved against his
cousin's grand design, the crown so far of all his efforts, and had
been defeated. There was no place for him any longer in the
Bowater organisation.

On 7 April 1953 Ian Bowater resigned from the Board of the
Bowater Paper Corporation. He found other business interests,
including 'The Compleat Angler' hotel at Marlow, and developed
his civic activities in the City. In 1969–70 he was Lord Mayor of
London, being the fourth of his family, in two generations, to hold
that office.

On 13 October 1952 Sir Eric Bowater and Sir John Keeling were
both in New York. Inston, in London, sent a cablegram to A. B.
Meyer: 'Inform President* and Keeling speediest that approximate
Tennessee figures are rights subscriptions five million one hundred
thousand odd and excess applications two million.'[61] The last financial obstacle was out of the way and the building of the Tennessee
mill could go ahead in security.

11.4 'THE CROWNING JOY'

On 30 September 1952 a North American province of the Bowater
empire was formally inaugurated by the transfer to a newly formed
Canadian company based in Montreal, the Bowater Corporation of
North America Ltd, of all the investments held in North America by
the Bowater Paper Corporation, which itself was the sole owner of
the Montreal company. Sir Eric Bowater, the President, and Sir
John Keeling represented the parent company on the Board and the

---

* The President, presumably, of the Bowater Corporation of North America not of the
United States.

other directors, with G. S. Currie as Vice-President, were either full-time executives of Bowater companies in North America or non-executive directors drawn from New York, Montreal and Newfoundland.[62]

This arrangement provided a measure of co-ordination of the activities of the two very large pulp and paper mills in North America and the selling company which acted for both of them. The Montreal company was also intended to become the medium through which dollar finance would in future be raised, and that was a very important reason for setting it up, since dollar finance would be needed for all future development of the Bowater business in North America.[63]

Looking ahead at about the time when the Montreal company was being set up, Eric Bowater decided that 'the Organisation has now reached proportions where it is essential that there is a complete interchange of information and ideas between the Managements of its various constituent parts'. He therefore ordained, in his most imperial style, that managers from North America, the United Kingdom and Scandinavia should be brought together twice a year. 'It is my wish that such meetings, at which Mr. K. N. Linforth will preside, should be held at regular six-monthly intervals, . . . alternately in London and in Montreal.'[64] Only the royal 'we' is missing.

Contractors moved on to the Calhoun site in June 1952. For Bowaters, Karl O. Elderkin, Vice-President and General Manager

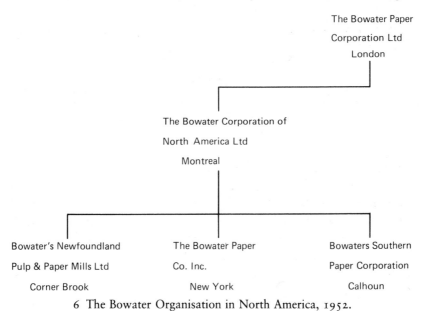

6 The Bowater Organisation in North America, 1952.

of Bowaters Southern, took charge of construction, having previously been manager of Crossett Paper Mills in Arkansas. Much earlier he had worked at Mersey mill in Nova Scotia and at Corner Brook before becoming an independent consultant in Montreal. In that capacity in 1938, acting for the Commission of Government in Newfoundland, or more specifically for L. E. Emerson, Commissioner for Justice, he prepared a sharply critical report on the agreement which the Commission was about to conclude with Bowaters. In 1952, when he was on Bowaters' side of the fence, he was held in high regard. Why, he once enquired, did Eric Bowater never say 'No' to him?[65]

Probably it was because of his all-round competence. Not only did he conduct negotiations with Federal officials; not only did he oversee the immensely intricate construction project so that it ran remarkably smoothly; but he played a leading part in developing a system for storing six weeks' supply of logs under water (southern pine deteriorates rapidly in air) in a pond containing enough water to float a ten-thousand-ton ship and furnished with elaborate equipment for recovering the logs and sending them on their way to the mill.[66]

The mill was designed for the complete process of receiving

Calhoun, 1954. Note the vast circular log-pond, reputedly large enough to float a 10,000 ton ship. Immersion in water prolongs the storage life of southern pine logs.

timber, preparing mechanical pulp and kraft pulp and manufacturing newsprint. Two 232-inch newsprint machines were installed, designed to work at speeds up to 2,000 feet per minute. The main building, 1,200 feet long and mounted on 7,200 piles, contained 13 million cubic feet of space.[67] Kraft pulp came into production from May 1954 onwards and No. 1 newsprint machine started in July. 'Of one thing we are certain', the directors remarked in their minutes – it sounds like Elderkin speaking – 'we have a beautiful paper machine.' On 21 August, No. 2 machine started and the Board minutes record 'fine teamwork by all concerned with the excellent start-up of the mill'.[68] By April 1955 newsprint production was running at 145,000 tons a year against the designed rate of 130,000 and kraft pulp was being produced at a rate of 60,000 tons instead of 50,000 tons a year.[69]

On 9 October 1954 five hundred people gathered at Calhoun Mill. Many were American newspaper publishers and their wives. There was a strong contingent from the United Kingdom. Other guests represented the local community and other interested parties. Eric Bowater, with his strong theatrical sense, arranged for messages to arrive from R. A. Butler, Chancellor of the Exchequer, from George M. Humphrey, Secretary of the United States Treasury, and from the Lord Mayor of London, Sir Noel Bowater. A plaque to commemorate the opening of the first independently financed newsprint mill in the South was unveiled jointly by the President of the Southern Newspaper Publishers Association and the Governor of the State of Tennessee. Thus the mill was ceremonially 'dedicated'. For Eric Bowater, if for no one else, the significance of the occasion was more than purely practical: almost mystical, and certainly deeply emotional, imbued with warmth by the achievement of a long-held ambition.

Addressing the gathering on the evening of the day of dedication, he made his feelings clear in a speech as deeply charged with a sense of personal fulfilment as with pride in corporate achievement. He began by saying: 'This is the proudest and one of the happiest days of my life.' He spoke of 'this great new plant' as 'the culmination of one of the fondest and most cherished dreams of my life' and remarked: 'at one time it seemed only a pipe smoker's dream and one too beset with difficulties ever to be realised'. He acknowledged the work of engineering consultants, main contractors, over 150 other firms and four individuals whom he mentioned in terms which suggest varying degrees of intimacy: Arthur Baker, Gus Meyer, Charlie Hicks and K. O. Elderkin. In his peroration, his own intense commitment to the Tennessee venture once again broke through the ceremonial trimmings:

To become, as we now have, a part of the great economy of the United States is a source of immense pleasure, pride and happiness to all of us of the Bowater Organisation and particularly to myself who since my first visit to this country as a youngster in 1922 have always enjoyed the warmth and fullness of your great hospitality. To you all I again extend my humble and grateful thanks for the several ways in which you have helped us in the realization of our dream and the crowning joy of my business life.[70]

CHAPTER TWELVE

Zenith 1954–1956

12.1 OPTIMISM UNLIMITED

For about ten years at mid-century, say from 1947 to 1957, Sir Eric Bowater, aged sixty in 1955, was at the peak of his career. The Bowater Organisation was the largest producer of newsprint in the world. Its mills were working to capacity, their capacity was being extended, demand for newsprint was still rising and if Bowaters needed capital for expansion investors in London, New York and Montreal were happy to provide it.

In such a climate, Eric Bowater's urge for growth burgeoned as never before and, with it, a display of personal and corporate magnificence which combined with his dominance of the affairs of the Corporation and of virtually everyone who had dealings with him to build about him a veil of legend. To a degree, it was distasteful to him. In private he expressed his dislike for public appearances and he was very apprehensive of such duties as making speeches to employees, especially when what he had to say was not pleasant, or delivering his address to Bowaters' Annual Meeting. Nevertheless he was well aware of the dignity of his position and would have been thoroughly in sympathy with a seventeenth century Earl of Bristol, commemorated in Sherborne Abbey, whose epitaph says he was 'carefull to keep up the port of his Quality'.

Eric did it, or it was done for him, in various ways. At a gathering of long-service employees in 1957 his appearance was heralded by trumpeters of the Household Cavalry. His entertaining overseas, in the houses provided for corporate use by the companies of which he was the head, may not have been out of keeping with the standards of the circles in which he was accustomed to move. It was grand enough, nevertheless, when a number of newspaper publishers visited Strawberry Hill, for an accompanying American journalist to find it rather overwhelming. 'At dinner', he wrote half-incredulously, 'there were 20 pieces of silver on the table besides the cutlery, five ash trays, two candelabras [sic], two cigarette "trunks", two lighters and three sets of salt, pepper and mustard – all identical. When the butler brought a message, a letter or a pair of glasses, it was on a silver tray.'[1] All this, not in London, New York, or Montreal, but in the wilds of Newfoundland.

Nearer home, from 1954 onward, the Bowater Paper Corporation's Annual Meetings were transformed from small, sedate gatherings into annual outings for thousands of shareholders. The idea of these large gatherings was to make the shareholders less remote from their company and to give them a glimpse of its operations, either by staging exhibitions or by showing them round the factories. At the same time, those who worked in the factories were occasionally to be given the opportunity to see and perhaps meet some of the shareholders, which might help to dispel the sedulously cultivated image of a 'shareholder' as a top-hatted, be-spatted oppressor of the working class.

It followed that Bowaters' Annual Meetings, from 1954 onward, were not invariably held in London. At the Chairman's own suggestion, the 1954 meeting was held at Sittingbourne. Its success was much greater, almost embarrassingly greater, than anyone had anticipated and after that meetings were held at Chester and Croydon, both of which were conveniently placed for mill visits, at Northfleet, Ellesmere Port and Gillingham. Three – in 1958, 1960, 1961 – were held in the Royal Festival Hall in London, where the Chairman's entrance was elaborately stage-managed to give him a lonely pre-eminence.

The transport of shareholders to these meetings presented considerable problems of logistics, rather like moving several regiments of troops without the support of military discipline. Transport was organised in fleets of coaches, special trains or, in 1957, in the Thames steamers *Royal Daffodil* and *Royal Sovereign*, and ballots were held to determine the lucky ones who were offered places. For the meeting at Mersey in 1959, journalists were brought in a chartered Viscount airliner.

The first of these agreeable extravaganzas was held while Sir Noel Bowater, a Vice-Chairman of the Corporation, was also Lord Mayor of London. His cousin, adept at seizing an occasion, welcomed him in both capacities. 'The association', said Sir Eric, 'of our family and the Corporation that bears its name, with the City of London has now become almost traditional, for Sir Noel Bowater is no less than the third member of that family and of your Board who has held the high office of Lord Mayor.' It is just possible that the

Stanier Pacific No. 46225 *Duchess of Gloucester*, suitably embellished, heads the 9.00 Euston–Chester special, one of four trains taking Bowater shareholders to the AGM of 25 May 1955. The meeting was followed by a tour of the Ellesmere Port paper and packaging complex.

'The decade just ended was a memorable one for Bowater . . .' Sir Eric addresses the AGM of 2 June 1960 in the Royal Festival Hall.

Sir Noel V. Bowater as Lord Mayor of London, 1954. Sir Vansittart, Sir Frank and,
most recently, Sir Ian also held the office.

City, always a trifle suspicious of Eric's flamboyance, was a little
less pleased than he was.

Shareholders, whether they went to the Annual Meeting or not,
received elaborately printed and illustrated publications containing
not only the statutory Report and Accounts but much other information about the Bowater Organisation, well-written and
attractively presented. There was no lack, either, of other published
material, all produced to a very high standard. In some circles the
meetings and all that went with them were decried as needless

extravagance, though the cost was a tiny fraction of the Corporation's revenue. They generated publicity and, among a less austere audience, widespread goodwill for Bowaters. They also, unintentionally and perhaps to Eric's annoyance, contributed extra voltage to the aura of aristocratic magnificence which emanated from Bowaters' Chairman.

The surge which carried the Corporation forward in the mid-fifties was the culmination of the rise in demand for newsprint, ahead of the capacity to supply it, which had persisted since the end of the war. It seems to have arisen chiefly because the Canadian newsprint producers, collectively the largest in the world, being mindful of the ruinous thirties when so much plant had stood idle in their mills, were willing to speed up their existing machines but very chary of making the heavy investment needed for new ones.[2] As a consequence, newspaper publishers in the USA, where most of the demand arose, were forever short of newsprint and forever indignant at what they saw, perhaps not without justification, as the grasping policy of the Canadian suppliers. Their indignation spilt over into evidence before one congressional committee after another. Excess of demand over capacity, the root of their complaints, reached its peak in 1956.[3]

On the crest of this wave of rising demand the Tennessee venture was launched. On the expectation of its continuance, and with little regard, it seems, for the risk of over-capacity, Bowaters' policy for the production of newsprint in the later fifties and beyond was founded. It was a policy of ambitious expansion on both sides of the Atlantic, for Eric Bowater's post-war mood of disenchantment with the prospect before the newsprint industry in the United Kingdom seems to have passed away as Government control of the industry was gradually relaxed.

12.2 EXPANSION IN NORTH AMERICA: THE MERSEY MILL (NOVA SCOTIA)

In North America control of Bowaters' business lay formally in Canada with the Bowater Corporation of North America. Relations with the Bank of Montreal were close, and George Currie (see p. 173 above) was one of Eric Bowater's leading advisers. Moreover until the late fifties Corner Brook, supplying newsprint for the USA and pulp for Bowaters' mills in the United Kingdom, remained the largest producing unit – over 300,000 tons of newsprint a year – in the Bowater Organisation, though plans for expansion rested on

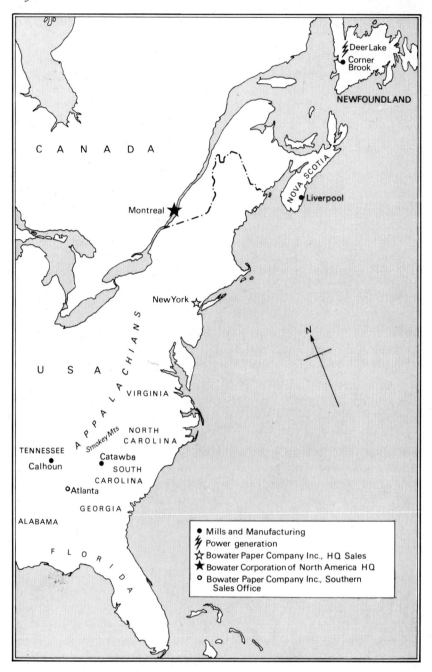

Bowater in North America, 1962.

improvement of existing equipment rather than on massive new installations.

After the war the question of Newfoundland's constitutional status – the Commission of Government had never been intended for permanence – came up for decision. Bowaters' dislike of the proposal for union with Canada, forcefully expressed by H. M. S. Lewin, caused friction with J. R. Smallwood, later Prime Minister of the new Province. Union came, and with it loss, in 1950, of the Corner Brook company's tax privileges; a loss which Bowaters fought unsuccessfully before the Supreme Court of Canada. In spite of the increased tax burden Corner Brook's financial health remained good. In 1955, with Can.$18,628,800 in cash raised by the sale of its hydro-electric assets to a newly formed public company, which remained a Bowater subsidiary, Corner Brook's entire funded debt was paid off. Thus freed from funded debt, Corner Brook, described as 'the Crown Jewel', reinforced Bowaters' credit in North America.[4]

In 1956 the Canadian side of Bowaters' business was enlarged by taking over the Mersey Paper Co. of Liverpool, Nova Scotia. Eric Bowater had tried to buy the business in 1934 (pp. 104–6 above) and when, twenty years later, he heard that there might be another chance he mounted another attempt, code-named 'Killjoy', to try to persuade Isaak Walton Killam to sell. In spite of strenuous efforts by Eric himself in the spring of 1954 – 'Walton at present in hospital on account, he says, of his last six-hour meeting with me but I am going to see him this evening'[5] – this attempt also failed. In August 1955 Killam died and with almost indecent haste Gordon Ball of the Bank of Montreal, on Bowaters' behalf, approached the executors. The final decision would lie with Killam's widow, who had no intention of letting her large shareholding go cheaply.

Mersey had two paper machines and Eric contemplated a third, but the main attraction was the possibility of putting up a new, highly efficient, mill to produce 100,000 tons of groundwood pulp a year. At least, this was the consideration advanced by Eric as a justification for buying the mill to Meyer, Currie and Lewin who were dubious of its value to Bowaters purely as a paper mill. As time went on and the price that would have to be offered for the shares climbed steadily from $170 or so to well over $200, Meyer and Currie became less and less enthusiastic about the proposition. They both had in mind that, as the Mersey negotiations were going on, Bowaters were also trying to finance large developments in the United States.

'It is a curious thing', Meyer wrote to Eric on 8 May 1956,

that while in the past I have always been enthusiastic about development and expansion, almost everything within me 'screams' against 'Killjoy'. I think a lot of it is 'hunch' and is probably not supported by a great deal of logic . . . I have the feeling that we may be acquiring two very efficient newsprint machines plus a site for a groundwood mill at the sacrifice of possibly diversifying the way I had hoped we would in this country. I am not now thinking so much of the long pull as I am looking ahead, say, five years. I think the additional debt in connection with 'Killjoy' may bring us to a point where (i) we will find ourselves in the position where it is inadvisable to try to incur additional debt and (ii) it may be impossible for us to raise money for the things that we might like to do. Therefore, the importance of 'Killjoy' as a groundwood mill site looms up so largely.

He then attempted to justify the purchase of Mersey as a ground-wood mill site, but evidently without much conviction. 'I think', he concluded,

One of the things that we should consider is that the per ton earnings of 'Killjoy' are now probably at a peak the same as they are in all newsprint mills possibly for the next three or four years. I think with the new production that is earmarked over the next three years this industry is going to be less inclined to raise prices to meet increased costs. Therefore, I doubt whether I would expect increased profit from 'Killjoy' without the necessary capital investment to provide for increased production – namely, the speeding up of the existing machines.

He ended his letter with characteristic modesty:

All of the above may be somewhat trite and academic but I am trying to analyze my coolness towards the project. In any case, I feel that all of us have reached the point where we should, at least, give you an expression of our views and hunches, and I can assure you that if, in your own wisdom, you decide to go ahead with 'Killjoy' certainly you will get full enthusiasm from your lieutenants. The thing that possibly bothers me and worries me more in extending my views to you is that you have been so right in the past and I have the uncomfortable feeling that you feel 'Killjoy' is another step in the right direction.[6]

In a letter written a few days earlier, he had indicated Morgan Stanley's view: 'Morgan Stanley still . . . advise very strongly that we do not buy "Killjoy" unless we have permanent financing arranged ahead of time'[7] – which they had not, although they had the support of the Bank of Montreal.

Against the strongly expressed views of George Currie, Eric did go ahead. He offered Mrs Killam and the minority holders $230 a share, requiring a cash payment of nearly $52m. 'The price per share which we have in mind', wrote Currie, 'is to my mind greatly in excess of the value of the company . . . and can only be justified as an acquisition of raw materials and productive facilities for future expansion . . . I feel it my duty to express these views and that you expect them from me under the circumstances.'[8]

High though the offer was, there was no certainty that the lady would accept. She was staying in one of her houses in the Bahamas and, when John V. Walters of the Bank of Montreal arrived with documents for her signature, she bade him stay with her during the time allowed for clearing final details. Some of these she discussed with him for an hour while they swam side by side in her Olympic-sized swimming pool soon after he arrived. After two days (7–8 June 1956) of teasing, which she evidently thoroughly enjoyed, Mrs Killam invited Walters to a late supper. Still, for nearly three hours, she announced no decision. 'At about fifteen minutes to midnight', Walters wrote in 1978, 'Mrs. Killam burst into a smile and said to me "It's a deal! Let's sign the documents!" This was done and I sent a previously prepared cable to Montreal. Then she snapped her fingers and champagne appeared out of the darkness and we toasted each other with great goodwill.'[9]

Thus the decision was announced which brought another 140,000 tons a year of newsprint capacity within the Bowater

Mersey mill, Nova Scotia. *Sherman Hines Photo.*

Organisation. The whole transaction was characteristic of Sir Eric Bowater's methods. He saw an opportunity of achieving an objective which he had long desired and he let nothing stand in his way: not the doubts of his closest confidants, nor the opinion of his professional advisers, nor uncertainty about long-term finance, nor the risk of throwing other development plans, far longer and more carefully prepared, into disarray. It was a triumph of personality over prudence.

The groundwood pulp mill was never built.

Notwithstanding the heavy Canadian weighting of Bowaters' North American business, it was apparent from 1952 onward, not least in Corner Brook, that the most ambitious developments were going to be in the United States. The two original machines at Calhoun were barely running before measures were being taken to speed them up and plans were soon put in hand for a third and then a fourth machine. A large part of the finance for these major investments would be forthcoming, it was hoped, from the American insurance companies and banks who had lent money for the original two machines.

With plans for raising the output of newsprint for the USA went plans, considered by Eric Bowater equally or more important, to manufacture sulphate pulp in large quantities in America for Bowaters' mills in the United Kingdom. Meyer worried about the possible effect of the Mersey purchase on these developments. They interacted also upon each other and they are considered together below (pp. 244ff).

12.3 EXPANSION IN THE UNITED KINGDOM: NEWSPRINT AND PACKAGING (EBURITE)

Plans for newsprint in the United Kingdom were, if anything, even more ambitious. Between 1949 and 1956 – when Government control over the newsprint industry at last ended, nearly eleven years after the war which had brought it into being – machines were speeded up and the long-anticipated, long-postponed No. 6 machine at Kemsley was installed. Beyond that, in 1955 a Master Plan for the United Kingdom was formulated to provide for no less than four new machines for newsprint and magazine paper, two each at the Mersey mill and at Northfleet, giving extra capacity, between them, of 200,000 to 240,000 tons a year. To support them new power plant would be needed, new office buildings and, at Northfleet, a deep-water jetty. At Northfleet there were also plans for building new Central Research Laboratories, a new office and drawing offices for the Chief Engineer, and a new large transport depot.[10]

Great hopes were placed, in the United Kingdom, on the development of magazine paper – a superior quality of newsprint – because these were prosperous years for periodicals such as *Woman*, *Woman's Own* and *Woman's Realm*, as well as *Radio Times* and the newly launched *TV Times*. Free at last from paper control, supported by abundant advertising, scarcely yet affected by competition from television, they could respond with rising circulation and lively competition amongst themselves to the higher incomes, especially among women going out to work, which were generated by economic growth.

The double programme of expansion on both sides of the Atlantic was intended to give the Bowater Organisation, by the early sixties, capacity for producing 840,000 tons of newsprint in North America and 860,000 tons of various kinds of paper, about 75 per cent newsprint, in the United Kingdom (Table 24), an increase on the 1956 capacity of 40 per cent in the United Kingdom and nearly 59 per cent in North America. It was devised at a time when, as Eric Bowater observed, 'the paper industry as a whole was passing through a period of great prosperity',[11] and it represented a hearty vote of confidence that 'great prosperity' would go on.

These very large plans for newsprint by no means marked the limit of Bowaters' expansion plans for the late fifties. Although Eric Bowater had overcome his misgivings about the future of newsprint in the United Kingdom, he was still determined to press on with diversification. Plans were made, alongside the plans for newsprint, to advance Bowaters' interests in three main fields: building products, packaging, tissues. In building products Bowaters could extend from the business in wallboards acquired with Lloyds in 1936 and the Irish Wallboard Co. acquired in 1950. Their experience in packaging was short. In tissues, they had to buy experience in.

The marketing opportunities presented by these activities were attractive: most of all, perhaps, in packaging. During the fifties, as Harold Macmillan inelegantly remarked, consumers had never had it so good. Standards of living were rising. New products of all kinds and new versions of old ones were flooding into the shops. The shops themselves and the whole nature of the shopkeeper's trade were being transformed by self-service. In the midst of all this was packaging, both the cartons in which goods reached the shops and the innumerable varieties of containers in which retail

TABLE 24. *Bowater's expansion programme (paper only)*

	Thousands of tons	
	Year to December 1956	On completion of programme
USA		
Calhoun, Tennessee	195	435
Canada		
Corner Brook, Newfoundland	300	340
Mersey, Nova Scotia	97	165
(1956 production for eight months only)	397	505
Total North America	592	940
Equivalent long tons (all newsprint)	529	840
United Kingdom		
Thames ⎫		
Mersey ⎪		
Kemsley ⎬	615	860
Sittingbourne ⎭		
Grand totals (long tons)	1,144	1,700
Division of total production		
North America	$46\frac{1}{4}$	$49\frac{1}{2}$
United Kingdom	$53\frac{3}{4}$	$50\frac{1}{2}$
	100%	100%

Compared with 1956, production will increase in N. America by $58\frac{3}{4}$ per cent
Compared with 1956, production will increase in United Kingdom by 40 per cent

Source: Table 1 in 'A memorandum on Bowater Paper Corporation Limited'
　　prepared by Hedderwick Hunt Cox & Co., September 1957.

customers picked them off the shelves or in which they were handed across counters.

For manufacturer, retailer and consumer alike, packaging has advantages. It guarantees origins, hygiene, quality, weight, freshness. It is handy. It advertises the product inside it, builds readily into displays and can carry instructions for use. Packaging can be made from many different materials and, during the fifties, the more modern kinds of plastic were for the first time becoming cheap and plentiful, thanks largely to advances in heavy organic chemistry based on cheap petroleum. Plastics and the older materials could be used either alone or in combination and amongst the older materials were tinplate, metal foil, paper and paper board.

If Bowaters wanted, as they did, to move from papermaking to paper-conversion, thereby securing to themselves some of the value added by the conversion process, here in packaging was an obvious opening. Apart, however, from their undoubted skill in the manufacture of some kinds of packaging materials, they had little to contribute to the industry in the way of experience, technical knowledge, or innovation. Moreover, the opening that was obvious to Bowaters was equally obvious to other firms which fancied their chances of taking advantage of it and, during the fifties, packaging became not only a growth industry but a crowded one.

The crowd was varied. There were firms specialising in one branch of packaging, as it might be corrugated cases, fibre drums or paper bags. There was the Metal Box Co. Ltd, determined to expand from the kind of products its name implied towards the fields opened up by modern plastics and into paper conversion – a most formidable opponent, under Sir Robert Barlow, if its interests were threatened.[12] There were other paper firms, including E. S. & A. Robinson and Reeds, seeking, like Bowaters themselves, to convert their own primary products. There was Courtaulds, as intent on diversification as Bowaters themselves and having a parallel interest in wood pulp.[13] There was ICI, beginning to produce polythene and other plastics in very large quantities and seeking uses for them. There was Thames Board Mills, owned as to 50 per cent by Unilever. In spite of such great names as these, however, the packaging industry was not one in which size automatically conferred advantage. The fabrication of polythene film and one or two other activities, needing little in the way of capital or specialised knowledge, were seized upon with glee by small, nimble producers with a very sharp eye for the main chance and not over-burdened, some of them, with any great weight of scruple.

The beginnings of Bowaters' advance into packaging have been discussed in Chapter 10.2 above. The Master Plan of 1955 made provision for considerable expansion, including a factory on Merseyside for producing corrugated cases, the most successful of Bowaters' packaging products so far. At the same time, another leading firm in the industry, Eburite Corrugated Containers Ltd, had similar plans in mind. Faced thus with the danger of creating excess capacity, and for reasons arising from Eburite's internal politics, Bowaters and Eburite began to negotiate with each other for a union of interests.

Eburite had a corrugator factory in Glasgow and another in Acton, North London. A subsidiary, Autolex Ltd, made crimped cups and aluminium bottle caps at Sunbury-on-Thames, and another London subsidiary, Alfred Kent Ltd, made folding cartons and set-up boxes. The profits (net trading profit before taxation), after a sharp fall in 1952, were substantial and rising steeply:

1950	£ 484,531
1951	£ 971,336
1952	£ 474,236
1953	£ 720,439
1954	£1,143,271

The capital structure was simple: just 160,000 7 per cent Preference shares of 10s. each (£80,000) and 3,440,252 Ordinary shares of 5s. each (£860,062). Of the Ordinary capital, about 22 per cent was in the hands of five directors and their families:

John F. Fielding and others	294,509	8.6 per cent
Sir Geoffrey Byass and others	85,803	2.5
Norman Gold and others	124,234	3.6
Reginald Popham and others	42,024	1.2
J. M. C. Ritchie and others	196,883	5.7
Total	743,453	21.6
Other holdings	2,696,799	78.4
Total, 5s. Ordinary shares	3,440,252	100.0

Fielding, who was Chairman, and Popham were both close to retirement but Popham had a son, C. F. Popham, in the business. Ritchie, not yet forty, was ambitious and belonged to the family which had owned Eburite's Glasgow subsidiary, Andrew Ritchie & Co. The Board, in spite of Eburite's prosperity, was not harmonious.[14]

The negotiations were long, difficult, occasionally acrimonious – 'Suggestions regarding manipulation of share markets are both childish and insulting', Eric Bowater cabled to Charles Rye in February 1956 when something of the sort had been hinted at by Eburite[15] – but they ended in agreement. In July 1956 Eburite took over Bowaters Fibre Containers Ltd (formerly Acme) and changed its own name to Bowater-Eburite. Bowaters received 988,000 shares in Bowater-Eburite in exchange for the equity capital of their subsidiary and they subscribed £787,500 for a further 350,000 shares, thus providing cash for the development plans of the new joint company.[16]

In setting up Bowater-Eburite, Bowaters were inspired by the businessman's normal desire to eliminate dangerous competition and by a desire to widen the geographical spread of their manufacturing activities. They certainly were not setting out to change the nature of their own business but that was what, in due process of time, the new joint company did. Eburite was a strong, prosperous company. Its negotiators could look Bowaters in the eye, and did so. Eric Bowater was so provoked, in February 1956, that he exclaimed to Rye: 'Finally, the time has arrived when you can let Popham' – of Eburite – 'know, in no uncertain terms, that I have no intention that Brighton* should be in the saddle.'[17] The final agreement only gave Bowaters a minority holding in the new joint company's Ordinary capital, which is indicative of Eburite's bargaining strength. Bowaters, however, were much the largest shareholders, and with 28 per cent – which they immediately began to increase – they had no need to fear any likely combination against them: a position which they had aimed at from the start of the negotiations.

Eburite brought into Bowaters' business managers who, in their own opinion, knew their own trade far better than anyone in Bowaters knew it, who were not beholden in any way to Sir Eric Bowater and who saw no reason why they should invariably defer to him or to his close advisers. The effect of the Eburite incursion into the Bowater Organisation, during the remainder of Eric Bowater's lifetime and beyond, was profound.

12.4 EXPANSION IN THE UNITED KINGDOM: BOWATER-SCOTT

For tissues Bowaters needed access to American experience and a manufacturing base, neither of which was speedily acquired, so that they were a good deal later into tissues than into packaging, though both had figured in the early diversification plans. Talks in the late forties with Kimberly-Clark, the American owners of 'Kleenex', broke down and Kimberly-Clark allied themselves with Reeds. There were also talks with Kimberly-Clark's competitors – Scott Paper Company of Chester, Pennsylvania – which at that time came to nothing. On Bowaters' side, several years of intermittent and indecisive deliberation followed, until in January 1955 Bowaters provided themselves with the manufacturing base they needed by paying £4 each for 135,000 shares (the whole of the share capital) in the company that owned St Andrew Mills, Walthamstow, in North-East London.[18] The mills' principal product, undignified but indispensable, was 'Andrex' toilet tissue. Bowaters had looked at the business more than once over a period of at least three years.[19]

When St Andrew was bought, Bowaters had for some time been in treaty with Scott Paper Co. for access to the technical and

---

* Bowaters' code-name for Eburite, used during the negotiations.

marketing skill needed for an advance into the growing market for facial tissues, paper towels and other products of that kind, essentially substitutes for products of the textile industry. Scotts, having plans of their own for their own home market, were not at first very encouraging but St Andrew gave Bowaters a foothold in the United Kingdom market and, by the autumn of 1955, 'Tissue Developments' had found a place in Bowaters' Master Plan, and plans for a joint company with Scotts, in the United Kingdom, were being discussed in New York by Sir Eric Bowater and the President of Scott Paper, Thomas B. McCabe (b. 1893), who was also the largest individual stockholder.

McCabe, about the same age as Eric Bowater, was of a similarly masterful disposition and had been at the head of Scotts' business, as Eric had been at the head of Bowaters', since 1927. Eric was not personally attracted to McCabe and the feeling may have been mutual but they seem to have had no great difficulty in laying down, at their meeting in New York, general principles which their negotiators should follow in arriving at the substantive agreement. Nothing seems to have been written down except a ten-point memorandum, prepared for McCabe, which was read over to Eric and to which, apparently, he verbally agreed.

McCabe, said an American journalist, had 'built up one of the finest management teams of any company in American industry . . . young, able, aggressive and dedicated'.[20] In November 1955 he sent three of these formidably qualified executives to London 'with full authority to negotiate agreements . . . in spirit of partnership we discussed in New York'.[21] Eric Bowater entrusted Bowaters' side of the negotiations to a similar team, including J. Kirwan-Taylor, Charles Rye and, from the company's solicitors, G. W. R. Morley. When Scotts' men went back to America, in the last week of November, McCabe, according to his own account, did not even read the draft agreements they brought with them, saying 'he had simply told his team what you [E. V. B.] and he had agreed upon and instructed his team to work out an agreement on that basis and he was satisfied with whatever they had worked out'.[22]

Eric Bowater, on the other hand, read the agreements thoroughly and demanded material alterations, notably a provision that the Chairman of the joint company should always be a Bowater man and should always have a casting vote at Board meetings. Later, he challenged a clause giving Scotts control of market research on which marketing policy was to be based. Evidently Eric was sceptical of the accuracy of market research but to Scotts it was one of the essential foundations of their whole technique of marketing, which was to be one of their main contributions to the new joint company's assets.

McCabe, furious, told A. B. Meyer

he did not like this method of doing business and he did not like the method of master-minding behind the scenes – that might be the English method of doing business but it was not his way of doing business. He said if this was our idea of a partnership he wanted out . . . He said he had been warned that he could expect just this sort of treatment from our organisation.

Meyer, reporting this tirade – and much else – to Eric Bowater in January 1956, said he thought the whole deal was probably on the verge of breaking up.[23]

It did not break up. After strenuous efforts by Meyer and others on the second level of seniority an agreement was reached which both the men at the top would ratify. The episode demonstrates the dangers which might arise from the kind of summitry practised by McCabe and Eric Bowater, and especially from their omission to put together any joint statement of what they thought they had agreed. It demonstrates also Eric Bowater's reluctance to let any real power slip from his hands. There was no doubt a good deal of truth in McCabe's reference to 'master-minding behind the scenes'.

This was the unpromising prelude to the formation, in April 1956, of the Bowater-Scott Corporation, an English company owned fifty-fifty by Bowaters and Scotts, which turned out far more successful than such joint ventures usually are. The original capital of £3m was provided during the first year or so of the company's existence by Bowaters putting in St Andrew and subscribing £900,000 in cash and by Scotts subscribing £1.5m for half the Ordinary shares at par (see Table 25). The Chairman was Sir Eric

TABLE 25. *Bowater-Scott Corporation, initial capitalisation, 1956–7*

	£	%
£3,000,000 in £1 Ordinary shares at par of which:		
600,000 issued to Bowaters for St Andrew		
900,000 issued to Bowaters for cash	1,500,000	50
1,500,000 issued to Scott Paper Co. for cash	1,500,000	50
Total	3,000,000	100

Source: Comptroller to Chief Cashier, Bank of England, 9 December 1955.

Bowater but for General Manager he chose T. H. N. Whitehurst, who had first come to his notice as his doctor in Surrey. Whitehurst, first invited into Bowaters to reorganise medical services at Corner Brook, was launched through Bowater-Scott into a career in general management leading eventually to the Board of the Corporation. In choosing managers Eric Bowater relied entirely on his own judgment, matured over a period of months or years, and it rarely let him down.

Softness that matters to your family

Here's a new kind of softness—Andrex softness—and it's important to *all* your family. Andrex is entirely different from ordinary toilet papers, even the best of them. Think of facial tissues, soft and gently absorbent. Andrex has that same firm softness, but it is strong, too, with two fine sheets joined together for luxurious depth and strength. Andrex is better for all the family—more hygienic, more efficient, much nicer to have in the house. Get Andrex for your family today!

Andrex

The most luxurious toilet tissue in the world

Bowater-Scott advertisements: from *Woman's Realm*, 1960.

When Bowater-Scott was formed, one new paper machine had already been ordered, to be erected, along with slitters, wrapping machines and other equipment, at Northfleet. Another machine and ancillary equipment, probably requiring another £1.5m capital, was in contemplation. Scotts, besides granting trade mark and patent rights, offered the joint company access to research and development work, technical advice (which turned out very necessary) and the kind of marketing management, directed principally

from *Mother*, 1979.

at housewives and other buyers of consumer goods, of which Bowaters had no experience.[24] As one of McCabe's men said of McCabe, 'What he is interested in is the company operating on the right basis and making as much money as possible.'[25]

From the general tone of surviving papers there is no doubt that at the level of operating management, from A. B. Meyer downwards, there was great enthusiasm for the project on both sides of the Atlantic, the more so since representatives of the two companies liked and respected each other, in spite of the thunder and lightning discharged at Olympian heights above them. 'If we can survive the negotiations that have taken place to date', one of Scotts' men told A. B. Meyer at the height of the storm, '. . . our relationship should be a very happy and successful one.'[26] Only Sir Eric Bowater, for inscrutable reasons of his own, seemed determined at one time to press the negotiations to irretrievable breakdown.

12.5 SELF-SUFFICIENCY: SULPHATE PULP AT CATAWBA

Bowaters' expansion policy in the mid-fifties, sketched in brief outline above, was carrying the business towards a point where, in the early sixties, the Corporation's output of paper would be over 1.6 million tons a year and of packaging products nearly 300,000 tons. These were very large figures. The Chairman, nevertheless, was as determined as ever that the Corporation's control over raw material supplies should match them. 'Our policy', he told Kirwan-Taylor in December 1956, 'is, and remains, that we control not less than 60% of our requirements of all raw materials.'[27]

Eric Bowater's policy of self-sufficiency, extended in 1955 from raw materials to ocean transport (Chapter 12.6 below), arose directly from his experiences in 1937 (Chapter 7 above). He considered that his business had been blackmailed and he had himself been humiliated by Scandinavian machinations, and he was never going to expose himself to that kind of risk again. His belief in the necessity of self-sufficiency was emotional as well as rational, as little likely to be shaken by argument as any other article of faith, equally firmly held.

As long as prices for wood pulp on the world market ruled high, Eric Bowater had little need to defend his views. As prices began to drop in the later fifties, the case was altered, especially as demand for newsprint was falling short of supply. The policy of self-sufficiency became highly debatable and was much debated within and outside Bowaters.

The policy looked very different on the two sides of the Atlantic. In North America it was a matter of siting mills to take advantage of inexhaustible supplies of suitable timber and then managing the forests and the mills so as to produce pulp of good quality at an economic cost. For the mills in the United Kingdom matters were far otherwise. Their position was extremely weak. They depended for survival almost entirely on imported supplies of pulpwood and wood pulp, and the price was crucial, because if it ran much higher than world prices generally the mills would not be able to compete with imported paper. It was of the utmost importance, therefore, in providing sources of supply within the Bowater Organisation, that transfer prices should be kept low.

Within the Bowater Organisation the sources of supply, until 1954, were in Scandinavia, for mechanical pulp, and in Newfoundland for timber and sulphite pulp. Then the pulp mill at Calhoun came into operation, producing sulphate pulp for the two original machines at Calhoun and for mills in the United Kingdom as well (p. 223 above). There was never any intention of leaving Calhoun with two machines only and before the end of 1954 a third machine was being discussed.[28] 'Financial considerations', Eric Bowater admitted, 'had to be studied in some detail', but the success of Bowaters Southern in its first two years was so great and the prospects before the newsprint industry seemed so attractive that it turned out not to be too difficult to persuade the insurance companies and the bankers to lend $20m of the $30m required for a third machine and other measures to increase production, including the installation of a mill to make pulp from hardwood instead of pine.[29] Then in December 1956, before the third machine was working, proposals for a fourth machine were put forward which, with the purchase of additional timberlands, would require $26m.[30] Once again the American institutions were prepared to put up $20m though not, this time, with quite such alacrity as formerly.

When the fourth machine came into operation, a critical point would be reached, since the four machines at Calhoun would take up so much of the pulp produced at Calhoun that there would not be enough left for export to the United Kingdom mills. But exports to the United Kingdom mills there must be, even though that meant building a pulp mill in America for no other purpose. 'The supply of pulp to the United Kingdom mills of the Bowater Organisation is . . . essential', says a document prepared by Morgan Stanley, 'Consequently, arrangements are being made to construct a pulp mill . . . to meet this requirement.'[31]

Plans for the fourth machine, code-named 'Danube' (the third machine had been 'Vienna') and for a new pulp mill to produce 134,000 tons of sulphate pulp a year, code-named 'Dogwood', therefore went forward together. Eric Bowater must have been clear in his own mind that of the two projects 'Dogwood', safeguarding supplies to the United Kingdom, was more important than 'Danube', providing more productive capacity in Tennessee, for he made it clear that if he could not have Dogwood he would not have Danube either, and he used this threat as a stick to beat down estimates. 'Estimates relating to Danube and Dogwood', he cabled across the Atlantic in June 1956, '. . . came as a very great shock to me especially that relating to Dogwood. On basis of these estimates, there is not going to be any Dogwood, and it follows therefore that neither can there be any Danube.'[32]

Dogwood was very expensive: so expensive as to suggest that Eric Bowater's concern for securing supplies was coming danger-ously close to an obsession. He thought long and hard, and con-sulted with Charles Rye and Robert Knight in one final examination of the figures before he committed Bowaters to go forward with it. The total estimated cost, including $2.55m for 'contingencies, in-cluding escalation', came to $38m, or about 68 per cent of the combined cost of the two new machines at Calhoun, which were profit-earning assets rather than part of the services provided by the Bowater Organisation for its members. It was not at all the kind of proposition which the American institutions would be easily per-suaded to accept, but their support was vital.[33]

Nor did it come before them at a propitious moment. Morgan Stanley, acting for Bowaters, put Danube and Dogwood to the insurance companies and the banks during the summer and autumn of 1956, hoping to borrow some 75 per cent of the capital required. In April, in another part of the financial field – Montreal – Bowaters' North American company had raised $Can.17.5m to provide

TABLE 26. *Catawba sulphate mill, summarised estimate of con-struction cost, 1956*

	$
Mill, steam and power plant, site and timberlands, other facilities, engineering	32,950,000
Interest during construction	1,500,000
Contingencies, including escalation	2,550,000
Working capital	1,000,000
Total	38,000,000

Source: Morgan Stanley, 'Bowaters Carolina Corporation', 15 December 1956, p. 7.

equity capital for the third and fourth machines at Calhoun, for the pulp mill, and for a fibreboard mill which was at an advanced stage of planning.[34] On top of that came the Mersey purchase (Chapter 12.2 above), requiring another $52m in cash from the Montreal company for the equity shares (p. 254 below); how it was to be raised was still unsure. It is hardly surprising, in the circumstances, that the prospective lenders looked hard at Danube and Dogwood, especially at Dogwood: the more so after the Suez fiasco jangled their nerves in November. 'Stuart Cragin [of J. P. Morgan]', Kirwan-Taylor reported to Eric Bowater on 22 November, 'spent some time explaining that the "boom" is over and there is no longer an abundance of money available.'[35] There is evidence also that neither Kirwan-Taylor himself, nor Currie, nor Meyer were entirely happy about Dogwood but the Chairman – or rather, in North America, the President – overrode them.[36]

The mill was to be set in about 1,300 acres along the Catawba River, about eight miles from the small town of Rock Hill (25,000 inhabitants), South Carolina. It had water, good communications, good access to coal, natural gas and pulpwood. Bowaters Carolina Corporation was set up to run it and it came into production in July 1959.[37]

The mill's whole output, up to 134,000 tons a year, was to be sold for twenty years to the Bowater Corporation of North America, which in turn contracted to sell it to Bowater Paper Corporation in England. The price to be charged by the mill company, and agreed by both the other parties, was to be the general contract price for semi-bleached pulp at the time of delivery but if the North American Corporation bought less than 134,000 tons a year, or if the price fell below $125 a ton, then the North American Corporation undertook to lend the mill company enough money to offset losses or to keep its working capital at $1m after making all payments due for the service of the loan capital. Moreover, the Bowater Paper Corporation, if it failed to buy all the pulp contracted for, similarly undertook to maintain the mill company's working capital at $1m.[38]

These contracts, with their related guarantees of the price of pulp and of Carolina's working capital, were insisted upon by the American institutions as a condition of making the loans – up to $26m in $5\frac{3}{4}$ per cent Mortgage Bonds: $3.2m in $4\frac{3}{4}$ per cent Notes – which the mill company needed. Under these conditions, the loans were as nearly risk-free as they could be and it may be thought that they bore interest at an ample rate. This, however, was the price Eric Bowater agreed to pay for the Catawba pulp supplies and, at the time he agreed to pay it, there seemed to be no reason to fear that the guarantees would ever operate.

12.6 SELF-SUFFICIENCY: THE BOWATER STEAMSHIP COMPANY

One of Sir Eric Bowater's successors remarked that every great man wishes either to own a newspaper or to own ships. Eric Bowater, so far as newspapers were concerned, was content to supply the paper they were printed on but in the early fifties he began to show a desire to become, through Bowaters, an owner of ships, which was what prompted Martin Ritchie's remark. Exactly what prompted the desire is uncertain. Those who knew him have suggested that, just as in 1937 he was provoked into seeking sources of raw materials by the excessive prices asked by foreign suppliers, so at the time of the Korean war he was provoked into the idea of owning ships by the excessive rates Bowaters were then obliged to pay. Certainly the result was the same. It became his settled policy that just as Bowaters ought to control their own sources of raw materials, so they should control ships for carrying raw materials and for finished goods. What is equally certain is that, once Bowaters had their ships, Eric showed every sign of enjoying the possibilities they opened up for him. He used one, once, for a private cruise in the Caribbean and they added to the resources at his and the Corporation's disposal for sumptuous entertaining.

Ship-owning was not entirely a new departure for Bowaters. Newsprint always had to leave Newfoundland by sea and for many years the company had owned ships – seven or more during the Second World War, of which four were sunk – to carry it. In 1954 they had only one ship, SS *Corner Brook*, which was about to be scrapped, but to replace her two vessels were being built in Dennys' yard at Dumbarton. At Corner Brook, however, they knew their limitations. The company owned ships but did not manage them. That function they prudently contracted out to Furness, Withy & Co.

The conception forming in Eric Bowater's mind, early in 1954, was of something far grander than the relatively modest Corner Brook operations. It began to take written shape, as Eric's conceptions about this time were apt to do, in a document prepared by Kirwan-Taylor. He analysed Bowaters' use of sea transport at considerable length and concluded that it might be advisable to form a new subsidiary company to own the two ships then building, of 7,000 tons each, one new medium-size ship and five new smaller ones, requiring in all a capital investment of some £2m for the six new ships he proposed. The two 7,000 ton ships – semi-icebreakers – would carry newsprint, as already planned, between Corner Brook and the United States' Atlantic seaboard. The rest would provide about half the ships required to carry raw materials produced by Bowater companies in Scandinavia and North America, and they would be designed to adapt to as many likely kinds of cargo as possible: timber, wood pulp or paper. As to management, the Corner Brook precedent should be followed, though not necessarily with Furness, Withy.[39]

Much discussion followed and much advice was sought, within and outside the business. H. M. S. Lewin, writing in July 1954, favoured a subsidiary which would control the ships as well as owning them and the Chairman scribbled agreement in the margin.[40] That probably settled the matter but final decisions were not taken until nearly the end of the year. At a Corporation Board meeting in December,

the Chairman said that for some long time past he had been deeply concerned at the vulnerable position of the Organisation in regard to shipping when it was borne in mind that (i) the Corner Brook mill relied wholly on shipping for its existence, (ii) similar circumstances applied to our Scandinavian mills and (iii) the whole of the output of saleable pulp from our new Tennessee mill would be shipped to the United Kingdom. Moreover, raw material requirements . . . would be considerably stepped up . . . and in one form or another upwards of one million tons of raw materials would have to be carried in ships each year, of which more than half came from our own sources.

Then, broadly speaking, he adopted Kirwan-Taylor's proposals for the composition and purposes of the Bowater fleet, saying that the total investment required, taking the two ships already building along with the rest, would probably reach between £3½m and £4m, which 'might be obtained from fixed loans through the banks or finance houses dealing primarily with the shipping trade, and/or circulating acceptances'.[41]

An Office Memorandum of 21 January 1955 announced the formation of the Bowater Steamship Co. Ltd.[42] It was a wholly-owned subsidiary of the Corporation and its first ship, named *Margaret Bowater* after the Chairman's wife, was about to leave on her maiden voyage to Corner Brook. Before the year was out *Sarah Bowater*, named after the Chairman's daughter, followed *Margaret Bowater* to sea. In the Corporation's Annual Report for 1955 it was announced that five new diesel-driven vessels each of 4,750 tons

The *Sarah Bowater* prepared for launching at Dumbarton, May 1955. *Scotnews*

deadweight had been designed 'for our regular traffic between the United Kingdom, North America and particularly Scandinavia'. There would soon be a Bowater fleet in being.

12.7 THE FINANCE OF OPTIMISM

In September 1957 Hedderwick Hunt Cox & Co., London stock-brokers, helped by Kirwan-Taylor, computed the cost of the expansion programme undertaken by Bowaters about 1952 and expected to be completed eight or nine years later. They put the total at

£124.5m, of which £88m had been or would be invested in North
America and £36.5m in the United Kingdom. Sums invested else-
where, presumably up to that date insignificant, they ignored (see
Table 27).

This analysis betrays immense optimism about Bowaters' profitability during the years covered by the expansion programme.
'Prior charge issues' provided about 72 per cent of the total capital
sum required. Very healthy and rising profits would be needed to
service the loan capital, to provide depreciation on the new plant
installed and to generate £26.25m 'internal resources', to say
nothing of providing dividends for the stockholders.

This was entirely in the Bowater tradition. From its earliest days
the business had been built up by daring expansion financed by
heavy borrowing, and always the assumption had been that the
returns from a growing market would outpace the cost of servicing
loans, of depreciation and of other inescapable calls on the company's revenue. This was still the assumption underlying the expansion planned for both sides of the Atlantic in the mid-fifties. Sir Eric,
at the height of his career, discussed Bowaters' plans for the United
Kingdom in his address to the Annual Meeting at Chester in 1955
when a fleet of fifty coaches took about 1,400 stockholders to visit
the Mersey Paper Mills and the Multiwall Sack Factory at Ellesmere
Port. 'Few programmes on this scale', he said,

TABLE 27. *Bowater Paper Corporation, capital costs of expansion,
actual or projected, 1952–61 (approx.)*

	North America £m	United Kingdom £m	Total £m
Already provided			
Prior Charge issues	70.00	20.00	90.00
Ordinary share issues		8.25[a]	8.25
Total	70.00	28.25	98.25
Sum transferred to			
N. America[b]	+10.75	−10.75	
Total	80.75	17.50	98.25
Found or to be found from			
internal resources	7.25	19.00	26.25
Total required to completion	88.00	36.50	124.50

[a] Represents proceeds of rights issue, 1955.
[b] Represents $30m provided by BPC through Bowater Corporation of North
America for equity investment in Tennessee and South Carolina.

Source: Table on p. 10 of 'A memorandum on Bowater Paper Corporation
Limited', prepared by Hedderwick Hunt Cox & Co., September 1957.

– and few such exist – can ever have received such prolonged consideration and been the subject of scrutiny from so many aspects, technical and
otherwise. The plan, as it stands today, has been modified to meet the
pattern of sales and of consumption of our products, as we now see it, for a
considerable time ahead and let me say that we consider it vital to the
maintenance of our rightful place in the sun.

That required, as Hedderwick Hunt made plain, a great deal of
capital. We must consider the arrangements for raising it, both in
the United Kingdom and in North America.

The United Kingdom

A great deal of money-raising was done through subsidiaries,
especially in North America, but it was in the Bowater Paper
Corporation in London that the guiding financial strategy was
determined, because it was with the Corporation that the ultimate
financial responsibility lay. 'The Corporation', as the members of a
high-level committee put the matter in 1960, 'could not allow a
subsidiary to fail to meet its obligations',[43] and that held true
outside the United Kingdom as well as within.

The Corporation's closest concern, nevertheless, was with the
business in the United Kingdom and with the United Kingdom
Development Plan, accepted in principle early in December 1954
and elaborated during 1955. It was expected to be completed in two
stages within five years and to require, according to the preliminary
estimates, about £21m, a figure to which more detailed calcu-
lations, twelve months later, added another £5m, with promise of
more to come on account of what the Chief Engineer called 'possible escalation' and of 'possible further expenditure' – £3.6m –
'which might arise before 1960 on major schemes already under
review by the Chief Engineer or for early consideration'.[44]

Raising the money, in the prosperous atmosphere of 1954–5,
seemed to present no great difficulty. 'As regards the amount,
means and method of raising the new capital', said Eric Bowater in
December 1954 with, perhaps, even greater self-confidence than
usual, '. . . obviously during the course of the coming year advantage would be taken of any favourable opportunity which may
arise.'[45] A cash forecast prepared for him, he said, 'indicated that if
Stage I of the scheme was completed [by the end of 1958] the new
capital required, even after taking care of the substantial amounts
still outstanding on current projects . . ., would be at maximum
£7/8 million and the remainder, which was not an inconsiderable
part of the whole, would be found out of our own resources'.

In 1954 about £1.8m had been raised by a rights issue of Ordinary shares, presumably to take care of the 'substantial amounts still outstanding on current projects'. The new capital required for the UK Development Plan was brought in by another rights issue, in June 1955, of 2.4 million Ordinary shares at 70s., which provided about £8.2m.[46] That left a considerably larger sum, and a sum, moreover, which was showing a marked propensity to rise as the months went by, to be found from Bowaters' own resources.

Eric Bowater, as we have seen, was confident that it could be done. So was Charles Rye, who had been Comptroller since 1952. In July 1955 he was optimistic enough to recall

that when we took into account Stage II of the capital expansion we anticipated that we would be more than able to meet that expenditure out of accruing resources and that by 1962 or 1963 we would have in fact covered the whole of the capital expenditure from such accruing resources *theoretically* leaving the whole of the £8.2 million free.

Those were brave days! Table 27 shows that by September 1957 the total capital requirement for the UK had gone up to £36.50m, of which £19m was to be found internally. The rights issue was followed, in October 1955, by a capital reorganisation in which half-a-dozen Preference issues of the Corporation and its United Kingdom subsidiaries were consolidated into one issue of $5\frac{1}{2}$ per cent Cumulative Preference stock of the Corporation; the issued Ordinary capital of the Corporation was doubled by capitalisation of £9.6m from reserves; and the authorised share capital of BPC was increased to £35m, of which £26.445m was in issue. At the same time the three mill companies in England were amalgamated into Bowaters United Kingdom Pulp & Paper Mills Ltd.[47]

'Poor old Jack Keeling', wrote Eric Bowater on 14 September 1955, 'has had a nervous breakdown and has been ordered complete rest for several months.'[48] For Eric Bowater there could scarcely have been a heavier blow either in business or privately. Sir John Keeling, Vice-Chairman of the Corporation since 1948, had been at Eric's side since his earliest days as head of the business. 'His absence from his office at this time', the letter goes on, 'is a cause for some anxiety and I shall miss him a very great deal. I can only hope and pray that he will recover fully but I am fearful he may not.' Sir John never, in fact, returned to quite so central a position in Bowaters' counsels. For the last seven years, the most demanding years of his career, Eric Bowater was deprived, to a large extent, of his oldest and closest adviser's help and support.

North America

Bowaters' hunger for capital was even greater in North America than in the United Kingdom. As well as the developments in Tennessee from the buying of the site to the start-up of the fourth machine it included the acquisition of Mersey Paper Co., the construction of the sulphate mill at Catawba, mills for building board and groundwood, and speeding-up of machines at Corner Brook and Mersey. In 1957 the total cost, by the time it was all finished, was expected to reach $246m – £88m – against £36.5m for expansion at home.[49]

Bowaters' intention was that all the capital they needed in America, apart from the original equity investment in Tennessee, should be found in America by methods radically different from those they employed in England. About 75 per cent of the money, as we have seen, was to be borrowed from American insurance companies and banks. The remaining 25 per cent was to be equity capital, supplied either by the Bowater Corporation of North America or from retained profits. Behind the North American Corporation stood the Bowater Paper Corporation but only as a last resort. The general assumption was that the North American Corporation, when necessary, would go to the market on its own side of the Atlantic.

These plans were dislocated by the decision to buy Mersey. It was precipitated by the death of I. W. Killam and no provision had been made for it. It had to be fitted in alongside the difficult negotiations for loans for the fourth machine at Calhoun and the Catawba pulp mill (Chapter 12.5 above). The equity capital for these projects and others was to be provided from $17.5m raised by the North American Corporation from an issue of 5 per cent Cumulative Redeemable Preference shares in April 1956 (pp. 246–7 above), but that issue had not long been made when Mrs Killam, on 8 June 1956, accepted Bowaters' offer for her holding in Mersey (p. 233 above).

For Mersey Bowaters had to pay $53,754,501, of which they had to find $51,760,290 in cash – a formidable undertaking in itself and doubly formidable when this sum was added to the $26m they needed for the fourth machine at Calhoun and the $38m for the pulp mill at Catawba. Since the proceeds of NAC's Preference issue were opportunely to hand, $15m intended for Tennessee and Carolina was promptly diverted towards Nova Scotia, by way of an issue of Common stock taken up by NAC in a new Mersey company formed to buy the assets of the old one, but that $15m would have to be replaced and the balance of the Mersey purchase money (about $36m) would have to be found.

During the early summer of 1956 plans were worked out for raising $9.9m by a public issue of $5\frac{1}{2}$ per cent Cumulative Preference shares in the new Mersey company and for a private placing in New York of $26m twenty-year $4\frac{7}{8}$ per cent Series A First Mortgage Bonds of the same company. Meanwhile the Bank of Montreal lent new Mersey the $36m needed to complete the purchase of old Mersey.

This very large sum was lent by the Bank, on the authority of its President, Gordon Ball, with no more formality than the verbal assurances of Eric Bowater and George Currie, thus demonstrating once again the solidity of Bowaters' credit in North America. As to the prospect of raising permanent finance in the summer of 1956, Ball was not encouraging. The money market, he told Currie on 16 August, 'had worsened during the last two weeks' and the prime rate for commercial loans would go up $\frac{1}{4}$ per cent in four days' time. Of the proposed Mersey Preference issue 'he said that his advice . . . if given to-day would be that such an issue could not be marketed on reasonable terms' and he asked what the issue was for. 'I told him', Currie reported, 'it was to replace the investment in the equity of the Mersey Company, thus replacing funds intended for expansion in the south.' Ball responded with a warning against the danger of over-expansion. 'He ventured to advise that he thought we should go slow in the expansion of plants and re-appraise the future.'[50]

As doubts thickened around his expansion plans, Eric Bowater suffered another heavy loss from his small circle of close advisers. In September 1956 Herbert Inston died. 'I was more or less expecting it', Eric wrote,

but it came as a shock to realise I had lost my most trusted counsellor and helper. I find it difficult to realise that I must do without him too. He was the one to whom I always talked about all my problems and difficulties and whose advice I sought most. Also I tried things out on him, and he helped me with my speeches and A.G.M.s, etc. He was a wise, gentle creature and I shall greatly miss him. I was fond of him, too, and feel more alone than ever without him.[51]

No matter what the future might hold, and for the first time since the thirties a threat of over-capacity in the newsprint industry was beginning to appear, Eric Bowater was determined, in the autumn of 1956, that Bowaters' American expansion should go ahead as planned (pp. 235–6 above). That meant that $15m would have to be found, in the difficult money markets of 1956–7, to replace the sum diverted to Mersey. The Mersey Preference issue, made at the end of August 1956, went well enough. Why not follow it, not later than March 1957, with a $15m issue of NAC Preference shares, thus duplicating the issue of which the proceeds had been diverted?[52]

In mid-November NAC made an issue of 5½ per cent Cumulative Redeemable Preference shares. It was not designed to raise $15m but to raise $7,162,500 ($7.5m nominal), at a price yielding 5¾ per cent. The prospectus simply said that the proceeds would be used 'to provide $6,000,000 additional capital for Bowaters Southern Paper Corporation required . . . in connection with the installation of a fourth newsprint machine and other work, and for other corporate purposes of the Company'.

The reception of the issue, not warm, suggested that Canadian investors shared Gordon Ball's misgivings about Bowaters' expansion. It became clear that the full $15m required for NAC's subsidiaries could not be found in North America. Unless it were found somewhere, Bowaters' North American expansion could not go on, for no loan capital would be forthcoming until the equity capital had been provided. Therefore the financial wheel came full circle. The Bowater Paper Corporation found itself obliged to provide the cash, just as the Corporation had found it for the original equity capital of Bowaters Southern. 'It has become clear', Rye wrote to L. G. Pearce at the Bank of England in December 1956, 'that further finance cannot be raised in North America unless and until there is injected into the North American Corporation some new equity capital by this U.K. Parent Corporation.'[53]

The means chosen for raising the money was an issue by BPC of £15m 5¾ per cent Convertible Unsecured Loan stock. The sum raised would be far greater than was needed in North America but by the autumn of 1956 it was clear, in Eric Bowater's words to the BPC Board, 'that because of capital expenditure cash resources would be running into a deficit commencing from next year'.[54] Bowaters' profits as a whole, that is to say, were not rising fast enough to stand the strain put upon them by the demands of the expansion programme. In 1957 the trading surplus of the group turned out 6 per cent greater than in 1956 but, by the time loan interest and depreciation had been provided for, the profit before tax was nearly 4 per cent less. Lloyds Bank were as willing as ever to give temporary help but, for permanent expansion, permanent capital would be needed and, if it was not being generated plentifully enough internally, it would have to be raised on the market.

Morgan Stanley, before the issue, ventured to criticise it. They were uneasy, as always, about the amount of debt the Bowater

Organisation carried. Eric, probably under considerable strain, was irritated and let his irritation be known in a telephone call. Kirwan-Taylor, writing in an aeroplane between New York and Montreal, did his best to calm the Chairman down – 'having aired their views and heard our replies position is now better understood and I feel sure Morgastan and J.P.M. will co-operate fully'.[55] No doubt they did.

In February 1957 the loan stock was successfully offered to Bowater stockholders in the United Kingdom at £97. 10s. per cent, showing a yield of nearly 6 per cent. Investors were offered three opportunities of converting their holdings into Ordinary shares, on terms stated in the prospectus, in July of 1959, 1960 and 1961, so that, if the stock were fully converted, there would be no permanent addition to Bowaters' loan capital but considerably greater profits would have to be earned to keep up the value of dividends on the Ordinary stock.

The purpose of the issue, as stated in the prospectus, ranged widely. The aims of the United Kingdom Development Plan of 1955 were briefly rehearsed and to them were added provisions for

the acquisition and equipping of a factory to manufacture, under licence, an improved type of fibre drum in association with a subsidiary company of Continental Can Company Incorporated of the United States of America and for the Corporation's participation in the developments of the Bowater-Scott Corporation Limited and Bowater-Eburite Limited, important associated companies of the Corporation.

On the North American side, the prospectus spoke of 'an additional programme of development . . . at an estimated cost of some $60 million', including the sulphate pulp mill, the fibre-board mill, the abortive groundwood pulp mill at Mersey, Nova Scotia, and further speeding-up in Newfoundland and Nova Scotia. The intention disclosed in the prospectus was to put up new equity capital for the Montreal company. The sum required was £5.7m which, with Exchange Control permission, was to be used to provide Canadian dollars to take up three million Common shares. The shares were issued in March 1957 but, because of delays in engineering and construction in America, they were paid for by instalments and did not become fully-paid until sometime in 1959.[56]

In Bowaters' original plans for financing expansion in the United Kingdom and in North America the loan stock issue of 1957 had no place. It was forced upon them by disappointing profits in the United Kingdom and by the growing difficulty of raising loan capital, or indeed capital of any sort, in the United States and

Canada. These were all signs of the times: of that totally unexpected break in the growth of the newsprint market which was beginning to threaten the foundations of Bowaters' policy.

Bowaters' financial planning in its original form provided for separate financing on each side of the Atlantic. It had certainly never been contemplated at this stage that BPC should provide funds in any form for North America. The loan stock issue, by contrast, showed how interdependent the two sides of the business were, with one of the main links running through the pulp mills, designed as they were to supply pulp to Bowater mills in the United Kingdom. It was the prospect of not getting finance for the pulp mill at Catawba, above all else, which drove Bowaters to provide dollar capital with money raised in the United Kingdom. The technical skill displayed in the whole intricate operation reflected credit on the Chairman's advisers and staff on both sides of the Atlantic.

The American side of Bowaters' business, by 1957, was very important and becoming more so. It was regularly providing 65–70 per cent of Bowaters' total profits and the proportion was tending to grow (Table 28). It was also supplying a high and rising propor-

TABLE 28. *Bowater Paper Corporation, sources of profits,** 1950–61*

Year	UK companies (%)	Overseas companies (%)
To 30 Sept.		
1950	50–	50+
1951	57	43
1952	22	78
1953	44	56
To 31 Dec.		
1954 (15 month)	45	55
1955	35	65
1956	30	70
1957	29	71
1958	35	65
1959	33	67
1960	30	70
1961	22	78

* Trading surplus

Sources: 1954 AGM speech, 30 May 57.
1960 AGM speech, 1 June 61.
1961 Robert Knight to Chairman 24 May 62, 49/52.BC(i).
All other years – BPC Board minutes.

tion of the pulp and timber needed by the mills in the United Kingdom. That, to Eric Bowater, seems to have been almost more important than the contribution to profits. Hence his unwavering persistence in keeping the Catawba project alive and unpostponed.

CHAPTER THIRTEEN

Expansion into adversity
1957–1960

13.1 'A GREAT AND ALMOST REVOLUTIONARY CHANGE'

It was Sir Eric Bowater's custom, in January every year, to dine with Bowaters' staff in London and afterwards to deliver a forthright address on the state of the business. In 1958 his message was not pleasant. 'Since we dined here together last January', he said, 'a great and almost revolutionary change has come over the economic climate of the world. The change, of course, is very definitely one for the worse; and the nature of it a great deal more far-reaching in its adverse effects on industry than many had expected, myself, I'm frank to admit, included.'[1]

The 'great and almost revolutionary change' was not, by earlier and later standards, very severe. Nevertheless there were symptoms of recession in the USA during 1957–8 and again two or three years later. The long decline of the British economy was marked by 'credit squeezes' which carried the Bank Rate to 7 per cent in 1957–8 and in 1961, and in the late fifties and again in 1962–3 unemployment figures rose alarmingly, though briefly, to more than half a million – over 2 per cent of the working population – though they rapidly fell back to levels which, for nearly twenty years, had come to be accepted as right and proper: part of the natural order of things.

These mild ripples on what was still, for the industrial nations, a strongly rising tide of economic expansion could not have come at a worse moment for the newsprint industry. Both newspaper publishers and newsprint makers, Eric Bowater told his staff, 'anticipated a continuance of the steady yearly increase in consumption of about three and a half per cent which we had enjoyed, almost without a break, since the war; and both . . . planned accordingly'. When that anticipation was falsified by recession, the newsprint makers were far more awkwardly placed than the newspaper publishers. Plans for increasing production, involving construction programmes spread over several years, were far less readily reduced or cancelled than the newspaper publishers' plans for buying, especially spot buying. As a consequence productive capacity went on building up well in advance of demand, especially in North America, where in 1957 productive capacity for newsprint rose by about 10 per cent over 1956; in 1958, by 8 per cent over 1957 and the rise continued into the sixties. Meanwhile production, responding to slacker demand, was scarcely greater in 1957 than in 1956 and in 1958 it actually fell by nearly 4 per cent while buyers worked through their stocks (Table 29).

TABLE 29. *North America, newsprint capacity and production, 1956–60*

	Capacity 000 short tons	% change	Production 000 short tons	% change
1956	7,868		8,186	
1957	8,677	+10	8,223	=
1958	9,339	+ 8	7,854	− 4
1959	9,911	+ 6	8,538	+ 9
1960	10,010	+ 1	8,777	+ 3

Source: Canadian Pulp and Paper Association, as for Appendix I, Tables 2 and 3.

The mechanics of the process as they affected Bowaters were explained by Sir Eric:

The effects of inflation . . . suddenly became masters of the situation; money became scarce and expensive, people bought less, advertising naturally declined, circulations shrank or became static and publishers here and in the United States found themselves with very large stocks or inventories of newsprint on their hands. Moreover, the anticipated three and a half per cent increase in consumption did not materialise and stocks in publishers' hands will clearly have to be liquidated. All this obviously amounts to reduced orders to the mills, both here and in North America, which in turn means curtailment of production in those mills.[2]

In other words, the position of the newsprint makers, not only in North America but in the United Kingdom too, had suddenly reversed itself. In the mid-fifties, by enthusiastic speeding-up of machinery, not least in Bowaters' mills, they had barely kept pace with demand and for a year or two were working above their machines' rated capacity. Now, in 1958, world capacity had increased by 8 per cent over 1957 but demand had dropped by 2 per cent so that they found themselves faced with having to work

uneconomically far below the rated capacity: a predicament un-
comfortably reminiscent of the thirties.

It is difficult to over-emphasise the seriousness, for Bowaters, of
the rapid and lasting change which came over the balance of supply
and demand in the newsprint industry between 1956 and 1958. In
spite of Eburite, in spite of Bowater-Scott, newsprint was still much
the most important product of the Bowater Organisation and much
the most important source of profits. Accordingly all the most
ambitious expansion plans discussed in Chapter 12 – two new
machines at Mersey (England), two new machines at Northfleet,
two new machines in Tennessee; the buying of Mersey (Nova
Scotia); the setting-up of the Catawba pulp mill; the formation of
the Bowater Steamship Co. – were aimed at consolidating and
expanding Bowaters' position as the largest makers of newsprint in
the world.

They were founded, as Eric Bowater indicated to the staff, on a
calculated risk: that demand for newsprint would go on growing
for many years in the future at much the same rate – $3\frac{1}{2}$ per cent,
compound – as for many years in the past and that the rise in
capacity would not get very much out of step with it. Scarcely had
the expansion plans been put into execution than the underlying
calculation turned out to be false and Bowaters had to face the
consequences. Expansion, nevertheless, continued.

13.2 THE IMPACT OF EBURITE

Bowaters' packaging interests at the beginning of 1957, all in the
United Kingdom, consisted of three comparatively small undertakings – fibre drums, multiwall sacks, paper bags – all wholly-
owned through Associated Bowater Industries; and Bowater-
Eburite Ltd, in which Bowaters held no more than 40 per cent of the
Ordinary capital,* which owned the Eburite interests and Bowaters'
Fibre Containers, the largest of Bowaters' original packaging
enterprises (see Figure 7). Of the three wholly-owned businesses,
politely referred to as being 'in the development stage',[3] two –
multiwall sacks and paper bags – were consistent loss-makers.
Bowaters' Fibre Containers, on the other hand, was profitable but,
so long as Bowaters remained minority shareholders in Bowater-
Eburite, the greater part of its profits were liable to be diverted away
from the Corporation.

This was not a situation which Bowaters intended should be

---

* Increased from 28 per cent (p. 239 above) between July and December 1956 (BPC 29.xi.56).

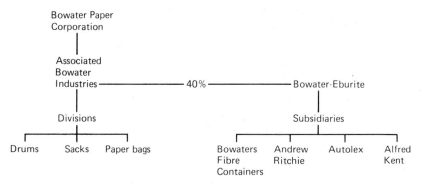

7 Bowaters' packaging interests at the beginning of 1957.

permanent. Early in 1957 they carried their plans a stage further. Rye, Kirwan-Taylor and W. R. T. Whatmore formulated a proposal for a reverse takeover, in which Bowater-Eburite would take over the three 'development' businesses from the Corporation but, in the process, would cease to be an associate of the Corporation and become its subsidiary. The plan was for Bowater-Eburite to take over ABI and its assets, issuing as consideration sufficient Ordinary shares to give the Corporation a majority holding in Bowater-Eburite's Ordinary capital. Among the assets would be £1m newly contributed in cash by the Corporation to finance extensions which the subsidiaries had already decided upon.[4]

This was a splendid proposition for the Bowater Paper Corporation: considerably less so for the other shareholders in Bowater-Eburite. They, who owned the majority of the shares, were being asked to give up their holding in a profitable undertaking in return for assets of which the best that could be said, and Charles Rye said it, was that 'the profit record is a matter of the future rather than the past'. It was felt, and again the phrase is Charles Rye's, 'that a "gimmick" [was] needed'. It took the form of a distribution by Bowater-Eburite of bonus shares, made possible by the capitalisation of reserves so greatly out of proportion to the nominal value of the issued capital as to allow for a distribution of more than three new shares for every one old share held. In the event the issue was on a basis of two for one.[5]

Whilst Bowaters were putting together a package which, they hoped, would satisfy the Bowater-Eburite shareholders, an opportunity arose for another acquisition in the packaging industry. Hunt Partners Ltd of London and South Wales, owned as to 60 per cent of the Ordinary capital by the Hunt family, though consistently profitable during the early fifties, was caught in the credit squeeze of 1957 and the directors, evidently, were open to offers. In May 1957 they accepted an offer from Bowaters, through ABI, for their company's 600,000 Ordinary shares. They were to receive the equivalent of £697,500 in 300,000 Bowater shares plus £37,500 in cash. Hunts' profits for five years to 31 March 1956 had averaged £118,000 a year and Bowaters expected a return of 14 per cent on their outlay 'but', said Eric Bowater, 'there is every reason to suppose that the potential earning capacity of the business should readily exceed its previous levels'.[6] The business was attractive to Bowaters because Hunts made folding cartons which would be complementary to corrugated cases made by Bowater-Eburite.

The reasoning behind the acquisition, based on the revolutionary changes that were coming over the food industries, was explained from the Chairman's office:

It has been evident for some time that in order to fully and effectively round off our case making businesses entry into the carton field is highly desirable. The corrugated case industry is closely allied to the carton industry in that approximately 70% of the consumer demand is for food packaging. In recent years there have been significant changes in the packaging of food and other products, particularly in view of the rapid growth of super-market or help-yourself stores and the introduction of frozen foods in this country, and these changes have led to a steady growth in pre-packaging and a greatly increased usage of cartons. It is anticipated that this growth will continue.

The note added that many of Bowaters' customers were large consumers of folding cartons, which, when filled, were packed into corrugated cases for bulk distribution, so that there were obvious advantages in being able to offer a combined service. Moreover 'by developing the corrugated box and the carton together, it may well be possible to produce worth while packaging economies and improvements in performance'.[7]

Hunts were added to the parcel of assets to be acquired by Bowater-Eburite, their shares being offered by the Corporation in exchange for shares in Bowater-Eburite. By the beginning of July 1957 negotiations between Bowaters and the non-Bowater directors of Bowater-Eburite had gone far enough for circulars to go out to Bowater-Eburite shareholders. Rye and others were nervous of their reaction to the revelation that their company was on the point of becoming a Bowater subsidiary but there seem to have been no serious objections. Perhaps Hunts' record of profitability helped; it must certainly have been welcome. On 24 July 1957 Bowaters duly emerged as owners of 55.2 per cent of Bowater-Eburite's Ordinary capital.

Between the summer of 1957 and the end of 1959 Bowaters proceeded with the swallowing of Eburite. ABI, having no longer any trading function, was abolished and Bowater-Eburite, on 1 October 1957, became a direct subsidiary of the Corporation, holding in turn the capital of subsidiaries producing fibre containers, bulk packaging (drums and sacks) and flexible packaging, including paper bags. Then, on 16 December 1959, the minority shareholders in Bowater-Eburite were given the opportunity of exchanging into BPC shares. Holders of over 99 per cent of the outstanding shares accepted and Bowater-Eburite became a wholly-owned subsidiary of the Corporation. In June 1960 the name Eburite disappeared, as years before the name Lloyd had disappeared, and Bowater Packaging Ltd was set up. To outward appearances, the swallowing was complete.

To swallow is one thing, to digest another, and so Bowaters were to find with Eburite, by far their most important acquisition in the United Kingdom since Lloyds more than twenty years earlier. Lloyds was the larger acquisition of the two, being in fact larger than Bowaters themselves, but it belonged essentially to the newsprint industry, which Bowaters thoroughly understood, and it marked no real change of emphasis within the group. Moreover, with Lloyds, no managers, except perhaps Percy Denson, entered Bowaters who could conceivably challenge the existing authorities and their methods of running the business. With Eburite, matters were far otherwise. Eburite brought increased weight to the packaging side of Bowaters, and although Eburite was dead, its soul went marching on in the persons of Martin Ritchie, Chairman of Bowater Packaging, and C. F. Popham, that company's General Manager.

The soul of Eburite was essentially a simple soul: that of a business single-mindedly engaged in the conversion of paper products, and to a lesser degree other materials, into various forms of packaging. That soul had now entered the body of a vertically integrated combine which took pride in being active in every phase of the paper industry from the forest to the finished product and which, as well as producing papermakers' raw materials and finished products, also carried them in ocean-going ships at sea and fleets of motor vehicles on land. Into this wide-ranging and complex pattern Bowater Packaging was expected to fit.

This meant, in the first place, strong pressure to purchase materials for conversion from Bowater mills, themselves under strong pressure to take their pulp supplies from other Bowater mills one stage further back along the chain of integration. On this point Eric

Bowater's views were strong and unequivocal. 'He would be reluctant,' he said in 1954, 'to agree to purchase from outside any paper
supplies which are already made within the Organisation', and
about six weeks later he laid down that 'we must ourselves manufacture the full raw material requirements in the form of kraft
products and straw products for all of our conversion plants'.[8]

Next, the incomers to Bowaters were faced with a far more
centralised system of administration than they had been used to. In
matters of finance and accounting, the Eburite companies had been
virtually autonomous. Now, like Lloyd before them, they were
required to accept standardised methods and control from London.
'While there was a degree of resistance at that time and subsequently', said Martin Ritchie in 1962, in phrases which suggest
careful understatement, '. . . it was agreed that in all the circumstances it was logical to do so.'[9]

Ritchie also looked with some scepticism on Bowaters' central
services as a whole and on the London head office from which they
were directed. About seven hundred people worked there, housed
until 1958 in Stratton Street, Mayfair, and after that in an imposing
block, newly built astride the road from Knightsbridge into Hyde
Park, with a flat for the Chairman on the fourteenth floor commanding a wide view northward across Hyde Park towards the

Bowater House, Knightsbridge, the Corporation's head office since 1958.

Hampstead ridge, and guarded, on the Park side, by a ferocious Epstein sculpture of a mythical hunt. An Economy Committee in 1958, having calculated that head office expenses would rise from £270 a head per year in Stratton Street to £620 in Knightsbridge, commented: 'the Knightsbridge building allows for considerable future expansion':[10] a prospect which Ritchie probably regarded more as a threat than a promise.

Ritchie's view of head office and the central services associated with it was one that is not uncommon among managers of operating companies in large organisations. He felt that his own company – the Packaging Company – was being obliged to bear the cost of activities which either it could perform better itself or which were not necessary at all. If he persisted in these views, he would find himself in opposition to the whole system of administration, built up over many years, through which the Bowater business in the United Kingdom was run, at the centre of which were the Director in charge of Finance and Administration, Charles Rye, and the Comptroller, Robert Knight. They had the full confidence of the Chairman and they were not lightly to be challenged.

The position of a packaging subsidiary in the Bowater Organisation no doubt had disadvantages which Ritchie, looking back on his independent past, took frequent opportunity to deplore. At the same time it offered the possibility of much greater, or at any rate faster, expansion than Eburite would have been able to undertake on its own and expansion was as much to Martin Ritchie's taste as it was to Eric Bowater's.

13.3 THE ADVANCE INTO EUROPE: PACKAGING

One promising direction for expansion, about the time Bowater-Eburite became a Bowater subsidiary, was Western Europe. On 25 March 1957 the Treaty of Rome brought into existence the original European Economic Community of six members: West Germany, France, Italy, the Netherlands, Belgium, Luxembourg. The Government of the United Kingdom held aloof, then tried to establish a European Free Trade Area linking the EEC with seven countries – Austria, Denmark, Norway, Portugal, Sweden, Switzerland, the United Kingdom – which were not members. When the attempted linking of EFTA with the EEC broke down in 1959, EFTA became a scarcely veiled rival organisation to the EEC.

For Bowaters and other firms in the British paper and board industry, EFTA represented a threat rather than a promise, because the products of powerful Scandinavian competitors could come

into the United Kingdom duty-free whereas at the frontiers of the
EEC they would face a duty of 18 per cent. The EEC, on the other
hand, promised the kind of business opportunities which had previously only existed in the USA: a market notoriously hard to break
into.

To get over the EEC tariff barrier it would be necessary to acquire
factories inside it – a problem which for most British firms bristled
with difficulties. They were accustomed enough to establishing
themselves as manufacturers in distant continents, particularly in
Australia and South Africa, but the Continent was foreign territory
indeed with – as Bowaters were to find out – not only different
languages and different laws but a different conception of business
life and methods altogether. As a guide through this daunting
labyrinth Bowaters took on B. G. Alexander, a barrister and an
official of the United Nations who knew his way in Europe, and set
up a committee under C. G. Rye which included Alexander and
representatives of newsprint, packaging and Bowater-Scott.[11]

A year's investigations convinced Alexander and J. M. Ritchie, by
April 1959, that 'the Common Market countries are on the
threshold of a development in packaging, similar to that which took
place in the United States and Great Britain some ten to twelve years
ago'; that by 1975 the standard of living in Europe would have
reached 'the standard prevailing in the United States at the present
time'; and that it was 'possible to envisage an operation in Europe
in the field of packaging comparable to that which the Bowater
Organisation undertook in the United States in the field of paper
production'.[12]

The first stage in this ambitious programme was to be 'the direct
acquisition of existing plants sufficiently modern in themselves to
be able to provide a firm basis of expansion' and, by the time those
words were written, negotiations for two such plants were already
well under way. The businesses to be acquired were to be controlled
by a new Bowater holding company based in Europe, just as the
enterprises in Canada and USA were controlled from Montreal by
the Bowater Corporation of North America. Finance was to be
raised in Europe also, for among the unfamiliar inhabitants of this
strange new world were bankers prepared – indeed, anxious – to
lend at very low rates of interest. An unnamed voice from within the
Bank of England warned Rye that bankers in the Common Market
'seem to have lost all sense of their usual banking procedure' and
suggested that Bowaters should 'exercise considerable care' and
avoid unduly restrictive conditions for borrowing[13] but it is clear
that Rye and his colleagues were not to be deterred. They were eager

to explore the banking territory of continental Europe and they contemplated a pattern of finance on the American model – 75 per cent loan capital to 25 per cent equity.

By the early Autumn of 1959 the beginnings of a Bowater enterprise within the European Economic Community were taking shape. On 19 October Bowater Europe SA was set up in Brussels and immediately opened a loan account for the equivalent of £4m with the Banque de Bruxelles. This new holding company already had three subsidiaries: Bowater-Cello, making folding boxes at Ghent in Belgium; Bowater-Perrone, making corrugated containers at Genoa in Italy; Bowater-Prot (not yet wholly-owned), making folding cartons at Rheims in France. The cost of all three to Bowaters was about £1.3m,[14] but that was only the start, for all were 'intended to be bridgeheads from which it was the intention to expand in two directions, firstly through their internal development and secondly through future acquisitions', and in both directions moves were already being made.[15]

Late in 1959, as the group under Bowater Europe was being brought into existence, Bowater-Scott, the Corporation's 50-per-cent associate, was pushing towards Belgium and Italy, so that in less than two years Bowaters had created in Europe a rapidly expanding organisation which was already of respectable proportions. The wholly-owned part of it was so far entirely in packaging, emphasising the strategy of diversification and the part played in it by the formation of Bowater-Eburite. An approach to the European newsprint industry was also in preparation, but to that we shall return.

13.4 THE UNITED KINGDOM – GROWTH
IN PACKAGING

The business of Bowater Packaging, as it took shape in the United Kingdom after the absorption of Eburite, was widespread and diverse. There were factories in Scotland, on Merseyside and elsewhere in north-western England, in South Wales and in the London area. They made products which included the corrugated containers which had originally brought Bowaters and Eburite together; fibre drums, multiwall sacks, paper bags and waxed paper brought in from the Bowater side; crimped cups, bottle caps, foil trays and dishes, folding cartons and set-up boxes from Eburite. To these were added, in 1957, Hunts' cartons and, in 1959, 'Perga' waxed cartons for milk and fruit juices. Sales by 1960 (United Kingdom and Europe together) were running at about 250,000 tons

Multiwall sacks made and printed at Ellesmere Port, 1957.

out of 2,229,000 tons of paper, paper products and pulp sold by the Organisation, and the packaging company, with a trading surplus of £1,796,000, contributed 7.6 per cent of the Organisation's total trading surplus of £23,494,000.[16]

The largest and most successful branch of Bowaters' packaging business was the production of corrugated containers. The cornerstone of Bowaters' business in corrugated containers was the factory at Croydon. There was a distinct danger, however, in the late fifties, that the manufacture of corrugated containers would become an overcrowded occupation. 'The entire industry in this country', Ritchie told the GPC in March 1957, '. . . was modernising its equipment and installing plant which would increase output far beyond current demand and, as a result, competition was becoming fierce and prices were falling.' For the future he was reasonably optimistic, expecting a 14 per cent increase in demand between 1958 and 1960 which would bring demand and supply into balance again. It was unfortunate, nonetheless, that Bowaters' largest exercise so far in diversification away from newsprint should have brought them into an industry which was showing disturbing signs of following newsprint along the road to over-capacity.

During Bowater Packaging's early years it was engaged in two major capital projects which had emerged from a variety of plans formulated, originally, by Associated Bowater Industries and continued by the new management. They were characterised by a certain vagueness of intention and imprecision in planning which caused both of them, as time went on, to grow both in scope and expenditure far beyond anything originally envisaged. One, in its final form, was a factory for corrugated containers at Stevenage in Hertfordshire, where one of the original attractions of the site was the promise of assistance from the local authority, intent on developing Stevenage New Town. The other, again in its final form, was a factory for 'Flexible Packaging', later 'Paper Products', at Gillingham in Kent.

The Stevenage project began, in 1956, with a plan to lease the site and build on it, *quickly*, a factory to produce, under licence from Continental Can, the 'Leverpak', a drum with a greatly improved closing device which was regarded as a sure tonic for the not very robust fibre drum business. After a good deal of vacillation, commented upon both by Charles Rye and Stanley Bell,[17] that plan was given up in favour of making Leverpak drums elsewhere and, in August 1959, some three years after it had first engaged the attention of the General Purposes Committee, the Stevenage project emerged in its final – and more costly – form as a scheme for building a factory, at a capital cost of some £2m, to make corrugated containers, in spite of the fact that in 1956 Ritchie had said that 'he and his colleagues were not attracted by Stevenage as a location'.[18]

Fitness for purpose, indeed, seems in the end to have had little to do with the choice of the Stevenage site for new corrugating plant and the timing of the proposal was forced upon Bowaters by the terms of their agreement with Stevenage local authority. 'Mr Bell said that the proposal . . . would not have been put forward at the present time and in fact could have been postponed for two or three years yet, were it not for the necessity to fulfil Bowater-Eburite's obligation to commence the erection of a factory in Stevenage by July 1960.'[19] That date was not in fact met and, by the time estimates for the proposal had been worked out in detail, not without a certain lack of co-ordination between Containers Division and Engineering Division, the predicted cost had risen to £2.75m. No wonder Stanley Bell, in opening the GPC's discussion of the estimates, 'said that this was a very big project . . . [and] added that he was becoming more and more concerned at the magnitude of the continuing capital expenditure put forward by the various Divisions of the Organisation'.[20]

The history of the Gillingham project was very similar. It began in 1958 with a proposal, estimated to cost about £700,000, to expand certain activities in flexible packaging, hitherto under the control of the mill company at Sittingbourne, and set them up in a factory of their own, preferably at Kemsley. Here Kenneth Linforth, Director in charge of Operations, intervened. Flexible packaging involved printing and print unions were trying to insist on printers' rates of pay. If they succeeded, their success might unsettle the labour force in any nearby paper mill, and that would never do.[21] Another site must therefore be found, and by August 1959 it had been found at Gillingham.[22]

By the time a detailed proposal was put forward, in July 1960, the plan had expanded from a factory producing flexible packaging, meaning chiefly packaging papers of various types, including laminations with foil and plastic, to a factory producing paper products, meaning both packaging papers and cartons of the type made by Hunt Partners, whose activities were to be transferred from Clapton. The estimated capital expenditure had risen to £1.9 m and to that, at a very late stage, to the sharp displeasure of the Chairman, almost £950,000 had been added, giving a total estimate not far short of £3m, about four-and-a-half times as great as the sum named in the original proposal.[23]

It is difficult not to feel that this kind of exuberantly expansionary planning and unco-ordinated estimating, of which the projects at Stevenage and Gillingham were not the only examples, shows a slackening of control from the top. The plans themselves were no doubt soundly enough conceived. Those who produced them were doing their proper job in pointing out where, in their view, the business could and should be expanded and they backed their proposals with sales surveys, profit forecasts, figures of market share, ominous references to the doings of competitors. It was not for them to calculate the effect on the finances of the Corporation if too much capital expenditure were sanctioned in too short a time, or at the wrong time. It was the function of the central management of the Corporation to control these matters, which in turn caused the operators to complain of interference.

The plans in themselves may all have been desirable, but it was for the higher management to choose between desirable alternatives, having regard to the resources available. Was the higher management of Bowaters, in the late fifties, doing this part of its job? Was there the organisation necessary for it to do this part of its job? The Chairman's General Purposes Committee was not a committee of the Board and, although its pronouncements and recommendations carried a good deal of weight, it had always been told very firmly that it had no executive powers. Its function was to examine individual projects, to advise, to recommend, not to the Board but to the Chairman. It does not seem to have been encouraged to compare one project with another, to calculate the cumulative effect of several projects on the finances of the Corporation as a whole, though repeated remarks by Stanley Bell suggest that he, at least, was becoming worried, in the late fifties, at the piling of scheme on scheme, of expenditure on expenditure. The decision, however, always lay with Eric Bowater, whose judgment for thirty years had been almost uncannily sound and whose instinct was always in favour of expansion, however much, from time to time, he might complain about the cost of it. If, in the end, capital expenditure were sanctioned before revenue had been generated to pay for the upkeep of the buildings, machinery, ships and other assets which were being brought into existence, then the results would be serious.

13.5 NEWSPRINT IN THE UNITED KINGDOM AND EUROPE: ST MORITZ AND LA CHAPELLE

While the packaging projects at Stevenage and Gillingham were taking shape and growing, grave doubts were beginning to emerge, on the newsprint side of the business in the United Kingdom, about the wisdom of pursuing the Master Plan according to the original timetable: the more so since, in newsprint as in packaging, expenditure showed an alarming propensity to rise far beyond the levels allowed for in the estimates. It was evident by the beginning of 1957 that the big projects for new machines at Kemsley and Northfleet were going to cost about £1m more than had been expected and, at a meeting of the GPC in June, 'the main discussion was devoted to the expediency of proceeding with the entire development programme under the present contracting market conditions'.[24]

After that the brakes came on. Linforth, in September 1957, arranged with Walmsleys that a machine intended as No. 5 at Northfleet should go instead as No. 6 to Mersey, so that work on the building intended for it could be reduced.[25] At the Staff Dinner in January 1958 the Chairman announced a decision to defer – 'I use the word "defer" advisedly and expressly' – the installation of 'some of our machines in Britain'. In May 1958 it was reported that, out of fixed assets valued at £19m, £11.3m in the United Kingdom and £7.7m in North America were not yet earning revenue. They were nearly all on the newsprint side of the business.[26] By the end of 1959 Nos. 5 and 6 machines at Northfleet, in Robert Knight's words to the GPC, 'were in abeyance'.[27]

Knight thus signalled the end of the Master Plan, put in hand so hopefully in 1955, for the expansion of Bowaters' newsprint capacity in the United Kingdom. It was killed by over-expansion of newsprint capacity in the world generally. Its monument was a huge building put up at Northfleet for two machines which were never installed there – a building which for twenty years stood forlorn and purposeless, a constant reminder of the reality of risk in business enterprise.

The expansion of Bowaters' newsprint business in the United Kingdom might be ending in 1959 but in Europe it was just about to begin. In the original plans for going into the EEC packaging had been given priority (Chapter 13.3 above) but newsprint had never been far behind. In 1960 it was brought right to the fore with a proposal to gain control of the largest paper mill in France, Les Papeteries de la Chapelle at St Etienne-de-Rouvray near Rouen which, with five machines, had an annual output of 180,000 to 190,000 metric tons of newsprint and coated magazine paper.[28]

La Chapelle had been losing money and was controlled by Aktiengesellschaft fuer Unternehmungen der Papier-Industrie, St Moritz, which came to be known to Bowaters as Paper Industries

Ltd of St Moritz, or simply 'St Moritz', the shares of which were listed on the Zürich Stock Exchange. St Moritz held 56 per cent of the capital of La Chapelle and had holdings also in two French pulp mills: La Cellulose de Strasbourg (100 per cent) and La Cellulose du Rhône (10 per cent).

In conditions of great secrecy a deputy general manager of the Union Bank of Switzerland, W. Fankhauser, made it clear to Alexander and Kirwan-Taylor that the only way Bowaters could gain control of La Chapelle would be by gaining control of St Moritz itself and its other two subsidiaries. La Chapelle was not for sale on its own.[29] This was a considerably larger transaction than Bowaters had contemplated and they were to be offered no opportunity of following their usual practice when a company was acquired: that is, getting a report from Peat, Marwick, Mitchell on La Chapelle. Nevertheless, as John Kirwan-Taylor put it, 'The idea of controlling La Chapelle is, I think, very attractive and would place us in the forefront in Europe.'

The shares in St Moritz, in the Continental fashion, were bearer shares, so that the names of the holders were not registered and a takeover bid of the English type was impossible. Fankhauser, 'who is everything that I' – Kirwan-Taylor – 'have always understood a rugged Swiss banker to be', therefore put forward a plan to buy shares quietly on the market which would give Bowaters the 51 per cent they needed for control. This was not the kind of transaction Bowaters were used to but they accepted it as a particular situation and allowed Fankhauser to proceed, though not without some misgivings as the price of St Moritz shares rose.[30] On 9 June 1960 the required number of shares were delivered and paid for – the total cost was £4.9m[31] – and control of St Moritz, carrying with it control of La Chapelle, passed into Bowaters' hands.[32] Very shortly afterwards, and probably not by coincidence, Fankhauser left the employment of the Union Bank.

The St Moritz purchase had a sequel. Unknown, apparently, to Bowaters there had been a rival buyer, and a very formidable one – F. Béghin, one of the most powerful businessmen in France, who among many other interests, including sugar refining, owned paper mills. Fankhauser had approached Béghin as well as Bowaters but had been rebuffed because, Béghin said, 'the price suggested was outrageous'[33] and without Fankhauser's help Béghin had bought about 30 per cent of the St Moritz shares.

When Béghin found that Bowaters had beaten him to control, he was extremely angry and the anger of so powerful a figure would be dangerous to Bowaters in France, the more so because at least one major French banker – the General Manager of the Banque de Paris et des Pays-Bas – was 'upset about the way things have happened' and in a general way there was resentment that French businesses – La Chapelle and the two pulp mills – had been sold into English ownership by a Swiss banker. Late in June 1960, in an effort at gastronomic diplomacy, Eric Bowater entertained Béghin's confidential agent (Béghin himself was not available) to lunch and offered to buy Béghin's holding of 18,825 St Moritz shares at their cost to Béghin plus 10 per cent, which worked out at Sw.Frs.1,500 a share.[34] This was about Frs.400 a share less than Bowaters had paid Fankhauser, on average, but presumably Béghin did not know this. He accepted the offer. He seems to have been pacified but not altogether appeased. Almost a year later, Ritchie suggested nervously that there was a risk of Béghin buying up publications in France, 'thus depriving La Chapelle of their customers'.[35]

The total cost to Bowaters of gaining control of La Chapelle, which was the original object of gaining control of St Moritz, was £7.2m, made up of £4.9m for Fankhauser's collection and £2.3m for Béghin's shares.[36] To these sums, early in 1961, were added a further £0.5m required to gain full ownership of St Moritz by purchasing the 11,000 or so shares still outstanding in return for forty-two BPC Ordinary shares, plus Sw.Frs.20 in cash, for each St Moritz share.[37]

For their outlay Bowaters gained not only control of La Chapelle but control of La Cellulose de Strasbourg also, giving them their own pulp mill in France. That had been no part of the original intention. It simply showed how one thing can lead on to another.

Bowaters' advance into the EEC was widespread and rapid. By the end of 1960 Bowater Europe SA, in Brussels, with issued capital equivalent to £5m, headed a group of businesses, all set up or acquired by Bowaters in less than two years, which was spread over Belgium, Switzerland, France and Italy.[38] Bowater companies were producing chemical pulp and commercial alcohol at Strasbourg, and at La Chapelle newsprint, magazine papers and coated papers. La Chapelle's output of coated papers, increasingly in demand, was 22,500 tons, estimated to represent about 75 per cent of total French production.[39] On the packaging side they were chiefly producing cartons and corrugated containers. Alongside the wholly-owned businesses were three associates – Bowater-Scott in Belgium, Burgo-Bowater-Scott in Italy and Bowater-Philips in Belgium, which was being set up at Ghent to supply Philips of Eindhoven and other customers with corrugated cartons. All these enterprises had been launched with development in mind and work was going on

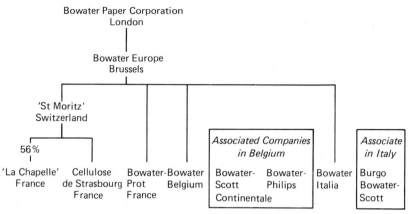

8 Bowaters' major subsidiaries and associates in Belgium, Switzerland, France and Italy, December 1960.

on building the container plant at Ghent and on planning a similar plant at Rheims in France which was never built. Perhaps most ambitious of all, a plan was coming forward for increasing La Chapelle's capacity for coated paper from 24,000 tons a year to 64,000, at a cost of £1,330,000. Despite Bowaters' original intention to concentrate, in Europe, on packaging, the lure of paper in some form seemed irresistible. In spite of predictions of over-capacity for coated papers in France by 1962, 'la Chapelle were confident that they could capture and hold the market, and fill the extra capacity within two years of installing the new machine, since the magazine publishers in France were expected to turn over more and more to coated papers'.[40]

13.6 NEWSPRINT IN AUSTRALASIA: THE TASMAN PARTNERSHIP

At much the same time as Bowaters were developing their European policy they were considering the possibility of going into newsprint manufacture in Australia or New Zealand. Australia had always been the most important destination for exports of Bowater newsprint and, in the middle and late fifties, it was being shipped there at rates of 90,000 to 100,000 tons a year from the United Kingdom and Corner Brook. Bowaters therefore were very sensitive to any change in conditions in the Australian market and, in particular, to the emergence of new competition, either from other importers, chiefly Canadian, or from local manufacturers, who might always hope to get Government preference in one way or another.

Except in special circumstances, setting up in manufacture in

Australasia was not likely to be a very attractive proposition to Bowaters so long as exporting remained profitable. Briefly, Australia had a market for newsprint but virtually no trees to make it from; New Zealand had the trees but virtually no market. It was difficult, therefore, to decide on a good site for a newsprint mill – whether it should be near the market or near the raw material – and in 1950 Eric Bowater had turned down a proposal for a New Zealand venture, backed by the New Zealand Government, in favour of his project in Tennessee (p. 202 above).

In 1955 Reeds stepped in where Bowaters had refused to tread. They went into partnership with the New Zealand Government and with New Zealand business interests in an enterprise rather similar to the one rejected by Eric Bowater in 1950. The Tasman Pulp & Paper Co., formed to develop the resources of the Kaingaroa State Forest, was putting up integrated plant incorporating newsprint, pulp and timber mills. Reeds agreed to take up 1.5 million £1 shares at par, to supply a Director of Operations for Tasman and to give Tasman employees technical help and training.[41]

Bowaters showed signs of perturbation and the GPC looked at possibilities of manufacture in Australia after Stanley Bell had asserted firmly and unconvincingly that their motive was 'not fear of Reeds' influence in that part of the world and a consequent desire to get in at all costs'.[42] The search for a site was still going on, or going on again, in 1958. Meanwhile the market turned against the newsprint makers, Tasman lost £1.7m in 1956 and £1m in 1957 and some members of the Tasman Board turned against Reeds.

Reeds, early in 1959, came to Bowaters with a suggestion for joint action. They suggested a second machine at Tasman, installed with the backing of Reeds and Bowaters, which would have the double effect of making Tasman's business profitable and providing Bowaters with the productive capacity in Australasia which they had for so long been seeking.[43] Moreover, competition between Bowaters and Tasman would be abolished.

Negotiations in New Zealand early in 1959 were conducted for Bowaters by their chief representative in Australia, Arthur Lissenden, with Stanley Bell and Charles Rye taking a close interest from London and Eric Bowater from wherever he happened to be. Bowaters' position was strong. 'I remain convinced', Eric cabled from a holiday house at Palm Beach, Florida, in March 1959, 'that all trump cards are in our hands and, while not wishing to ride roughshod over any other interested parties, am determined that our participation must be on our terms or we withdraw.'[44]

Participation was indeed very much on Bowaters' terms. Before any binding agreement was made, an Anglo-American Bowater team, including K. O. Elderkin and V. J. Sutton, went to New Zealand to investigate Tasman's operations, management, sales, development programme (including the proposal for a second machine) and legal and financial matters. Fortified by that team's report, Rye, Linforth, Kirwan-Taylor and one of Bowaters' lawyers went to New Zealand to negotiate the final arrangement, embodied in four agreements executed between September 1959 and October 1960.[45]

The effect of these agreements, so far as the outside world was aware, was to establish Bowaters and Reeds as equal partners in Tasman by virtue of equal holdings, amounting to about 17 per cent each, in Tasman's share capital, which gave them joint rights over the appointment of four directors out of twelve and of the Managing Director and over the management of the company and the training of New Zealand personnel.

Privately, agreements between the equal partners made Bowaters much the more equal of the two. For ten years, Bowaters had the right to appoint the Managing Director and their first nominee was D. W. Timmis, Eric Bowater's nephew, from Tennessee. They had the right to choose management and tuition teams for New Zealand and, again, they chose them from Tennessee. They were to deal with all matters concerning the installation of the second paper machine,

Briefing at Bowater House for the American management team before their installation at Tasman, January 1960. The picture includes K. N. Linforth (at head of table); on his left, Stanley Bell; Charles Rye (fourth from right); W. E. J. Miles (second from right); and, next to Miles, Denis Timmis.

expected to require from Tasman an investment of about £10m.
Above all, Tasman agreed to appoint Bowaters' Australian sales
company as their sole selling agent; an arrangement which not only
brought in about $250,000 a year in commission but, more impor-
tant, promoted Bowaters' name as suppliers of newsprint in
Australia.[46]

Bowaters' triumph over Reeds in New Zealand seems almost to
have been thrust upon them in spite of themselves, or in spite of Eric
Bowater. Bowaters could have established themselves in New
Zealand in 1950 but Eric rejected the opportunity and few will
doubt the soundness of his judgment, though it was not universally
appreciated at the time. Later, he rejected a possible partnership
with New Zealand Forest Products, perhaps less wisely.[47] Then
Reeds, seeing the opportunity of managing the Tasman business,
took it. The door seemed shut against Bowaters but Tasman's early
misfortunes, by casting doubt on the efficiency of Reeds' management, opened it again and Bowaters marched through. It almost
seems as if Eric Bowater was determined not to go into New
Zealand but that New Zealand was determined Bowaters should
come.

13.7 NORTH AMERICA: EXPANSION AND DIVERSIFICATION

Earlier sections of this chapter have shown how Bowaters' ambitious plans for the expansion of their newsprint business in the
United Kingdom were thwarted, during the late fifties, by the sudden change in market conditions described by Eric Bowater at the
Staff Dinner in 1958. Other projects, nevertheless, were still pushed
rapidly ahead, so that by 1960, when the advance into Europe
culminated in unexpectedly heavy expenditure on gaining control
of La Chapelle, far the greater part of Bowaters' expansion was
planned to take place outside the United Kingdom. In March 1960
£24,864,000 of capital expenditure was contemplated, though not
all approved, and the geographical distribution was:[48]

United Kingdom	£ 3,822,000	15.4 per cent
Europe	£ 9,500,000	38.2
North America	£11,542,000	46.4
Total	£24,864,000	100.0

These figures lead our attention back to North America and
first to the crowning achievement of Eric Bowater's career: the
Tennessee venture. Upon its earning power and upon the con-

fidence which that inspired in American financial institutions the development of Bowaters' North American business would chiefly depend and the North American business, as the figures set out above show, was much the most important profit centre in the Bowater Organisation.

Of the twin pillars of Bowaters' North American business, at Calhoun in Tennessee and at Corner Brook in Newfoundland, Calhoun in the late fifties was conspicuously the more successful (Table 30). Operations at Corner Brook were seriously hampered by a fire in April 1957 which, added to worsening conditions in the market, had a disastrous effect on profits. At Calhoun, by contrast, productive capacity rose as two new machines started up – No. 3 in January 1957 and No. 4 in December 1958 – and profits, despite the difficulties of the newsprint industry, remained buoyant.

In December 1959, as predicted when the Calhoun mill opened, Bowaters Southern paid their first dividend – $2,340,000 – to the Bowater Corporation of North America. The conditions precedent to the payment of any dividend, insisted upon by the providers of loan capital (pp. 213–14 above), were strict: that Southern's equity capital (reinforced in July 1959 by $7m subordinated debentures taken up by the Montreal company) and reserves should be equal in amount to the loan capital and that there should be not less than $3.5m working capital. To pay a dividend under those conditions, in the circumstances of 1959, was creditable and Southern's success was the more welcome because H. M. S. Lewin had been making gloomy noises about the outlook for Corner Brook and the other Canadian companies. 'My dear Eric', he wrote in August 1959,

I have been reviewing the latest projections of profits of the Canadian units of the Bowater Organisation for 1959. They do not make happy reading. . . . In 1959 Corner Brook's earnings after Preference dividends will fall considerably short of last year's Common dividend; and Mersey will only just make it . . . I see no reason for getting in a flap, but the situation certainly needs careful scrutiny.[49]

Canadian forebodings were not allowed to interfere with plans for expansion in the South, both at Calhoun and also, increasingly at Catawba, where the building of the sulphate pulp mill ('Dogwood') operated by Bowaters Carolina Corporation had been made possible by the confidence generated in American financial circles by the manifest success of Bowaters Southern – confidence which the American insurance companies and banks were careful to underpin with a contract from Bowaters for 134,000 tons of pulp a year at a price guaranteed never to drop below $125 a ton

TABLE 30. *Profits and newsprint production,*[a] *Corner Brook and Calhoun, 1955–9*

	Corner Brook				Calhoun			
	Profits ($Can.ooo)	Change (per cent)	Newsprint production (short tons)	Change (per cent)	Profits ($USooo)	Change (per cent)	Newsprint production (short tons)	Change (per cent)
1955	7,563		297,188		7,389		164,953	
1956	6,935	− 8	300,351	+ 1	8,719	+18	194,749	+18
1957	5,308	−23 [b]	275,798	− 8	10,962	+26	298,879 [c]	+53
1958	4,578	−14	253,534	− 8	10,441	− 5	290,852	− 3
1959	5,559	+21	263,697	+ 4	11,381	+ 9	352,607 [d]	+21

Notes: [a] Profits after depreciation but before interest on loan capital and taxation.
[b] Fire in April 1957.
[c] No. 3 machine started up January 1957.
[d] No. 4 machine started up December 1958.

Source: Profits – Corner Brook Reports and Accounts.
Calhoun, Bowater Southern Reports and Accounts.
Production – Corner Brook, Balloch, Newfoundland Operations Review, 6 February 1961, Corner Brook archives.
Calhoun, Bowater Southern archives.

(p. 247 above). The mill came into production in August 1959 and for the moment we may leave the matter there, remarking only that by then the price of chemical pulp on the open market was heading firmly downwards.

Alongside the pulp mill, in 1959, another project was taking shape at Catawba: a mill to produce hardboard for industrial users, chiefly in the furniture trade. It was to be financed by Southern, with help, by way of equity capital, from NAC: a method which would have the advantage of increasing Southern's net worth and making easier the payment of a dividend.

The origins of the venture ran back to 1955, when the Calhoun management were seeking a use for hardwood chips produced from trees in their forests and the management of Bowaters' North American business in general were seeking diversification. C. G. Cullen, who had many years' experience of hardboard in the United Kingdom, with Edward Lloyd first and then with Bowaters, came over to survey the market. 'There is undoubtedly', he reported, 'a very good and expanding market for both Hardboard and Insulation Board in the United States.' Eric Bowater's response was: 'Let us attend the official opening within two years.'[50]

The hardboard mill did not, in fact, come into operation until more than five years later, in September 1960. Why the delay? Partly, it would seem, because elaborate market surveys and, because the manufacturing process was a new one, technical research, including work on a pilot plant in Oregon, were needed;[51] partly because a decision was taken in or about August 1957, largely at A. B. Meyer's instance, to postpone building for a year in order to relieve the strain on Bowaters' finances;[52] partly, perhaps, because a great many people were associated with the project but no clear line of responsibility for its development seems to have been laid down. 'Mr Kirwan-Taylor', wrote Sam Mann, Controller of NAC, in 1955, 'I feel I am sitting at the apex of a very long triangle with you and Denis [Timmis, Secretary of Bowaters Southern] at the other two ends. Are there any more gaps which you can fill in for me?'[53] As the years passed, the estimated cost of the project rose steadily. In the early days, when Kirwan-Taylor patronisingly called it 'quite a modest venture', the figure was put at $5.5m. By the time the mill opened it had cost at least $7m and more was to come.[54]

Those responsible for Bowaters' business in North America were by no means content merely with the sulphate pulp mill and the hardboard mill at Catawba. At Mersey they were obliged to spend heavily, replacing plant which was near the end of its useful life. By the beginning of 1962, $6.5m, had been laid out, including $3.5m for complete modernisation of the electrical system, put in hand in 1960–1 and executed by Bowaters' Engineering and Development Co.[55] In the South, the minds of the management teemed with ideas. At various times in 1959 they discussed among themselves and with others projects for a chemical plant at Calhoun ($6m at first estimate in March, rising to $8.25m by October),[56] for an extension to the sulphate pulp mill at Calhoun ($13.8m),[57] and, in December 1959, for acquiring St Mary's Kraft Corporation at St Mary's, Georgia, which produced sulphate pulp, kraft paper, board, bags and sacks.

This last was an extremely ambitious project which immediately excited Eric Bowater's enthusiasm. 'This business', he said, 'would fit nicely into our development programme' – it would provide both diversification and a supply of kraft pulp – 'and I would like to pursue the matter vigorously.'[58] On 14 January 1960, in London, he tentatively agreed with the owner, Charles Gilman, to buy St Mary's for $100m. Then, after investigations and valuations his eagerness abated, to the extent of reducing the offer to $55m, which Gilman would not consider.[59] In May 1960 the negotiations collapsed, to the great relief of A. B. Meyer. 'I am so glad that this is your final decision', he wrote to Eric.

I have the uncomfortable feeling that things are not as good as we had hoped they would be . . . I do not think we really ought to buy anything to-day that is not a real bargain no matter . . . how anxious we are to diversify . . . As you know only too well, I have the unique record for being wrong most of the time but I have that peculiar and uncomfortable feeling that the moment for caution is at hand.[60]

So had Charles Rye. The Americans were moving too fast for his peace of mind, in too many directions at once and without co-ordination. In the South they were preparing cash projections and financial plans without regard for the position of the North American Corporation; still less for that of the Bowater Organisation as a whole. A. B. Meyer, in spite of his position on the Board of NAC and in spite of his habitually cautious mentality, was much addicted to this kind of activity. In November 1959 he and Charles E. Opdyke, respectively President and Controller-Treasurer of Bowaters Southern, called on Stuart Cragin of Morgan Guaranty in New York, thereby causing displeasure at Morgan Stanley.[61]

That brought matters to a head. Eric Bowater, complaining that 'some confusion [was] developing in relation to finances for the various projects in the South', said,

I think the best course now to pursue . . . is to allow the matter to rest . . . until . . . our new financial forecasts are available in the New Year and then for John [Kirwan-]Taylor to go out to New York with the object of properly co-ordinating the whole matter. This would be in accord with our previous practice and obviate any possible confusion and crossing of wires.

Rye was more explicit. 'The difficulty of the situation', he wrote, '... is that we have again reached the point of too many independent projections, so that quite frankly neither I nor I am sure anybody else has any real idea of the current N.A.C. consolidated position.'[62] This observation illustrates the difficulty of devising an organisation for co-ordinating the policy of the various companies in North America and for keeping North American policy as a whole in line with policy in the United Kingdom.

The two major provinces of Bowaters' empire, as we observed earlier (p. 172 above), were united for policy-making purposes only at the head, through Eric Bowater acting on one side of the Atlantic as Chairman of the Bowater Paper Corporation and on the other as Chairman of the Board and Chief Executive Officer of each North American company.* In this way he kept the ultimate direction of affairs to himself: a sound enough arrangement as long as he had capable advisers and his own judgment remained unimpaired. The weakness of the system lay in the absence from North America of the provisions which existed in the United Kingdom for central discussion of policy in the GPC and for the accumulation and processing of information by the central financial/secretarial network under the Director in charge of Finance and the Comptroller, both of whom could and from time to time did offer advice and utter warnings based on their knowledge of the business as a whole.

The Chairman's North American Committee was set up in 1960 but until then there was nowhere for the discussion of North American affairs as a whole, nor – and this may have been even more important – was there any equivalent to the financial and secretarial services in the United Kingdom: hence Rye's outburst quoted above. He and Knight in the United Kingdom, and Sam Mann, Controller and Secretary-Treasurer of the Montreal company, were always anxious, when Eric was on his trips, that he might agree, as sometimes he did, to some previously unconsidered project put to him by enthusiastic managers in one or other of the North American companies.

* Based on the list given in the 1957 Bowater Report. The titles varied from time to time and there does not appear to have been a Chief Executive Officer in the Bowater Paper Co. New York.

At length, from the welter of proposals under debate in the South in 1959, there emerged one project of outstanding importance: to put up at Catawba an entirely new mill for the production of the light-weight coated paper which periodical publishers were using in greater and greater quantities. As against newsprint, coated paper had the supreme merit, from Bowaters' point of view, that demand was greater than supply. It would also help them, in a big way, to diversify their range of products.

The project began in quite a small way and then, as Bowater projects at this period were apt to do, developed a momentum of growth. The original suggestion was to coat newsprint made at Calhoun – a suggestion welcomed by Meyer because he felt sure it was 'going to be very difficult to keep the four newsprint machines running fully . . . during the next two or three years'. The capital cost, he thought, 'would not be less than $2,000,000 and might be as much as $2,500,000'.[63]

This was in January 1959. As the year went on a much larger proposition was formulated, namely that Bowaters should enter into a long-term contract with a large buyer of coated paper and that a mill should be built at Catawba to supply it, financed on the security of the contract. The similarity of the plan for building the mill at Calhoun, which Meyer had done so much to bring to success, is obvious. The trouble was that nearly all the really large magazine publishers, who were the only possible candidates for the kind of contract which Bowaters must have, already either owned mills or had arrangements with outside suppliers who gave them a price advantage over smaller buyers. One, however, and that one among the largest consumers of coated paper, using about 200,000 tons a year, had no such arrangement: McCall's.

McCall's strength lay in the growing market for women's magazines and their leading publications, *McCall's Magazine* and *Redbook*, were distributed throughout the United States. The owner of the business, Norton Simon, was remote and formidable. He worked by choice through subordinates but his authority within McCall's was as absolute as Eric Bowater's authority within Bowaters.

On 8 December, Meyer reported to Eric on 'such efforts as I have made to date on long-term contracts for coated paper from Catawba'. *Time* and *Life*, he said, were not interested. McCall's, on the other hand, were prepared to go ahead on a fifteen-year contract for 40,000 tons a year, delivery to begin in 1962, 'but they are not interested unless a special price can be worked out'. This was inevitable, since the whole object of the transaction, from McCall's point of view, was to put them on a level footing with their major competitors, all of whom had 'special prices'. McCall's wanted a price about 10 per cent below the going market price of $230 a ton delivered.[64]

Early in 1960 an agreement was worked out which guaranteed McCall's an average price, calculated over a five-year period, which would not be greater than an 'average standard price' which was set at $10 below the market price. With that settled, a fifteen-year contract was signed on 3 March 1960 under which Bowaters agreed to put up plant to produce not 40,000 but 75,000 tons a year of coated and supercalendered paper and McCall's agreed to take the whole output.[65]

By the time this contract was signed Bowaters' ideas had expanded yet again. The Catawba mill was to contain, by a date unspecified, not one machine of 75,000 tons' capacity but two, giving a total rated capacity of 150,000 tons of coated paper a year. By siting the new paper mill near the existing pulp mill economies would arise from sharing facilities but it was not intended that pulp from the existing plant should be diverted next door. The new machines would be fed from new plant provided for in the construction programme, which was drawn up by Bowater engineers and was aimed at completion of the first machine in about two years.[66]

The cost of the first stage of the project – the installation of the first machine – was estimated at $36m and the financial plan followed familiar Bowater lines – 75 per cent in loans from insurance companies and banks; 25 per cent in equity from NAC. Morgan Stanley proposed to raise the money as follows:

Twenty-year 6 per cent First Mortgage Bonds, Series B, of Bowater Carolina Corporation	$24m
5½ per cent Bank Loan	$ 3m
Equity securities	$ 9m
Total	$36m

With the McCall contract to back their arguments, Morgan Stanley found no great difficulty in placing either the bonds with insurance companies or the loan with banks. By 1 June 1960 their job was done. The building of the Catawba paper mill could go ahead.

The total cost of both stages of the mill was expected to be $61.5m. Thus had the coated paper project at Catawba grown, in a matter of fifteen months or so, from the original proposal for an outlay of $2–2.5m at Calhoun.

13.8 BOWATER IN 1960

In 1960 The Bowater Organisation produced about 1,500,000 tons of paper, chiefly newsprint; 450,000 tons of baled pulp; 256,000 tons of packaging materials and other products. It had about 60 per cent of its assets in North America; less than one-third in the United Kingdom. Its sales and its profits were both greater than in 1959 and it was expanding all its activities except newsprint in the United Kingdom, where machines were being turned to the production of coated paper or packaging materials. This widespread expansion was much to the Chairman's taste. Wherever he looked he saw factories being built, businesses being bought, ships sliding down the ways (nine were launched for the Bowater Steamship Co. between 1954 and 1961, though none actually in 1960). *Bowaters Annual Report 1960*, produced with a lengthy text and many coloured illustrations on the lavish scale which was usual for Bowater publications, was sub-titled, with perfect justification, *Progress in the world's market places*.

Nevertheless all was not well with Bowaters, as the Chairman guardedly admitted in his address to the shareholders in 1961 and

Directors and officials of Bowater, 1960. Left to right: W. E. J. Miles (Secretary), J. Martin Ritchie, Robert Knight (Comptroller), Charles Rye, Sir John Keeling, EVB, Sir Noel Bowater, Stanley Bell, A. B. Meyer, K. N. Linforth, G. W. Shaw, and R. J. Smith (Chief Accountant). *The Times*

as anyone could see who studied the published figures for 1960. First, although sales and profits were both rising, profits were rising more slowly than sales. That is to say, as Eric Bowater pointed out, the value of sales in 1960 was 21 per cent greater than in 1959 but the trading surplus (and also the consolidated profit before tax) was only 17 per cent greater. Profit margins were therefore being squeezed – serious at any time but particularly at a time of high capital expenditure, when revenue was badly needed for dividends, for the service of borrowings and for the construction and upkeep of plant, buildings, ships and other assets which were not yet earning revenue themselves. The measure of the problem, and Eric Bowater drew attention to it, was given by the rise in the charge for depreciation. It was 25 per cent higher than in 1959 – 'a relatively high increase', the Chairman said, 'by comparison with the increase in trading surplus'. All in all the implication of the Chairman's statement, barely concealed beneath the surface meaning of his words, was that Bowaters by 1960 were coming dangerously close to living beyond their means.

For this there were three main reasons or sets of reasons. One, probably the least important and in any case quite beyond Bowaters' control, was the unpromising state of the economy in general, in the United States and in the United Kingdom, during the latter part of 1960. That was temporary and would pass but with it might perhaps be grouped the permanently unstable exchange relationship between United States and Canadian dollars, which could very readily alter either to Bowaters' advantage or disadvantage, and against disadvantage they had no defence.

More disturbing than these general economic influences was the state of the newsprint industry itself and of the packaging industry, in which for some time over-capacity had been leading to rates of production uneconomically low, to sharp competition – especially, in the United Kingdom, from importers – and to a rigid level of prices against which profit margins were being squeezed by rising costs.

In spite of the attempts which Bowaters had made, since 1945, to diversify, the newsprint industry was still overwhelmingly important to them, especially in North America. The Organisation relied on newsprint, in 1960, for 57 per cent of its total production and the 1,200,000 tons or so which Bowater companies made represented about 10 per cent of the total tonnage of newsprint produced in non-Communist countries.[67] Bowaters were therefore very vulnerable to the threat posed by over-production of newsprint and the outlook was made gloomier by the declining health of many newspapers. To the traditional hazards of the newspapers' existence, always perilous, had been added the competition of television, biting both into readership and into advertising revenue. Moreover union pressure, abetted perhaps by weak management, kept their print-rooms overmanned. During 1960, in the United Kingdom, four newspapers disappeared: the *News Chronicle*, the *Star*, the *Empire News*, the *Sunday Graphic*. They were all Bowater customers and, although most of their circulation was picked up by other papers, so that the net loss of demand was not very great, their disappearance was ominous, not least because customers were required who were strong enough to be willing to pay the premium price needed to support the British newsprint industry against foreign competition.

The third group of reasons for Bowaters' looming difficulties, hinted at by the Chairman in 1961, comprised certain aspects of his own policies: his insistence on self-sufficiency, or something near it, in raw materials and sea transport; and his determination to keep on expanding the business in thoroughly adverse circumstances. The development of self-sufficiency and the headlong progress of expansion have been described in the last chapter and in this. In the last two years of his life, when his health was poor, Eric Bowater had to face their less desirable consequences. To that final episode in his career, bringing an end to his domination of Bowaters' affairs, we must now turn.

CHAPTER FOURTEEN

The cash crisis 1961–1962

14.1 PREMONITIONS

The city of San Francisco is said to be bound, at some time, to suffer another earthquake. The only question is: When?

The Bowater Organisation at the end of the fifties, as certain features of the results for 1960 and the Chairman's comments on them make clear, was in a rather similar situation. If matters went on as they were, it was evident that a crisis in the Organisation's affairs was overwhelmingly likely, for it was not making money fast enough in the late fifties to support expansion at the pace which had been set, as Chapters 12 and 13 show, in the mid-fifties. The only question was: would the crisis come sooner or later? In the event, it came in 1961–2, against an economic background which included, in the late summer of 1961, one of the United Kingdom's recurrent sterling crises followed by a credit squeeze with Bank Rate at 7 per cent.

The direction in which Bowaters' affairs were going, and the dangers inherent in it, were confirmed, during 1960, by an enormous rise in the Corporation's issued Ordinary capital, which grew by 78 per cent, from £23.1m at the start of the year to £41.2m early in 1961. Some of the increase came from buying out the minority holders in Bowater-Eburite early in the year; some from a one-for-five scrip issue in June; some from conversion, in July, of some of the Unsecured Loan stock issued in 1957 (pp. 256–7 above); some from a one-for-six rights issue in October; some from buying out minority interests in Continental subsidiaries.[1]

The rights issue was recommended by a committee set up in July 1960 to advise the Chairman whether the Organisation needed new money, how much it might need under varying circumstances, and how it might be raised. The members of the committee, from Bowaters, were J. Kirwan-Taylor, R. Knight, L. G. Pearce (lately of the Bank of England): from their professional advisers, W. R. T.

('Boss') Whatmore, A. C. Unthank and J. A. B. Keeling, Sir John
Keeling's son. They calculated that the need for cash would reach its
peak in March 1962, when it would amount to £16m. In considering how to raise it they touched on the weight of the Corporation's
loan capital. At the end of 1959 it stood at £68m, without taking
account of borrowings from banks or from Rothschilds. It represented some 40 per cent of total assets employed. They commented: 'any increase now in United Kingdom borrowings would
make further borrowings in North America (the Organisation's
traditional method of finance there) difficult to arrange'. This remark echoed persistent rumblings of misgiving, over the years, from
Morgan Stanley, although they continued to arrange loan finance.
The committee suggested raising £12m Ordinary capital and also
borrowing £3m on the Continent to meet Continental commitments. 'This is as much', they said, 'as Bowater-Europe can reasonably be expected to service out of its own resources.' The Corporation would have to guarantee the loan. 'Such a guarantee', the
committee added reassuringly, 'would not appear in the consolidated balance sheet but would be referred to by way of a note in the
accounts.'[2]

Eric Bowater accepted both recommendations. He was encouraged, no doubt, by an estimate that the Corporation's trading
surplus would rise in every year from 1961 to 1964. The estimate
also showed, naturally, a rising charge for depreciation but that he
had to accept if he wanted Bowaters to go on expanding, though he
must have recognised the danger of lower net earnings.[3] The new
money was therefore raised, the Ordinary capital in October 1960
and the Continental loan, for the equivalent of £5m rather than
£3m, during 1961.

On the Ordinary capital, as increased by the rights issue, an
increased dividend was paid – 2s. 9d. per £1 stock unit (13.75 per
cent) for 1960 against 2s. 6d. (12.50 per cent) for 1959. This was
extremely risky. It would set a level of expectation for 1961 which
would not be justifiable unless the Organisation's profits rose by at
least the sum estimated by Robert Knight but, by the time the
directors came to recommend the dividend for 1960, the indications
were that the profits for 1961 might fall. Eric Bowater was at pains
to make sure the shareholders understood the situation. 'Figures
and data available to date', he said at the Annual Meeting in June
1961, 'indicate that . . . as a consequence of shrinking profit margins . . . our current earnings have not reached the record levels of
the corresponding period of last year. The probability is . . . that
trading surplus for the year will be at much the same level as that

for 1960, although it is too early yet to make any accurate forecast.'[4]

Distress signals had in fact been flying in Bowaters several months before the Chairman spoke. In April 1961 he caused Rye to issue a strictly confidential Head Office Circular which expressed his dissatisfaction with the budgets of subsidiary companies for the year in prospect: 1961. 'The Chairman', said the circular, 'has indicated that the budgets are not acceptable, even as a minimum level, and has directed me to inform all senior executives concerned with operations, sales and supplies that such budgets must be improved upon.' Rye commented that the circular was not directed to any particular company, division or unit, but to all, and that the companies in North America had already been given this direction. He said, furthermore, that, even where individual companies' budgets had shown an improvement over the previous year, the memorandum was addressed equally to them. 'it will be appreciated', the circular pointed out, 'that the high level of capital expenditure incurred over recent years has carried with it increasing requirements for depreciation; in addition, the costs of capital developments and taxation are such that the parent Corporation must now more than ever before look to every constituent unit to achieve the maximum level of trading profits.' The fact that 'the high level of capital expenditure' had been set without consulting the 'constituent units' was ignored. Only one concession was made to them. They were not to be held responsible for costs imposed upon them from Bowater House. 'As regards costs', the circular said, 'it is concerned with those elements over which you and your teams have control and is not directly concerned with supplies (as regards the U.K.) and with inter-company charges for services, administration, engineering, research and the like, for the companies responsible for such matters have also been directed to . . . effect economies.'[5]

It was on the newsprint side of the business in the United Kingdom, described in 1962 as 'still the life blood of Bowaters',[6] that the worst of Bowaters' troubles lay and, early in 1961, a takeover bid by Daily Mirror Newspapers for Odhams Press Ltd, one of Bowaters' most important United Kingdom customers, suddenly threatened to make those troubles worse. Cecil King, at the head of Daily Mirror Newspapers, had been provoked into making the bid by Roy Thomson, later Lord Thomson of Fleet, who, wishing to add magazines, especially large-circulation women's magazines (*Woman*, *Woman's Realm*, *Woman's Own* and others), to his newspapers and television interests, had made an offer for Odhams.

To Bowaters the Thomson bid presented no threat but the bid from Daily Mirror Newspapers was very disturbing because of the possibility that Bowaters' business with Odham publications would be transferred, as contracts ran out, to Albert E. Reed in which Daily Mirror newspapers had a large holding. So great was Bowaters' alarm that early in February 1961 they hastily prepared plans for taking over Odhams themselves, in partnership with Thomsons: a proposition requiring about £13m cash and a large issue of Ordinary capital.[7]

Eric Bowater then warned King of Bowaters' intentions, emphasising that they had no desire to own Odhams but were determined to protect their interests. King, evidently unwilling to fight Bowaters as well as Thomsons and Odhams, offered to protect Bowaters' interests himself – a possibility which had already occurred to Eric and his advisers.[8] King agreed that, if Daily Mirror Newspapers took over Odhams, Bowaters' contracts with Odhams should stand and that for ten years Bowaters and Reeds should be given the opportunity of sharing between themselves any new business with Odhams or Daily Mirror Newspapers that might arise.[9] Bowaters, no doubt much relieved – the ownership of a large publishing business was a diversification which Eric Bowater did not seek – withdrew, leaving Roy Thomson and Cecil King to fight for Odhams between themselves.

In the late fifties, as Table 31 shows, the performance of Bowaters United Kingdom Pulp and Paper Mills Limited was patchy. In 1960 demand was brisk, giving rise to optimism about 1961. It turned out to be unjustified. In 1961 'there was a fall in demand for all the

TABLE 31. *Bowater's United Kingdom Pulp & Paper Mills, trading surplus and depreciation, 1956–61*

	Trading surplus & other revenue		Depreciation charge	
	£	% change	£	% change
1956	3,835,199		650,000	
1957	3,512,459	− 8	725,000	+11
1958	3,780,421	+ 8	900,000	+24
1959	3,577,911	− 5	1,035,000	+15
1960	4,373,720	+22	1,230,000	+19
1961	3,364,730	−23	1,270,000	+ 3

Source: Bowaters United Kingdom Pulp & Paper Mills Ltd Board minutes 29.iii.57, 31.iii.58, 18.iii.59, 18.iii.60, 29.iii.61.

Company's products and turnover was £1.7 million lower than 1960, at £42 million'.[10]

During all this period, nevertheless, the costs of expansion had to be borne, in the form of depreciation charges on new plant installed under the Master Plan. Even when the trading surplus fell, depreciation charges rose. In 1961, when the trading surplus was at its lowest for five years, the cost of depreciation had never been higher. Eric Bowater's anxiety at the beginning of the year is easy to understand.

He had cause for anxiety and so had everyone else in the British newsprint industry. On 1 January 1959 the price of newsprint in the United Kingdom had come down from £60 a ton (delivered) to £58. 10s. That price, in July 1961, was returning Bowaters profit at the rate of £4. 5s. or 7¼ per cent a ton, after absorbing increased costs, since the price was fixed, of £1. 12s. a ton, thus demonstrating painfully what was meant by 'erosion of profit margins'.[11] Moreover, although the profit on newsprint, as a mass-produced commodity, is very sensitive to reduction in the level of production, yet in the autumn of 1961 demand was so weak that Bowaters felt obliged to stop one of the machines at Kemsley.

At £58. 10s., it was reported in the spring of 1962, the Canadians could undersell Bowaters by almost £2 a ton, Scandinavians by almost £4.[12] There was consequently no hope of raising the selling price and all Bowaters' efforts were directed to postponing a further fall, which was regarded in the long run as inevitable.[13] For Bowaters, the position was thus extremely serious, for, although British newspaper owners had traditionally been willing to support the home newsprint industry by paying a premium for service, there was a limit to how far they could or would go, especially in their own not very robust state of prosperity.

The inherent weakness of the British newsprint industry, in competition against the Canadians and the Scandinavians with their abundant timber supplies and their cheap power, had been masked in the thirties by the low cost of pulp and in the forties and early fifties by the excess of demand over supply. In the early sixties slack demand, combined with over-capacity and rising costs, began to reveal this weakness as it had never been revealed during the whole of Bowaters' previous existence as a manufacturing concern. Moreover, excess capacity was still building up in other parts of the world and there was no indication when, if ever, easier conditions for the British newsprint maker would return.

All this was beyond Bowaters' control. In addition, however, there were disturbing indications that Bowaters' mills in the United

Kingdom were not, by international standards, very efficient. Labour relations were uneasy. At Kemsley and Sittingbourne, early in 1960, what Linforth called 'union troubles' were interfering with maintenance by preventing weekend work. At Mersey and Thames, the following year, labour turnover was reported to be very high – 35 per cent at Mersey, 30 per cent at Thames, against 12 per cent at Kemsley and Sittingbourne.[14] In the summer of 1961 Bowaters' Central Work Study Division produced an unflattering comparison between the three United Kingdom pulp and paper mills and Corner Brook. Wherever they could compare operations, and in many cases comparisons were not possible, they found the United Kingdom mills using 50 per cent more labour than Corner Brook and working a great deal of overtime also. They suggested that by the application of work study, output could be greatly increased with the existing labour force, or alternatively the labour force could be reduced. 'In either event', they said with remarkable confidence, 'the result is the same; reduced costs. These could well be of the order of £750,000 per annum minimum.' Finally, they discovered that over the preceding fifteen months – to July 1961 – hourly paid workers' pay had risen, taking basic rates and bonus together, by 24 per cent. 'Coupled with excess overtime hours now varying between 10% and 28%, and no significant increase in productivity, the present situation is untenable and alarming. Work – effective work – must be related to wages.'[15]

The packaging side of Bowaters in the United Kingdom, in 1961–2, was no happier than the newsprint side and for similar reasons: excess capacity in the industry, weak demand, sharp competition, labour troubles. Attention focused on the new, ambitious project at Gillingham, so hungry for capital. At a meeting of the GPC in September 1961, Rye and Knight criticised the projected return on expenditure, saying '10% was not good enough, and 20% should be regarded as the practical minimum'. Ritchie found himself forced to accept 'that the anticipated return was too low and said that every effort would be made to improve the results'. Ritchie, however, was not one to lie passive under attack, especially attack from the general direction of the central departments in Bowater House. 'He added that much thought needed to be given to the extent of the headquarters expenses since he felt that competitors were not being called upon to absorb such large sums as the Bowater packaging units.'[16] This was a theme to which, as we shall see (p. 310 below), he was soon to return much more aggressively.

14.2 THE AMERICAN MARKET: HARDBOARD AND PAPER

With the main Bowater businesses in the United Kingdom relatively unprofitable and with the European businesses, representing about 8 per cent of total net assets, still in the stage of absorbing capital rather than generating new revenue, it was evident at least as early as the summer of 1961 that a cash crisis was impending. The importance of North America as the main profit centre for the Bowater Organisation – Corner Brook and Southern were each earning more than Bowaters United Kingdom Pulp & Paper Co. – was therefore greater than ever. It was imperative that every dollar of their earnings which could be spared from the North American companies' own essential purposes, including, in the case of Southern, a heavy element of debt repayment, should flow to the Bowater Paper Corporation.

It was imperative, in particular, that Southern should pay a dividend to NAC and hence to BPC but Southern, an eminently successful enterprise, had other uses for its profits, including the purchase of woodland, highly desirable as the most tangible of tangible assets. This inclination had to be curbed. 'You must . . . remember', Meyer wrote in September 1961 to Charles Opdyke, whose expansionary instincts were well known, 'that Tennessee must not fail to pay a dividend of $3,000,000 per annum and that no capital expenditures must be undertaken which will jeopardize that dividend. Not any penny of capital expenditure must be incurred that is not absolutely necessary to keep the mills operating efficiently.'[17] There was also the matter of working capital. It must not be allowed to fall below $3.5m or a dividend would not be permissible under the agreement with the providers of loan capital.

Meyer, in August, was not optimistic about Southern's sales of newsprint in 1961. Orders were not easy to get and Southern's agents, the Bowater Paper Co., found that customers in Mexico and Australia insisted on paper from Corner Brook because, they said, it was better than Southern's. He thought the best Southern was likely to achieve would be 'something between 390,000 and 400,000 tons'.[18] In fact it turned out to be about 395,000 tons. 'The outlook', he wrote to Eric Bowater, 'is not exhilarating', and in the letter quoted in the last paragraph he advised Opdyke 'to predicate all our expenditures on the basis of 90% operations'.

Any threat there might be to Southern's dividend, however, did not arise from newsprint. 'The sad results of the board mill', Meyer told Eric Bowater, 'and the heavy capital expenditures we have had to make to get the board mill into satisfactory operation is largely

responsible for the poor cash position of the Southern Corporation.' To Charles Opdyke he complained that something would
have to be done to prevent dust from the hardboard mill interfering
with the coated paper process which was also being installed at
Catawba. 'The Lord only knows', he commented gloomily, 'what
the cost of this will be.'

The hardboard venture seems to have been misconceived from
the start and a dreadful warning of the dangers of diversification:
that is, of diversifying into a market already occupied by powerful
and efficient competitors. There were unforeseen difficulties with
the process, leading to unforeseen capital expenditure and to un-
reliable quality in the product.[19] The market, in spite of repeated
surveys, never seems to have been thoroughly understood.[20] Financial, operational and selling responsibilities were split between
Southern, Carolina and Bowater Paper Co. Personal relations were
not happy between V. J. Sutton, General Manager at Calhoun and a
Vice-President at Catawba, and T. C. Bannister, General Manager
at Catawba and also a Vice-President.[21] Probably the essence of the
problem lies in a remark in an introductory letter to the report of a
committee set up in 1962, by Bannister, 'to investigate all phases of
the hardboard operation'. Simply and damningly, the letter says:
'From the very beginning, it was apparent that neither the members
of the Committee nor the Bowater Organization in the United
States, to our knowledge possessed the professional experience to
evaluate and solve the several problems present.'[22]

Faced with the board mill's losses and continual need for fresh
spending, Southern in 1961 was finding it difficult, if not impossible, to provide cash for a dividend as well as for unavoidable
capital expenditure and for the repayment of funded debt, which
required $4.1m a year in order to repay the Series A 4¾ per cent
Mortgage Bonds by 1967. In October 1961 Cecil Unthank of
Barton, Mayhew and Robert Knight arrived in North America to
review Southern's affairs. Their proposal, in order to improve the
cash flow and provide additional funds for capital expenditure and
the dividend which BPC so sorely needed, was to slow down the
repayment of the Series A Mortgage Bonds.[23] This of course would
require the consent of the bondholders and might shake Bowaters'
credit in the United States. That any such proposal should have
been entertained shows how desperate BPC's need for cash was
becoming.

The proposal was discussed with Ed Vollmers of Morgan Stanley
and by the Southern Board. 'I have read many dismal and depressing reports in my life', Eric Bowater cabled to August Meyer,

but none so dismal and depressing as your memorandum to the Southern Board Meeting of November 20th. I am bound to confess that your report relating to the hardboard mill comes as something of a surprise and of course a great disappointment. I agree with you it would appear highly important that insurance companies be asked to reduce annual sinking fund on Series A Bonds, provided you and Vollmers are satisfied that this can be done without prejudicing our prestige and standing with those companies. I do not need to remind you of the importance of maintaining dividends... I can only hope and pray that the 1962 budget will at least be realised.[24]

In the midst of this anguished message, it deserves to be recorded, Eric went out of his way to praise two members of the staff of the board mill, George Jackson and Joe Hahn, who appeared to be doing well in what Eric himself called 'the dismal picture'.

On 15 January 1962 a cable arrived from Meyer: 'To give you a little cheer Southern's net earnings after tax turn out to be 3,140,000 which as you know is better than the original budget. Insurance Companies have all agreed to halving sinking fund payments of A bonds, rate however will be increased from $4\frac{3}{4}$% to 5%.'[25]

Southern's essential soundness was thus demonstrated and its immediate difficulties were relieved. A dividend of $2.7m was paid for 1961.

For Southern, however, and for Bowaters' North American business in general 1962 was no more exhilarating than 1961. In June a General Sales Meeting in New York discussed how best to share misery equitably by distributing cuts in production among the various mills, not only in 1962 but in 1963 also.[26] In that year, the Tasman agreement would make it inevitable that Corner Brook would suffer, for its terms would oblige Bowaters' selling company in Australia to give Tasman preference over Corner Brook in supplying Australian customers. Meyer estimated that 'with the loss of Australasian business at Corner Brook and the general reduction in all our overseas business' Corner Brook, Mersey and Tennessee might have to operate at 85 to 90 per cent of capacity – a grossly uneconomic rate.[27] 'It's too depressing for words;' commented Rye, 'let us hope we really do get somewhere with coated papers and specialties.'[28]

'Coated papers' began to come off the mill at Catawba, for sale to McCall's, about a month before Rye uttered his hope. It was not fulfilled. The quality of the paper did not satisfy McCall's and by 13 July Meyer's early optimism about putting it right had turned to acute anxiety. 'Am concerned', he wired to T. C. Bannister, 'that I have not heard anything from you . . . since the recent start-up. Are we getting rid of the big holes and have we solved the question of pin holes? How is the coater running now – are we getting production? Is the quality we are now making up to standard . . . I am anxious to see samples.'[29] A long dispute followed, into which McCall's inserted demands for revision of the price clauses of their contract. Bowaters, at an irremediable disadvantage by reason of the undeniably poor quality of their product, eventually accepted a settlement, in May 1963, which required a payment by them of $100,000.[30] T. C. Bannister was replaced at Catawba by V. J. Sutton. Though in the long run successful, the coated paper project was in its beginnings just one more problem for the harassed Bowater management of the early sixties. The second coating machine was never built.

'Specialties', by contrast, provided a little relief, being superior grades of newsprint for which there turned out to be a lively demand, chiefly for use in telephone directories and mail order catalogues, provoking, naturally, lively competition. 'Everybody is after us on this specialty business', said Meyer in June 1962, adding ominously:

Great Northern, St Croix, and the Canadian mills are beating the bushes for this type of paper and we found that during this past year we lost certain good customers because our competitors are making a better sheet of paper than we can make. If this continues for another year we may find that our present volume of specialties will be sharply reduced.[31]

It seems he was right, because about six months later he said he had been disappointed in specialty sales during 1962 and added: 'Unfortunately all our newsprint competitors are following our lead . . . and I am afraid most of them can really make better specialties than we can.'[32]

Complaints of quality are plentiful in the records of Bowaters' North American business in the early sixties. They run through the whole range of products, from Tennessee newsprint to Corner Brook sulphite pulp. Some of the trouble may have arisen from new equipment before it was run in, and it is in the nature of customers to complain, but the suspicion remains that quality control may not have been as strict as it should have been.

The poor quality of the specialty papers may have been a consequence of the drive to keep down capital expenditure. In May 1962 Meyer told Kirwan-Taylor he was sure they were going to have 'an immediate requirement of not less than $2,000,000 to put Tennessee in a position to make the proper and higher priced groundwood papers which ... we need so vitally to keep all of the North American mills running substantially full'.[33] A month or so later a figure of $3.5m was being talked about. In the end no money was spent in 1962; almost certainly false economy because, in his letter of January 1963, quoted above, Meyer said they had authorised expenditure of $1m on No. 2 machine at Calhoun 'and we hope this will enable us to regain our position and make some progress'.

Another conspicuous casualty of the ban on spending was an office building for Calhoun which had been planned for years but never built. It required about $750,000. 'Postponing the Administration Building', said Meyer, 'has now [May 1962] reached the point where I am sure it is bad for the morale of the Organization.'[34] Postponed it was. It was not built until the mid-sixties.

14.3 THE AMERICAN MARKET: A SURFEIT OF PULP

In July 1959 the sulphate pulp mill at Catawba, erected at Eric Bowater's urgent insistence (Chapter 12.5 above) and designed to produce at least 134,000 tons a year exclusively for Bowaters' paper and board mills in the United Kingdom, came into production. It could hardly have done so at a more embarrassing moment. There were already two sources of chemical pulp within the Bowater Organisation – for sulphite pulp at Corner Brook and for sulphate pulp, mainly for internal use, at Calhoun – and it had been evident since 1957 that in the changing state of the newsprint market, with supply in excess of demand, their output was from time to time more than sufficient for the Organisation's needs. By the same token, in the weak state of the market, it was impossible to sell excess Bowater pulp at a profit outside the Organisation.[35] Stanley Bell went so far as to suggest closing the sulphite mill at Corner Brook for a year – a suggestion which, as he knew, was full of political dynamite. It was not acted upon then but H. M. S. Lewin put it forward in August 1958 and, in 1959, there was a suggestion that, if it were necessary to restrict pulp production, 'the most obvious course ... would be to eliminate the production of Corner Brook sulphite because of its poor quality'.[36]

Before the Catawba mill opened in 1959, estimates of Bowaters' likely sales of newsprint and production of pulp over the years from 1960 to 1964 suggested that the Organisation would produce about 90,000 tons of pulp a year more than it needed, partly because the mill at Calhoun, contrary to expectations, would produce at least 20,000 tons a year more than Calhoun could use. In 1960, 45,000 to 50,000 tons *might* be sold on the open market but no forecast was made beyond that. Sales turned out to be over-estimated and production of pulp under-estimated, so the problem was even worse in reality than in the estimates but they gave clear warning of the way things were going.[37]

The warning proved only too accurate. As soon as the Catawba mill came into production, the contract on which the financing had been based took effect. The Montreal company, through the Bowater Paper Co., were obliged to take 134,000 tons of pulp a year, and Bowaters in the United Kingdom, in turn, found themselves with far more North American pulp – for it came in from Corner Brook and Calhoun as well as from Catawba – than they had any use for. Moreover, it was expensive pulp, for costs at the Bowater mills were high, and when Scandinavian prices began to fall they could not follow them down. Worst of all, perhaps, Bell and Ritchie made it quite clear to the GPC, in the autumn of 1959, that if they had their way they would not buy pulp from Calhoun or Catawba at all, at any rate for making kraft. Scandinavian pulp, they said, was much better for making sack kraft, and Ritchie went so far as to say that, if the Mersey mill in England did not use some Scandinavian pulp in making kraft, 'there would inevitably be a loss of business to Bowater-Eburite'.[38]

Production of marketable pulp at Calhoun was on a fairly small scale and after 1959 it fell. Production at Catawba, on the other hand, supported by the UK contract and by considerable sales, through Bulkley Dunton, on the open market in the United States, rose far above the 134,000 tons which the mill had originally been designed to produce (Table 32).

Use of Catawba pulp in the reluctant English mills remained far below the contract figure. In 1960 it only amounted to 75,798 tons, semi-bleached and unbleached. For making kraft, the mills used

TABLE 32. *Production of marketable pulp at Calhoun and Catawba, 1959–63 (short tons, air dry)*

	Calhoun	Catawba
1959	51,811	41,853
1960	40,012	150,498
1961	42,993	165,070
1962	44,035	160,484
1963	39,420	192,114

Source: Calhoun – BS
Catawba – Carolina archives

24,758 tons of unbleached pulp from Catawba, 287 tons from Calhoun and 33,480 tons from elsewhere, presumably Scandinavia. In all, during 1960, Bowaters' United Kingdom mills used 411,444 tons of all kinds of pulp, mechanical and chemical, of which 260,454 tons – 63 per cent – came from their own mills, including 145,955 tons of mechanical pulp from Sofiehem and Risor.[39]

Between 1956 and 1961 the price charged to Bowaters in the United Kingdom for chemical pulp produced by Bowaters in North America varied, from year to year, between 10 per cent and 26 per cent higher than prices charged in the open market. There was also a difference, very much smaller and sometimes in the paper mills' favour, between the price of mechanical pulp from the two sources. The consequence for Bowater paper mills of using Bowater pulp was therefore a higher cost of production than might otherwise have been necessary.

This was a point which interested the Royal Commission on the Press which, under Lord Shawcross, sat during 1961 and 1962. Figures prepared for the Royal Commission by Bowaters showed that, if chemical pulp purchased at the market price had been used for newsprint between 1956 and 1961, Bowaters' production figures might have been lower by figures ranging between £1.44 a ton (1956) and £2.49 (1959), yielding total savings on production costs ranging between £597,232 and £1,066,497. The corresponding figures for mechanical pulp, £0.34 and £0.80, would have yielded savings of £141,423 and £314,016 (Table 33).

These figures suggest that Bowaters were paying dearly for the Chairman's policy of controlling raw material supplies: a suggestion which members of the Royal Commission did not fail to take up, being concerned, they said, 'as to why the price of newsprint is high' – a reading of the situation with which Bowaters profoundly disagreed. Linforth, who, along with Rye and Robert Knight, gave oral evidence to the Royal Commission, pointed out that Bowaters' policy was intended to give them 'some control over prices so that we were not "taken for a ride" in times of shortage when prices might go sky-high ... This was a long-term plan, and ... one obviously has from time to time to take the rough with the smooth.' Rye added that the Scandinavian prices might have been higher if Bowaters, instead of having 300,000 tons of pulp a year of their own, had had to go into the market and buy it, thus forcing the price up against themselves and their competitors. It might, besides, have been possible to get relatively small quantities of pulp at low 'spot' prices but it would have been difficult or impossible to contract

TABLE 33. Bowater UK Paper Mills: theoretical effect on newsprint production costs of using pulp bought on the open market, 1956–61

	1956	1957	1958	1959	1960	1961 (nine months)
Chemical pulp						
Average market price (£)	51.75	50.50	47.25	45.00	45.50	48.50
Decrease in total production costs (£)	597,232	799,528	966,135	1,066,497	931,229	485,676
Total tons produced (long tons)	413,603	439,383	390,723	428,468	469,954	333,499
Decrease in cost per ton (£)	1.44	1.82	2.47	2.49	1.98	1.46
Mechanical pulp						
Average Market Price (£)	33.12	32.50	29.62	28.50	28.50	28.50
Decrease in total production costs (£)	141,423	247,940	314,016	320,403	314,583	149,621
Total tons produced (long tons)	413,603	439,383	390,723	428,468	469,954	333,499
Decrease in cost per ton (£)	0.3	0.56	0.80	0.75	0.67	0.45
Newsprint price per ton (£)	58.50	59.75	60.00	58.50	58.50	58.50

Note: These are combined figures for Kemsley, Thames and Mersey mills. The prices charged for 'pulp furnished' vary from £56.13 (Kemsley, 1961) to £63.74 (Thames, 1956), for chemical pulp, and from £28.43 (Kemsley, 1961) to £34.65 (Mersey, 1956) for mechanical pulp.

Source: Papers prepared by Bowaters for the Royal Commission on the Press 1961–2.

forward at such prices for the very large quantities Bowater needed.[40]

These were valid points but Bowaters' raw material policy, which covered pulpwood from Newfoundland and Labrador as well as the various kinds of wood pulp, had been conceived when prices were rising, supplies were scarce and protection was needed, as Linforth said, against being 'taken for a ride'. It looked very different and much more expensive when prices were falling and supplies were plentiful, especially as applied to the sulphite mill at Corner Brook and to the sulphate mill at Catawba.

Both had to be kept going at a profit, the sulphite mill for reasons of Newfoundland politics and the mill at Catawba because the arrangements for financing its construction required the uninterrupted maintenance of working capital at a certain level and the service of funded debt. Neither could match the Scandinavian prices which set the general level of the market and at which it was desirable that the paper mills should work. Both, therefore, were subsidised, chiefly by Bowaters in the United Kingdom, roughly to the extent of the difference between the price at which they could earn a profit and the market price.[41]

There was also an element of subsidy in ocean transport costs. North American supplies crossed the Atlantic in Bowater ships at the expense of the receiving Bowater companies, which was good business for the ships. It was also unnecessary, since equivalent supplies could have been brought from Scandinavia at very much lower transport costs.

These subsidised operations, it was later recognised, confused and distorted inter-company transactions within the Organisation. They inflated the profits of subsidised companies unrealistically and deflated profits elsewhere. Moreover, for the newsprint side of the business in the United Kingdom they were a heavy burden in years when profits of any kind were not easily made.

The trading relationship between Bowater companies and the intricate system of accounting which went with it became the subject of a conference between the most senior executives on each side of the Atlantic in 1963.[42] In 1961 a more urgent problem was over-production of sulphate pulp at Catawba and Calhoun which was causing stocks to mount beyond any near prospect of consumption in the United Kingdom or of sale on the open market.

This problem was not peculiar to Bowaters. The Bulkley, Dunton Pulp Co. of New York, who handled the sales of Bowater pulp outside Bowaters, warned Meyer in September 1961 that, at 30 June, the stocks of pulp held at producing mills (not the mills of consumers) in North America and Scandinavia had been 77 per cent greater than a year earlier. As Meyer commented, these figures were 'indeed alarming'. He forecast that, by the end of 1961, pulp stocks at Calhoun and Catawba would stand about 4,000 tons higher than at the end of 1960 – at 26,000 to 27,000 tons, a higher tonnage than had been expected because sales to Europe through Bulkley, Dunton were likely to fall short of estimates by 6,000 to 7,000 tons. 'Actually', said Meyer charitably, 'I think an exceptionally good sales job has been done for us by Bulkley, Dunton.' Production at Catawba and Calhoun was running at a rate which would yield 14,500 tons more than they had budgeted for but only about 4,000 tons would remain unsold.[43]

That, though Meyer did not say so, can only have meant one thing: large stocks of pulp piling up at the expense of Bowaters in the United Kingdom, showing how Bowaters' system of internal trading, if it got out of hand, could work simultaneously to the advantage of some parts of the Organisation, in this case Catawba and Calhoun, and to the disadvantage of others, in this case the paper mills in the United Kingdom. Certainly Charles Rye thought the system was getting out of hand. Before Meyer wrote from New York, Rye, in London, was writing to Robert Knight. 'I am writing this note', he wrote on 27 September 1961,

because it looks as though one way or another we are going to get ourselves completely tied up again . . . I am most disturbed to find that the latest weekly cash position memo. discloses an overdraft now well over £7 million, which means we are already approaching £2 million over the figure we really thought should be the maximum for 1961. I do not doubt there are a number of reasons for this, but both of us are fully aware of the main one, namely the raw material stock position . . . To me this is a matter of top policy, and I am wondering whether the Chairman, but certainly Gus Meyer, should *now* be warned by me that we must, repeat must, order a slowing down in pulp production at Carolina and Calhoun. What do you think??[44]

The reason for Rye's hesitation in approaching the Chairman was ominous. On his regular autumn visit to Corner Brook, early in September 1961, he was taken ill; evidence, no doubt, of strain and increasing age – he had his sixty-sixth birthday in January 1961. From Corner Brook, following the advice of Dr Harley, a local practitioner, he went by way of Montreal and New York to California where for a month, he told Harley later, he 'had a complete rest and did nothing'. He came back through New York to London where a neurologist's prognosis was encouraging: if he took things easily for the time being there was no reason why he should not regain '98–99% completely normal health'. By mid-November, he said, he had not regained complete control of his right leg but he was 'infinitely better and improving every day'. He added that he got rather tired and was only going to London two days a week.[45] During the remaining months of his life, although his authority was never questioned and his recovery was good, he can scarcely have been fit to withstand the pressures of his position at a peculiarly difficult time and, indeed, by the early summer of 1962 ill-health of a different sort was closing round him again.

Rye's urgent demand that the production of pulp should be cut down was echoed a few days later by the General Manager of BPC's Raw Materials and Shipping Group, J. A. Colvin. 'Bearing in mind', he said, 'we can still buy Scandinavian pulp at £10. o. o. per ton below the landed cost of Southern pulp the cessation or temporary cessation of pulp production at Calhoun may be worth considering in all its aspects.'[46] Rye duly wrote to the Chairman, allegedly doing nothing in California, suggesting that Robert Knight should investigate 'the Carolina and Tennessee pulp position with a view to asking you to direct that . . . the production of those mills should definitely be slowed down'. He pointed out that although it was very satisfactory for Tennessee and Carolina to earn substantial profits and reduce their loan capital, yet on the other hand pulp bought had to be paid for, 'and the United Kingdom is not in the position to do so unless we . . . go to the maximum Lloyds Bank credit limit in 1961, which I think it would be wrong to do from many points of view'.[47]

Eric Bowater, apparently with some reluctance, agreed. 'If', he said, 'Meyer is unable to dispose of further quantities, then both mills must if necessary cut back production even at the expense of their respective profits, but happen what may, Tennessee's dividend must remain inviolate. Please so inform Meyer.'[48] Rye hastened to do so. 'I fear', he told Meyer,

this is just another of those problems for 1961, and in one direction or another all of us have really had enough of them for this year . . . The Chairman is conversant with this situation and I can tell you that whilst he is relying upon us to try to find ways and means of avoiding any cutback at our pulp mills, he has indicated that he fully approves of a programme of reduced production if that is the only alternative.[49]

Meyer's response to Eric Bowater's directive was optimistic. Sales, he said, had 'kept reasonable pace' with the excess over budgeted production of pulp for 1961, which he now put at 15,000 to 16,000 tons, largely because sales gained in the United States had

balanced sales lost, on price, in Europe. 'I would, therefore, at this
stage of the game strongly recommend against a cutback in production at either Carolina or Tennessee.' 'I agree. E.V.B.' appears in the
margin.[50] In 1962 the production of pulp at Catawba was 3 per cent
lower than in 1961; at Calhoun, 2 per cent greater (Table 32
above). These adjustments, presumably reflecting falling demand in
the United Kingdom balanced by sales on the open market, were no
doubt designed to relieve pressure on Bowaters' finances in the
United Kingdom without inflicting too much damage on Calhoun
or Catawba.

14.4 AT THE CENTRE

Sir Eric Bowater never seriously contemplated retirement, though
he had occasional fantasies about a cottage in the country with a
delightful companion, and he had an even greater dread of death,
perhaps, than most people.[51] He made no provision for a successor
as Chairman and no one else presumed to do it for him. On 11
February 1961 Stanley Bell – a possible successor to Eric Bowater –
died.

His place on the Board, but not his function in the business, was
filled by John Kirwan-Taylor. Bell's death left a gaping hole, particularly on Bowaters' United Kingdom side, for his knowledge of the
newsprint industry, its customers and its raw materials was very
wide.

In May, Eric approached Sir Christopher Chancellor, Chairman
of Odhams Press. He was the son of an illustrious figure of the latter
days of Empire, Sir John Chancellor (1870–1952), who had been
the first Governor of Southern Rhodesia and later High Commissioner in Palestine. Christopher had been at Eton and Trinity
College, Cambridge, where he took a first-class degree in History.
Then he was with Reuters, from 1930 to 1939 as Chief Correspondent and General Manager in the Far East and from 1944 to 1959 as
General Manager of Reuters Ltd. He went to Odhams in 1960,
disliked the *Daily Mirror* takeover and left, as he told Eric, 'without
regret' in June 1961.[52]

After some hesitation on account of his age – fifty-seven – Chancellor agreed to join the Board of the Bowater Paper Corporation as
a full-time executive director. In his family background, in his
education, in his career, he stood apart from his new colleagues but
he had the qualifications they sought in a replacement for Stanley
Bell. 'I very much doubt', said K. N. Linforth, 'if there is anybody at
present available in the U.K. whose knowledge of and personal

contact with the newspaper proprietors and publishers, not only at home but overseas, can equal that of Christopher Chancellor.'[53]

Coming into Bowaters as he did, at the top, Chancellor could survey the Organisation with a fresh and critical eye. He saw a very large business dominated to an extraordinary degree by the Chairman, who acted in many ways as if he owned it. The business, with very doubtful prospects before it in the United Kingdom for newsprint, was in the grip of a cash crisis brought on by over-exuberant and, in some cases, ill-judged expansion and by over-production of chemical pulp in North America. It was saddled with overhead costs which, in Chancellor's view, were too heavy, particularly in prestige advertising and public relations activities, of which the most conspicuous was the Annual General Meeting and all that went with it. Against all that there was the solid and growing strength of Eric Bowater's masterpiece: the Bowater business in North America. In 1961 it contributed nearly four-fifths of the Organisation's trading surplus of £21.9m.

J. M. Ritchie, also an incomer to Bowaters at a high level, held views, as we have seen in previous chapters, which on many matters coincided with Chancellor's. Essentially what these two observers saw was that the expansion of Bowaters, continuous and rapid over many years, had far outrun the development of the central administration of the business. This was an observation most disagreeable to members of the central administration who had devoted themselves with exemplary loyalty to the development of Bowaters along lines which, until very recently, had led time after time to success. To go beyond observation to action and to challenge the system which for so many years had brought such rewards and, by implication, to challenge the autocrat at the head of it – Sir Eric Bowater – would be a serious undertaking.

To issue such a challenge in prosperous times would have been to invite rebuff and as lately as 1958, when the turn in the tide of Bowaters' affairs was already perceptible, recommendations for reform offered by Associated Industrial Consultants had not been gratefully received. By the beginning of 1962 the outlook, especially in the United Kingdom, was much darker. Linforth, in January, said 'a further newsprint machine must immediately be taken out of production' and Ritchie said 'the outlook for Packaging Group also appeared more gloomy than was anticipated in the Profit Budget forecast'.[54]

About a fortnight later Robert Knight painted the general picture in sombre tones. Radical changes in 'certain sales forecasts', he said, 'would mean major changes in the profits budgets', which would come on top of heavy initial losses at Gillingham, losses arising from the transfer of certain activities to Stevenage and the late start-up of a coated-paper machine (No. 16) at Sittingbourne. For all these reasons 'he could not look for increased profits in the coming months to improve the situation', though he hoped for some relief by running down stocks of raw materials and paper which, at the end of December 1961, had been keeping £11m tied up. Lack of cash, caused by lack of profits, would mean that the bank overdraft in the United Kingdom, which had risen between the end of December and the beginning of February from £5.3m to £6.7m, would rise to about £10m by the end of the summer, although it was hoped it would fall to £8m by December 1962.[55]

In these alarming circumstances, calling evidently for radical measures, J. M. Ritchie handed to the Chairman a paper in which he 'suggested that the whole system of administrative control be radically changed and a considerable degree of autonomy and de-centralisation be effected'.[56] He concentrated on the business in the United Kingdom and within the United Kingdom on packaging but as his remarks were directed to matters of principle as well as to recommendations for practice they had a much wider application.

Briefly, what he wanted to see was the transfer of a wide range of executive authority from Bowater House to the operating units, so that it would be possible 'to very substantially reorganise the function and responsibilities of the headquarters personnel with a consequent sharp reduction in the numbers employed'. There were already, he claimed, models within Bowater – 'both in North America and in Europe individual companies and units are virtually autonomous, and while a small headquarters staff has been established it is mainly advisory but is responsible for the co-ordination of policy and the consolidation of individual company accounts'.[57]

He proposed setting up in the United Kingdom companies endowed with 'every function of management . . . including finance and administration' to run the UK pulp and paper mills, Bowater Packaging, Bowater-Scott and the building products business. Bowaters Sales Co. he would scrap, thus giving final victory to the various operating groups in their long vendetta against centralised control of sales. 'Constant criticism', he said, 'by sales of operations and vice versa could, under this set-up, no longer obtain.'[58] This was a shaft directed to the very heart of the traditional organisation, for Bowater Sales was the direct descendant of the ancestor of all Bowater companies, W. V. Bowater & Sons. Bell had been its Chairman and, after him, Weimar Cross, one of Eric Bowater's oldest associates, who died in New York on 25 October 1961.

Having put his proposals for the liberation of the operating units from the imperialism of Bowater House, Ritchie turned his attention to Bowater House itself, where 834 people were employed, and to the central administration and services generally, which were costing £2.6m a year to run.[59] His recommendations were drastic. The system of financial accounts and administration, built up over many years, would cease to be the control centre of the Organisation and 'very substantial reductions' could be effected in the numbers employed at Bowater House. He looked with an equally cold eye on a wide range of other departments, including Management Audit, Office Management and Services, Registration, Travel, Personnel and Management Training, Engineering, Research and Development, Publicity, suggesting that they should be cut down, abolished, physically removed, reorganised, or otherwise man-handled in the cause of de-centralisation and lower overhead expenses, especially those charged out to operating units, and most especially of all those which were resented by Bowater Packaging.

There was nothing out of the ordinary or unreasonable in Ritchie's general approach, whatever might be thought of some of the detailed proposals. In large concerns, tension naturally arises between the operating units and the central administration, and the arguments for and against autonomy for the units and authority for the centre are so finely balanced, and vary in force so much with circumstances, that large industrial groups commonly swing from one phase to the other, sometimes repeatedly. What is unusual in Bowaters' case is that the demand for devolution came so late and that it was made, as Ritchie said in opening his paper, in response to the emergence of severe competition, which more commonly makes operating units thankful for the everlasting arms beneath them and gives rise to a strengthening of central authority.[60]

Ritchie's proposals, carrying an implicit challenge to Eric Bowater's authority, had only one precedent – Ian Bowater's revolt in 1952 – and that was not encouraging. Eric, however, received the proposals with a good grace; a measure, perhaps of his anxieties. In March he gave them to Rye to circulate to members of the General Purposes Committee. He had already given instructions that expenses should be cut by 10 per cent.

Rye was closely identified with the established Bowater system, had given it devoted service and must have been deeply committed to it emotionally. He introduced Ritchie's proposals to his colleagues in a letter which is a model of fair-minded balance. He asked them to read Ritchie's paper before they read his own comments, which were few but shrewd. 'This is in many important respects', he

said, 'a controversial document . . . but there is too much at stake
for the Committee to fail to take it seriously and in the spirit in
which it is submitted.' He briefly defended the existing system,
saying it had been built up over the years 'on a basis which seem-
ingly best met our requirements', but he admitted that it did not
necessarily follow that it was appropriate to current and future
conditions, 'but the Committee would have to be abundantly satisfied concerning the soundness of new principles before recommend-
ing the breaking down of any existing structure'. He observed that
'de-centralisation is not as simple as it sounds', pointed out that
some of Ritchie's recommendations had been put forward by AIC
and rejected, and remarked 'possibly circumstances have changed,
but you must note that in certain fundamental respects the decisions
are not more than three years old. Furthermore, it is for consideration whether size and/or diversification do in fact change fundamental principles.' At the end of the letter, guardedly and indirectly
but unmistakably, he let his own deep feelings emerge: 'Finally, we
must take all possible steps to deal with this on an impersonal basis,
which for some members of the Chairman's Committee is not an
easy assignment.'[61]

On 5 June 1962 Sir Eric Bowater took the chair for the last time at
Bowaters' Annual General Meeting, held in a huge marquee outside
the new packaging plant at Gillingham, which in spite of its losses
Eric had decided to show to the shareholders. Three thousand of
them had applied for seats in chartered coaches and a ballot had
been held. Some 1,200 had said they would come in their own or
public transport. The whole of the gathering was escorted around
the works and everyone had a packed lunch, including a quarter-
bottle of wine.

It was the last glitter of the old glory. Eric himself was not in good
health and only his will-power propelled him to the meeting. The
account he had to give of 1961, for reasons that have been sufficiently examined, was not a happy one. Sales were higher than
ever before but profit margins were thin. The trading surplus was 7
per cent higher than in 1960, depreciation charges were nearly 10
per cent higher and the consolidated profit after depreciation and
interest but before tax was lower by almost 19 per cent. The
Chairman could not even be encouraging about 1962. 'The figures
and data available to date', he said, 'show a further decline in
earnings in the United Kingdom, whilst those of our overseas interests . . . are running at substantially the same level as for the
corresponding period of last year.' The dividend remained unchanged at 2s. 9d. in the pound – 13¾ per cent – but if that was

boldness for 1960 it was bravado for 1961, for Robert Knight had warned the Chairman in March that it could not be covered out of the year's earnings.[62]

Despite the sombre tone of the Chairman's address, the shareholders received it as warmly as usual, thus demonstrating their confidence in him and in the company. At the end of the day's proceedings, Eric's cousin, Ian, proposed a vote of thanks and, in doing so, expressed the view that Eric's judgment had been sounder than his in the decision to set Bowaters up in Tennessee. That was at the same time a handsome public gesture and an acknowledgement of the most lasting monument to Eric's genius as a businessman: the Bowater enterprise in North America.

Sir Eric Vansittart Bowater died of cancer at Dene Place in his sixty-eighth year, after about two months' illness, on 30 August 1962. His authority was unquestioned, his views were sought, his mind was clear, until a very few days before the last, so that until the last he remained, despite the shaking of the ground beneath his feet, 'the man who was Bowaters'.

CHAPTER FIFTEEN

Bowaters in outline
1962–1980

15.1 AFTER SIR ERIC

Without Sir Eric Bowater, the Bowater Organisation would not have come into existence. That he was a greater man than any of his colleagues none of them would have been likely to deny. None of them would have denied, either, that at his death his policy had reached the end of the road – had, indeed, travelled beyond it, so far as cash was concerned – and that the need for change was urgent. Eric's character being what it was, however, could he have brought himself to make the changes that were necessary? If not, would he willingly have given way to those who would have made the changes for him?

The measure of his dominance of Bowaters' affairs was apparent as soon as he died. He left no directions as to who was to succeed him and the Board had taken no steps to choose a successor them-selves, although they had known for some months that, in all probability, a successor would soon be necessary. Not only Eric, it seems, but also his close colleagues were unwilling to face the possibility that he might not be immortal. After a series of consul-tations, those of the directors who were on the spot summoned Sir Christopher Chancellor from Italy, where he was on holiday, to take the vacant Chair.

In this matter of the succession Eric Bowater might reasonably have expected his wishes, if he had expressed any, to carry weight but he had no right of nomination. As soon as he was gone, it was not only the right but the duty of the Board to find his successor, having regard only to the interest of the business as they saw it, yet they seem to have been thrown into confusion when they found he had not done their job for them.

The Board expected Eric to act as if he owned the business, which was the way he had been acting for the past thirty-five years or so, except for the years from 1930 to 1932 when Rothermere and Beaverbrook showed him who, at that time, the real owners of the

Sir Christopher Chancellor, Chairman 1962–9.

business were. Eric himself never came near such a position, for the shares he held were never more than a tiny fraction of the whole. Nevertheless, as the course of this narrative has shown, he assumed total authority in the direction of Bowaters' affairs, exercised it through the force of his personality and his ability, and considered himself justified in relying on the business to provide him, against payment, with the means of living as a rich man, which he enjoyed. His salary was substantial but, at his insistence, remained unaltered for many years and he did not seek to build a large personal fortune. In 1954, without prompting from Eric, the shareholders voted him an option on 150,000 shares, but an alteration in the tax laws

J. Martin Ritchie, Chairman and Chief Executive 1969–73.

prevented him from taking it up. It is doubtful whether money for its own sake had much attraction for him. As well as claiming total authority, he accepted total responsibility, the weight of which, as private correspondence makes clear, he felt very keenly. Towards the end of his life the tide of prosperity turned and his judgment began to fail but there is no evidence of his blaming either the advisers whom he consulted before framing policy or the subordinates to whom he gave instructions for carrying it out. He did not delegate authority but he did not delegate responsibility either and the strain upon him was severe.

Lord Erroll of Hale, Chairman since 1973.

The period immediately after Eric Bowater's death was bleak. In Bowaters' markets over-capacity ruled, so that profits were hard to come by, but charges for depreciation and loan interest, Eric's legacies, remained high, so that the need for ever-increasing earnings remained as urgent as ever. 'This is the time for a pause', said the new Chairman, addressing Bowaters' shareholders for the first time, and announced a lower dividend. No fleets of coaches had brought his audience to that meeting and the presentation of the Report and Accounts, much slimmer and more restrained than in the recent past, signalled the new austerity.

After Eric had received Ritchie's paper on Bowaters' administration, he had taken counsel with Charles Rye and invited W. R. T. Whatmore, with two other partners of Peat, Marwick, Mitchell, to take an arm's-length view of the same subject. Their report[1] was submitted about a fortnight before Eric died and three weeks after the death of 'Boss' Whatmore, one of Eric's few remaining close advisers. The outside investigators' report carried much the same message as Ritchie's paper, and with Ritchie as Managing Director — jointly, for a time, with Rye — words swiftly became deeds.

A very cold wind indeed swept through Bowater House and the central administration generally, carrying jobs away with it and leaving office space to let, and the organisation in the United Kingdom was considerably de-centralised. Early in 1963 a conference was held in London to promote an assault on the established system of inter-company trading and subsidisation.[2] At about the same time, shipping experts from the British & Commonwealth Group were invited to investigate the running of the Bowater Steamship Co., which as a result was handed over to British & Commonwealth for management.[3] Mindful, perhaps, of 'de mortuis . . .', the British & Commonwealth experts accepted the principle that Bowaters should own ships to carry their own goods but over the succeeding years as the ships in turn became obsolete the fleet was run down until, in 1977, the last of Bowaters' ships, Nina Bowater, was sold. 'Far-called, our navies melt away . . .'

These measures, important though they were, were tactical. They did not touch Bowaters' abiding strategic problem: too much newsprint capacity in the United Kingdom. The form and the scale of this problem, as the successors of Eric Bowater inherited it, were the direct result of Eric's own policy as expressed in the Master Plan of the mid-fifties (Chapter 12 above). Before that, in the immediate post-war years, Eric had announced that Bowaters would rely on packaging rather than on newsprint for expansion in the United

Kingdom (p. 184 above), but that policy had been reversed and plans had been made for four new machines and an increase of 40 per cent in papermaking capacity, from 615,000 to 860,000 tons a year, of which about three-quarters was to be newsprint.[4]

This plan, as we have seen, never came fully into effect. Two of the projected machines were never built. In so far as it did come into effect, however, it did so just in time to add its contribution to the over-capacity which plagued the world's newsprint makers from the late fifties onward. From 1958 to the time of writing the demand for newsprint in the world has ranged from 85–86 per cent of capacity in bad years to 93–96 per cent in good ones, although 96 per cent was only reached in 1974 (Table 34). Newsprint manufacture is quintessentially a mass-production industry in which the scale of operations is crucial to the costs of production and a machine running below 95 per cent of its capacity rapidly starts losing money.

The figures in Table 34 present a picture of a highly competitive industry in which, unless demand again comes close to outrunning supply, as it did in the forties and early fifties, British newsprint makers are permanently ill-placed to compete, having neither abundant raw materials nor cheap power nor tariff protection. Their only defenders, who contributed powerfully to Bowaters' success in the thirties, are strong newspaper and magazine proprietors, willing and able to pay a premium price for service, especially the daily delivery of supplies direct to the Press rooms, and to preserve the British newsprint industry as a counter-balance to the Canadians

TABLE 34. *World demand for newsprint as a percentage of capacity, 1955–77*

Date	%	Date	%
1955	100	1967	88
1956	102	1968	88
1957	95	1969	93
1958	86	1970	91
1959	85	1971	89
1960	88	1972	91
1961	87	1973	93
1962	87	1974	96
1963	85	1975	86
1964	89	1976	86
1965	92	1977	89
1966	93		

Source: Canadian Pulp and Paper Association, as for Appendix I, Table 1.

and Scandinavians. Newspaper and magazine owners, however, have for a good many years been hard pressed to ensure their own industry's survival, let alone their suppliers'. Meanwhile the traditional absence of a tariff has left the British market wide open to importers backed by immense natural advantages, and the Scandinavians, wanting a product with greater value added than wood pulp, have sought to send in newsprint rather than pulp, using price policy – relatively cheap newsprint, relatively dear pulp – to further their aims.

Eric Bowater's answer to the problem of the British newsprint industry, long before it became so severe as it was when he died and later, was to diversify into packaging. Packaging also, in the late fifties, began to suffer from over-capacity, sharp competition and low profit margins. Again, like the newsprint industry and for the same reasons, it was an attractive target for the supply of raw materials by foreigners, especially, after EFTA was set up, by the Scandinavians.

Bowaters, in packaging as in newsprint, enthusiastically made the problem of over-capacity worse by expansion. As late as 1965 their splendid new flexible packaging plant at Gillingham was still unprofitable, four years after opening, and Chancellor said they were trying to find another use for it. Nevertheless the business in corrugated containers, in the mid-sixties, was encouraging enough for Bowaters to make a major acquisition in February 1966: Hugh Stevenson & Sons, with 4,000 employees and factories in Manchester, London, Newport (Mon.), Birmingham, Lichfield, Darlington, Glasgow and Edinburgh.

The history of Bowaters' incursion into the EEC, concentrated as it was on newsprint, pulp and packaging, was brief and unhappy. A misconceived venture into packaging in South Italy, Bowater Europea, lasted only from 1962 until the spring of 1965, ending with a sit-in at the factory near Rome. In 1966 Bowater Italia opened a new corrugated container factory at Modena and in December 1968 La Chapelle, in France, was merged with Papeteries Darblay to give Bowaters the largest French papermaking group, with capacity of more than 450,000 tons a year. That was Bowaters' European zenith. The French Government steadily refused to allow Bowaters to raise their prices to what they considered a reasonable level, losses became insupportable and in 1971 the whole papermaking enterprise, which had cost Bowaters £7.2m in 1960 (p. 276 above) and a great deal more thereafter, was sold to a Swiss subsidiary of the Banque de Paris et des Pays-Bas for 'a sum of the order of £1 million'.[5] After that, one by one, the businesses acquired in the EEC in the late sixties were inconspicuously disposed of until only one was left: the joint venture with Philips into making corrugated containers in Belgium. Bowaters, it is clear, never felt at home on the Continent.

Amid the gloom encircling the paper industry in the United Kingdom there was in the sixties one bright spot: tissues, including toilet tissues (in British lavatories, hard papers were being replaced by soft tissues – more soothing but less reliable), and household papers, principally kitchen towels. The main beneficiaries of rising demand for these goods, some 10 per cent a year, which they did their best to stimulate by aggressive marketing and advertising, were Reeds, in alliance with Kimberly-Clark (Kleenex), and Bowater-Scott (Andrex, Scotties), an outstanding and unqualified success among the businesses in the United Kingdom bequeathed by Eric Bowater to Bowaters.

Bowater-Scott paid their first dividend in 1963, Andrex being by then the largest-selling brand of toilet tissue in the United Kingdom, with 25 per cent of the market. A new high-speed paper machine – 4,000 feet per minute – began to run in the summer of 1965 and in the summer of 1966, Bowater-Scott's best year so far, a decision was announced to put up a completely new mill at Barrow-in-Furness. By the time it was officially opened, in May 1968, a second machine had been ordered and plans were in hand for a third; by March 1975 four machines were in operation.

By October 1970 Bowater-Scott also had a three-machine mill running in Australia, at Melbourne. Outside Europe, except in North America, Bowaters' main interests were in selling paper rather than making it and they did not go into manufacture except in joint enterprises, of which Bowater-Scott in Australia was much the most substantial and enduring. In enterprises in New Zealand and South Africa they took minority holdings, saw to getting the mills established and then withdrew, having no desire to stay in enterprises which they could not control. In New Zealand they sold their 17 per cent of Tasman (p. 279 above) in 1973, though the consultancy agreement and the sales agency both ran on until 1979. In 1973 Bowaters also sold their minority holding in a joint company with Anglo-American Corporation, established in 1968 to set up a mill, to be built by Bowaters, near Durban. No doubt their decisions were influenced, in New Zealand, by the knowledge that the Government would never allow them to acquire a really large holding, and in South Africa by the political outlook which always deterred Eric (p. 203 above) and after this time grew steadily worse. In South Africa and in Australia, traditional export markets for

Bowater-Scott Australia's tissue mill, Melbourne.

British goods, Bowaters had sales companies, of which the Bowater
Paper Co. Pty Ltd in Australia was much the larger.

All Eric Bowater's successors have had to look for ways of escape
from the consequences of one of the few miscalculations of his
business life: the decision to expand Bowaters' newsprint business
in the United Kingdom in the fifties. All of them, equally, have been
indebted to the far-sighted boldness of his decisions to expand in
North America, first in Newfoundland and later in Tennessee, for
without those decisions it is difficult to see how the Bowater
Organisation could have survived, let alone prospered.

Bowaters' success in North America depended heavily on per-
suading American financiers to back an English enterprise, repeatedly and heavily, with loan capital, and that in turn depended on
the personality of Eric Bowater and the respect which he inspired,
not once or occasionally but continuously. The North American
success would have been remarkable at any time but it shines all the
more brightly in a period when success seems to be something

which people no longer expect from British business. The stakes and the risks were both high and in making both the fundamental decisions – to take over Corner Brook in 1938 and to set up in Tennessee in 1952 – Eric Bowater flew in the face of conventional wisdom and displayed the highest level of commercial courage.

Within this strategic success there were tactical failures. Meyer thought that the purchase of the Mersey mill and the building of the pulp mill at Catawba were 'serious mistakes which might take Bowaters ten years to get over'.[6] Mersey, though an expensive purchase, was never unprofitable, and Catawba in the seventies became very profitable indeed, but to Meyer's list might be added the hardboard mill and the early operations in coated paper which led to the quarrel with McCall's (pp. 299–300). All these problems had to be faced by the new management. In 1962 they sold a 49 per cent interest in Mersey to the *Washington Post*, which eased the financial strain and, as Chancellor said, guaranteed 'a high level of operation for many years to come'. At Catawba nothing that was done – a great deal was tried – could make the hardboard mill profitable and in 1964 it was sold. The quarrel with McCall's was settled after a great deal of coming and going between London and the United States. In 1966 the Catawba Newsprint Co. was set up, rather after the pattern set by the deal with the *Washington Post*, in partnership with the Newhouse Newspaper Group, owners of twenty-one titles. To serve the partnership the largest newsprint machine in the world, designed to produce 180,000 short tons a year, was built at Catawba. It started up on 26 November 1968 and immediately became known, for no reason that anyone can be sure of, as Ol' Blue, a name frequently given to quick-running hunting hounds in the Southern States.

A. B. Meyer, aged 71, died in April 1964, just before he had intended to retire. Since the revival of Bowaters' North American business in 1938 (p. 172) he had been one of the central figures in it, but his acquaintance with Eric Bowater ran back to the early twenties, giving him exceptional influence not only in North America but in London also – influence which he exercised, after Eric's death, in the choice of Eric's successor.[7]

Meyer's death, followed in the Autumn of 1965 by the death of his successor, Charles T. Hicks, left a vacuum at the head of the Bowater Paper Co. in New York which was occupied, but not filled, by a succession of incumbents until the autumn of 1968. Then Hugh K. Joyce, a forty-seven-year-old Canadian, reached the position by way of Mersey and Corner Brook. His first task was to repair the damage inflicted on morale in the company by the four-

The wet end: Ol' Blue, largest newsprint machine in the world, Catawba.

The dry end: a reel of finished newsprint nears completion at one of Bowater's
Canadian mills.

year interregnum and to re-invigorate Bowaters' North American sales organisation. Also in 1968 Bowater Inc. was formed in the United States with Victor J. Sutton as President to manage the North American business as a whole. Sutton was followed by Sam Mann and in 1972 Joyce became President.

It is a measure of the soundness of Bowaters' North American business that this prolonged lack of effective authority on the sales side seems to have done no lasting harm. Certainly the difference between the position of firms in the newsprint industry in the United Kingdom and in North America is profound. In the United Kingdom, with no natural advantages, they need special circumstances for survival. In North America, firms can go through severe spells of low demand or over-capacity and come out on the other side into renewed prosperity, as many did in the extreme conditions of the thirties and in the far less severe cyclical fluctuations which afflicted them every four years or so in the sixties and seventies.

In 1965 Bowaters launched into massive expansion in British Columbia, that other home of the paper industry which they had investigated in the late forties and early fifties before Eric decided on Tennessee. Their reason for doing so, fully in the tradition set by Eric Bowater, was to safeguard their future supplies of raw materials. A world shortage of timber was forecast before the end of the century, and British Columbia was said to be the last source of timber suitable for pulp. Bowaters joined with Bathurst Paper of Montreal, leading manufacturers of packaging paper and packaging products, to take control of the Bulkley Valley Pulp & Timber Co. In 1966 Bathurst merged with Consolidated Paper to become Consolidated Bathurst and the joint venture was renamed Bulkley Valley Forest Industries.

British Columbia's Minister of Lands and Forests had granted the Bulkley Valley company exclusive pulpwood-harvesting rights over some six million acres around Houston in the northern part of the province. Relying on these rights, the partners proposed to build a pulp and paper mill which by 1971 would have a daily output 'in the range of 600 to 1,000 tons', though the precise nature of its products were to be decided 'in the light of supply and demand conditions when the time comes'.[8] As a single undertaking, it was more ambitious than any which Eric in his prime had ever contemplated.

It did not follow the course intended. Feasibility studies suggested that there would be no immediate market for the output of the pulp and paper mill, so the building of the mill was postponed. During 1969 work began on building a very large sawmill, intended as the first phase of a project which in the fullness of time would include pulp and paper-making as well, using residue from the sawmill as cheap raw material. The sawmill came into operation in the summer of 1970.

In 1969 Sir Christopher Chancellor retired and J. M. Ritchie, aged fifty-two, took his place, remaining also Managing Director, so that like Sir Eric Bowater before him he was both Chairman and Chief Executive. He greatly desired the position, but it was hardly an enviable one, for although Bowaters' business in North America was so strong that there were rumours in the Press of a plan for Bowater Inc. to take over the rest of the group,[9] yet the outlook in other directions, to say the least, was uncertain.

In 1969 Bowaters' profits, £19.2m before tax, were greater than they had ever been but in the United Kingdom less money was made from newsprint, although more newsprint was sold, than in 1968. On the Continent, difficulties with the Government in France were already threatening the prosperity of the very large newsprint group which had just been formed there. Even in North America, Corner Brook, for the time being, was not prosperous and the radical alteration in the phasing of the Bulkley Valley project was hardly calculated to promote confidence in its future. If Bowaters were to do well in the years immediately ahead, many things would have to go well for them. Several things, unfortunately, showed signs of going badly.

15.2 'THE NADIR OF OUR FORTUNES'

What Bowater needed when Martin Ritchie took over as Chairman was a run of luck; instead, misfortunes came crowding in.

First, there was the persistent *malaise* of the newsprint industry to contend with. During 1970 demand for newsprint in the United States fell by nearly 3 per cent, though elsewhere it rose. The consequences for Bowaters' profits illustrated dramatically the contrast between their strength in the USA and their weakness in the United Kingdom. In the USA, despite the general fall in demand, Bowaters' new machine at Catawba produced 5,000 tons more than its designed output and Bowaters' North American business as a whole, exceptionally among North American newsprint businesses in 1970, made £1m more profit than in 1969. In the United Kingdom, on the other hand, Bowaters and Reeds, by the end of the year, were discussing the possibility of merging their British newsprint businesses, presumably in the belief that trouble shared is trouble halved. The idea of the merger was not warmly received by the Monopolies Commission, or by *The Economist* ('the result will be a classical monopoly').[10] Reeds, according to *The Economist*, put the profit ratio between the two sides at 70:30 in Reeds' favour; Bowaters said that it was nearer 55:45, that their plant was more modern than Reeds' and their outlook brighter in the long run.[11] Negotiations ceased in March 1971.

In 1970 Bowaters sold about 470,000 tons of newsprint in the United Kingdom, some 5 per cent less than the high figure of 1969. The selling price went up in two stages by £5 a ton – 7.6 per cent – to £70.75 but that was not enough to make up for rising costs, especially of imported raw materials and wages. During 1971 three machines were closed down at Kemsley. This drastic action, though the necessity for it was deplorable, was part of a continuous pattern and cannot have been unpredictable. What made the situation far worse, in 1970–2, than it had ever been before was the convergence of a series of other blows on the newsprint side of the business.

There was first of all, early in 1971, the sale of Bowaters' interest in Chapelle-Darblay (p. 320 above). The sale removed the incentive for owning the sulphite pulp mill at Strasbourg which had been acquired by accident in the course of gaining control of La Chapelle (p. 276 above). In the face of falling profits at Strasbourg in 1971 and the certainty of heavy expenditure to comply with increasingly strict pollution control regulations, the mill was sold early in 1972.

As well as these French divestments, representing a major retreat from the ambitious Continental strategy of the late fifties and early sixties, there were disturbing developments on the other side of the Atlantic, where most of Bowaters' profits came from. In May 1970 the Canadian dollar was allowed to 'float'. It promptly rose, and continued rising, against the United States dollar, with the result that newsprint exported from Canada to the USA, where it was sold for American dollars, returned steadily fewer Canadian dollars to the producing mills. This might not have been serious if prices could have been adjusted to allow for it as well as for rising costs, but adequate prices were difficult or impossible for two reasons: the competitive situation, with a world surplus of newsprint, in 1971, of three million tons; and the action of the American Government, in August 1971, in 'freezing' prices, including newsprint prices, thus preventing an increase which had been arranged. Between 1970 and 1972 the combined effect of 'frozen' prices and a Canadian dollar on its way up from 95c to $1.01 to the American dollar was that for the producing mill the price of a ton of newsprint sent from Canada to the States was the equivalent, in American dollars, of $Can.164 in January 1970 and $Can.161 at the end of 1971. 'In these days of exceptional inflation', Martin Ritchie observed rather bitterly at Bowaters' Annual Meeting in 1972, 'there must be few commodities which at the end of 1971 realised a sale value below the level ruling two years before.'

This was especially sad for Corner Brook, which for a long time had scarcely been Bowaters' favourite child, since the mills in the South were far better placed to supply American demand, especially when it was falling. Corner Brook suffered, too, when Tasman came into production in New Zealand. Its plant was ageing, it had suffered fire and drought, its costs were high and the rise of the Canadian dollar was more than Corner Brook could stand. Its results tumbled over into heavy loss (Table 35).

TABLE 35. *Corner Brook, losses, 1970–2 (in $Can.)*

1970	252,000
1971	4,646,000
1972	2,312,000

Source: OG.

Bowaters' response, in 1971, was first to import 100,000 tons of newsprint into the United Kingdom from Corner Brook to replace output from the three machines shut down at Kemsley and then, when that proved insufficient, to announce that at the end of October 1971 they would shut down No. 7 machine, the last and largest machine installed, in the late forties, at Corner Brook. The Prime Minister of Newfoundland, 'Joey' Smallwood, 'took exception', in Martin Ritchie's words, 'to this closure, and . . . stated that his Government had powers to nationalise the Corner Brook mill'.[12] Bowaters were pleased to hear it, especially when the Newfoundland Government paid them $200,000 for an option to make an offer, which Bowaters would be under no compulsion to accept, exercisable until 30 June 1972. Bowater, in return, agreed not to close the machine until the end of December 1971.

No. 7 machine was shut down; the option, after a change of Government, was not exercised; but until 1974 or thereabouts, when conditions in the newsprint market began to improve, Corner Brook was up for sale – no reasonable offer refused. As it turned out, no refusal was necessary. By the late seventies the mill was again very profitable (Table 36).

The decision to cut production of newsprint in the United Kingdom reacted not only on Corner Brook but on Bowaters' Swedish

TABLE 36. *Corner Brook, profits, before tax, 1973–8 (in $Can.)*

1973	4,037,000
1974	11,451,000
1975	2,028,000*
1976	716,000*
1977	19,051,000
1978	25,264,000

* Profits affected by strikes.

Source: OG.

groundwood pulp mill at Sofiehem. Far less pulp was needed for Bowaters' business and, since there was an even deeper recession in the market for pulp than in the market for paper, it was very difficult to find other customers for the pulp that should have gone to the United Kingdom. In North America the chemical pulp mill at Catawba no longer supplied the Bowater mills in the United Kingdom, but in the open market in the United States, where most of its output was sold, price-cutting reduced the mill's profits for 1971 by more than half. Eric Bowater's policy of self-sufficiency in raw materials had advantages for Bowaters while prices ruled high and supplies were tight but, in 1971, a thoroughly bad year, it added the problems of the pulp producers to the problems they already had as producers of newsprint.

Bowaters' worst disaster in the disastrous years of the early seventies was the collapse of the Bulkley Valley project. Throughout 1971 the new sawmill was 'beset by considerable production difficulties'.[13] Bowaters and their partners, Consolidated-Bathhurst, found themselves in a not entirely unfamiliar predicament, namely, that the costs of reaching an economical level of production were going to be far greater than they had expected. Even if these costs were accepted, there would still be no near prospect of expanding into pulp and paper production, the original object of the project.

The partners sold out to Northwood Pulp Ltd. Bowaters' share of the losses came to £7.5m, plus £3.9m that might have to be found, over a period of ten years, to meet payments guaranteed by Bowaters' Canadian Corporation.

By the beginning of 1972 the closing of No. 7 machine at Corner Brook and what Ritchie called 'the newsprint rationalisation programme carried out in the United Kingdom' – the closure of the three machines at Kemsley – had reduced Bowaters' capacity for newsprint production in the United Kingdom and North America by 300,000 tons. So far as the United Kingdom was concerned there was no likelihood that the reduction would ever be made good and its permanence was emphasised in 1973, when the diminishing production of newsprint finally ceased at Thames Mill, Northfleet, where Bowater's Paper Mills had first gone into business in 1926.

When Martin Ritchie surveyed Bowaters' results for 1971, at the Annual Meeting of 1972, he could take comfort from packaging ('a good year' – 7,200 employees and twenty plants in the United Kingdom, with £50m turnover); from building products ('an excellent year': £14m turnover); from tissues ('a difficult year but . . . the earnings of Bowater-Scott rose by some 14 per cent'); and from the performance of the companies in Australia and New Zealand; but precious little from newsprint anywhere. Consolidated profits, at £9,519,000 before tax, were 41 per cent lower than in 1970. No final dividend for 1971 was paid, partly because, on top of everything else, a strike by coal-miners in the United Kingdom had seriously affected earnings in February and March 1972. With stark frankness, Ritchie set out the main activities in which profits had fallen below the 1970 level:

United Kingdom	Newsprint, magazine and coated papers	£3.5m
Canada	Newsprint	£1.8
United States	Newsprint and coated papers	£1.0
	Pulp	£1.3
Sweden	Pulp	£0.5

'1971', said Ritchie, 'has been, in many respects, the worst the paper industry has experienced for a very long time.' He added that he believed it would prove to be 'the nadir of our fortunes' and expressed 'some guarded optimism' about the results for 1972. The shareholders passed a resolution submitted by the Board removing the word 'Paper' from their company's title, leaving it simply the Bowater Corporation Ltd.

15.3 RALLI AND BEYOND

About three weeks before Bowaters' Annual Meeting in 1972, just after their 1971 results had come out, Michael Braham interviewed Ritchie for *The Observer*. The price of Bowaters' shares, 154p, was barely half their value three years earlier, yet their very solid backing, including a great deal of freehold land, was calculated by Braham to give an asset value of 200p a share. Slater Walker, at the height of their prestige and influence, were known to have been buying and a takeover bid was not impossible. Braham put the point to Ritchie. 'We're too heavily indebted', was the reply, 'we don't even own our head office. Quite frankly, if I were one of those chaps prowling around I would not be very keen on getting involved in this industry.'[14]

Still it was evident, within Bowaters and outside, that Bowaters' business ought not to go on as it was. McKinseys, the management consultants, as fashionable in their field as Slater Walker in theirs, commissioned to review Bowaters' affairs, confirmed that they were too heavily involved in the production of newsprint: a point which had occurred to Eric Bowater about a quarter of a century earlier, but he had misguidedly ignored it later. McKinseys also confirmed the correctness of Bowaters' plans for developing their other product groups, such as building products and packaging. Why Bowaters felt they needed expensive confirmation of their own good judgment is not obvious but evidently it made them feel better.

Good judgment pointed, as it had pointed since the late thirties, towards diversification and as far away from newsprint, or indeed paper generally, as possible; hence the alteration in the Corporation's title. The general atmosphere of the sixties and early seventies, too, was favourable to such a policy.[15] Bigger was generally thought to be better, not least by Anthony Wedgwood Benn, and there was a bright faith in the omnicompetence of management. The word 'synergy', not hitherto prominent in the vocabulary of business, became fashionable. Tobacco companies became cosmeticians, owners of department stores, purveyors of potato crisps. Unilever and Allied Breweries nearly merged, being rescued only by the intervention of the Monopolies Commission, which delayed matters until movements in share prices upset the deal. Why not, then, a move sideways for Bowaters?

One signpost pointed in the general direction of building products. Bowaters had been established in a corner of that field ever since they acquired Lloyds' business in wallboards in 1936 (p. 114 above), and since 1959 they had owned Flexpipe, making pitch-fibre pipes as an alternative to salt-glazed pipes for drainage, sewage and electrical conduits. Both activities, like papermaking, were based on wood fibre and waste paper.

It was not, therefore, a very long step from wallboard and Flexpipe to household equipment and furniture, similarly reliant on timber, and in 1969 Bowaters acquired the issued share capital of F. Hills & Sons Ltd, who made doors, industrialised building components and specialised wood products in factories at Stockton-on-Tees and in Ayrshire. They followed up that acquisition, early in 1970, by taking over Limelight built-in and fitted furniture. All these businesses, in wallboards, flexible piping, building components and furniture, were consolidated into Bowaters Building Products Ltd which by 1971 was a small but exceedingly profitable part of Bowaters' business as a whole.[16]

Encouraged by these results, though not unmindful of the cyclical nature of the furniture industry – 'at present the industry is going through a boom period but it is fairly certain that past cycles will be repeated'[17] – Bowaters made a major investment. For a consideration valued at £11m they took over, in August 1972, Beautility Ltd. Its operations were varied. Beautility itself made furniture and, through subsidiaries, controlled timber merchanting and the production of bathroom and kitchen units, veneers, coffins (bought in and then beautified), cabinets made from chipboard, and carpets which provided about £500,000 of the group's £968,000 profits for 1971. Beautility was a large firm in an industry mainly carried on by small ones and the takeover made Bowaters a significant force in it. The price was thought by some to be high but, at a time when consumers were spending freely, Bowaters could see few clouds on Beautility's horizon.

The Beautility acquisition was barely completed before it was over-shadowed. On 26 September 1972 Bowaters announced to an uncomprehending world that their Board and the Board of Ralli International Ltd had completed negotiations for a merger. It took the form of a takeover of Ralli by Bowaters and the terms, eleven Bowater Ordinary shares for ten Ralli Ordinaries, put a value of about £80m on Ralli, though no cash was to pass. On the face of it, no merger could have been more unlikely. Bowaters were manufacturers, their capital employed in the most tangible of assets: factories, land, forests, huge paper machines, ships, stocks of raw materials and finished goods. Ralli, although they had manufacturing interests, were primarily commodity traders – rubber, jute, sisal, coffee, above all cotton and, apart from their stock-in-trade, their most important assets were the knowledge, judgment and instant decisiveness of the successful merchant.

In origin, it was a financier's merger, based not on any consideration of the complementarity or compatibility of the parties' activities but on a shrewd valuation of Bowaters' assets and the use they might be put to by a management with cash and an eye to any opportunities that might exist or be created. The initiative did not come from Bowaters but from Jim Slater and his associates, who in so many ways embodied the spirit of the 'swinging sixties' as it expressed itself in Stock Market operations directed by the higher flights of the financial imagination.

Ralli International was controlled by two youngish men of very different background – the ninth Earl of Carrick (forty-one) and Malcolm Horsman (thirty-nine). They owed their position to their abilities, backed by large loans from Slater to enable them to buy into the equity of the company.[18] It had been formed by a merger between two subsidiaries of Slater Walker – Ralli Brothers (Trading) Ltd and Oriental Carpet Manufacturers, one of the world's largest manufacturers and distributors of carpets from Romania, Turkey, the Caucasus, Iran, Russian Turkestan, Afghanistan, Pakistan, India, Nepal and China. The merged company, under the title Ralli International Ltd, was floated publicly with great success in November 1969. The whole operation was a classic example of company promotion. The financial manoeuvres which led up to it and accompanied it were intricate and very profitable; they have been described in detail by Charles Raw and in considerably less detail by Slater himself.[19]

In rather less than three years of independent life Ralli International's growth, under Malcolm Horsman, was very fast indeed. Takeover followed takeover, in pursuit of what Horsman called 'a basic strategy of developing in areas of relative political stability and growth'. His Chairman's statement to the Annual Meeting in 1972 reads rather like the setting for a James Bond novel, as yet unpublished. He takes his shareholders through commodity trading, chiefly in Australia and the Far East, banking, bill broking, retail jewellery in the USA, and river transport on the Rhine. Hong Kong, Temenggong and Memphis, Tennessee, are called to mind. A 'major profit centre in the United States of America' is 'reversed into a company quoted on the American Stock Exchange'. It is exotic, dramatic, the action never stops. In 1971, that year of gloom for Bowaters, Ralli's profits, £5,577,000 before tax, were 61 per cent greater than in 1970 and the earnings per share had more than doubled in two years.

Yet Bowater had a solidity – and a respectability – which Ralli could not match. Ralli, to pass to another literary image, was like a palace in the *Arabian Nights*: all its glories might vanish in an instant. The same could hardly be said of Calhoun, Catawba, Corner Brook, Gillingham. In other words, Ralli had cash, Bowater assets, as Slater had noticed before he began to buy in. By September 1972 Slater Walker held 12 per cent of Bowaters' Ordinary capital; of Ralli's, 15. Why not put the two together?

One evening in September 1972 Slater put the idea to Sir Kenneth Keith, Chairman of Hill Samuel, Bowaters' merchant bankers, and to Robert Clark, his deputy, who was on Bowaters' Board. They were favourable. The plan was then put before Bowaters' directors. On 1 November 1972 Trafalgar House Ltd, under Nigel Broackes, cut clean across the Bowater-Ralli negotiations by making a bid valued at £126m for the Bowater Corporation itself. Nearly three weeks of noisy battle followed and then on 17 November Bowaters' shareholders voted to go ahead with the Ralli takeover and reject Broackes's offer. It was withdrawn on 20 November.

By the beginning of 1973, Ralli International became a subsidiary of the Bowater Corporation and was radically changed thereby. Slater commented,

The outcome was a very satisfactory one for Slater Walker as we had underpinned the assets per share of Ralli International in which we had a substantial holding; activated our shareholding in Bowater; realized about £11 million in cash by the sale of [Bowater] shares to Hill Samuel [Hill Samuel had insisted] and earned a sizeable merchant banking fee for advising Ralli on the merger.[20]

It is a curious reflection that Slater could bring about wholesale changes in the balance and composition of a very large industrial undertaking for reasons which had nothing to do with its industrial purposes at all but a great deal to do with the value of its assets.

Martin Ritchie did not see the new order in. He announced his resignation on 6 December 1972, to take effect on 31 January 1973. During his brief and stressful Chairmanship he was not easy to work with, having, in spite of his earlier representations to Eric Bowater, something of Eric's liking for centralised power. Against that, it should be borne in mind that it fell to him, during one of the down-swings in the paper industry's trade cycle, to contend with the consequences of errors in past policy amid general circumstances which were beyond his control – he could not, for instance, influence the exchange rate of the Canadian dollar – and full of difficulty. He saw Bowater through the worst, and an upturn in the Corporation's affairs was not long delayed.

On the reconstituted Board of Bowaters, Ralli was strongly represented. The new Chairman, however, was non-executive and neutral as between Ralli and Bowater, for he was Lord Erroll of Hale, an engineer by profession who, as a Conservative politician, had served as President of the Board of Trade and Minister of Power between 1961 and 1964 and had gone back into business after Harold Wilson's first Labour Government took office. The Chief Executive's position was divided. Malcolm Horsman came in as Deputy Chairman and joint Managing Director with Colin Popham, who was also one of two Vice-Chairmen, the other being

Robert Knight. The three together formed the executive Committee of the Board. Lord Carrick and David Slater (unrelated to Jim) also joined the Board from Ralli.

Malcolm Horsman, having headed the charge of new forces into Bowater, did not stay for very long. In 1972 Bowaters' profits were rising again. Reinforced by Ralli's they reached £26.5m, much their highest figure up to that date, and in 1974 they reached £59.5m. Horsman, however, resigned his executive positions early in 1976 and soon afterwards left Bowater altogether. His ways were not the ways of Bowater and it may be doubted whether he was ever at home in surroundings so different from those in which he had made his name.

The Ralli merger, nevertheless, altered the shape and nature of Bowaters' business more radically than anything that had been done to it since Eric Bowater, in 1926, transformed his father's and his uncles' cosy little paper shop into a large-scale manufacturing enterprise. In 1972 Bowaters' sales were immediately more than doubled, though the capital employed rose by only 38 per cent, demonstrating the difference between manufacturing and trading. The great increase in sales came from 'international trading' which was greater in value than the whole of Bowaters' sales in 1971. Sales of paper and pulp, the traditional Bowater products, stood in 1972 at a figure little more than half as large as the figure for international trading (Table 37). If diversification was the object of Bowaters' policy, as for so long it had been, then the object had at last been achieved.

TABLE 37. *The Bowater Corporation, sales after the merger, 1972*

	£m	%
Paper and pulp	163	27
Packaging	57	10
Building products, furniture, carpets	22	4
Tissue products	44	7
International trading and other	309	52
Total	595	100
Total 1971	254	

Source: 1972 Annual Report. In previous reports inter-company sales were included, so that the originally published figure for 1971 was £271m.

The pattern of Bowaters' business, after nearly a hundred years, is displayed in the figures set out in Table 38. Two points immediately stand out. One is the abiding importance to Bowaters of pulp and paper. Forty years after Eric Bowater's first thoughts about diversification, eight years after the Ralli merger, in the shadow of the decline of the newsprint industry in the United Kingdom, pulp and paper still provide the Corporation and its subsidiaries with 26 per cent of the value of their sales and 64 per cent of their profits. The other point is the preponderance of North America in Bowaters' affairs. In 1979 21 per cent of the value of their sales arose in North America: 57 per cent of their trading profit.

In North America Bowaters have not only, among their paper machines, the largest and fastest newsprints machine in the world. They have also large areas of timberland in Newfoundland, Nova Scotia, Tennessee and South Carolina. In these last two areas, trees planted in the fifties will be ready for harvest during the mid-eighties, and after that the forest will continually supply natural resources constantly harvested and constantly renewed. There may also be an unexpected bonus, in Eastern Tennessee, from oil and gas below the surface. The pulp business at Catawba, in total contrast to its position in the early sixties when it was bound by the onerous clauses of the original contracts (p. 247 above), has become, in good years, handsomely profitable from sales on the open market. In the paper business itself, Bowaters are the largest newsprint makers in the United States: a remarkable distinction for a British firm and perhaps some slight corrective to the prevailing lack of national self-confidence.

Pulp and paper represent almost the whole of Bowaters' North American business: in 1979, 75 per cent of the value of sales and 97 per cent of the profits. International trading, on the other hand, is relatively small in the North American business: 18 per cent of the value of 1979 sales: practically no profit. In Bowaters' business as a whole, international trading looms very large indeed: 46 per cent of the 1979 sales, but only 4 per cent of the profits.

Other interests – packaging in the United Kingdom; building products in the United Kingdom, Europe and Australia; tissues in the United Kingdom, North America, Australasia – contributed between them 27 per cent of the value of Bowaters' sales and 32 per cent of their trading profits in 1979. All derive more or less directly from the forests and packaging and tissues are both branches of the paper industry, so to that extent they do not carry Bowaters so far along the path of diversification as the Ralli merger did. On the other hand, the markets they serve are so diverse in their nature and

TABLE 38. *The Bowater Corporation, sales and trading profit, 1979*

	Total		United Kingdom		North America		Australasia, Europe, Far East etc.	
	£m	%	£m	%	£m	%	£m	%
Sales								
Paper and pulp	454	26	164	20	276	75	14	3
Packaging	160	9	160	19				
Building products*	158	9	78	9	10	3	70	14
Tissue products	156	9	110	13	13	3	33	6
International trading, freight services etc.	795	46	326	39	67	18	402	77
Total	1,723	100	838	100	366	100	519	100
Trading profit								
Paper and pulp	72.4	64.1	7.7	23.9	62.8	96.8	1.9	12.0
Packaging	13.1	11.6	13.0	40.4			0.1	0.6
Building products*	7.0	6.2	2.1	6.5	0.7	1.1	4.2	26.6
Tissue products	16.8	14.9	12.3	38.2	1.0	1.5	3.5	22.2
International trading, freight sevices etc.	3.6	3.2	(2.9)	(9.0)	0.4	0.6	6.1	38.6
Total	112.9	100.0	32.2	100.0	64.9	100.0	15.8	100.0

* Includes additionally lumber, furniture and carpets

Sources: Annual report for 1979, p. 18.

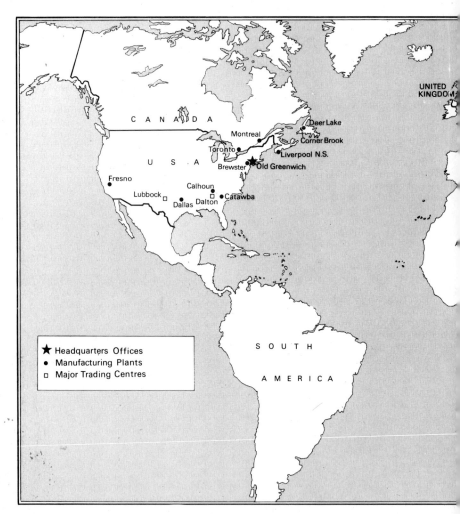

Principal Bowater activities world wide, 1980. For UK, see over.

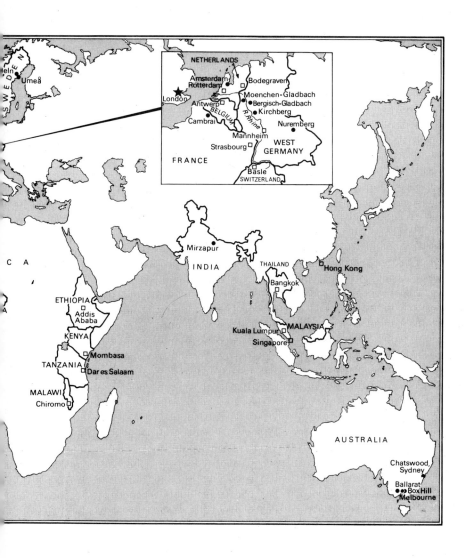

Principal Bowater activities in the United Kingdom, 1980.

so widespread about the world that all these products serve a purpose which, as we have seen, has for forty years been a consistent aim of Bowater policy: to offset some of the risks of dependence on the newsprint industry. The situation as it was in 1979–80 will be radically altered by the proposed sale, in 1981, of the commodity trading interests. Bowater after the sale will be a manufacturing group with substantial interests in service industries, chiefly freight and general trading.

Looking along the perspective of nearly sixty years, it is possible now to see that Bowaters' early success as manufacturers and their astonishingly rapid expansion in the British newsprint industry of the twenties and thirties, though based on an accurate – and bold – judgment of the market at the time, was on insecure foundations. Bowaters prospered for two reasons, both temporary. One reason was that the price of pulp in Canada and Scandinavia was falling faster than the price of newsprint in the United Kingdom. The other was that British newspaper owners, not yet weakened either by competition from television or by inordinate demands from their print-room staff, were able and willing to pay rather higher prices for British-made newsprint than for imports in order to keep the British newsprint industry healthy.

This was the situation which gave Eric Bowater the opportunity he was seeking to enlarge and transform his family's business. His father's death may have thrust him to the head of the business sooner than he would have otherwise have got there, and perhaps he got there a little too soon, though anything he may have lacked in the way of experience he soon made good and ability he never lacked. He probably had encouragement from Rothermere: perhaps also from Beaverbrook. He certainly had a connection with Armstrong, Whitworth. To say all this is only to say that no man is an island, and when it has been said Eric Bowater emerges as a businessman of exceptional force, daring and creativeness.

No doubt, in the late twenties, the newspaper magnates needed fresh newsprint capacity in the United Kingdom. No doubt, if Eric had not been available, they would have found someone else to create it for them. The Berry brothers even went some way to creating it for themselves after they took over Lloyds. All this is speculation. What is fact is that Eric Bowater was the man for the moment. Every great man needs luck and the way he uses it shows his qualities. Eric's luck lay in being in the newsprint business when conditions were right for expansion. The business he proceeded to construct in these conditions, between 1926 and 1939, was an extremely personal creation and an extremely large one. Without

Logging in Newfoundland, 1970s.

his achievement, it is almost certain that far more of the newsprint used in Britain in the thirties would have been imported from Canada.

Perhaps, in the light of conditions forty years later, that would have been as well, but that is not a valid criticism of Eric Bowater's business judgment, which in the circumstances was remarkably sound. What is even more remarkable is that at the height of his early success, with 60 per cent of the United Kingdom's production of newsprint under Bowaters' control, Eric was looking beyond it, and in two ways. First, he was uneasy about total commitment to newsprint in the United Kingdom, partly because he disliked dependence on a very narrow ring of powerful customers and partly because he distrusted the Scandinavian pulp cartels. Secondly, he was looking for even larger opportunities than he could find in the United Kingdom. Both these considerations pointed the same way – across the Atlantic – and we have seen (Chapter 8 above) how, partly by design and partly by accident, Bowaters established themselves in North America in 1938.

The decision to take over Corner Brook was probably the most fundamental business decision Eric Bowater ever made, for the original decision to build Bowater's Paper Mills was not his alone. It pointed Bowaters not only towards North America but towards the United States. By so doing it prepared the way for the even larger decision, fourteen years later, to build the Calhoun mill in Tennessee. Upon this decision, its risks and its opportunities, it is unnecessary here to enlarge (see Chapter 11). No one is likely to deny, first, that it was an extremely bold decision or, secondly, that it established the main foundation for Bowaters' confidence in the future. Without that decision to build in Tennessee in the fifties, by the eighties Bowaters' continued existence might have been seriously in doubt.

Eric Bowater is the hero of this book and it would be easy to write as if the foundation and progress of Bowaters, up to the time of his death, were a single-handed achievement. That, besides being ridiculous, would be scandalously unfair. He made no major move without advice and he was well advised. Moreover he was well served, particularly in technical and financial matters. The list of names is long and they will be found in their place in the body of the book. At the head of the list in the United Kingdom would stand Sir John Keeling, Arthur Baker, Earle Duffin, Herbert Inston and certain professional advisers; in North America, A. B. Meyer and George Currie. It is noticeable and probably not coincidental that, as some of his closest advisers disappeared, the quality of his decisions declined.

The weakest point in Bowaters' business is in the industry which gave it birth: the newsprint industry in the United Kingdom. 'Inevitable' is not a word which historians ought to use but it thrusts itself again and again into the mind in connection with the decline of the British newsprint industry. Certainly no one who has followed this narrative thus far can be in doubt of the reasons for it, or that it was long foreshadowed. It is equally evident, and again this narrative has set out the evidence, that in dealing with the difficulties which, late in life, beset him in the United Kingdom, Eric Bowater was less sure in his judgment than in seizing his earlier opportunities. As a consequence the difficulties which Bowaters would in any case have had to face after his death were increased rather than lessened. His successors, accordingly, faced a daunting task and some of the paths they took in search of a secure future would have surprised him. Nevertheless, if part of his legacy to the business which he created was difficulty, by far the greater part was opportunity, especially in North America. On the solid assets in North America all else has come to rest, and as it was to Eric Bowater that the present Bowater business owed its foundation, so it is to him that the business owes its best hope for future prosperity.

General statistics

1. *World demand and capacity for newsprint, 1930–76 (in thousand short tons)*

Year	Total demand	Total capacity	Amount of reserve capacity	Demand as per cent of capacity
1930	6,500	8,300	1,800	78
1931	6,300	8,700	2,400	72
1932	6,000	8,900	2,900	67
1933	6,100	9,000	2,900	68
1934	6,900	9,300	2,400	74
1935	7,100	9,300	2,200	76
1936	7,800	9,300	1,500	84
1937	8,500	9,500	1,000	89
1938	7,000	9,500	2,500	74
1939	7,500	9,700	2,200	77
1946	6,652	8,485	1,833	78
1947	7,366	8,649	1,283	85
1948	7,854	8,812	958	89
1949	8,589	9,145	556	94
1950	9,185	9,482	297	97
1951	9,660	9,749	89	99
1952	9,965	10,236	271	97
1953	10,230	10,591	361	97
1954*	10,827	11,143	316	97
1955	12,255	12,298	43	100
1956	13,156	12,959	−197	102
1957	13,371	14,144	773	95

Year	Total demand	Total capacity	Amount of reserve capacity	Demand as per cent of capacity
1958	13,125	15,329	2,204	86
1959	14,040	16,447	2,407	85
1960	14,901	16,866	1,965	88
1961	15,367	17,639	2,272	87
1962	15,707	18,100	2,393	87
1963	15,985	18,787	2,802	85
1964	17,355	19,447	2,092	89
1965	18,145	19,789	1,644	92
1966	19,371	20,821	1,450	93
1967	19,564	22,228	2,664	88
1968	20,586	23,443	2,857	88
1969	22,480	24,286	1,806	93
1970	22,976	25,164	2,188	91
1971	22,609	25,543	2,935	89
1972	23,535	25,922	2,381	91
1973	24,692	26,450	1,758	93
1974	25,025	26,009	984	96
1975	22,574	26,265	3,691	86
1976	23,844	26,852	3,008	89

* Figures for the years prior to 1955 exclude some Communist countries for which information is not available. There are no reliable figures for the war years 1940–5.

Source: Canadian Pulp and Paper Association, *Newsprint Data 1977* (Montreal, 1978).

2. *United States capacity, production and consumption: newsprint, 1913–79 (in thousand short tons)*

Year	Capacity	Production	Consumption
1913	–	1,305	1,473
1914	–	1,313	1,547
1915	–	1,239	1,509
1916	–	1,315	1,690
1917	–	1,359	1,779
1918	1,450	1,260	1,752
1919	1,388	1,375	1,892

Year	Capacity	Production	Consumption
1920	1,548	1,512	2,197
1921	1,668	1,225	2,043
1922	1,639	1,448	2,439
1923	1,578	1,485	2,777
1924	1,632	1,481	2,847
1925	1,721	1,530	3,014
1926	1,763	1,684	3,410
1927	1,788	1,485	3,427
1928	1,735	1,418	3,586
1929	1,741	1,392	3,758
1930	1,687	1,282	3,599
1931	1,768	1,157	3,242
1932	1,771	1,009	2,832
1933	1,735	946	2,693
1934	1,714	961	3,107
1935	1,504	912	3,345
1936	1,471	921	3,692
1937	1,464	946	3,825
1938	1,094	820	3,422
1939	972	939	3,520
1940	1,081	1,013	3,731
1941	1,085	1,015	3,930
1942	1,126	953	3,816
1943	1,033	805	3,627
1944	1,033	720	3,243
1945	981	724	3,481
1946	839	771	4,296
1947	845	826	4,753
1948	850	867	5,141
1949	876	899	5,529
1950	992	1,015	5,937
1951	1,050	1,125	5,975
1952	1,165	1,147	5,988
1953	1,170	1,084	6,143
1954	1,280	1,211	6,163
1955	1,409	1,552	6,638
1956	1,625	1,717	6,899

Year	Capacity	Production	Consumption
1957	1,921	1,826	6,865
1958	2,100	1,758	6,644
1959	2,390	1,964	7,151
1960	2,399	2,038	7,426
1961	2,376	2,094	7,380
1962	2,471	2,154	7,486
1963	2,461	2,218	7,547
1964	2,469	2,261	8,042
1965	2,372	2,245	8,550
1966	2,545	2,483	9,161
1967	2,844	2,709	9,222
1968	3,176	3,045	9,330
1969	3,374	3,362	9,884
1970	3,533	3,464	9,727
1971	3,642	3,476	9,829
1972	3,694	3,636	10,513
1973	3,819	3,678	10,755
1974 Eq.*	3,889	3,606	10,614
1974	3,715	3,553	10,261
1975	3,940	3,683	9,235
1976	4,005	3,728	9,591
1977	4,060	3,862	10,207
1978	4,081	3,760	10,850
1979	4,154	4,054	11,217

* Until 1974 standard newsprint was 52 g/m^2. In 1974 many mills changed to 48.8 g/m^2. A given area of 48.8 gram paper weighs less than the same area of 52 gram paper, so the tonnages quoted for 1974–9 understate the actual growth in newsprint usage. Figures for 1974 are given on a basis comparable to 1973 and are denoted by '1974 Eq.'.

Sources: Figures for the years 1913–74 inclusive are taken from the *Annual newsprint supplement 1975*, published by the Canadian Pulp and Paper Association, Montreal. Figures for the years 1975–9 inclusive are converted from those given in the 1979 edition. Domestic production is supplemented by imports, mostly from Canada (Table 3 below).

3. *Canadian capacity, production and shipments: newsprint, 1913–79 (in thousand short tons)*

Year	Capacity	Production	Shipments	
			USA	Total
1913	–	402	218	–
1914	–	470	275	–
1915	–	549	329	–
1916	–	662	438	–
1917	–	722	491	–
1918	837	770	602	–
1919	905	849	628	–
1920	1,016	938	679	949
1921	1,151	852	656	848
1922	1,277	1,143	896	1,161
1923	1,465	1,330	1,108	1,313
1924	1,638	1,418	1,201	1,416
1925	1,823	1,619	1,315	1,587
1926	2,121	2,068	1,751	2,080
1927	2,716	2,290	1,865	2,280
1928	3,262	2,612	2,041	2,604
1929	3,512	2,984	2,327	2,977
1930	3,902	2,791	2,145	2,749
1931	4,127	2,516	1,916	2,488
1932	4,142	2,186	1,647	2,179
1933	4,149	2,282	1,715	2,323
1934	4,182	2,911	2,114	2,913
1935	4,263	3,083	2,122	3,050
1936	4,218	3,535	2,551	3,592
1937	4,211	3,998	3,044	4,032
1938	4,535	2,893	1,940	2,780
1939	4,633	3,175	2,281	3,125
1940	4,716	3,770	2,741	3,804
1941	4,218	3,771	2,987	3,802
1942	4,211	3,455	3,007	3,489
1943	4,535	3,219	2,681	3,273
1944	4,633	3,625	2,530	3,271
1945	4,672	3,592	2,666	3,553

Year	Capacity	Production	Shipments USA	Total
1946	4,641	4,506	3,563	4,496
1947	4,729	4,820	3,897	4,873
1948	4,883	4,983	4,128	4,967
1949	5,113	5,176	4,380	5,164
1950	5,227	5,279	4,748	5,311
1951	5,360	5,516	4,784	5,504
1952	5,510	5,687	4,835	5,666
1953	5,723	5,721	4,861	5,733
1954	5,920	5,984	4,875	5,970
1955	6,064	6,191	5,070	6,236
1956	6,243	6,469	5,230	6,449
1957	6,756	6,397	5,055	6,364
1958	7,239	6,096	4,827	6,043
1959	7,521	6,394	5,118	6,425
1960	7,611	6,739	5,279	6,752
1961	7,734	6,735	5,226	6,707
1962	7,844	6,691	5,229	6,680
1963	8,055	6,630	5,180	6,622
1964	8,274	7,301	5,648	7,310
1965	8,421	7,720	6,093	7,747
1966	8,878	8,419	6,610	8,385
1967	9,294	8,051	6,263	7,968
1968	9,655	8,031	6,107	8,096
1969	9,675	8,818	6,431	8,797
1970	9,617	8,701	6,150	8,686
1971	9,995	8,437	6,134	8,345
1972	9,974	8,801	6,416	8,883
1973	10,009	9,121	6,841	9,180
1974 Eq.*	10,209	9,925	7,224	9,977
1974	9,789	9,528	6,934	9,577
1975	9,878	7,662	5,478	7,711
1976	9,900	8,897	6,238	8,693
1977	9,881	8,969	6,326	8,985
1978	9,841	9,692	7,087	9,804
1979	9,969	9,632	7,008	9,657

* See note to Table 2.

Sources: Figures for the years 1913–69 inclusive are taken from the *Annual newsprint supplement 1975* (Canadian Pulp and Paper Association, Montreal). Figures for the years 1970–9 inclusive are converted from those given in the 1979 edition. Note that the figures shown in column 1 for 1970 and subsequent years are based on revised methods for calculating capacity and are not comparable to those shown for prior years.

4. *United Kingdom capacity, production, imports and consumption: newsprint, 1930–79 (in thousand short tons)*

Year	Capacity	Production	Imports		Consumption
			Total	From Canada	
1930	–	608	392	256	911
1931	–	719	359	244	1,012
1932	–	790	350	214	1,046
1933	–	830	386	260	1,127
1934	–	940	417	286	1,290
1935	–	970	410	292	1,301
1936	–	1,004	460	337	1,378
1937	–	1,033	527	389	1,496
1938	–	954	500	364	1,391
1939	1,100	848	474	350	1,280
1940	–	333	267	248	592
1941	–	168	137	136	304
1942	–	156	75	75	231
1943	–	145	107	107	251
1944	–	169	151	151	320
1945	–	181	208	208	386
1946	–	330	117	111	430
1947	896	282	137	116	416
1948	896	336	141	111	455
1949	896	529	203	151	665
1950	896	609	155	20	650
1951	672	590	192	77	676
1952	672	601	293	128	812
1953	705	675	262	170	798
1954	730	686	367	249	910
1955	730	694	449	285	988
1956	730	720	538	350	1,106
1957	730	732	554	388	1,150
1958	780	703	584	387	1,170
1959	860	753	570	399	1,232

			Imports		
Year	Capacity	Production	Total	From Canada	Consumption
1960	990	831	689	460	1,464
1961	1,010	799	686	443	1,455
1962	1,027	734	727	495	1,434
1963	1,010	753	720	458	1,447
1964	858	840	754	477	1,575
1965	890	860	658	382	1,515
1966	890	825	708	379	1,530
1967	944	788	673	355	1,459
1968	944	811	755	414	1,566
1969	955	876	844	501	1,719
1970	980	834	855	443	1,688
1971	700	634	890	387	1,526
1972	520	515	1,242	580	1,760
1973	495	484	1,282	517	1,768
1974	460	420	1,404	493	1,822
1975	430	348	1,179	383	1,521
1976	397	359	1,250	480	1,598
1977	397	330	1,060	519	1,377
1978	397	351	1,124	499	1,452
1979	397	400	1,187	457	1,555

Sources: The figures for production, imports and consumption for the years 1930–67 inclusive are taken from the *Annual newsprint supplement 1968*, published by the Newsprint Association of Canada. Figures for the years 1968–79 inclusive are taken from the 1979 edition, published by the Canadian Pulp and Paper Association. The figures for capacity are taken from the respective annual editions of *Newsprint data*, published until 1970 by the NAC and subsequently by the CPPA.

5. *United States capacity, production and consumption: wood pulp, all grades, 1869–1972 (in thousand short tons, air dry weight)*

Year	Capacity	Production	Consumption paper and board
1869	–	1	–
1879	–	23	–
1889	–	306	–
1899	–	1,180	1,173

Year	Capacity	Production	Consumption paper and board
1904	—	1,922	2,019
1907	—	2,547	2,832
1908	—	2,119	2,358
1909	—	2,496	2,827
1910	—	2,534	—
1911	—	2,686	—
1914	—	2,893	3,490
1916	—	3,435	—
1917	—	3,509	—
1918	—	3,313	—
1919	—	3,518	4,020
1920	—	3,821	—
1921	—	2,875	—
1922	—	3,522	—
1923	—	3,789	—
1924	—	3,723	—
1925	—	3,962	—
1926	—	4,395	—
1927	—	4,313	—
1928	—	4,510	—
1929	—	4,863	6,289
1930	—	4,630	—
1931	—	4,409	—
1932	—	3,760	—
1933	—	4,276	—
1934	—	4,436	—
1935	—	4,926	6,442
1936	—	5,695	—
1937	—	6,573	—
1938	—	5,934	—
1939	—	6,993	8,650
1940	—	8,960	9,782
1941	—	10,375	11,364
1942	—	10,783	11,038
1943	—	9,680	10,635
1944	—	10,108	10,502

Year	Capacity	Production	Consumption paper and board
1945	–	10,167	10,825
1946	12,130	10,607	12,092
1947	12,789	10,946	13,253
1948	14,106	12,872	14,375
1949	15,018	12,207	13,636
1950	16,167	14,849	16,509
1951	17,668	16,524	17,737
1952	18,771	16,473	17,286
1953	19,497	17,537	18,684
1954	21,039	18,302	18,989
1955	22,407	20,740	21,454
1956	24,198	22,131	22,998
1957	26,152	21,800	22,459
1958	27,717	21,796	22,483
1959	28,374	24,383	25,155
1960	29,536	25,316	25,700
1961	30,711	26,523	26,683
1962	31,958	27,908	28,598
1963	32,826	29,439	30,220
1964	33,822	31,911	32,088
1965	35,758	33,296	34,006
1966	38,602	35,636	36,922
1967	41,062	36,355	36,994
1968	43,120	39,196	41,303
1969	44,834	40,990	43,670
1970	45,863	42,216	43,192
1971	47,107	43,744	44,183
1972	48,970	46,604	46,949

Source: American Paper Institute Inc., *Wood pulp statistics* (New York, 1973).

6. *Canada capacity, production, consumption and exports: wood pulp,
all grades, 1908–72 (in thousand short tons, air dry weight)*

Year	Capacity	Production	Consumption in paper and board	Exports
1908	–	363	–	240
1920	–	1,960	–	820
1921	–	1,549	–	527
1922	–	2,150	–	818
1923	–	2,476	–	875
1924	–	2,465	–	782
1925	–	2,773	–	961
1926	–	3,230	–	1,006
1927	–	3,279	–	879
1928	–	3,608	–	864
1929	–	4,021	–	831
1930	–	3,619	–	760
1931	–	3,168	–	623
1932	–	2,663	–	452
1933	–	2,980	–	609
1934	–	3,636	–	606
1935	–	3,868	–	662
1936	–	4,485	–	754
1937	–	5,142	4,253	871
1938	–	3,668	–	554
1939	–	4,166	3,461	706
1940	–	5,291	–	1,069
1941	–	5,721	–	1,412
1942	–	5,607	–	1,511
1943	–	5,273	–	1,556
1944	–	5,271	–	1,408
1945	–	5,601	–	1,435
1946	–	6,615	–	1,419
1947	–	7,254	–	1,699
1948	–	7,675	–	1,798
1949	–	7,853	–	1,557
1950	–	8,473	6,592	1,846
1951	–	9,315	–	2,243

Year	Capacity	Production	Consumption in paper and board	Exports
1952	–	8,968	–	1,941
1953	–	9,077	–	1,950
1954	–	9,673	–	2,180
1955	–	10,151	7,800	2,366
1956	–	10,734	8,339	2,374
1957	–	10,425	8,143	2,283
1958	–	10,137	7,882	2,219
1959	–	10,832	8,367	2,450
1960	13,183	11,461	8,833	2,601
1961	13,602	11,779	8,874	2,869
1962	14,147	12,133	9,004	3,044
1963	14,663	12,474	9,120	3,339
1964	15,446	13,742	10,045	3,636
1965	16,216	14,573	10,679	3,853
1966	17,487	15,958	11,699	4,096
1967	18,981	15,857	11,413	4,269
1968	20,078	16,762	11,635	4,971
1969	21,409	18,590	12,814	5,795
1970	21,679	18,308	12,771	5,581
1971	22,844	18,234	12,475	5,671
1972	22,620	19,091	–	6,102

Source: American Paper Institute Inc., *Wood pulp statistics* (New York, 1973).

7. *United Kingdom production and imports: wood pulp, all grades, 1925–72 (in thousand short tons, air dry weight)*

Year	Production	Imports
1925	98	1,664
1927	129	1,676
1928	117	978
1929	129	1,279
1930	113	1,192
1931	108	1,113
1932	102	1,363

Year	Production	Imports
1933	111	1,403
1934	121	1,621
1935	125	1,612
1936	129	1,761
1937	157	2,090
1938	218	1,901
1939	158	1,858
1940	84	769
1941	56	422
1942	45	548
1943	37	466
1944	28	448
1945	22	821
1946	19	984
1947	35	965
1948	63	1,300
1949	86	1,478
1950	137	1,603
1951	159	1,872
1952	154	1,611
1953	142	1,797
1954	159	2,148
1955	149	2,512
1956	160	2,464
1957	178	2,395
1958	178	2,357
1959	206	2,495
1960	206	3,037
1961	258	2,890
1962	224	2,724
1963	280	2,953
1964	358	3,326
1965	358	3,278
1966	317	3,257
1967	342	3,029
1968	414	3,309
1969	466	3,283

Year	Production	Imports
1970	477	3,428
1971	416	2,616
1972	393	2,855

Source: American Paper Institute Inc., *Wood pulp statistics* (New York, 1973). Figures for production are unofficial estimates of total domestic production, supplied by the British Paper and Board Makers' Association. 'Imports' include imports of dissolving grades for industrial purposes. Exports have been negligible and there is no domestic production of dissolving grades.

8. *United Kingdom comparative prices of pulp and newsprint, 1901–69*

Year	Price of mechanical pulp per air dry ton (£)	Price of chemical pulp per dry unbleached ton (£)	Approx. cost of fibre at 80% mech., 20% chem. (£)	Price of newsprint (£)
1901	5.76	8.70	6.35	
1902	4.86	8.17	5.52	
1903	4.52	7.77	5.17	
1904	4.46	7.75	5.12	
1905	4.44	8.53	5.26	
1906	4.44	8.42	5.24	
1907	4.62	8.19	5.34	
1908	5.08	8.26	5.71	
1909	4.98	7.49	5.48	
1910	4.62	8.44	5.39	
1911	4.52	7.67	5.15	
1912	4.60	7.78	5.23	
1913	4.50	8.09	5.22	
1914	5.30	8.23	5.89	
1915	5.56	9.42	6.33	
1916				25.67
1917				33.83
1918				43.75
1919	16.55	25.11	18.24	36.17
1920	33.80	37.78	34.60	50.95
1921	13.80	37.35	18.51	30.52
1922	9.00	13.00	9.80	19.25
1923	10.75	15.00	11.60	18.50
1924	8.50	12.50	9.30	18.00
1925	7.78	12.62	8.74	17.50
1926	8.12	13.38	9.18	16.25

Year	Price of mechanical pulp per air dry ton (£)	Price of chemical pulp per dry unbleached ton (£)	Approx. cost of fibre at 80% mech., 20% chem. (£)	Price of newsprint (£)
1927	6.50	12.00	7.60	15.50
1928	6.10	11.37	7.15	14.25
1929	6.50	11.88	7.58	13.25
1930	6.50	11.25	7.45	14.00
1931	5.47	8.77	6.13	13.25
1932	4.48	8.50	5.28	12.00
1933	4.60	7.50	5.18	11.75
1934	4.67	8.10	5.36	9.75
1935	4.00	7.10	4.62	10.00
1936	4.62	8.50	5.40	10.00
1937	7.21	14.63	8.70	10.00
1938	5.50	8.19	6.04	11.50?
1939	5.97	10.12	6.80	13.04
1940	12.74	20.75	14.34	22.46
1941	16.65	28.32	18.98	30.29
1942	16.65	28.32	18.98	34.00
1943	16.65	28.32	18.98	34.12
1944	16.65	28.32	18.98	34.12
1945	16.65	28.32	18.98	34.12
1946	17.50	28.32	19.66	31.60
1947	20.25	33.83	22.97	35.81
1948	27.50	47.50	31.50	46.17
1949	23.23	36.21	25.82	37.78
1950	19.62	35.50	22.80	34.47
1951	38.80	70.98	45.24	57.75
1952	41.98	63.92	46.36	61.78
1953	27.50	41.50	30.30	51.25
1954	27.50	46.25	31.25	51.50
1955	29.13	49.50	33.20	53.75
1956	33.12	51.75	36.85	58.50
1957	32.50	50.50	36.10	59.75
1958	29.62	47.25	33.15	60.00
1959	28.50	45.00	31.80	58.50
1960	28.50	45.50	31.90	58.50
1961	28.50	48.50	32.50	58.50
1962	28.50	44.37	31.67	58.50
1963	28.30	44.50	31.54	56.75
1964	28.50	48.00	32.40	56.75
1965	30.50	49.88	34.38	56.75
1966	30.00	48.00	33.60	56.75
1967	31.50	49.12	35.02	58.75
1968	36.00	52.50	39.30	65.75
1969	36.00	55.25	39.85	65.75

Sources: Pulp – 1901–15 from *Papermakers' Journal*, 15 February 1916; 1919–
38 from letter, E. A. Holmes of Price & Pierce Ltd to J. A. Colvin,
Bowater, 21 July 1961 (except chemical pulp prices 1919–21, which are
calculated from Price & Pierce table of import statistics for those years);
1939–61 from Bowater records (1940–9 Paper Control re-issue prices,
annual averages; 1950–2 industry weighted averages; 1953–61 average
market prices); 1960–9 J & JW tables, yearly averages.

Newsprint – 1916–21 approximate average prices from Bowater records; 1922–38 from letter, Holmes to Colvin, 21 July 1961; 1939–69
annual average prices from Bowater records.

Bowater statistics

1. *Consolidated profits, 1926–79*

Financial Year	Consolidated trading surplus (£000s)	Depreciation (£000s)	Consolidated profits after depreciation (£000s)	Interest on loan capital (£000s)	Consolidated profit before taxation (£000s)
To December 1926 (16 months)	44	3	–	–	41
December 1927	129	19	110	19	91
September 1928 (9 months)	133	16	117	14	103
September 1929	165	26	139	47	92
1930	215	40	175	90	85
1931	235	41	194	91	103
1932	353	67	286	87	199
1933	304	68	236	83	153
1934	253	74	179	75	104
1935	364	85	279	72	207
1936	485	132	353	81	272
1937	853	264	589	73	516
1938	835	298	537	108	429
1939	1,292	475	817	376	441
1940	2,115	519	1,596	397	1,199
1941	1,975	611	1,364	396	968
1942	1,526	577	949	389	560
1943	1,528	578	950	362	588
1944	1,723	590	1,133	348	785
1945	1,774	593	1,181	341	840
1946	2,139	643	1,496	350	1,146
1947	2,732	648	2,084	339	1,745
1948	3,734	1,004	2,730	335	2,395
1949	3,693	921	2,772	329	2,443
1950	5,395	1,445	3,950	371	3,579
1951	10,276	1,451	8,825	363	8,462
1952	6,708	1,477	5,231	358	4,873
1953	8,184	1,631	6,553	629	5,924
December 1954 (15 months)	13,095	2,658	10,437	1,301	9,136

Financial Year	Consolidated trading surplus (£000s)	Depreciation (£000s)	Consolidated profits after depreciation (£000s)	Interest on loan capital (£000s)	Consolidated profit before taxation (£000s)
December 1955	13,210	3,342	9,868	1,412	8,456
1956	16,129	3,946	12,183	1,812	10,371
1957	17,152	4,741	12,411	2,427	9,984
1958	18,145	5,247	12,898	2,968	9,930
1959	20,070	6,260	13,810	3,257	10,553
1960	23,494	7,828	15,666	3,323	12,343
1961	21,867	8,595	13,272	3,265	10,007
1962	22,047	9,223	12,824	3,515	9,309
1963	25,400	10,400	15,000	3,800	11,200
1964	29,100	10,900	18,300	3,700	14,600
1965	31,100	11,000	20,100	3,700	16,400
1966	32,900	11,800	21,000	3,700	17,400
1967	34,300	13,500	20,800	4,300	16,500
1968	34,900	13,000	21,900	4,600	17,300
1969	41,600	16,300	25,200	6,000	19,200
1970	39,500	17,400	22,100	5,900	16,200
1971	29,800	15,100	14,700	5,200	9,500
1972	51,600	18,100	33,500	7,000	26,500
1973	77,200	20,200	57,000	9,300	47,700
1974	94,600	21,900	72,700	13,200	59,500
1975	94,900	24,300	70,600	17,700	52,900
1976	130,000	30,800	99,200	20,900	78,300
1977	139,900	32,100	107,800	20,800	87,000
1978	141,700	30,900	110,800	20,800	90,000
1979	142,000	33,700	108,300	17,000	91,300

Notes: Because of changes in presentation, figures are not always strictly comparable year on year. Figures for the years 1970–9 include attributable profits of associated companies.

Sources: Figures for the years 1926–45 inclusive have been consolidated by Robert Knight. Figures for subsequent years are taken from published accounts.

2. *Sales, profits and capital employed, 1946–79*

Year	Sales (£m)	Profits after depreciation but before tax and interest (£m)	Capital employed (£m)	Return on capital employed (% profits to capital)
To 30 September				
1946	n.a.	1.5	21.2	7.1
1947	n.a.	2.1	23.4	9.0
1948	n.a.	2.7	24.8	10.9
1949	29.4	2.7	26.6	10.1
1950	35.3	3.9	30.7	12.7

Year	Sales (£m)	Profits after depreciation but before tax and interest (£m)	Capital employed (£m)	Return on capital employed (% profits to capital)
1951	54.1	8.8	35.3	24.9
1952	64.2	5.2	37.3	13.9
1953	57.3	6.5	52.4	12.4
To 31 December				
1954 (fifteen months)	84.4	10.4	65.6	15.8
1955	82.8	9.9	93.7	10.6
1956	95.3	12.2	125.8	9.7
1957	102.5	12.4	143.7	8.6
1958	107.2	13.0	158.6	8.2
1959	117.0	13.8	167.8	8.2
1960	142.1	15.7	187.8	8.4
1961	148.4	13.3	186.2	7.1
1962	150.8	12.8	195.0	6.6
1963	138.8	15.0	197.7	7.6
1964	152.5	18.3	196.6	9.3
1965	166.0	20.1	200.6	10.0
1966	189.0	21.0	203.9	10.3
1967	200.0	20.8	234.2	8.9
1968	214.0	21.9	254.9	8.6
1969	268.0	25.2	278.5	9.0
1970	294.0	22.1	269.4	8.2
1971	254.0	14.7	246.4	6.0
1972	595.0	33.5	339.8	9.9
1973	999.0	57.0	385.8	14.8
1974	1,194.0	72.7	434.6	16.7
1975	1,107.0	70.6	519.7	13.6
1976	1,548.0	99.2	600.6	16.5
1977	1,723.0	107.8	628.4	17.2
1978	1,564.0	110.8	612.6	18.1
1979	1,723.0	108.3	590.0	18.4

n.a. = not available

Notes: Because of changes in presentation, figures are not always strictly comparable year on year. In 1963 the presentation of sales figures was changed. In 1970 the attributable profits of associated companies were brought into consolidation.

Source: Published accounts. Profits/capital employed percentages calculated by the author.

3. *Production of newsprint, 1927–76 (in thousand short tons)*

Year	(1) UK	(2) North America	(3) Total[a]
1927[b]	56		56
1928	56		56
1929	134		134
1930	196		196
1931	202		202
1932	268		268
1933	268		268
1934	268		268
1935	268		268
1936	576		576
1937	599		599
1938	545	113	658
1939	465	152	617
1940[c]		203	
1941		197	
1942		175	
1943		138	
1944		161	
1945[d]		153	
1946[e]		196	
1947		193	
1948	178	202	380
1949	311	248	559
1950	392	278	670
1951	384	296	680
1952	386	300	686
1953	396	295	691
1954[f]	530	432	962
1955	435	462	897
1956	461	592	1,053
1957	492	721	1,213
1958	435	689	1,124
1959	484	759	1,243

Year	(1) UK	(2) North America	(3) Total[a]
1960	524	847	1,371
1961	499	864	1,363
1962	448	844	1,292
1963	451	837	1,288
1964	496	914	1,410
1965	534	936	1,470
1966	523	1,024	1,547
1967	512	990	1,502
1968	503	958	1,461
1969	550	1,137	1,687
1970	525	1,222	1,747
1971	374	1,109	1,483
1972	281	1,149	1,430
1973	267	1,270	1,537
1974	249	1,233	1,482
1975	218	1,036	1,254
1976	206	1,157	1,363

Notes: [a] Totals shown do not include figures for Papeteries de la Chapelle, acquired in 1960, or Papeteries Darblay, merged with La Chapelle in 1968. The approximate annual output of the Chapelle mill was 120,000 tons, and of the combined Chapelle-Darblay group, 250,000 tons. Chapelle-Darblay was sold on 1 January 1971. Figures for Tasman (New Zealand) and Mondi (South Africa), in which Bowater owned minority holdings, are also excluded.

[b] The figures in column 1 for the years 1927–36 inclusive are approximate.

[c] During the years 1940–56 the British Government restricted domestic newsprint production to a given percentage of normal pre-war output, i.e. output recorded for the twelve months ended 31 August 1939. Bowater's 'reference period tonnage', thus defined, was 522,640 tons; the Government limit was set in February 1940 at 60 per cent of this rate, and was revised as follows:

April 1940	30 per cent
June 1940	20
April 1941	$17\frac{1}{2}$
December 1942	15
November 1943	$18\frac{1}{2}$
November 1945	$33\frac{1}{2}$
January 1946	35
July 1947	$33\frac{1}{2}$

January 1948   20
March 1948   24

Thereafter the maximum permitted volume was greatly increased until the final abolition of Government controls. No figures are available for the actual output achieved during 1940–7.

[d] 1945: nine months ended 30 September
[e] 1946–53: twelve months ended 30 September
[f] 1954: fifteen months ended 31 December

Source: Bowater internal statistics.

4. *Total production of paper and packaging, 1949–69 (in thousand short tons)*

Year	Paper	Packaging etc.
1949[a]	678	40
1950	843	49
1951	836	59
1952	837	66
1953	851	74
1954[b]	1,205	132
1955	1,113	125
1956	1,281	85
1957	1,422	120
1958	1,347	220
1959	1,455	236
1960	1,706	286
1961	1,820	304
1962	1,817	331
1963	1,848	366
1964	2,022	383
1965	2,103	389
1966	2,184	508
1967	2,143	536
1968	2,017	579
1969	2,707	639

Notes: [a] 1950–3: twelve months to 30 September
[b] 1954: fifteen months to 31 December

Source: Annual reports.

5. *Number of employees (selected years)*

Year	Total	UK	Overseas
1953	15,578	8,361	7,217
1960	23,000	–	–
1964	29,000	–	–
1967	30,000	17,348	12,652
1971	25,000	17,071	7,929
1976	36,000	19,945	16,055
1979	37,600	23,178	14,422

1936 Estimated: Bowater 1,400
Lloyd 3,000
Total 4,400

Sources: Annual Reports; Bowater internal statistics

Directors, Secretaries and Comptrollers of the parent Bowater company 1910–80

DIRECTORS

Alexander, B. G.	1970–7	
Baker, Arthur	1932–59	Joint Managing Director 1932–47
Balloch, A. E.	1967–80	
Bell, Stanley	1947–61 (d)	
Bowater, Sir Eric	1918–62 (d)	Joint Managing Director 1926–7, Chairman and Joint Managing Director 1927–47, Chairman and Chief Executive 1947–62
Bowater, Frank	1910–27	Joint Managing Director 1910–24, Managing Director 1924–6, Joint Managing Director 1926–7
Bowater, Sir Frederick	1910–24 (d)	Joint Managing Director
Bowater, Sir Ian	1947–53	
Bowater, Sir Noël	1918–64	Joint Managing Director 1926–32, Vice-Chairman 1952–64
Bowater, Rainald	1918–26	
Bowater, Sir Thomas	1910–27	Chairman
Carrick, 9th Earl of	1972–	
Chancellor, Sir Christopher	1961–9	Chairman 1962–9
Clark, R. A.	1970–3	
Denson, P. G.	1936–40	Vice-Chairman 1936–40
Duffin, E. C.	1931–49 (d)	
Erroll of Hale, 1st Baron	1973–	Chairman
Fifoot, E. L.	1936–52 (d)	
Fitt, P. R. J.	1932–3, 1947–56	
Gammie, A. P.	1971–	
Greenborough, Sir John	1979–	
Hicks, C. T.	1964–5 (d)	
Horsman, Malcolm	1972–7	Deputy Chairman and Joint Managing Director 1973–6
Howard, J. W.	1931–2	
Inston, H. J.	1929–56 (d)	
Jones, J. H. Mowbray	1963–70	
Joyce, H. K.	1972–	

Keeling, Sir John	1939–67	Vice-Chairman 1948–67
Keeling, J. A. B.	1968–	
Kirwan-Taylor, W. J.	1961–4	
Knight, Robert	1964–79	Vice-Chairman 1969–76
Lee, Sir Frank	1963–70	
Lenton, A. I.	1979–	Managing Director 1981–
Lewin, H. M. S.	1955–62	
Linforth, A. E.	1927–36	
Linforth, K. N.	1947–71	Vice-Chairman 1962–71
Lissenden, A.	1967–78	
Maddrell, G. K.	1978–	
Mann, Sam	1968–73	
Meyer, A. B.	1955–64 (d)	
Mitchell, Sir Derek	1979–	
Morley, Sir Godfrey	1968–79	
Popham, C. F.	1963–81	Vice-Chairman 1971–9, Joint Joint Managing Director 1973–6, Managing Director 1976–81, Deputy Chairman 1979–81
Ritchie, J. Martin	1959–73	Joint Managing Director 1962–3, Managing Director 1963–9, Deputy Chairman 1967–9, Chairman and Chief Executive 1969–73
Rutherford, H.	1933–47	
Rye, C. G.	1956–63	Joint Managing Director 1962–3
Shaw, G. W.	1952–64	
Shortis, F. R. A.	1926–32	
Slater, D. J. H.	1972–	
Sutton, V. J.	1964–73	
Tegner, I. N.	1971–	
Tutt, L. E.	1978–	
Young, B. W.	1932–3	
Whitehurst, Neville	1963–70	

SECRETARIES

1910–26	Rainald Bowater
1926–7	G. S. Myles
1928–32	H. J. Inston
1932–5	H. Rutherford
1935–44	H. J. Inston
1944–54	C. G. Rye
1954–60	Robert Knight
1960–77	W. E. J. Miles
1977–	D. A. Rees

COMPTROLLERS*

1944–52	H. J. Inston
1952–7	C. G. Rye

1957–64   Robert Knight
1964–7   Sam Mann

* Post created 1944, abolished 1967.
(d) indicates death in service.

Notes: The parent company was W. V. Bowater & Sons from 1910 to 1932
(becoming a public company in 1926); Bowater's Paper Mills from 1932 to
1947; the Bowater Paper Corporation from 1947 to 1972; and the
Bowater Corporation from 1972.

Glossary

This glossary has been compiled by Robert Knight with technical assistance from K. C. Saunders.

PULP, PAPER AND PACKAGING

Air dry is a term applied to wood pulp and is equivalent to 90 per cent bone dry.

Bleached mechanical pulp is now produced for use in intermediate printing grades, including some coated papers. *See also* Groundwood pulp.

Calender is a part of the papermaking machine and comprises a set(s) of chilled iron rolls stacked vertically which smooth out irregularities on the surface of the paper and impart a slight gloss to it. *See also* Supercalender.

Cellulose is the main constituent of wood and other fibres suitable for papermaking.

Chemical pulp is pulp produced by cooking pulpwood chips or other fibrous raw materials with certain types of chemicals which dissolve the lignin but do not dissolve the cellulose.

China clay is used in paper manufacture as a 'loading', i.e. as a 'filler' between the fibres to provide a better and smoother surface for printing as well as improved opacity. China clay can also be used as a pigment in the surface coating of paper and board.

Chipboard is made from waste paper and commonly used as an inner liner for corrugated containers and fittings.

Coated paper in the printing sense is paper which has been coated with china clay and starch or other admixtures, in order to provide a superior printing surface. The coating process can either be 'on the (paper) machine' or a totally separate operation 'off the machine'.

Corrugated containers are generally made from two outer liners of kraft liner or similar board, with a middle layer of fluted paper (fluting medium). This type of packaging is widely used for safe transit between the supplier and the wholesaler/retailer and also for display, and is very often printed with promotional material in colour.

Esparto is a cellulose fibre which comes from esparto grass, grown mainly in North Africa. The grass was baled and shipped in large quantities at one time, and processed and used in British paper mills to make a wide range of fine papers. The fibres are short and the yield is only about 40 per cent of the original weight. In more recent times esparto has tended to be converted into pulp in the countries where the grass grows, and shipped as bleached esparto pulp.

Fibre drums are drums made from kraft liner and other papers with or without steel reinforcement.

Flash dried pulp: moist pulp 'crumbs' are sprayed into a stream of hot air, the dried fibres are then collected and compressed into blocks (i.e. baled) form. This drying process is a modern alternative to the drying of pulp in thick sheet form.

Fluting, also called corrugating medium, is paper made from semi-chemical or waste paper and used for the middle layer of corrugated containers.

Fourdrinier is the name applied to the most common type of papermaking machine. It was invented by Nicolas Louis Robert in France about 1798, and developed by the brothers Henry and Sealy Fourdrinier in Britain with the help of one Bryan Donkin, a well-known engineer and inventor. The machine was erected around 1804 and was the first to make paper on a continuous web. Prior to that paper was hand made in sheets and now, 175 years later, the basic principles of the original Fourdrinier machine are still applicable. The word 'fourdrinier' is also applied to that part of the paper machine where the wet sheet is formed on the machine wire, and it is sometimes also called the 'wet end'.

Fully bleached chemical pulp is used for higher grade printing and other papers where whiteness is important. GE (*see under* Pulp brightness) around 85–92 per cent.

Groundwood (or mechanical) pulp is pulp produced by a 'mechanical' process (as distinct from a 'chemical'). The pulp is made by pressing the pulpwood logs against a grindstone, in the presence of water, in a machine called a 'grinder'. Since the lignin is not removed as in a chemical process, mechanical pulp is typically a pale yellowish-brown in colour and is relatively weak.

Kamyr press is a proprietary machine similar to parts of a paper machine, and makes wood pulp into thick sheets for baling and shipment.

Kamyr process is one of many proprietary methods for producing chemical pulp.

Kraft liner is a very strong kraft paper used mainly as the outer liner for corrugated containers where printability and abrasive resistance are also important requirements.

Kraft paper. See Kraft liner and Sack kraft.

Lignin is a chemical component of wood or plant fibre. Lignin is almost completely removed in a chemical pulping operation but not in a mechanical pulping process.

Magazine paper is a type of uncoated printing paper – superior to news-print – used mainly for the popular magazines.

Moist (or wet) pulp: traditionally pulp was made and shipped in sheets of moist pulp approximately 50 per cent air dry, and until the beginning of the Second World War the selling price was invariably quoted 'per wet ton'.

The freight cost handicap with wet pulp was offset by the avoidance of drying costs at the pulp mill and re-processing advantages during the later papermaking operation. Changing circumstances have since favoured the production and shipment of 'dry' pulp (90 per cent air dry).

Multiwall sacks are sacks made from a layer or a number of layers of sack kraft paper or plastic or other material, for bulk packaging.

Newsprint is the paper on which newspapers are printed. It is normally manufactured from virgin fibre in a mixture of about 70/80 per cent mechanical wood pulp and 20–30 per cent chemical wood pulp but it is also nowadays made from secondary fibre, e.g. de-inked waste paper.

Pulp brightness is measured by photometers against a standard of pure white in theory 100. A common scale is General Electric (GE).

Pulping is the name of the process which separates the wood fibres in such a way as to enable a sheet of paper to be formed.

Pulpwood is wood suitable for pulping. Of the amount used in the paper and board industry about 75 per cent is coniferous, i.e. pine, spruce and fir, and the remainder various types of hardwood.

Pures. See Woodfree paper.

Refiner groundwood is a modern variant of mechanical pulp and is made from wood chips passed through a refiner. The refiner typically consists of two grooved discs which are contra-rotating at high speed.

Sack kraft is paper made from kraft sulphate pulp and used for multiwall sacks, bags, etc.

Semi-bleached (sulphate) pulp is normally used in newsprint and similar papers. GE (*see* Pulp brightness) 60–70 per cent.

Slush pulp is pulp fibre suspended in water, i.e. up to about 5 per cent pulp, and is the term normally applied to pulp used directly for the manufac-ture of paper as distinct from pulp first converted into baled form for shipment, i.e. *baled pulp*.

Strawpaper is named after the straw pulp from which it was partly made. Typically used to make corrugated strawpaper for packaging, and as a corrugating medium for corrugated board and containers. Strawpaper has now largely been superseded by semi-chemical fluting medium and waste paper based substitutes.

Sulphate (or Kraft) pulp is prepared with an 'alkaline' cooking solution (effectively sodium sulphate) which provides a very strong pulp brown in colour in the unbleached form.

Sulphite pulp is prepared with an 'acidic' cooking solution (usually based on calcium, sodium or magnesium bi-sulphite) which provides a strong but essentially 'white' pulp even before bleaching.

Supercalender is a calendering machine separate from the paper machine and is used to impart a high gloss finish as well as to give a greater degree of smoothness to the finished sheet. The vertical stack in this case consists of both iron rolls and 'soft rolls', the latter so-called 'bowls' usually having a paper or cotton surface composition. *See also* Calender.

Tailings are course fibres rejected by screening.

Test liner is a quality of paper or board made from waste paper but with a top layer of kraft used in corrugated cases as a substitute for pure kraft liner.

Thermo mechanical pulp ('*TMP*') is pulp made by a process which is a later development of the refiner method. In TMP the wood chips are steamed under pressure before being refined.

Unbleached chemical pulp is used for paper or board where strength is the main requirement and colour or brightness are not of importance.

Woodfree paper is made using chemical pulp. The absence of 'groundwood' pulp led to the abbreviated term 'woodfree', but an alternative designation for this grade of paper is 'Pures'.

FINANCIAL AND GENERAL TERMS

Accelerated depreciation. Depreciation at a higher than the normal rate for the type of asset – sometimes provided in order to gain additional reliefs for tax purposes, e.g. in the case of the original plant at Bowater Southern through the Certificate of Necessity.

Affiliate. A company closely associated with another. A United States term for a British 'associated company'.

Amortization. (a) Gradual provision over a period for retirement of a debt by sinking fund or by payment to the lender.

(b) Reduction in book value of a fixed asset, e.g. a long lease.

CIC. Capital Issues Committee, the UK body through which all issues of capital in the war and post-war period had to be authorised.

Certificate of Necessity. An authorisation by a US Government agency (Section 168 of the Inland Revenue Code) permitting accelerated depreciation over a sixty-month period, of plant and facilities deemed to be essential in a period of emergency.

cif. 'Cost Insurance and Freight' means that the selling price includes these items of cost up to the foreign port. Title normally passes to the buyer when the goods are delivered to the ship.

Consolidated accounts (sometimes also referred to as 'group accounts') are accounts which show the whole of a group of companies as if it were a single unit. Consolidation is the method by which the assets and liabilities and the statement of profit and loss of the holding company is combined with the related items of the companies it owns or controls.

GLOSSARY

Credit agreement. An agreement between a bank and a borrower covering a firm loan and setting out the limitations and restrictions, and the rate of interest and of repayments, e.g. Southern, Carolina.

Debenture. A written acknowledgment of a debt, normally in the form of a deed promising to repay money lent, together with interest thereon and subject to certain special conditions. Sometimes the debenture gives the lender as security a charge or mortgage over given property, in which case it is referred to as a Mortgage Debenture.

Debt and equity ratio. Long-term debt divided by net worth (shareholders' equity.) *See under* Equity, shareholders'.

Depletion. Normally the annual amount provided in the accounts for the exhaustion of a natural resource, e.g. timberlands.

Depreciation. The diminution in value in use of a fixed asset.

Earned surplus. American term for retained earnings but the latter term is now in more common use.

Equity, shareholders'. The sum of the Ordinary shares plus retained earnings and other reserves.

FTC (Federal Trade Commission). A quasi-judicial administrative agency of the US Government, charged with the general responsibility of maintaining the freedom of business enterprise, curbing monopolies and unfair business practices and keeping competition 'both free and fair'.

fob. 'Free on board' means the selling price includes costs up to the port of shipment, and insurance and freight will be for the account of the buyer.

Funded debt. Debt evidenced by outstanding bonds or long-term notes.

Holding company. A controlling company holding shares in subsidiaries and confining its activities primarily to their management.

Indenture. In this book a financial agreement setting out rights and duties of the parties in respect of a long term debt.

Minority interest. That part of the shareholders' equity (*see* Equity, shareholders') of a subsidiary company not owned within the holding group.

Mortgage bond. A bond or series of bonds secured by a mortgage on specific assets, e.g. the 'A' Mortgage Bonds of Bowater Southern.

Net current assets. Working capital.

n.p.v. No par value, i.e. shares without a stated value.

SEC. The Securities and Exchange Commission, a regulating body of the Federal Government in the United States, dealing with the issue and registration of stocks and shares and related matters.

Subordinated debentures. A promise to repay money borrowed but interest and repayment subordinated to prior ranking securities.

Working capital. The excess of current assets (cash, stocks and accounts receivable) over current liabilities (accounts payable and other short-term debts).

UNITS OF MEASUREMENTS

One long ton	=	2,240 lb
One short ton	=	2,000 lb
One tonne	=	1,000 kilos = 2,204.62 lb
One fathom	=	216 cubic feet
One cord	=	128 cubic feet
One cunit	=	100 cubic feet

Notes

For abbreviations used in the notes, see the Bibliography. Where no specific source is given, the document is in the archives of the Bowater Corporation.

1. THE PUBLISHING REVOLUTION AND THE FAMILY FIRM

1 Charles Wilson, 'Economy and society in late Victorian Britain', *Economic History Review*, 2nd series, XVIII (1965), 183; Peter Mathias, *The first industrial nation* (London, 1969), pp. 404–31.
2 Information on Harmsworth part-works kindly supplied by Hon. T. Harmsworth.
3 Reginald Pound and Geoffrey Harmsworth, *Northcliffe* (London, 1959), p. 137.
4 In general, A. P. Wadsworth, 'Newspaper circulations 1800–1954', unpublished paper to the Manchester Statistical Society, 1955; for the *Daily Express*, see W. T. Stead, 'Cyril Arthur Pearson', *Review of Reviews*, XXI (1900), 420–8.
5 Census of England and Wales 1881, general report and tables, Parliamentary Papers 1883, LXXX, 583; Census of England and Wales 1911, summary tables, Cd 7929, Parliamentary Papers 1914–16, LXXXI, 385.
6 E. Haylock, 'Paper', in Trevor Williams (ed.), *The twentieth century*, History of Technology, vols. 6–7 (Oxford, 1978), vol. 7, p. 619.
7 A. H. Shorter, *Paper making in the British Isles* (Newton Abbot, 1971), p. 142.
8 Pound and Harmsworth, *Northcliffe*, pp. 146, 197, 216; Paul Ferris, *The house of Northcliffe* (London, 1971), p. 45.
9 Pound and Harmsworth, *Northcliffe*, p. 173.
10 Northcliffe to F. W. Bowater, 28 September 1915, NP CLXXVII.
11 Private information; *Paper Makers' Monthly Journal*, February 1881 and November 1881; Kelly's Directories Ltd, *London Post Office Directory 1900*.

12 *World's Paper Trade Review*, 27 December 1889, 5.
13 *Ibid.*, 11 October 1889, 2.
14 *Ibid.*, 25 October 1889, 1.
15 'The father of the cheap press. The interesting story of Mr Edward Lloyd', *Fortunes made in business* (part-work, London, n.d., c. 1902), p. 265.
16 'A visit to Lloyd's mills at Sittingbourne', *The Paper-Maker and British Paper Trade Journal*, November 1902, 3–19.
17 *Ibid.*
18 Stead, 'Pearson', p. 428.
19 Private information.
20 *Ibid.*; Kelly's *London*.
21 Cornford to G. A. Sutton, 30 December 1908, NP; *Daily Mail*, 12 May 1928.
22 'A brief history of the Bowater Organisation', typescript, n.d., Legal Dept.
23 WVB AM, 22 February 1911; WVB 21.xii.10, 20.i.11, 22.ii.11.
24 WVB 28.iv.11, 8.xi.11, 2.xii.12, 1.x.13, 2.i.14.

2. THE EXPANDING MARKET AND THE URGE TO MANUFACTURE

1 Wadsworth, 'Newspaper circulations', p. 26.
2 Pound and Harmsworth, *Northcliffe*, p. 495.
3 G. Ward Price, *Fifty years of the 'Daily Mail', 1896–1946* (privately printed, 1946), Ch. 8.
4 Pound and Harmsworth, *Northcliffe*, pp. 769, 837.
5 A. J. P. Taylor, *Beaverbrook* (London, 1972), pp. 99, 132–3.
6 *Ibid.*, pp. 213–14.
7 Royal Commission on the Press 1947–9, Report, Cmd 7700, Parliamentary Papers 1948–9, xx, Ch. 7; see also Viscount Camrose, *British newspapers and their controllers* (London, 1947).
8 Harold Hobson, Philip Knightley, and Leonard Russell, *The pearl of days: an intimate memoir of the 'Sunday Times' 1822–1972* (London, 1972), pp. 80–3.
9 PEP (Political and Economic Planning), *Report on the British Press* (London, 1938), p. 103; Camrose, *British newspapers*, p. 43.
10 Private information; Alan Peters, 'His "logic" built an £80 million business', *Business*, May 1955.
11 F. W. Bowater to Northcliffe, 25 September 1915, NP CLXXVIII.
12 Private information.
13 Augustus Muir, *The British Paper and Board Makers' Association 1872–1972: a centenary history* (privately printed, 1972), pp. 26–7; *The Times*, 18 February 1916.
14 WVB 19.v.16, 2.viii.17, 11.iv.19.
15 WVB 31.iii.16, 27.x.16, 26.iv.17, 24.v.18.

16 WVB 23.vi.16, 4.viii.16; Hudson Packing & Paper Co., Certificate of
   Incorporation, 9 September 1916, OG; Hudson Board minutes
   18.ix.16, 6.x.16, 19.ix.17 and AGM minutes 19.ix.17, OG.
17 WVB 28.ix.17.
18 WVB various dates.
19 WVB 30.ix.19, 4.vi.20; Peters, '£80m business'.
20 'Note on newsprint market conditions', attached to letter to Sir Joseph
   Napier, 7 December 1926, BPM/Sec/9.
21 Peters, '£80m business'.
22 Private information.
23 WVB 3.vii.23.

3. MERCHANTS INTO MANUFACTURERS

1 EL 12.iii.19, 31.iii.19, 27.ii.20; *The Paper-Maker and British Paper
   Trade Journal*, January 1919.
2 Amalgamated Press, *The machinery of a vast undertaking*, brochure,
   n.d. (c. 1912), pp. 11–20.
3 Sutton to Northcliffe, 20 July 1919, NP xxxiv.
4 Amalgamated Press, *Vast undertaking*, pp. 22–6.
5 Sutton to Northcliffe, 2 July 1919, NP xxxiv.
6 Sutton to Northcliffe, 23 January 1919, in *ibid.*
7 Northcliffe to Sutton, 28 January 1919, in *ibid.*
8 Rothermere to Sutton, 26 June 1919, in *ibid.*
9 Sutton to Northcliffe, 18 July 1919, in *ibid.*
10 Northcliffe to Sutton, 22 July 1919, in *ibid.*
11 Private information.
12 Allied Newspapers Ltd, Chairman's speech to AGM, 12 June 1928.
13 Private information.
14 See Appendix I, Tables 2 and 3.
15 Beaverbrook to Rothermere, 21 September 1927, BbK c/284.
16 Beaverbrook to A. R. Graustein, 6 November 1928, BbK h/64.
17 J. D. Scott, *Vickers: a history* (London, 1962), p. 89.
18 *Ibid.*, p. 153.
19 Newfoundland Products Corporation Act, 6 Geo. V cap 4, Newfoundland Legislative Acts 1915.
20 Minutes of Newfoundland Executive Council 25.xi.22, Nfd GN/5,
   254 C.
21 *Corner Brook: 25 years of progress, 1923–1948* (Corner Brook,
   1948), p. 2.
22 D. C. Jennings to Sir R. Squires, 30 June 1922, Nfd GN/5, 254 C.
23 W. Preston to H. D. Reid, 8 July 1921, Reid Papers, Newfoundland,
   File 22.
24 'Report on pulp and paper mills for the Newfoundland Products
   Corporation Ltd', 7 November 1921, Reid Papers, Newfoundland,
   File 497.

25 Scott, *Vickers,* p. 153.
26 R. S. Sayers, *The Bank of England 1891–1944* (3 vols., Cambridge, 1976), vol. 1, pp. 315–16.
27 E. V. Bowater to Angus Reid, 20 November 1923, Reid Papers, Newfoundland, File 305.
28 See Appendix 1, Table 2.
29 'Stipulation of facts', 7 March 1947, 8, 'Anti-trust' file, OG.
30 *Ibid.,* Appendix B.
31 Bowater Paper Co. Inc., minutes of meeting 21.ix.23, Board minutes 15.viii.25; Hudson Packing & Paper Co., AGM minutes 21.ix.23 and Board minutes 17.x.23; all OG.
32 BPM 16.vii.23; Newfoundland Products Corporation Act; Reid to Jennings, 5 July 1922, Reid Papers, Newfoundland, File 22; Jennings' letter at BPM 30.ix.26.
33 Bowaters' Paper Mills Ltd and Sir W. G. Armstrong, Whitworth & Co. Ltd, Contract for the construction of works at Northfleet, Kent, 4 April 1924, BPM/Sec/2; 'Newsprint manufacture in bulk', *The Power Engineer,* February 1927; *Bowater's News,* 18 December 1929.
34 WVB 3.vii.23, 7.iii.24; BPM 29.ii.24, 11.iii.24, 4.iv.24.
35 BPM and Armstrong, Whitworth, Contract for the construction of works at Northfleet.
36 WVB 11.iii.24.
37 WVB 11.iii.24, 18.iv.24.
38 Sir T. V. Bowater to Armstrong, Whitworth, 8 May 1925, BPM/Sec/4.
39 BPM 28.iv.24, 8.v.24, 23.v.24.
40 Sir John Clapham, *An economic history of modern Britain* (3 vols., Cambridge, 1926–38), vol. 3, pp. 234–6.
41 Muir, *Centenary history,* p. 36; private information.
42 Arthur Baker's retirement speech, 1960, supplied by Eric Baker.
43 BPM 27.vi.24.
44 Letter of agreement, 20 August 1924, BPM/Sec/8.
45 Arthur Baker's retirement speech.
46 BPM 6.x.24, 21.x.24, 10.xii.24.
47 BPM 10.xii.24.
48 BPM 25.ix.24.
49 Armstrong, Whitworth to Bowater's Paper Mills, 1 May 1925, BPM/Sec/4.
50 Correspondence between Armstrong, Whitworth and James Byrom Ltd, 1–16 June 1925, BPM/Sec/4.
51 Bowater's Paper Mills and Armstrong, Whitworth, Contract, BPM/Sec/4.
52 BPM AM, 16 June 1926.
53 Sir T. V. Bowater to Armstrong, Whitworth, 8 May 1925, BPM/Sec/4.
54 Scott, *Vickers,* pp. 154, 161.
55 Report by Batten & Co. on Bowater's Paper Mills Contract, 22 September 1926, BE SMT 8/9.

56 Sir Henry Clay, *Lord Norman* (London, 1957), pp. 319; Sayers, *Bank of England*, vol. 1, pp. 314–17.

57 BPM 13.i.26.

58 BPM 25.ii.26.

59 BPM 22.ii.26; WVB 24.iii.26.

60 W. V. Bowater & Sons (1926) Ltd, Prospectus for issue of 8 per cent Participating Preferred Ordinary shares, 23 January 1926.

61 BPM 25.ii.26; WVB 24.iii.26, 16.iv.26, 28.iv.26.

62 *Bowater's News*, 18 December 1929; *Gravesend and Dartford Reporter*, May 1926; private information.

63 Sir Alfred Mond, *Industry and politics* (London, 1927), pp. 2–3.

64 BPM 14.ix.26; BPM AM 16 June 1926, 15 March 1928.

65 Bowater's Paper Mills, Prospectus for issue of $7\frac{1}{2}$ per cent Cumulative Participating Preference shares, 2 April 1927; BPM AM, 16 June 1926.

66 Batten Report, BE SMT 8/9.

67 Scott, *Vickers*, pp. 161–2; private information.

68 J. Frater Taylor and Sir Gilbert Garnsey, 'Report on Armstrong, Whitworth & Co.', 30 March 1926, BE SMT 7/2.

69 BPM 14.vi.26.

70 BPM 23.vi.26.

71 BPM 4.viii.26.

72 BPM 19.viii.26.

73 Draft letter to Price Waterhouse at BPM 19.viii. 26; Frater Taylor to Price Waterhouse, 4 September 1926, at BPM 14.ix.26.

74 BPM 14.ix.26.

75 BPM 14.ix.26.

76 Frater Taylor to Baring Brothers, 24 September 1926; Frater Taylor to Garnsey, 24 September 1926; Frater Taylor to E. Peacock, 27 September 1926; Notes of meeting at the Bank of England, 28 October 1926; all BE SMT 8/9.

77 Scott, *Vickers*, pp. 163–6.

78 BPM 13.x.26.

79 Bowater's Paper Mills, Prospectus for issue of $7\frac{1}{2}$ per cent Cumulative Participating Preference shares, 2 April 1927; Bowater's Paper Mills and Power Securities Corporation Ltd, Supplemental Trust Deed, 14 June 1927, BPM/Sec/2.

80 E. Victor Morgan and W. A. Thomas, *The Stock Exchange: its history and functions* (London, 1962), pp. 204, 248.

81 Bowater's Paper Mills, Prospectus for issue of $7\frac{1}{2}$ per cent Cumulative Participating Preference shares, 2 April 1927.

82 *Ibid.*; Supplemental Trust Deed, 14 June 1927, BPM/Sec/2; WVB 30.iii.27.

83 BPM AM, 24 June 1927.

84 Edward Rushton, Son & Kenyon to Directors of Bowater's Paper Mills, 7 December 1926, BPM/Sec/2.

85 Frater Taylor, Report to Armstrong, Whitworth Advisory Committee, 11 April 1927, BE SMT 8/10.
86 BPM 30.iii.27.
87 BPM 15.iv.26.

4. ERIC AND THE BARONS

1 Daily Mirror Newspapers Ltd, Board minutes, 26.viii.27.
2 WVB 10.xi.27, 1.xii.27; BPM 10.xi.27, 1.xii.27; EVB to H. Rutherford, 4 November 1927, BPM/Sec/9.
3 Bowater's Paper Mills Ltd, Prospectus for issue of 6 per cent Debenture stock, 18 October 1928.
4 BPM 3.viii.27.
5 List of customers, 19 March 1928, BPM/Sec/7.
6 BPM 15.v.28, 22.v.28.
7 BPM 15.vi.28, 21.viii.28, 18.ix.28; Bowater's Paper Mills to Charles Walmsley & Co. Ltd, 21 September 1928, BPM/Sec/13.
8 Bowater's Paper Mills Ltd, Prospectus for issue of 6 per cent Debenture stock, 18 October 1928 BPM 11.x.28; Proposals, 22 August 1928, BPM/Sec/13.
9 BPM AM, 28 December 1928; Bowater's Paper Mills Ltd, Prospectus for issue of 6 per cent Debenture stock, 18 October 1928.
10 BPM AM, 17 December 1929.
11 BPM 18.ix.28.
12 BPM AM, 17 December 1929; BPM 17.xii.29, 4.ii.30.
13 WVB 15.v.28, 18.ix.28, 16.x.28, 12.iii.29, 25.vi.29.
14 WVB 27.iii.30.
15 WVB 6.v.30.
16 WVB 27.iii.30.
17 WVB 3.vi.30.
18 WVB 28.x.30, 27.i.31, 2.vi.31, 29.ix.31, 27.x.31.
19 Daily Mirror Newspapers, Board minutes, 2.x.30.
20 Beaverbrook to Rothermere, 21 September 1927, BbK C/284.
21 International Paper Company Ltd, Contract with the London Express Newspaper Ltd and The Evening Standard Ltd, 23 July 1929, BbK H/64.
22 Peters, '£80m business'; private information.
23 Beaverbrook to EVB, 2 July 1929, EVB to Beaverbrook, 3 July 1929, BbKc/53.
24 WVB 18.vii.29.
25 H. G. Phillips, 'A visit to Bowater's Mersey Paper Mills Ltd', *The Paper-Maker and British Paper Trade Journal*, December 1930, 13; BMPM 21.viii.29, 10.ix.29.
26 Bowater's Mersey Paper Mills Ltd and London Express Newspapers, Agreement, 19 July 1931, BPM/Sec/16.
27 Table 8 is drawn from Bowater's Mersey Paper Mills, prospectus for

issue of 6½ per cent First Mortgage Debenture stock, 23 July 1929; and BMPM 26.viii.31, 10.ix.29; Daily Mirror Newspapers, Board minutes, 9.ix.29.

28 Taylor, *Beaverbrook*, p. 250.
29 BMPM 19.vii.29; private information.
30 Phillips, 'Visit to Mersey', p. 17.
31 Private information.
32 Correspondence in Mersey archives file EVB/KNL 1929/36.
33 H. W. Richardson, *Economic recovery in Britain 1932–39* (London, 1967), p. 16.
34 BMPM 11.ii.30.
35 BMPM 18.iii.30; A. W. Rider, Report to the Directors of the London Express Newspaper Ltd, covered by letter Beaverbrook to Cowley, 11 December 1930, BbK H/63.
36 Beaverbrook to Graustein, 24 September 1930, BbK H/64.
37 Correspondence between Beaverbrook and EVB, BbK C/53.
38 H. J. Inston to A. Baker, 19 August 1930, BPM/Sec/19; BMPM 13.i.31, 28.xi.33.
39 BMPM 27.viii.30, 18.ix.30, 13.i.31.
40 BMPM 18.ix.30; EVB to E. J. Robertson, 7 November 1930, BbK C/53.
41 BMPM 3.ix.30.
42 BMPM 13.i.31.
43 EVB to Robertson, 7 November 1930 (second letter), BbK C/53; A. W. Rider, Report to the Directors, BbK H/63.
44 WVB 25.xi.30.
45 J. Cowley to Beaverbrook, 19 December 1930, BbK H/63.
46 Beaverbrook to Graustein, 25 November 1930, BbK H/64.
47 Graustein to Beaverbrook, 26 November 1930, in *ibid.*
48 EVB to Beaverbrook, 24 December 1930, BbK C/53.
49 Beaverbrook to Cowley, 14 January 1931, BbK H/ 63.
50 BMPM 13.i.31; Cowley to Beaverbrook, 15 January 1931, BbK H/63.
51 Cowley to Beaverbrook, 20 January 1931, in *ibid.*
52 Beaverbrook to Cowley, 21 January 1931, in *ibid.*
53 *Ibid.*
54 BMPM 29.xii.30.
55 BMPM 29.xii.30, 27.i.31.
56 BMPM 22.x.31, 11.xi.31.
57 See Appendix 1, Tables 2 and 3.
58 PEP, *British Press*, p. 307.
59 See Appendix 1, Table 8.
60 Bowater's Mersey Paper Mills to London Express Newspaper, 3 September 1931, at BMPM 28.ix.31.
61 BMPM 28.ix.31, 13.i.32.
62 Bowater's Paper Mills, Prospectus for issue of 6½ per cent Cumulative Preference shares, 27 May 1932.

63 Beaverbrook to Rothermere, 11 May 1932, Rothermere to Beaver-brook, 12 May 1932, BbK H/63.
64 Royal S. Kellogg, *Newsprint paper in North America* (New York, 1948), p. 25; PEP, *British Press*, pp. 61, 98; Camrose, *British Newspapers*, p. 64.
65 BPM 11.v.32; Bowater's Paper Mills, Prospectus for issue of 6½ per cent Cumulative Preference shares, 27 May 1932.
66 *Ibid.*; see also WVB 11.v.32.
67 Cowley to Beaverbrook, 13 May 1932, BbK H/63.
68 Beaverbrook to Robertson, 22 May 1932, in *ibid.*

5. THE BOWATER GROUP IN THE THIRTIES

1 PEP, *British Press*, pp. 96–108.
2 *Ibid.*, p. 306.
3 Royal Commission on the Press 1947–9, Report, Cmd. 7700, Appendix III; PEP, *British Press*, p. 84.
4 Royal Commission on the Press 1947–9, Report, Appendix III PEP, *British Press*, pp. 84, 99, 101; Camrose, *British newspapers*, p. 31.
5 PEP, *British Press*, pp. 53–6, 86–90; private information.
6 PEP, *British Press*, p. 307.
7 'The Gander Valley Power and Paper Company of Newfoundland: general report' (typescript, 31 October 1925), Table XIX.
8 See Appendix 1, Table 4.
9 BPM 20.xi.34, 12.iii.35; 'Great Hawks Tor China Clays Ltd' memorandum, n.d., BPM minute book.
10 Speech to Preference shareholders at BMPM 14.xii.36.
11 BMPM 18.vii.34.
12 BMPM 20.ix.32.
13 WVB 15.xi.32.
14 WVB 30.v.33.
15 PEP, *British Press*, pp. 73–4.
16 Appendix 1, Table 8.
17 Bowater's Paper Mills and London Express Newspaper, Agreement, 23 May 1932, BPM/Sec/16; Edward Lloyd Ltd and Allied Newspapers, Agreement, 20 July 1936, Legal Dept. QC/6, *q.v.* also for other similar contracts.
18 Beaverbrook to EVB, 2 July 1929, BbK C/53.
19 Inston to Rutherford, 29 May 1931, BPM/Sec/21.
20 Inston to Rutherford, 11 February 1932, and following correspondence BPM/Sec/21.
21 UNESCO, *The problem of newsprint and other printing paper* (Paris, 1949), pp. 38, 48, and *Newsprint trends 1928–51* (Paris, 1954), p. 44.
22 BMPM 11.i.30, 22.x.31, 24.xi.31; WVB 11.v.32; Daily Mirror Newspapers, Board minutes, 11.v.32; BPM 20.xii.32.
23 PEP, *British Press*, p. 44.

24 BMPM 28.xi.33.
25 Bowater's Mersey Paper Mills, Prospectus for issue of 5½ per cent Cumulative Preference Shares, 30 November 1932, and letter to Debenture holders, 20 January 1933; BPM AM, 6 December 1932.
26 BMPM 20.iii.34.
27 BMPM 20.xi.34.
28 BMPM 10.xi.36.
29 BMPM 7.i.36.
30 BMPM 18.ii.36.
31 *The Economist*, 20 February 1932; *The World's Paper Trade Review*, 26 February 1932 and 4 March 1932; *The Paper-Maker and British Paper Trade Journal*, March 1932.
32 WVB AM, 31 March 1932. See also WVB AM, 31 March 1933; BPM AM, 8 December 1930, 1 January 1934.
33 Frater Taylor to A. A. Ritchie, 1 November 1937, BE SMT 2/223.
34 BPM AM, 1 January 1934.
35 Barton, Mayhew & Co., Report to the Chairman on the cost of production of paper for home and export orders, 26 March 1936, BPM/Sec/21.
36 Private information.
37 BPM 7.i.36.
38 Barton, Mayhew & Co., Report, 26 March 1936, BPM/Sec/21.
39 Bowater's Paper Mills to Price Brothers' Bondholders' Protection Committee, 28 September 1933, BPM minute book; BPM 31.x.33.
40 BPM 29.ix.33.
41 BPM 31.x.33; *Financial Post*, 27 January 1934.
42 BPM 28.xi.33, 6.ii.34, 20.iii.34, 24.iv.34.
43 BPM 12.vi.34.
44 BPM 8.vii.34.
45 Private information; Taylor, *Beaverbrook*, p. 15.
46 BPM 20.xi.34.
47 Private information.
48 BPM 20.xi.34.
49 Private information.
50 This and following extracts from BE SMT 2/229.

6. THE FALL OF THE HOUSE OF LLOYD

1 EL 12.iii.19, 31.iii.19, 27.ii.20.
2 Edward Lloyd Ltd, minutes of Extraordinary General Meeting, 26 January 1927.
3 Lloyds, Chairman's speech to AGM, 11 May 1923.
4 *Ibid.*, 12 May 1925, 15 March 1928, 14 March 1929.
5 *Ibid.*, 12 May 1927, 15 March 1928.
6 *Ibid.*, 15 May 1924.
7 *Ibid.*, 12 May 1925.

8 *Ibid.*, 12 May 1925, 30 June 1926.

9 'Souvenir-programme of a visit of members of the International Association of Journalists attending the London conference 1927 to Kemsley Mills and Garden Village', 5 July 1927, p. 17.

10 *Ibid.*, p. 23.

11 Charles Wilson, *The history of Unilever* (3 vols., London, 1954–68), vol. 1, pp. 146–7.

12 'Souvenir-programme', p. 3.

13 Allied Newspapers, Chairman's speech to AGM, 12 June 1928.

14 PEP, *British Press*, pp. 62, 99, 101.

15 Hobson *et al.*, *Pearl of days*, pp. 76–8.

16 Allied Newspapers, Chairman's speech to AGM, 12 June 1928.

17 Edward Lloyd Investment Co. Ltd, Prospectus for sale of Debenture stock, 3 December 1927.

18 *Ibid.*

19 Lloyds, Chairman's speech to AGM, 30 March 1932; EL 3.iv.28, 25.vii.28; Newsprint contracts, Legal Dept. QC/6.

20 Private information.

21 EL 6.vi.16, 21.xii.21, 11.x.27, 14.iii.28; private information. See also, on the Denson family, *The Paper-Maker and British Paper Trade Journal*, February 1928.

22 Edward Lloyd Investment Co., Board minutes, 19.v.33, and Prospectus for issue of Debenture stock, 19 May 1933, and as n. 24.

23 Lloyds, Chairman's speech to AGM, 8 May 1934.

24 Bowater's Paper Mills, Prospectus for issue of $7\frac{1}{2}$ per cent Cumulative Preference shares, 21 July 1936.

25 Bowater's Paper Mills, Chairman's speech to Extraordinary General Meeting, 20 July 1936.

26 WVB 10.xi.36.

27 BPM, Chairman's speech to Extraordinary General Meeting, 20 July 1936.

28 Edward Lloyd Investment Co., Share certificates, 31 March 1935, and other documents, Registrar's Department.

29 BPM 14.vii.36, 28.ix.36.

30 BPM 9.vi.36.

31 Edward Lloyd Investment Co., letter to Debenture holders, 20 July 1936, Bowater Issues Book.

32 BPM, Chairman's speech to Extraordinary General Meeting, 20 July 1936.

33 BPM 28.ix.36.

34 BPM 10.ii.37.

35 BPM, Prospectus for issue of $7\frac{1}{2}$ per cent Cumulative Preference shares, 21 July 1936.

36 BPM 9.vi.36.

37 BPM, Prospectus for issue of $7\frac{1}{2}$ per cent Cumulative Preference shares, 21 July 1936.

7. THE RAW MATERIALS CRISIS

1 Lloyds and the Daily News & News Chronicle Ltd, Agreement, 30 July 1936, Legal Dept. QC/2; BPM 10.ii.37.
2 AGM, 1 December 1936.
3 AGM, 30 December 1937.
4 EVB, 'Memorandum as to proposed purchase of the equity of I. P. & P. Co. of Newfoundland Ltd', 2 May 1938, BE SMT 2/230.
5 Financial News, 3 April 1937; PEP, British Press, pp. 57–8.
6 AGM, 30 December 1937.
7 D. C. Coleman, Courtaulds: an economic and social history (3 vols., Oxford, 1969–80), vol. 2, p. 172.
8 AGM, 30 December 1937.
9 EVB to Baker, 3 December 1936, Mersey archives, File EVB/KNL 1929–36.
10 BPM 10.ii.37.
11 Ibid.
12 The Economist, 14 August 1937.
13 BPM 14.ix.37.
14 The World's Paper Trade Review, 30 July 1937.
15 Financial Times, Financial News, 6 August 1937.
16 BPM 14.ix.37.
17 AGM, 30 December 1937.
18 BPM 21.vi.38.
19 EVB, 'Memorandum', 2 May 1938, BE SMT 2/230.
20 BPM 10.ii.37.
21 BPM 10.ii.37 The Times, Financial Times, Daily Telegraph, 10 February 1937.
22 Financial News, 3 April 1937.
23 BPM 10.ii.37, 16.iii.37, 14.ix.37; EL 20.i.39.
24 EL 16.iii.37.
25 B&LS 22.iv.37.
26 BPM 1.xii.37.
27 Wilson, Unilever, vol. 1, p. 159.

8. THE ROAD TO CORNER BROOK

1 EVB, 'Memorandum as to proposed purchase of the equity of I.P. & P. Co. of Newfoundland Ltd', 2 May 1938, BE SMT 2/230.
2 BPM 16.iii.37; Agreement of 27 May 1937, BPM/Sec/24.
3 BPM 22.iv.37, 22.vi.37
4 BPM 16.iii.37.
5 BPM 22.iv.37.
6 BPM 16.iii.37.
7 Agreement of 28 June 1939; C. Anker to H. S. Borchgrevink, 29 June

1939; both in 'Acquisition of A/S Risor Traemassefabriker' at BPM 1.xii.39.

8 EL 16.iii.37.
9 St John Chadwick, *Newfoundland* (Cambridge, 1967), p. 154 and generally.
10 Newfoundland Royal Commission, Report, Cmd 4480, 1933.
11 R. B. Ewbank, Speech re development of Gander area, 4 November 1937, Nfd 7–1.
12 *Ibid.*
13 *Ibid.*
14 BPM 14.ix.37.
15 Telegram to Secretary of State, 28 October 1937, Nfd 7–1.
16 Telegram to Secretary of State, 30 October 1937, *ibid.*
17 Telegram from Chief Ranger, Maj. Anderton, 2 November 1937, *ibid.*
18 Ewbank to Anderton, 2 November 1937, *ibid.*
19 Anon., 30 October 1937, *ibid.*
20 Ewbank, Speech re development of Gander area, 4 November 1937, Nfd 7–1.
21 Various documents in Nfd 7–1.
22 Draft communique, n.d. (c. January 1938), Nfd.
23 Bowater-Lloyd Act, second proof, 25 January 1938, and attached minute, Nfd.
24 Frater Taylor to EVB, 15 December 1937, BE SMT 2/223.
25 Frater Taylor to Montagu Norman, 11 January 1938, *ibid.*
26 Correspondence between Sir F. Phillips (Treasury) and Norman, 3–8 June 1937, *ibid.*
27 Frater Taylor to E. H. D. Skinner, 19 October 1937, *ibid.*
28 T. Lodge, *Dictatorship in Newfoundland* (London, 1939). Lodge, one of the original Commissioners, resigned in 1936.
29 'Memorandum as to International Power and Paper Company of Newfoundland Ltd', 16 January 1938, BE SMT 2/223.
30 EVB, 'Memorandum', 2 May 1938, BE SMT 2/230.
31 Memo, Frater Taylor to J. H. Keeling, 4 March 1938, BE SMT 2/223.
32 EVB, 'Memorandum', 2 May 1938, BE SMT 2/230.
33 *Ibid.*; Secretary of State to Governor, 13 May 1938, Nfd GN 1/3, 354 38.
34 See Appendix 1, Table 8.
35 Frater Taylor to Skinner, 14 May 1938, BE SMT 2/230.
36 Frater Taylor to EVB, 15 December 1937, BE SMT 2/223.
37 BPM 31.v.38.
38 Memorandum by the Commissioner of Finance, 4 June 1938, Nfd F52 38.
39 Chairman's circular letter to newspaper proprietors, 14 July 1938, BPM minute book; BPM 15.vii.38, 27.ix.38.
40 BPM 15.vii.38.
41 BPM 21.vi.38.

42 Ewbank, Draft speech on Bowater agreement, 16 November 1938, Nfd.

43 Chairman's circular letter to BPM stockholders, 2 June 1938, BPM minute book.

44 Private information.

45 BPM 15.vii.38; Bowater-Lloyd Newfoundland Ltd, Prospectus for issue of debentures, 21 July 1938.

46 AGM, 22 December 1938.

9. WAR AND PAPER CONTROL

1 Sir Andrew Duncan to Oliver Lyttelton, 8 September 1942, PRO BT/28/148, MOP Sec/16 Part 1.

2 H. J. Gray, 'Paper 1939–1943', PRO BT/131/105, p. 2.

3 *ibid.*, p. 3.

4 Frater Taylor to Skinner, 5 February 1940, BE SMT 2/231.

5 Vincent Massey to Anthony Eden, 16 January 1940 and 25 January 1940, PRO MT/59/819.

6 C. R. Attlee to Massey, 16 November 1942, in *ibid.*

7 Camrose, *British newspapers*, pp. 153–5; Evidence of Lord Layton and F. P. Bishop in Royal Commission on the Press 1947–9, Minutes of evidence, Cmd 7409, Parliamentary Papers 1947–8, xv.

8 BPM 11.x.40.

9 *Ibid.*

10 AGM, 27 December 1940, 12 February 1943, 16 February 1944; 'Note for the information of the President of the Board of Trade', 12 November 1945, PRO BT/28/148, MOP Sec/16 Part 2.

11 Note of meeting on 20 June 1945, in *ibid.*

12 BPM 22.vi.42; private information.

13 Evidence of Lord Layton and F. P. Bishop in Royal Commission on the Press 1947–9, Minutes of evidence.

14 H. J. Hutchinson to Sir William Palmer, 25 September 1942, PRO BT/28/148, MOP Sec/16 Part 1.

15 T. G. Lee to Gibson Graham, 14 October 1942, PRO MT/59/819.

16 *Ibid.*; Duncan to Lyttelton, 8 September 1942, PRO BT/28/148, MOP Sec/16 Part 1; Attlee to Massey, 16 November 1942, PRO MT/59/819; Newsprint Supply Co., Board minutes, 25.ix.42, 2.x.42, 23.x.42, 13.xi.42; P. A. Clutterbuck to F. D. N. Dunn, 21 November 1942, PRO BT/28/148, MOP Sec/16 Part1; and other papers.

17 AGM, 16 February 1944; Gray, in PRO BT/131/105, Appendix VI.

18 E. L. Hargreaves and M. M. Gowing, *Civil industry and trade* (London, 1952), Ch. 10; Gray, in PRO BT/131/105, p. 8.

19 AGM, 27 December 1940.

20 AGM, 23 March 1945.

21 AGM, 23 January 1942, 12 February 1943, 16 February 1944, 23 March 1945; GPC 6.ii.46.

22 Gray, in PRO BT/131/105, pp. 9–13.
23 Royal Commission on the Press 1947–9, Minutes of evidence, p. 22.
24 BPC Statistical Bureau, 'The United Kingdom paper industry 1939–53' (April 1954), Table 9.
25 Gray, in PRO BT/131/105, p. 4.
26 Col. Clifford D. Sheldon to A. Ralph Reed, 16 September 1943; Reed to Hutchinson, 21 September 1943; both PRO BT/28/148, MOP Sec/16 Part 1.
27 Camrose, *British newspapers*, p. 155.
28 Lloyds, Report of activities, in 'War contracts 1938–45'.
29 Chairman's Advisory Committee, Recommendation No. 1, 'Recommended policy for post-war newsprint operation', 29 June 1945.
30 Private information; Bowater's Paper Mills, 'Production totals of munition work carried out by the Bowater-Lloyd group', n.d.
31 BPM 27.ix.38, 11.x.40; AGM, 28 December 1939; private information.
32 *The Times, Financial Times*, 28 December 1939; *The Economist*, 28 December 1940.
33 BPM 21.xii.42.
34 AGM, 12 February 1943, 16 February 1944; BPM 21.xii.42; *Investor's Chronicle*, 30 January 1943.
35 Inston to EVB, 17 July 1946, File 'Capital reorganisation, 1947', RK.

10. THE WIDER OUTLOOK

1 See Appendix 1, Tables 2 and 4.
2 E. C. Duffin, 'Report on visit to New York-Montreal-Corner Brook, November 1943–February 1944', p. 6.
3 WVB 11.xii.28; Bowater Paper Co. Inc., Board minutes, 14.xi.29, 3.xi.30.
4 Bowater Paper Co. Inc., Board minutes, 23.vi.38.
5 EVB to Mrs M. L. Reay-Mackey, n.d. (c. 1948–9), RM.
6 Bowater's Newfoundland Act 1938, Part II.
7 BNPP 12.xii.39; Bank of Montreal to H. M. S. Lewin, 12 December 1939; BNPP balance sheet and directors' report, 31 December 1940.
8 See Appendix 1, Table 2.
9 American Newspaper Publishers' Association, *Newsprint now and in the next decade* (New York, 1951), Chart 10.
10 Bowater Paper Co. and International Paper Co., Sales Allocation Agreement, 17 July 1941, 'Anti-trust' file, OG.
11 Newfoundland Export & Shipping Co. to Bowater Paper Co., 1 December 1946, in 'Draft stipulation of facts', 3 July 1947, 'Anti-trust' file, OG.
12 Evidence of A. B. Meyer in United States Senate Committee on Interstate and Foreign Commerce, *Newsprint inquiry*, Report of proceedings, vol. 2 (Washington DC, 1957).

13 BNPP 4.iii.43.

14 N. V. Bowater to A. B. Meyer, 27 December 1944, 'Anti-trust' file, OG.

15 BNPP 4.iii.43; evidence of A. B. Meyer to US Senate Committee, *Newsprint inquiry*.

16 BNPP 20.ix.43.

17 EVB to G. S. Currie, 24 February 1943, Corner Brook archives.

18 Correspondence in BE SMT 2/237.

19 Norman to Governor, Bank of Canada, 11 March 1940, BE SMT 2/231.

20 Correspondence in BE SMT 2/231–5.

21 H. E. Brooks to Ira Wild, 18 August 1941, BE SMT 2/233.

22 Frater Taylor to Skinner, 18 March 1942; Ritchie to Brooks, 28 May 1942; Frater Taylor, Notes on interview with Governor, 1 June 1942; all BE SMT 2/237.

23 Skinner to Norman, 21 July 1942, in *ibid.*

24 Note by Brooks, 10 September 1941, in *ibid.*

25 BPM 7.x.42, 22.vi.45; Deputy Governor's note to Chairman, Capital Issues Committee, 30 September 1942, BE SMT 2/237.

26 Committee of Treasury minutes, 16.xii.42, BE CT 192.02.

27 Norman to Frater Taylor, 18 September 1942, BE SMT 2/236.

28 See Appendix 1, Table 2.

29 GPC 20.xii.44, 3.i.45; Inston to EVB, 29 August 1945, 'B-L P&D Policy'; BNPP 15.v.46.

30 BNPP 15.v.46.

31 BNPP 20.v.46.

32 EVB to Inston, 29 August 1945, 'B-L P&D Policy'.

33 Bowater-Lloyd Newfoundland, Board minutes, 11.iv.46.

34 AGM, 13 March 1947.

35 *Ibid.*

36 *Ibid.*

37 *Ibid.*

38 BPM 22.vi.42.

39 BPM 10.v.44.

40 *Ibid.*

41 The Acme Corrugated Paper & Box Co. Ltd, Minute book I, 1923–40, and II, 1940–5.

42 BPM 30.vii.47.

43 *Ibid.*

44 GPC 21.ii.50.

45 Riegel Paper Corporation and Bowater-Lloyd Pulp and Paper Mills, Agreement, 11 September 1951; BPC 12.xii.51.

46 Note of a meeting on 19 September 1945, PRO BOT 28/148, MOP Sec/16 Part 2.

47 AGM, 11 March 1948; private information.

48 AGM, 11 March 1948.

49 W. J. Reader, *Imperial Chemical Industries: a history* (2 vols., Oxford, 1970–5), vol. 2, p. 497, and *Metal Box: a history* (London, 1976), p. 234.
50 EVB to Inston, 30 August 1945, 'B-L P&D Policy'.
51 *World's Press News*, 3 August 1944.
52 OM 16, 13 March 1945.
53 OM 9, 11 July 1944.
54 AGM, 13 March 1947.
55 Pamphlet, 'The Bowater Organisation', March 1947, File 'Capital reorganisation 1947', RK.

11. THE TENNESSEE VENTURE

1 BNPP 16.i.50; Roscoe C. Martin, *From forest to front page* (Birmingham, Alabama, 1956), p. iii.
2 BPC 14.vii.48; Memorandum from London & Yorkshire Trust, 25 June 1948, BPC issues book.
3 EVB to MLR-M, 26 September 1949, 1 October 1949, 27 September 1950, RM.
4 Application to Capital Issues Committee, 1 June 1949, File 'Issue, Sept 1950', RK; BPC 26.vii.49, 11.ix.50; Letter to BPC stockholders, 13 September 1950, BPC issues book.
5 'The Bowater Organisation – new capital – 9 Jan 1952', File 'New capital, 1952', RK.
6 Martin, *Forest to front page*, pp. 1–2.
7 Dard Hunter, *Papermaking: the history and technique of an ancient craft* (London, 1947), pp. 398–9; Meyer to Duffin, 18 July 1947, 'Anti-trust' file, OG.
8 GPC 17.iii.48.
9 Baker to EVB, 9 June 1950, 'Chairman's file – Projects, April 1950–51', DD.
10 Meyer's correspondence with Lewin and Duffin, Mar.-Apr. 1947, 'Anti-trust' file, OG; Meyer to EVB, 6 June 1947, 'Visits, Chairman, 1945–49', DD; Meyer to EVB, 2 June 1950, 'Chairman's file – Projects, April 1950–51', DD.
11 GPC 11.xi.48.
12 GPC 29.xi.48.
13 GPC 5.ix.50, 8.xii.50.
14 Keeling to I. F. Bowater, 25 September 1950, GPC minutes; Memo, EVB to Stanley Bell, 13 December 1950, GPC Murupara file.
15 Meyer to EVB, 2 June 1950, 'Chairman's file – Projects, April 1950–51', DD.
16 Coverdale & Colpitts, 'Report on Bowaters Southern Paper Corporation', 1 October 1951, Appendix c.
17 See Appendix 1, Table 4.
18 Martin, *Forest to front page*, p. 3.

19 Morgan Stanley & Co., 'Bowaters Southern Paper Corporation', 30 January 1952, p. 7.
20 Martin, *Forest to front page*, p. iii; Coverdale & Colpitts, 'Report on Bowaters Southern', pp. 12–23.
21 Coverdale & Colpitts, 'Report on Bowaters Southern', pp. 3, 17–18.
22 'Invitation to Bowaters Southern Paper Corporation', 28 August 1951, BS; Martin, *Forest to front page*, p. 20; Resolutions of McMinn County Council, 11 February 1952, 21 April 1952, BS.
23 J. Kirwan-Taylor to L. G. Pearce, covering BPC to Bank of England, 3 April 1951, 172/447; Bank of England to BPC, 11 May 1951, 'Exchange control applications 1951&1969', RK.
24 Martin, *Forest to front page*, pp. 6–7.
25 Bowaters Southern, 'Summary of aide-memoire for a meeting on 26 November 1951', 172/447.
26 See Appendix 1, Tables 2 and 3.
27 Newsprint Sales Agreement, 1 May 1952, Schedule A, printed in Purchase Agreement for 4¾ per cent Sinking Fund 1st Mortgage Bonds Series A, 17 June 1952.
28 Morgan Stanley, 'Bowaters Southern Paper Corporation', 5 September 1951, p. 14.
29 Bowaters Southern, Certificate of Incorporation and Bye-laws; Martin, *Forest to front page*, p. 3.
30 Coverdale & Colpitts, 'Report on Bowaters Southern', p. 42.
31 *Ibid.*, p. 44.
32 Martin, *Forest to front page*, p. 20.
33 EVB to MLR-M, 5 October 1959, RM.
34 *Western Star*, 16 November 1951; Martin, *Forest to front page*, p. 24.
35 Martin, *Forest to front page*, p. 24.
36 Bowaters Southern, 'Summary of aide-memoire' EVB to Chief Cashier, Bank of England, 20 December 1951, 172/447.
37 EVB to Chief Cashier, Bank of England, 20 December 1951, and reply, 3 January 1952, p. 15.
38 Martin, *Forest to front page*, p. 27.
39 Morgan Stanley, 'Bowaters Southern', 30 January 1952, pp. 12–13.
40 EVB to Chief Cashier, Bank of England, 20 December 1951, 172/447.
41 Morgan Stanley, 'Bowaters Southern', 30 January 1952, pp. 12–13.
42 Kirwan-Taylor to G. H. Tansley, 24 April 1952, 'new capital, 1952', RK.
43 Oral tradition.
44 Purchase Agreement for 4¾ per cent Sinking Fund 1st Mortgage Bonds Series A, 17 June 1952.
45 BPC to Capital Issues Committee, 10 January 1952, 'New capital, 1952', RK.
46 Memo, EVB to Stanley Bell, 13 December 1950, GPC Murupara file; cable Preslon 335, EVB to Keeling, 16 September 1952, 'New capital, 1952', RK.

47 Cable Preslon 222, EVB to Keeling, 17 April 1951, 'Reorganisation of Preference capital, 1950–51', RK.
48 Cable Lonpres 265, Keeling to EVB, 18 April 1951, in *ibid*.
49 GPC 17.iv.51 and Chairman's comments.
50 See e.g. BPC 26.vii.51.
51 BPC to Capital Issues Committee, 20 December 1951, '1952 issues', RK.
52 BPC to Capital issues Committee, 10 January 1952, 'New capital, 1952', RK.
53 Memo, Chairman to Directors, 31 January 1952, 'New capital, 1952', RK.
54 Memo, Chairman to Directors, 20 May 1952, in *ibid*.
55 BPC 22.v.52, 12.vi.52.
56 BPC 16.vii.52.
57 BPC 12.vi.52.
58 BPC 28.viii.52.
59 Cable Preslon 323, EVB to Keeling, 10 September 1952, 'New capital, 1952', RK.
60 Cables Lonpres 390, Inston to EVB, 15 September 1952; Preslon 335, EVB to Keeling, 16 September 1952; both in *ibid*.
61 Cable Lonyork 907, Inston to Meyer, 13 October 1952, in *ibid*.
62 BPC 28.xi.52.
63 Chairman's speech to BPC Debenture holders, 2 June 1954.
64 OM 80, 21 November 1952.
65 Private information.
66 Martin, *Forest to front page,* pp. 28–9; Robert Sinclair, *Bowaters build a mill in Tennessee* (privately printed, n.d., c. 1954), p. 29.
67 Martin, *Forest to front page,* pp. 35–6; *Southern Pulp & Paper Manufacturer,* 10 November 1954; Sinclair, *Mill in Tennessee,* pp. 29–30.
68 BSPC 16.vii.54, 25.viii.54.
69 Bowaters Southern, Directors' report, 11 April, 1955, BS.
70 Sinclair, *Mill in Tennessee,* pp. 29–30.

12. ZENITH

1 Harry Hampton, 'A far country', *Woods and waters,* n.d. (c. July 1962).
2 Evidence of Cranston Williams, General Manager ANPA, in United States Senate Committee on Interstate and Foreign Commerce, *Newsprint inquiry,* Report of proceedings, vol. 1 (Washington DC, 1957), pp. 35–7.
3 See Appendix 1, Table 1.
4 Bowater Power Co., Prospectus for $15.5m 1st Mortgage $3\frac{3}{4}$ per cent Sinking Fund Bonds Series A, 6 May 1955, SO/10; Kirwan-Taylor to EVB, 8 June 1956, 'Mersey', OG.

5 Cable Preslon 472, EVB to Keeling, 16 April 1954, 'Mersey', OG.

6 Meyer to EVB, 8 May 1956, in *ibid.*

7 Meyer to EVB, 4 May 1956, in *ibid.*

8 Currie to EVB, 7 May 1956, in *ibid.*

9 John V. Walters, 'note on the acceptance of Bowater's offer to purchase Mersey Paper Co.', n.d. (1978).

10 BPC 16.xii.54, 20.xii.55.

11 BPC 6.iv.55.

12 Reader, *Metal Box*, pp. 157–73.

13 Coleman, *Courtaulds*, vol. 3, pp. 166–8.

14 Secretary ABI to General Manager ABI, 26 July 1955, and ABI to Director of Operations BPC, 29 July 1955, File 'Eburite Corrugated Containers Ltd'; Kirwan-Taylor, 'Brighton', 10 November 1955, FMD 37/1.

15 C. G. Rye to EVB, 22 February 1956; Cable Preslon 639, EVB to Rye, 28 February 1956; both in FMD 37/1.

16 Rye, 'Consolidating memorandum on proposals for merging of interests of Eburite Corrugated Containers Ltd. and Bowaters Fibre Containers Ltd', 17 May 1956; Letter to Ordinary shareholders in Eburite Corrugated Containers Ltd, 15 June 1956.

17 Cable Preslon 639, EVB to Rye, 28 February 1956, FMD 37/1.

18 Purchase Agreement 28 January 1955; BPC 6.iv.55.

19 GPC 29.i.52.

20 C. Norman Stabler's comments, n.d., on a survey of the Scott Paper Co. issued by Smith, Barney & Co., KT.

21 Cable, Thomas B. McCabe to EVB, 28 December 1955, KT.

22 Meyer to EVB, 10 January 1956, KT.

23 *Ibid.*

24 Comptroller BPC to Chief Cashier, Bank of England, 9 December 1955, KT.

25 Meyer to EVB, 10 January 1956, KT.

26 Meyer to EVB, 11 January 1956.

27 Cable, EVB to Kirwan-Taylor, 5 December 1956, 172/447.

28 BPC 16.xii.54.

29 Morgan Stanley, 'Bowaters Southern Paper Corporation'. 21 April 1955, pp. 2–3.

30 Morgan Stanley, 'Bowaters Southern Paper Corporation: second expansion programme', 10 December 1956, p. 5.

31 *Ibid.*, p. 3.

32 Cable Lonsouth 566, EVB to K. O. Elderkin, 15 June 1956, 172/447.

33 Morgan Stanley, 'Bowaters Carolina Corporation', 15 December 1956, p. 7.

34 Comptroller BPC to Chief Cashier, Bank of England, 29 March 1956, 172/455; Bowater Corporation of North America, Prospectus for issue of $17.5m 5 per cent Redeemable Cumulative Preference shares, 18 April 1956.

35 Kirwan-Taylor to EVB, 22 November 1956, 172/447.
36 Cable Kingfisher 311, Kirwan-Taylor to EVB, 4 December 1956; cable Lonyork 923, EVB to Kirwan-Taylor, 5 December 1956; both 172/447.
37 Morgan Stanley, 'Bowaters Carolina Corporation', 15 December 1956, pp. 4–5.
38 Ibid., pp. 6–7.
39 Kirwan-Taylor, 'Shipping survey', 18 May 1954, 172/332.
40 Lewin to Kirwan-Taylor, 15 July 1954, in ibid.
41 BPC 16.xii.54.
42 OM 88, 21 January 1955.
43 'Bowater Finance', 12 July 1960, p. 4, FMD 37/2.
44 BPC 16.xii.54, 20.xii.55.
45 BPC 16.xii.54.
46 Comptroller to Director of Finance, 'Cash position and capital expenditure', 19 July 1955, RK.
47 'The Bowater Organisation – Press Broadcast for publication 23rd and 24th October 1955', RK.
48 EVB to MLR-M, 14 September 1955, RM.
49 BPC, Prospectus for issue of £15m 5¾ per cent Convertible Unsecured Loan Stock, 1 February 1957, p. 2.
50 Currie to EVB, 16 August 1956, 172/445.
51 EVB to MLR-M, 9 September 1956, RM.
52 Rye to Currie, 22 August 1956, 172/445.
53 Rye to Pearce, 7 December 1956, 172/445.
54 BPC 29.xi.56.
55 Cables Yorklon 766, Kirwan-Taylor to EVB, 16 January 1957; Kingfisher 504, Kirwan-Taylor to EVB, 18 January 1957; both 172/445.
56 Comptroller BPC to Chief Cashier, Bank of England, 2 September 1957, 172/445.

13. EXPANSION INTO ADVERSITY

1 'Extract from the speech of the Chairman at the annual staff dinner on 24th January 1958', 49/32.
2 Ibid.
3 Rye, 'Bowater-Eburite and ABI', 8 February 1957, FMD 37/1.
4 Ibid.
5 Chairman, Bowater-Eburite, to Ordinary shareholders, 1 July 1957, FMD 37/1.
6 Draft memo from Chairman's office, 'Hunt Partners Ltd', 14 May 1957, in ibid.
7 BPC 22.viii.57; OM 118, 1 October 1957; BPC Annual Report 1959.
8 GPC 30.vi.54, 9.viii.54.
9 J. Martin Ritchie, 'The Bowater Paper Corporation Limited, Adminis-

trative and organisational structure', 29 January 1962, p. 2, FMD 37/3.

10 Economy Committee's report, 12 August 1958, RK.

11 Head Office Circular, 14 April 1958; OM 126, 'European Free Trade', 1 August 1958.

12 Martin Ritchie and B. G. Alexander, 'Note on the development in Europe of Bowaters' packaging interests', 13 April 1959, 47/32.

13 Rye to EVB, 22 May 1959, 47/32.

14 BPC 20.viii.59.

15 Alexander, 'Progress report on European development', October 1959, 47/32.

16 BPC 13.vi.61, Appendix A.

17 GPC 31.x.56, 29.i.57.

18 GPC 31.x.56.

19 GPC 7.viii.59.

20 *Ibid.*

21 GPC 25.ii.58, 25.vi.58.

22 GPC 7.viii.59.

23 Bowater Packaging Ltd, 'Gillingham', 1 July 1960, 49/28; GPC 4.vii.60.

24 GPC 29.i.57, 11.vi.57.

25 GPC 19.ix.57.

26 Comptroller to Chairman, 'Capital expenditure and commitments', 14 May 1958, 49/32.

27 GPC 29.xii.59.

28 Carl Thiel to Bowater Sales Co., 8 May 1959, 47/50.

29 Kirwan-Taylor to EVB, 1 March 1960, in *ibid.*

30 Rye, 'Memorandum on discussions of May 3rd/4th with the Banque de Bruxelles', 6 May 1960, in *ibid.*

31 'Bowater Finance', 12 July 1960, p. 4. FMD 37/2.

32 Rye to K. N. Linforth, 'Zürich', 2 June 1960, 47/50.

33 Alexander to EVB, 23 June 1960, in *ibid.*

34 EVB to F. Béghin, 27 June 1960; Agreement of 30 June 1960; both in *ibid.*

35 GPC 18.v.61.

36 'Bowater Finance', 12 July 1960, p. 3, FMD 37/2.

37 Bowater Organisation Press Release, 13 January 1961, 47/50.

38 OM 142, 6 December 1960.

39 GPC 18.v.61.

40 *Ibid.*

41 Agreement of 22 October 1954 between Tasman Pulp and Paper Co. and Albert E. Reed, 172/447.

42 GPC 25.i.55.

43 'Notes of discussion re possible R. & B. project', 7 January 1959, 172/447.

44 Cable Preslon 844, EVB to Bell and Rye, 5 March 1959, in *ibid.*

45 Heads of Agreement, 1 September 1959 and 17 November 1959; Sales Agreement and Newsprint Tonnage Agreement, 13 October 1959; all 'Tasman', Bowaters Secretary's Office.
46 Private information.
47 *Ibid.*
48 'Bowater Finance', 12 July 1960, p. 3, FMD 37/2.
49 Lewin to EVB, 6 August 1959, DD.
50 C. G. Cullen, 'The wallboard market in the USA', April 1955; Cullen to Meyer, 22 April 1955; both 172/447.
51 Bowaters Southern, 'Report of the general manager to the board of directors', 17 January 1956, pp. 10–11, in *ibid.*
52 Meyer to EVB, 20 August 1957; EVB to K. N. Linforth, 23 August 1957; both in *ibid.*
53 Sam Mann to D. W. Timmis, 17 November 1955, in *ibid.*
54 Kirwan-Taylor to H. E. Vollmers, 7 September 1955; 'Draft memorandum on Bowater Fibreboard Co. Inc.', 18 October 1955; 'Bowater board, a product of intensive research', n.d.; all in *ibid.*
55 A. E. Balloch to D. Duma, 21 February 1962, 48/3; Mersey Executive Committee minutes, 2.iii.60; J. H. Mowbray Jones in *Mersey Quarterly*, 27 November 1969.
56 'Notes on decisions at meetings with the Chairman, March 25th and 26th 1959', 48/23; similar 'Notes', 6–8 October 1959, 49/14.
57 C. E. Opdyke to Kirwan-Taylor, 10 July 1959, 48/23.
58 Cable Lonyork 1726, EVB to Meyer, 11 December 1959, 'Diversifications unsuitable', KT.
59 Kirwan-Taylor to EVB, 10 May 1962, in *ibid.*
60 Meyer to EVB, 9 May 1960, in *ibid.*
61 EVB to Meyer, 1 December 1959, 48/23.
62 *Ibid.*; Rye to Duma, 4 December 1959, in *ibid.*
63 Meyer to Timmis, 14 January 1959, in *ibid.*
64 Meyer to EVB, 8 December 1959, in *ibid.*
65 Morgan Stanley, 'Bowater Carolina Corporation: Paper mill', 9 March 1960, Exhibit D; C. T. Hicks, Memo, 1 April 1963, SO/B/19.
66 Morgan Stanley, 'Carolina paper mill', generally.
67 AGM, 1 June 1961; Bowater percentage of world total from Economist Intelligence Unit, *The national newspaper industry: a survey* (London, 1966), Part II, p. 92.

14. THE CASH CRISIS

1 AGM, 1 June 1961.
2 'Bowater Finance', 12 July 1960, FMD 37/2.
3 *Ibid.*, 'Addendum by Robert Knight for the Chairman and Mr Rye only'.
4 AGM, 1 June 1961.
5 Head Office Circular, 18 April 1961.

6 GPC 31.v.62.

7 Kirwan-Taylor, 'Note to the Chairman-Alice Scheme 2', 2 February 1961, KT.

8 Kirwan-Taylor, 'Alice – Aide-memoire for talk with Mr King', 3 February 1961, KT.

9 Draft of letter by Chairman of Daily Mirror Newspapers, February 1961, KT.

10 Bowater's Pulp & Paper Mills, Board minutes, 29.iii.62.

11 GPC 10.vii.61; Knight, 'Newsprint price, second half 1961', memo, RK.

12 GPC 31.v.62.

13 *Ibid.*

14 GPC 26.i.60, 2.ii.61.

15 GPC 28.vii.61.

16 GPC 18.ix.61.

17 Meyer to Opdyke, 25 September 1961, 48/10.

18 Meyer to EVB, 4 August 1961, in *ibid.*

19 See e.g. cable Yorklon 1844, Meyer to EVB, 21 November 1960; Duma to EVB, 24 April 1962, 'The Chairman 1960–62', DD; V. J. Sutton, Speech to senior staff dinner meeting, Rock Hill, 6 September 1963, Carolina archives.

20 J. G. Meiler, 'Report on program for hardboard mill', 15 June 1962, File 'BA & Bowater Inc. studies', FMD 23; Cullen and Meiler, 'Hardboard market survey', July 1957, 172/447.

21 Memo, Kirwan-Taylor to EVB, 22 April 1963, 174/447.

22 R. B. Reid to T. C. Bannister, Jr, 14 September 1962, 'BA & Bowater Inc. studies', FMD 23.

23 Report by A. C. Unthank of Barton, Mayhew, 9 November 1961, RK.

24 Cable Lonyork 2207, EVB to Meyer, 4 December 1961, 49/32.

25 Meyer to EVB, 15 January 1962, in *ibid.*

26 Mann to Rye, 25 June 1962, 48/3.

27 Meyer to Kirwan-Taylor, 14 May 1962, 172/447.

28 Rye to Mann, 16 July 1962, 48/3.

29 Cable Yorkscar 422, Meyer to Bannister, 13 July 1962, SO/B/19.

30 Bowater Paper Co. to McCall Corporation, 9 May 1963, 'McCall', RK.

31 'Memo on board meeting of Bowaters Southern Paper Corporation', 26 June 1962, 172/447.

32 Meyer to Sir Christopher Chancellor, 3 January 1963, 'CNAC', RK.

33 Meyer to Kirwan-Taylor, 14 May 1962, 172/447.

34 *Ibid.*

35 Meyer to EVB, 24 December 1957, 172/447.

36 Rye to Knight, 9 July 1957, 172/445; Lewin, 'Notes on the economics . . .', 8 August 1958, 172/445; 'Chemical pulp forecast 1960/1964, Summary of position', February 1959, 172/447.

37 *Ibid.*

38 GPC 2.x.59.

39 'Replies to questionnaire to papermakers submitted by The Bowater Paper Corporation Ltd', in Royal Commission on the Press 1961–2, Documentary evidence vol. 5, Cmnd 1812–8, Parliamentary Papers 1961–2, XXI, Bowater papers on Royal Commission on the Press.

40 'Evidence of The Bowater Paper Corporation Ltd', in Royal Commission on the Press, Oral evidence vol. 2, Cmnd. 1812–1, in *ibid.* (see esp. qq. 12548–56); private information.

41 V. J. Sutton, Speech to senior staff dinner meeting, Rock Hill, 6 September 1963, Carolina archives.

42 'Memorandum of a meeting on Monday 7th January 1963', 'CNAC', RK.

43 Meyer to Duma, 29 September 1961, with enc. copy letter, E. B. Vaughan to ABI, 25 September 1961, 49/14.

44 Rye to Knight, 27 September 1961, 49/32.

45 EVB to Dr Harley, 14 November 1961, 'The Chairman 1960–62', DD.

46 J. A. Colvin to Rye, 2 October 1961, 49/14.

47 Rye to Knight, 6 October 1961, in *ibid.*

48 *Ibid.*

49 Rye to Meyer, 6 October 1961, in *ibid.*

50 Meyer to EVB, 9 October 1961, in *ibid.*

51 Private information.

52 Sir Christopher Chancellor to EVB, 27 May 1961, FMD 37/3.

53 Memo, K. N. Linforth to EVB, 2 June 1961, KT.

54 GPC 23.i.62.

55 GPC 8.ii.62.

56 Martin Ritchie, 'Administrative and organisational structure', p. 4, FMD 37/3.

57 *Ibid.*, pp. 2–4.

58 *Ibid.*

59 *Ibid.*

60 *Ibid.*, pp. 5–9.

61 Rye to K. N. Linforth and others, 5 March 1962, RK.

62 Knight to EVB, 30 March 1962, 49/32.

15. BOWATERS IN OUTLINE

The sources for this chapter are chiefly published documents, in particular Bowater's annual Report and Accounts and Chairmen's statements.

1 Peat, Marwick, Mitchell & Co., 'The Bowater Corporation Limited: Report', 14 August 1962, FMD 57/3.

2 'Memorandum of a meeting on Monday 7 January 1963', 'CNAC', RK.

3 British & Commonwealth Shipping Co., 'Report on Bowater

Steamship Co. Ltd', April 1963, 172/332; OM 189, 8 July 1963.

4 Hedderwick, Hunt, Cox & Co., 'Memorandum on Bowater Paper Corporation Limted', September 1957.

5 AGM, 16 April 1971.

6 'Memorandum of a meeting on Monday 7 January 1963', 'CNAC', RK.

7 Private information.

8 Annual report for 1965, p. 4.

9 *Sunday Times*, 1 October 1972.

10 *The Economist*, 2 January 1971.

11 *Ibid.*, 6 March 1971.

12 Annual report for 1971, p. 7.

13 *Ibid.*, p. 9.

14 *The Observer*, 19 March 1972.

15 L. Hannah, *The rise of the corporate economy* (London, 1976), pp. 171–7; Charles Raw, *Slater Walker: investigation of a financial phenomenon* (London, 1977), pp. 193–5; Robert Jones and Oliver Marriott, *Anatomy of a merger: GEC, AEI, English Electric* (London, 1970), Chs. 14–16.

16 J. M. Astill, 'Bowater involvement in the furniture industry', 22 August 1972.

17 *Ibid.*

18 Jim Slater, *Return to Go* (London, 1977), p. 115.

19 *Ibid.*; Raw, *Slater Walker*, pp. 251–4; see also Ralli Brothers Ltd, *History and activities of the Ralli trading group* (privately printed, 1979).

20 Slater, *Return to Go*, pp. 170–1.

Bibliography

PUBLISHED SOURCES

Books and articles

American Newspaper Publishers' Association. *Newsprint now and in the next decade*. New York, 1951.

American Paper Institute Inc. *Wood pulp statistics*. New York, 1973.

Anonymous. 'A Frank Lloyd memorial', *World's Paper Trade Review*, 25 October 1929.

'A mammoth Kentish paper mill', *British and Colonial Printer and Stationer*, XXIII, 2, 11 July 1889.

'A visit to Lloyd's mills at Sittingbourne', *The Paper-Maker and British Paper Trade Journal*, November 1902, 3–19.

'Can the manufacturer do without the agent?', *World's Paper Trade Review*, 11 October 1889.

Corner Brook: 25 years of progress, 1923–1948. Corner Brook, 1948.

'Newsprint manufacture in bulk', *The Power Engineer*, February 1927.

'Social welfare of paper mill workers', *World's Paper Trade Review*, 15 November 1929.

'The father of the cheap press. The interesting story of Mr Edward Lloyd', *Fortunes made in business* (part-work, London, n.d., c. 1902), 255–65.

Camrose, 1st Viscount. *British newspapers and their controllers*. London, 1947.

Canadian Pulp and Paper Association. *Annual newsprint supplement*. Montreal, 1975 and 1979.

Newsprint data, annual edns. Montreal, 1970–9.

See also Newsprint Association of Canada.

Chadwick, St John. *Newfoundland*. Cambridge, 1967.

Clapham, Sir John. *An economic history of modern Britain*. 3 vols. Cambridge, 1926–38.

Clay, Sir Henry. *Lord Norman*. London, 1957.

Coleman, D. C. *Courtaulds: an economic and social history.* 3 vols. Oxford, 1969–80.

Cooke, Rev. S. H. *A history of Northfleet and its parish church.* London, 1942.

Economist Intelligence Unit. *The national newspaper industry: a survey.* London, 1966.

Ferris, Paul. *The house of Northcliffe.* London, 1971.

Hannah, L. *The rise of the corporate economy.* London, 1976.

Hargreaves, E. L. and Gowing, M. M. *Civil industry and trade.* London, 1952.

Haylock, E. 'Paper', in *The twentieth century,* ed. Trevor Williams. History of Technology, vols. 6–7 (Oxford, 1978), vol. 7, pp. 607–21.

Hobson, Harold; Knightley, Philip; Russell, Leonard, *The pearl of days: an intimate memoir of the 'Sunday Times' 1822–1972.* London, 1972.

Hunter, Dard. *Papermaking: the history and technique of an ancient craft.* London, 1947.

Jones, Robert and Marriott, Oliver. *Anatomy of a merger: GEC, AEI, English Electric.* London, 1970.

Kellogg, Royal S. *Newsprint paper in North America.* New York, 1948.

Kelly's Directories Ltd. *London Post Office directory 1900.*

Lewis, Peter W. 'Some aspects of papermaking in England and Wales up to 1865'. *The Paper Maker,* August, 1968.

Lodge, T. *Dictatorship in Newfoundland.* London, 1939.

Martin, Roscoe C. *From forest to front page.* Birmingham, Alabama, 1956.

Mathias, Peter. *The first industrial nation.* London, 1969.

Mond, Sir Alfred. *Industry and politics.* London 1927.

Morgan, E. Victor and Thomas, W. A. *The Stock Exchange: its history and functions.* London, 1962.

Newsprint Association of Canada. *Annual newsprint supplement.* Montreal, 1968.

Newsprint data, annual edns. Montreal, 1947–69.

Newsprint supply, pamphlet. Montreal, 10 June 1950.

Peters, Alan. 'His "logic" built an £80 million business', *Business,* May 1955, 89–92.

Phillips, H. G. 'A visit to Bowater's Mersey Paper Mills Ltd', *The Paper-Maker and British Paper Trade Journal,* December 1930, 9–18.

PEP (Political and Economic Planning). *Report on the British Press.* London, 1938.

Postan, M. M. *British war production.* London, 1952.

Pound, Reginald and Harmsworth, Geoffrey. *Northcliffe.* London, 1959.

Raw, Charles. *Slater Walker: investigation of a financial phenomenon.* London, 1977.

Reader, W. J. *Imperial Chemical Industries: a history.* 2 vols. Oxford, 1970–5.

Metal Box: a history. London, 1976.

Richardson, H. W. *Economic recovery in Britain 1932–39*. London, 1967.

Roach, D. J. 'A short account of the history and development of Bowater's mills at Sittingbourne and Kemsley', *East Kent Gazette*, 11 April 1952 and 18 April 1952.

Sayers, R. S. *The Bank of England 1891–1944*. 3 vols. Cambridge, 1976.

Scott, J. D. *Vickers: a history*. London, 1962.

Shorter, A. H. *Paper making in the British Isles*. Newton Abbot, 1971.

Slater, Jim. *Return to Go*. London, 1977.

Stead, W. T. 'Cyril Arthur Pearson', *Review of Reviews,* XXI (1900), 420–8.

Taylor, A. J. P. *Beaverbrook*. London, 1972.

Wilson, Charles. *The history of Unilever*. 3 vols. London, 1954–68.
'Economy and society in late Victorian Britain', *Economic History Review*, 2nd series, XVIII (1965), 180–211.

Official publications

Census of England and Wales 1881. Parliamentary Papers 1883, LXXX.

Census of England and Wales 1911, Cd 7929. Parliamentary Papers 1914–16, LXXXI.

Newfoundland Products Corporation Act, 6 Geo. V Ch. 4.
Newfoundland Legislative Acts 1915, Ch. 3.

Newfoundland Royal Commission. Report, Cmd 4480, 1933.

Royal Commission appointed to inquire into the depression of trade and industry 1885–6. Final report and minutes of evidence. Parliamentary Papers 1886, XXIII.

Royal Commission on the Press 1947–9. Minutes of evidence, Cmd 7409. Parliamentary Papers 1947–8, XV.
Report, Cmd 7700. Parliamentary Papers 1948–9, XX.

Royal Commission on the Press 1961–2. Report, Cmnd 1811, and minutes of evidence, Cmnd 1812. Parliamentary Papers 1961–2, XXI.

UNESCO. *Newsprint trends 1928–51*. Reports and papers on mass communication, vol. 10. Paris, 1954.
The problem of newsprint and other printing paper. Paris, 1949.

United States Senate Committee on Interstate and Foreign Commerce. *Newsprint inquiry*. Report of proceedings, vols. 1–3. Washington DC, 1957.

UNPUBLISHED SOURCES

The abbreviations used in the Notes are given in brackets.

External

Amalgamated Press. *The machinery of a vast undertaking*. Privately printed, n.d. (c. 1912).

Anonymous. 'The Gander Valley Power and Paper Company of New-
foundland: general report.' Typescript, 31 October 1925.
Bank of England Archives. (BE)
Beaverbrook Papers, House of Lords Record Office. (BbK)
Correspondence with Eric Bowater, kindly lent by Mrs M. L. Reay-
Mackey. (RM)
Daily Mirror Newspapers Ltd. Board minutes.
Ministry Records, Public Record Office. (PRO)
Muir, Augustus. *The British Paper and Board Makers' Association
1872–1972: a centenary history.* Privately printed, 1972.
Newfoundland Archives, St John's, Newfoundland. (Nfd)
Newsprint Supply Company. Minutes of directors' meetings.
Northcliffe Papers, British Library. (NP)
Price, G. Ward. *Fifty years of the 'Daily Mail', 1896–1946.* Privately
printed, 1946. Kindly made available by Librarian, *Daily Mail.*
Reid Papers, Newfoundland.
Wadsworth, A. P. 'Newspaper circulations 1800–1954'. Paper read to
the Manchester Statistical Society, 1955, and kindly supplied by the
Society.

Bowater

The main source was the archives in Bowater House but archival material
was also kindly supplied by:
  Mersey, Ellesmere Port, Kemsley, Sittingbourne
  Corner Brook
  Mersey, Nova Scotia
  Carolina
  Bowater Southern (BS)
  Bowater Inc., Old Greenwich (OG)
The main sources within the Bowater House archives were as follows:
Report and accounts of Corporation, subsidiaries and early companies;
issue prospectuses.
Chairman's speeches at annual general meetings after 1934. From 1935
onwards one speech was delivered covering the affairs of all the main
companies. (AGM)
Minutes of board meetings.
  Bowaters & Lloyds Sales Company (B&LS)
  Bowater's Mersey Paper Mills (BMPM)
  Bowater's Newfoundland Pulp & Paper Mills (BNPP)
  Bowater Paper Corporation (BPC)
  Bowater's Paper Mills (BPM)
  Edward Lloyd (EL)
  W. V. Bowater & Sons (WVB)
  Bowater Southern Paper Corporation (BSPC)
Minutes of AGMs and Chairman's speeches before 1935.

Bowater's Paper Mills   (BPM AM)
W. V. Bowater & Sons   (WVB AM)
Minutes and supporting papers of General Purposes Committee   (GPC)
    Chairman's office memoranda   (OM)
    Collected papers of Bowater personnel, including:
        Dervish Duma   (DD)
        John Kirwan-Taylor   (KT for unnumbered papers)
        Robert Knight   (RK for unnumbered papers)
Use was also made of house magazines, books and booklets, including:
Edward Lloyd Ltd. '*Lloyd's Weekly News*': a souvenir. Privately printed,
    1909.
    'Souvenir-programme of a visit of members of the International Asso-
    ciation of Journalists attending the London conference 1927 to Kemsley
    Mills and Garden Village', 5 July 1927.
Raddall, Thomas H. *The Mersey Story*. Privately printed, 1979.
Ralli Brothers Ltd. *History and activities of the Ralli trading group*.
    Privately printed, 1979.
Sinclair, Robert. *Bowaters build a mill in Tennessee*. Privately printed, n.d.
    (c. 1954).

Persons interviewed

B. G. Alexander   Malcolm Horsman
H. M. Archibald   J. H. Mowbray Jones
E. T. Baker*   Hugh K. Joyce
A. E. Balloch   W. J. Kirwan-Taylor*
R. A. Batchelor   Arthur Lissenden
E. W. Bostel   F. W. Lissenden
T. D. Botterill   Mrs G. M. Loly
Sir Ian Bowater   D. McLaren
Lady Margaret Bowater*   Ross McMaster
Sir Noël Bowater   Sam Mann
The Earl of Carrick   R. J. E. Martin
Sir Christopher Chancellor   W. E. J. Miles
Sir Eric Cheadle*   Sir Godfrey Morley*
Sir Henry Chisholm   W. D. Mulholland
J. A. Colvin   J. Austin Parker
C. W. Copelin   J. A. Paterson
D. Duma*   L. G. Pearce
Bob Fowler   Jack Price
George Goyder   Mrs M. L. Reay-Mackey
J. C. Goobie   I. D. Reid
H. J. Gray   Dr G. K. C. Rettie
J. G. Hall   J. Martin Ritchie
R. Herdman   M. W. Russell

Dr H. Schmuki   S. E. Walmsley
J. H. Smith   T. H. N. Whitehurst
Dr Philip Sykes   M. Zeier
G. F. Underhay

*also provided papers

Index

For financial aspects of companies, see under separate headings, e.g. capital expenditure, profits. If no name is given, Bowater is assumed.

King, Cecil, 293–4
Kirwan-Taylor, W. John, b. 1905: and
Bowater-Eburite, 263; and the Catawba
mill, 247, 283; main board director, 308;
member of committee on capital
requirements, 291; negotiations with
Reeds, 279; negotiations with Scott Paper
Co., 240; negotiations with Union Bank of
Switzerland, 275; partner in London &
Yorkshire Trust, 212; report on the cost of
expansion, 250; report on sea transport,
248–9
kitchen towels, see paper towels
kitchen units, 332
'Kleenex', see tissues
Kleinwort, Sons & Co., 48–9, 51–2
Knight, Robert, b. 1911: and Gillingham
packaging project, 296; and the Master
Plan, 274; and the need for reorganisation,
309; Comptroller, 267; evidence to the
Royal Commission on the Press, 303;
investigations of Tennessee and Carolina
pulp, 307; member of committee on
capital requirements, 291–2; review of
Bowaters Southern Corporation, 298;
Vice-Chairman and member of the Board
Executive Committee, 334–5
Knightsbridge building, see Bowater House
kraft liner board, 99, 102, 118, 165, 185,
201
kraft (paper), 185, 284, 302
kraft products, 266
kraft pulp, 199, 201, 207, 214, 223, 234,
245, 284, 302

labour and labour relations: and the print
unions, 272, 290; Central Work Study
Division report, 296; comparison with
Corner Brook Co., 295; in the packaging
industry, 296; turnover, 296; union
'troubles', 296; wages and productivity,
296
Labour Government, of 1945, 188
Labrador timber limits, 131, 133
laminated papers, 272
land, asset value of, 330
lawsuits, see litigation
Layton, 1st Baron (W. T. Layton),
1884–1966, 159
legislation (USA): tax concession under
emergency regulations, 208–9
Leverhulme, 1st Viscount (W. H. Lever),
1851–1925, 110, 128, 154
'Leverpak' drums, 271
Lewin, H. Montgomery (Monty) S.,
1900–71: and Corner Brook company,
281, 301; and expansion in the South
(USA), 201; and the Gander loggers' strike,
136; and Mersey Paper Co., Nova Scotia,
231; policy on sea transport, 249
Life Magazine, 286
lighterage and towing, 15, 23
Limelight Furniture Ltd, 331
Linforth, Arthur, E., 3, 65–6, 71–2, 91–2
Linforth, Kenneth N., 1903–76: and
meetings of UK and N. American

managers, 221; director of Bowater's
Mersey Paper Mills Ltd, 91–3; Director of
Operations, 272; evidence to the Royal
Commission on the Press, 303; general
manager of Bowater's Mersey Paper Mills
Ltd, 72, 91–3; negotiations with Reeds,
279; remuneration, 91; trusted adviser,
191
Linklaters & Paines, 53, 63
Lissenden, Arthur, 278
litigation: breach of contract suits, 20–1; suit
on tax concessions in Canada, 231
Liverpool, Nova Scotia timberland, 104–5
Lloyd, Edward, 10–12, 27, 114
Lloyd, Frank, 12, 19, 27, 30, 108–11
Lloyd, Edward, Ltd: acquisition by Berry
Group, 30–1, 111–16, 339; acquisition by
Bowaters, 83, 107, 116–21, 185, 263,
331; Bowater's first great agency, 12;
building products, 185, 235; in the
General Strike, 49; guarantee to
Bowater-Lloyd Newfoundland Ltd, 146,
151; Kemsley and Sittingbourne, 109–11;
newsprint capacity, 114; newsprint
contracts, 27, 31; original company, 27; in
wartime, 167
Lloyd, Edward, Investment Co. Ltd, 113,
116–17, 121, 168, 192, 194
Lloyd, Edward, Wallboard Ltd, 114, 116
Lloyds Bank Ltd, 21, 65–6, 81, 181, 219,
256, 307
Lloyd's Weekly, 3
loans: for Calhoun mills, 210, 213, 218,
234, 254, 287; for Catawba mill, 245,
254, 287, 297–9; for Corner Brook mill,
172, 174–5, 178, 181, 199, 231; for
European expansion, 268–9, 292; for
expansion programme 1952–61, 250–1,
256–7; for purchase of Empire mill, 65–6;
for purchase of Mersey Paper Co., Nova
Scotia, 255–6; for purchase of
Rothermere's shareholding, 81; raised on
paper and pulp stocks, 48–9, 51–2; for
ships, 249
log-ponds, see wood and timber
logs, see wood and timber
London & Yorkshire Trust, 48, 63, 81, 106,
183, 210, 212
London Express Newspaper Ltd, 18;
shareholding in Bowater's Mersey Paper
Mills Ltd, 69, 71, 73–8, 81–2, 93–4
long-service employees entertained, 225
Lord Mayor of London: Sir Frank Bowater,
228; Sir Ian Bowater, 228; Sir Noel
Bowater, 223, 226, 228; Sir Vansittart
Bowater, 16, 23, 228
Lufkin mill, Texas, 201
Lyttleton, Oliver, 157

MPSA, see Mechanical Pulp Suppliers'
Association
McCabe, Thomas B., b. 1893, 240–1, 244
McCall Corporation, 286–7, 299–300, 323
McCall's Magazine: paper contract, 286–7,
299–300
Macdonald Currie & Co., 136, 173